A GUIDE TO WRITING PROGRAMS:
Writing Centers, Peer Tutoring Programs, and Writing-Across-the-Curriculum

Tori Haring-Smith, General Editor

with

Nathaniel Hawkins
Elizabeth Morrison
Lise Stern
Robin Tatu

Brown University

Scott, Foresman and Company
Glenview, Illinois
London, England

Library of Congress Cataloging in Publication Data

Main entry under title:

A guide to writing programs.

Includes bibliographical references.
1. Writing centers—United States—Directories.
2. English language—Rhetoric—Study and teaching—United States—Directories.
3. Universities and colleges—United States—Curricula—Directories. I. Haring-Smith, Tori.
PE1405.U6G8 1984 808'.042'02573 84-14171
ISBN 0-673-18177-4

Printed in the United States of America.
12345678-EBI-9190898887868584

ACKNOWLEDGEMENTS

Over the past several months, as we gathered information for this book, we relied on a number of people for help. The book could not have been completed without the assistance of the many instructors and administrators who answered our questionnaire and responded to our subsequent queries about their programs. We are particularly thankful to those people who provided extensive information about their writing programs, helping us to better understand current trends in teaching writing. Lil Brannon of New York University, Joseph Gordon and Linda Peterson of Yale University, Stephen North of SUNY Albany, Kenneth Risdon of the University of Minnesota at Duluth, and Christopher Thaiss of George Mason University were generous with information about writing centers. We also spoke at length about the theory of peer tutoring with Kenneth Bruffee of CUNY/Brooklyn College, Thom Hawkins of the University of California at Berkeley, and Patricia Bizzell of the College of the Holy Cross. Toby Fulwiler of the University of Vermont, Lowell Johnson of St. Olaf College, Elaine Maimon of Beaver College, Timothy Martin of the University of Pennsylvania, Ina Reiter of Ottawa University, John Ruszkiewicz of the University of Texas at Austin, and Leigh Ryan of the University of Maryland were informative and forthcoming about their writing-across-the-curriculum programs. To all these instructors, we owe our thanks.

Brown University extended much support for the preparation of this book. Harriet Sheridan, Dean of the College, encouraged us in our endeavor and provided financial assistance, including a Salomon grant to cover postal and incidental expenses. We are also grateful to Brown University for use of the word processing facilities, which greatly expedited the writing and editing of this book.

Nathaniel Hawkins and Robin Tatu, who did all the final editing, would like to thank Constance Rajala, our editor at Scott, Foresman, for her patience and guidance. They are also indebted to Fran Slaton, Dave Rubin, Chris Croasdale, and particularly Lisa Hirschhorn, for their quick fingers, sharp eyesight and clear heads, as they helped type, proofread, and edit the manuscript.

Finally, we would all like to thank Bob Haring-Smith, who developed a data base for our information, meticulously proofread, assisted with the editing of the manuscript, and helped us through many late nights.

TABLE OF CONTENTS

INTRODUCTION

In 1983-84, four participants in the Undergraduate Writing Fellows Program at Brown University decided to undertake a survey of writing centers, peer tutoring programs, and writing across the curriculum in universities and colleges nationwide. We originally became interested in this study because, like many teachers of composition, we wanted to know how other people in other places teach writing. More specifically, we were interested in discovering what kinds of nontraditional writing programs exist across the country. We hoped to answer a number of questions: What sorts of new writing programs have been developed in recent years? How have current trends in the teaching of writing influenced the structure and purpose of these programs? How do older programs differ from those established within the last few years? And what sorts of programs have been the most successful, and why?

In order to gather the data needed to address these questions, we sent a detailed questionnaire to directors of composition at approximately 500 institutions, eliciting information about their writing centers, peer tutoring programs, and cross-curricular writing programs. In selecting the schools to survey, we sampled a fair cross-section of American colleges and universities. We sent questionnaires to the 220 schools designated by Barron's Profiles of American Colleges (13th edition) as "most competitive," "highly competitive," and "very competitive." In addition, we chose 280 more schools from diverse geographical locations. After compiling the information from the questionnaires, we sent respondents the manuscript pages describing their schools programs so that they could verify the the accuracy of our information.

Of the 500 schools surveyed, over half responded, and many provided additional information about their writing courses, composition faculty, and the success or failure of their programs. Responses came from 48 states, from schools whose student populations range from less than one hundred to over thirty thousand, from state universities and private colleges to "specialty" institutions focusing on such areas as maritime studies, insurance, or adult education. Though the 500 schools represent a fair sample, they also represent a relatively small percentage of the number of schools throughout the country. Consequently, there are undoubtedly schools with interesting and innovative programs that we were unable to reach. But this guide is not intended to determine the prevalence of various kinds of writing programs, but rather to describe how different types of schools implement these nontraditional writing programs. It is not a quantitative analysis but a descriptive index.

The main section of the book contains formatted descriptions of the programs at individual schools followed by brief paragraphs that synthesize the formatted information and provide any additional details reported by the schools. The format includes the names of the respondents, the number of full-time faculty and students at each school, and detailed factual information about each program, including its age, the faculty and students it involves, its availability to students, attitudes towards the program, and the program's goals.

By studying the information we gathered and examining current research, we began to draw conclusions about the history and theoretical foundations of writing centers, peer tutoring in writing, and writing-across-the-curriculum programs. The three essays in the first half of the book discuss these conclusions. Elizabeth Morrison and Robin Tatu describe the development and present state of writing centers in America, Nathaniel Hawkins focuses on the theory and practice of peer tutoring, and Tori Haring-Smith and Lise Stern discuss the growth and organization of writing-across-the-curriculum programs.

The general trends we discuss indicate that writing programs today are generally expanding both inside and outside of the English classroom, and that this expansion is likely to continue. Except where funding limits growth, schools seem determined to raise the writing proficiency of their students by developing new programs or enlarging existing ones. We found, for example, that over two-thirds of all responding institutions have some sort of nontraditional writing program, whether a writing center, a peer tutoring program, or some form of writing-across-the-curriculum program. Considering that many of these programs operate under budgetary constraints, their abundance is even more remarkable.

The amount of writing now being required of students is further evidence of the growing interest in college writing. More than nine in ten schools in our survey have some sort of writing requirement for graduation, and many of those that have no requirement do have a cross-disciplinary writing program of some kind. As David Hamilton of the University of Iowa has suggested, interdisciplinary writing is rapidly developing into a field all its own.[1] Few interdisciplinary writing programs existed ten years ago, and of those that did, fewer still existed in their present form. Some of our respondents indicated that although their writing centers operated before the late 1970s, they used to be little more than rarely frequented "tutoring rooms" staffed by a graduate student or two. Today, many of these same centers serve over a quarter of their school's students in large facilities with books, computer terminals, and audio-visual materials. Other programs have expanded in a similar fashion. Peer tutoring programs, which have struggled to overcome student distrust and opposition from faculty and administrators, are now more widely accepted and draw favorable responses from students. And writing-across-the-curriculum programs, which began to appear in the mid-seventies, now assume many forms and frequently affect 100% of a school's student population.

Crucial to the success of most nontraditional programs is the training of the instructors or tutors. Writing center tutors, whether faculty, graduates or undergraduates, must be able to respond to students' specific needs, including ESL instruction, remedial assistance, analysis of the writing process, or grammar help. Peer tutors require training not only in methods of addressing their tutees' specific writing problems, but also in how

---

1 David Hamilton, "Interdisciplinary Writing," <u>College English</u> 41 (March 1980), 780-96.

to remain peer tutors. Many writing-across-the-curriculum programs attempt to spread writing instruction to all disciplines by training faculty from departments other than English in the teaching of writing. And it appears that educators are becoming more aware of the importance of training, judging from the number of programs that have recently instituted or planned training courses, workshops, or seminars for tutors or faculty.

Part of the impetus for these new training programs is an increasing awareness of new pedagogies that view writing as a process rather than a product. Program administrators and contemporary theorists such as Anne J. Herrington, Randall R. Freisinger, C.H. Knoblauch, and Lil Brannon maintain that interdisciplinary writing and the focus on the process of writing are related in significant ways.[2] And our results support their assertions--many of our respondents indicated that their nontraditional programs provide process-oriented instruction that the traditional classroom does not offer.

Although these results concur with what theorists and teachers have suspected about current trends in the teaching of writing, there are limitations to what we can fairly infer from the information in a study of this type. We must not, for example, interpret the number of nontraditional programs described in the book as an indication that all colleges and universities are turning to nontraditional teaching methods. Of the 500 schools we sent questionnaires, we received responses from roughly 300. Of these 300, we chose to include 230 in our report because they had, or planned to have, some sort of nontraditional program. The 70 or so schools we decided not to include either failed to provide us with adequate information or did not have a writing program that fit into our study. In addition, we suspect that the vast majority of the 200 schools that did not return our questionnaire chose not to because they sensed that our interests did not correspond to their programs. We are also somewhat wary of the overwhelmingly positive attitudes presented by the respondents. Although we agree that these programs are generally successful, we realize that not all people involved with nontraditional programs are as enthusiastic as the people who run them.

Nevertheless, we hope our results are of value to faculty and administrators who are interested in nontraditional writing programs and current trends in the teaching of writing nationwide. And perhaps more importantly, the information in this book should prove helpful to schools planning to establish nontraditional programs and wishing to know how similar schools have fared with these programs. As teachers of writing, we can all benefit greatly from learning about how other colleges and universities teach writing.

Nathaniel Hawkins

Elizabeth Morrison

----

2 Anne J. Herrington, "Writing to Learn: Writing Across the Disciplines," College English 43 (April 1981), pp. 379-87; Randall R. Freisinger, "Cross-Disciplinary Writing Workshops: Theory and Practice," College English 42 (October 1980), pp. 154-66; and C.H. Knoblauch and Lil Brannon, "Writing as Learning Through the Curriculum," College English 45 (September 1983), pp. 465-74.

FRAGS TO RICHES: WRITING CENTERS GROW UP

In the short space of fifteen years, writing centers have become an integral part of post-secondary writing education. Once a rare phenomenon limited to a few innovative schools, the writing center or writing lab is now a common program in colleges and universities across the country. According to Thom Hawkins and Phyllis Brooks, over one thousand institutions have some sort of writing center.[1] As these centers have grown in number, they have grown up in other ways as well. They have become better known and often better respected; many writing centers today are used voluntarily by one-quarter of all students at their institutions. But having lost their initial novelty, these centers have had to find more permanent ways to justify their existence, to convince the administration that they deserve continued funding. While the writing center is becoming a standard feature in most colleges and universities and finding a more secure role in college education, this role is often limited to a "fix-it station" where writing problems find instant solutions. As writing centers expand their services and scope, they continue to combat the image of remedial labs that attend only to basic grammatical skills. In short, writing centers have exchanged one set of problems for another: the problems of getting started for the problems of continuing to grow.

These problems of growth have a long and complex history. As Stephen North has discovered, the development of writing clinics has been difficult, fraught with funding problems, administrative entanglements, and struggles with the "comma center" image.[2] Obviously, the problems writing centers face have not disappeared over time. In many ways centers are in even more trouble today, facing severe budget cut-backs and loss of federal and state financing. But current writing centers do have one advantage: they can look to historical models and learn from the experience of earlier centers. One way to understand better the difficulties writing centers face today is to examine their origins, the difficulties they have encountered, the teaching trends they have endured, and the various paths different centers have taken. Through this kind of research we can gain a clearer idea of how writing centers may develop in the future.

---

1 "Improving Writing Skills," ed. Thom Hawkins and Phyllis Brooks, New Directions for College Learning Assistance 3 (1981), p. vii.

2 See Stephen M. North, "Writing Centers: A Sourcebook" (Ph.D. diss., State University of New York at Albany, 1979).

Writing Centers Before 1974: The Roots

Although a few writing centers existed as early as the 1930s,[3] most were created in the past fifteen years, many in the past ten. Muriel Harris has noted that of the centers established before 1974, several were started in response to what was perceived as a "literacy crisis" across the nation.[4] In the late 60s and early 70s, as colleges and universities began to be flooded with more students who were less prepared for college writing, faculty and administrators came to believe that many students' problems went beyond the classroom. "The Writing Lab provides individual help for students whose writing problems cannot be dealt with adequately in regular courses," states the May 1978 Rhetoric Handbook from the University of Iowa. A place to deal with poor writers was needed, and the writing lab seemed to be an ideal solution--outside of the classroom, the lab was operated by "composition experts" ready to solve a student's writing problems. The emphasis on writing at this time was on "fixing" a problem. The very terms "writing lab" or "clinic" reflect this pragmatic approach: students would be sent to the laboratory, where their problems would be analyzed and diagnosed. A "cure" would then be prescribed, usually based on the notion that correct grammar is equivalent to good writing: if students cleared up their "frag"s and "sp"s, their prose would be acceptable. The complexity of the composing process was overlooked in the attempt to direct students toward error-free final products.

Many labs during the early 1970's, then, were first designed as "remedial" services, and "problem" students were required to seek their help. A typical example of this remedial designation is the original Learning Lab at Central Missouri State University. When first opened over a decade ago, Central Missouri's lab was created for students needing to improve their basic writing skills. Other writing centers were established not as remedial skills centers, but in order to address a need within the regular writing curriculum. In existence for over twelve years, the former Writing Lab at the University of Minnesota at Duluth was created as an indirect response to the "literacy crisis." When the university's writing requirement was lightened considerably in the early 70s, the English Department created the writing center to supplement what was perceived as a "weak" writing curriculum.

Yet it is a myth that all writing centers began as remedial workshops, or even as supplements to the curriculum. Some writing labs were developed not from a sense of need, but from a desire to provide the college community with an avenue for nontraditional writing instruction, as the Writing Place at George Mason University attests. Opened in 1974, the Writing Place, originally called the Writing Lab, was designed to serve a much broader range of students than those needing remedial help: "all students in all disciplines, graduate and undergraduate, native and non-native English speakers, full time and part time, currently enrolled at GMU," according to a university brochure. The writing instructors at George Mason recognized that writers at all levels need to work on their composition skills. Judging from the four-fold increase in clients in the past five years, this non-remedial focus has been quite popular. In fact, it was not until 1980 that George Mason felt the need to establish its Composition Tutorial Center for developmental writers

---

3 Lou Kelly, "One on One, Iowa City Style: Fifty Years of Individualized Instruction in Writing," The Writing Center Journal 1 (Fall/Winter 1980), pp. 4-19.

4 Muriel Harris, "Growing Pains: The Coming of Age of Writing Centers," The Writing Center Journal 2 (Fall/Winter 1982), pp. 1-8.

and its English Language Institute for ESL students.

No matter how they were started, most early writing centers faced opposition and had to struggle to gain acceptance from their universities and colleges. Often the most pressing difficulty for these centers was funding. When individual English departments refused to provide financial support for writing centers, those centers were forced to seek either university aid or outside grants. Many centers ran on shoestring budgets and were in the precarious position of not knowing whether they would receive funding from year to year.

Neither did financial stability ensure a writing center's continued existence: directors of these centers frequently had to fight for cooperation from faculty and administration, who did not recognize the need for individualized instruction in writing outside the classroom. Ironically, English departments often formed the most adamant opposition to these young writing labs. For the writing center, especially as a novel and untested approach to instruction, was perceived as a threatening addition to the curriculum. Establishing a writing center seemed to imply that English faculty were not performing their duty or that the curriculum was somehow lacking. In the 1970's, writing labs implied a pedagogical revolution as well: in switching the focus from literature to student writing itself, labs began to alter fundamental conceptions about how and where writing should be taught. Some English instructors felt that a freshman English course might be a student's only exposure to classic literature such as Shakespeare, and if writing was substituted for literature, college students would be no longer well-educated. To write well, these instructors argued, it was more important for students to read than to write. While acknowledging the value of literature, writing instructors countered that students learn to write by writing--practicing the skill they wished to improve. Many educators also feared that a writing center staff would ghostwrite student papers--that cheating would be more prevalent if writing was not supervised by the English department. In many cases, the main obstacle writing centers faced was in overcoming an undeserved, adverse image.

Writing Centers from 1974-1979: Redefining Their Roles

As writing centers continued to fight their poor images, defining their roles in education became increasingly important. While they gradually gained acceptance as "developmental" or remedial work stations, few centers were able to move beyond this position; more innovative writing techniques, such as brainstorming or freewriting, were labeled as frills, expensive experiments, or expressions of laissez faire. Yet even when writing labs fulfilled the limited role expected of them, they were disparaged as "comma centers" or "fix-it" stations. At the University of Michigan at Dearborn, attendance at the writing center remained low despite the center's long hours; students tended to regard the center as a remedial service designed for problem writers. A similar situation existed at Rutgers University's Cook College, where the writing center received a less-than-favorable reception from students required to attend its grammar and essay writing tutorials.

Yet as Jon Jonz and Jeanette Harris believe, writing centers were slowly able to break free from their historical restrictions:

> Even though writing centers were generally created to address one aspect or another of the 'literacy crisis,' the better centers have quickly moved from the role of being an institution's major response to the declining level of literacy

> into the less dramatic but more productive role of being a campus-wide support service. . . . Writing centers are no longer attempting single-handedly to resolve massive, irresolvable problems but are now supporting every discipline in the resolution of common problems.[5]

The writing center at Rensselaer Polytechnic Institute is a clear example of this sort of support service. Karen Burke LeFevre, director of RPI's center, reports that since the lab opened five years ago, it has made its services available to assist different people in the college community: graduates and undergraduates from all disciplines as well as international students, faculty members, and staff members.

At the same time that RPI was establishing its writing lab, Yale University was developing an innovative approach of its own: residentially based writing workplaces in which professional writers and editors set up their own tutoring programs. Located in each of Yale's twelve colleges, these workplaces are not centers or labs, according to Linda Peterson, the co-director of Yale's writing program. Yale decentralized its former writing center in 1979 because both the name "center" and the central location tended to make the center appear remedial. Since it shifted from a central to a residential focus and increased individual attention, the program has been highly successful, doubling its clientele over the past five years. Faculty response to the program has been equally positive, showing that a highly innovative program need not be threatening to faculty and administration. Instead, the program works as an integral part of the university, as does RPI's center. Programs like these two may be effective because they do work in harmony with existing programs and because they provide support for schools, rather than propose ultimate solutions to writing problems.

Writing Centers from 1979 to the Present: Covering New Ground

In addition to looking at writing programs like those at Yale and RPI as models, writing centers have been influenced by the recent theories on the teaching of writing. In the late 1970's many writing centers completely restructured their programs after investigating the "process" approach to writing. Led by Janet Emigh, Linda Flower, and John Hayes, theorists explored the steps a writer goes through during composition, rather than emphasizing the final written product. Instructors of writing became aware that writing is an on-going effort for all students, not a problem that can somehow be "fixed." Because this approach to writing made good sense in the writing center context--here students could receive individual attention to all stages of their writing without fear of being graded or judged--it was incorporated into many centers' programs. Rudolph Almasy and Stephen North are among those who believe that process has become a predominant writing lab pedagogy.[6]

---

5 Jon Jonz and Jeanette Harris, "Decisions, Records, and the Writing Lab," Tutoring Writing: A Sourcebook for Writing Labs, ed. Muriel Harris (Glenview, IL: Scott, Foresman, 1981), p. 216.

6 Rudolph Almasy, "The Nature of Writing-Laboratory Instruction for the Developing Student," and Stephen North, "Writing Center Diagnosis: The Composing Profile," in Tutoring Writing: A Sourcebook for Writing Labs, ed. Muriel Harris (Glenview, IL: Scott, Foresman, 1981), pp. 13-20 and 42-52.

One way "process" was incorporated into writing centers was through the use of peer tutoring programs. Although not all peer tutoring services are process-oriented, many do emphasize this approach and require their tutors to guide students through the stages of composition. Perhaps because this approach allows for such individual attention, or perhaps because students feel more comfortable with peers, peer tutoring has been an extremely successful addition to many writing centers. (For a more comprehensive discussion of peer tutoring, see Nathaniel Hawkins' essay below.)

The success of peer tutoring programs has encouraged institutions to experiment with other approaches in their writing centers. Some writing centers now offer either mini-courses or full academic courses in conjunction with English and other departments. Many writing centers conduct university-wide faculty seminars that explore strategies for teaching writing. Smith College, for example, has received outside funding over the past three years to bring diverse groups of faculty members together to discuss the teaching of writing. Other writing centers, like the one at Illinois State University, provide "grammar hotlines" for their students. Illinois State also offers workshops not only for their students and faculty, but for nearby high schools, community colleges, and universities. Georgetown University's writing center operates one of the largest outreach programs in the country; this center provides a number of programs, including dorm seminars, career panels, ESL instruction, community outreach programs, and summer seminars on writing techniques. As these different centers expand their services, they continue to de-emphasize the "fix-it" mentality and encourage thinking about writing from a variety of perspectives.

In addition to these various approaches, many schools choose to operate their writing centers as part of a more general "Learning Resource Center" or "Academic Skills Center." Linking a writing center with a general learning center can encourage students to consider writing as an integral part of their other studies, not isolated from reading or research skills. A learning center is often a pragmatic solution for those institutions that cannot currently afford a separate writing center. Mills College has recently moved to combine its writing center with a general tutoring center, partly to keep costs down, and partly in an attempt to reach more students. This strategy of appealing to a larger number of students is important, since peer tutoring, course-related activities, and community and campus-wide workshops can all help ensure that writing centers enjoy added popularity by showing students that the centers are not solely remedial.

While some writing centers have expanded their services and widened their focus, others choose to cater to a more specific audience. George Mason University's new Composition Tutorial Center (CTC), for example, has focused on developmental writers, while the specific focus of the writing center at Indiana State University at Terre Haute is foreign students needing help with ESL. Still other colleges and universities focus on freshmen, and some require attendance at the writing center as part of their introductory composition courses. San Francisco State University has designed its writing center to include all <u>but</u> seniors, while a number of schools, including Vanderbilt University and Wake Forest University, pay particular attention to athletes' writing skills.

Writing Centers in the Future: Expanding with Caution

Today almost every college and university has some kind of a writing center. Some are well-established and, like the center at Georgetown University, receive substantial federal, state, or institutional funding. Many centers also receive support and encouragement from English and humanities departments, and even from departments in the sciences and social sciences. But many more writing centers experience financial and political difficulties. To revive or sustain interest in their services, a number of writing centers have turned to recent innovations like computer-assisted instruction (CAI) since computers attract the attention of both students and faculty, and can encourage use of a center. At the University of Minnesota at Duluth, for instance, Tom Bacig and Kenneth Risdon are developing a new writing center that uses 25 IBM Personal Computers to teach writing. Shared by the remedial program and the Writing Program, the new Writing Lab will become a center for research in CAI as well as a teaching laboratory; Risdon and Bacig plan to use the lab as a workshop for developing educational software for writers.

But while many schools are currently embracing CAI--perhaps not only because it is an innovation, but also because it is aututorial and a relatively inexpensive form of instruction--several writing instructors fear its misuse. "In my nightmares the writing center has been made so 'efficient,'" writes Stephen North, "that all that's left is one central, federally-funded giant Gramma Phone, out of which a computer voice dispenses chapter and verse from The Harbrace Handbook."[7] Although the use of computer-assisted instruction may give the writing center a more secure position within an institution, it should probably be approached carefully. Universities need to avoid returning to the "fix-it" mentality of composition and should investigate not only the pedagogical approaches of various CAI programs, but also whether a particular program is appropriate for a given school or writing center. Rather than consider computer-assisted instruction in isolation, schools should investigate ways to incorporate it into existing writing instructions. At one Eastern college, the recently purchased computers are stored in a closet because none of the faculty knows how to use the software. This college might have done better to follow NYU's example and examine how other institutions have incorporated computers into writing programs, before buying machines and software. Many writing faculty are probably unaware, for example, that the University of Notre Dame has offered computer-assisted instruction for nearly ten years; surely Notre Dame's experience with computers could be valuable to writing faculty considering computers. York College is currently researching the role of computers in heuristics before beginning its CAI program, and Illinois Institute of Technology has not only adopted Bell Laboratories' "Writer's Workbench," but has also designed software specifically for its students. These schools did not rush into CAI just to add a more "flashy" component to their writing centers; as a result, York College and Illinois Institute of Technology will probably benefit, in the long run, from this cautious approach.

Although writing centers have great potential for expanding programs and enriching writing instruction, their movement into the future should be a cautious one. They must balance the needs of remedial and advanced students, of fixing individual essays and teaching students better writing procedures, of preserving traditional teaching methods and exploring innovative pedagogies. Certainly in sharing past experiences and exploring new options, writing centers can learn from one another's mistakes and successes.

Elizabeth Morrison

Robin Tatu

----

[7] North, "Writing Centers," p. 176.

AN INTRODUCTION TO THE HISTORY AND THEORY OF PEER TUTORING IN WRITING

The teaching and learning of writing has traditionally taken place in the English classroom, where the instructor teaches the entire class, and each student responds on an individual basis. The instructor imparts knowledge to a group of students, but evaluates individual student's acquisition of knowledge. Each student works only with the instructor while competing with fellow students. But as educators and writing theorists have written more and more in the last twenty years about poor student writing, they have raised questions about traditional notions of how writing should be taught. The establishment of writing centers and writing-across-the-curriculum programs has moved some writing instruction outside of the classroom or beyond the English curriculum, but neither has, by itself, significantly affected the traditional student-instructor relationship. Peer tutoring, however, has challenged this relationship and created a supplement to traditional teaching methods through its strong roots in collaborative learning.

Origins in Collaborative Learning

The concept of peer tutoring is based not on instruction or student competition, but on student <u>collaboration</u>, which has in the past been generally regarded as a form of cheating since it undercuts the importance of individual initiative and accomplishment. Students may learn collaboratively as they interact informally in dormitories, dining halls, after lectures, or in almost any campus setting. In the classroom, collaborative learning is somewhat more formal because collaboration must be directed towards helping students learn about a specific topic or approach a certain goal. In most cases the teacher will assign a task for students to work on in small group discussions or in a large class discussion. Through their exchange of ideas, students attempt to arrive at a consensus over the assigned topic. As the students collaborate, the teacher may stand aside completely, watch the students' progress, or facilitate discussion, but he must not appear as a class leader or critic. Ideally, the teacher is not a judge or a mere repository of knowledge, but a collaborator who sets goals and organizes discussion.[1]

----

[1] For a more detailed discussion of collaborative learning with practical models, see Kenneth A. Bruffee, <u>A Short Course in Writing</u> (Boston: Little, Brown and Company, 1980), pp. 103-134.

Although collaborative learning in the classroom has been accepted by a significant number of educators only in the last twenty years, the benefits of collaboration in education are by no means a new discovery. According to Kenneth A. Bruffee, director of CUNY/Brooklyn College's peer tutoring center, collaborative learning is "an old principle which wise teachers have known for ages--that students can often teach each other things which resist assimilation through the direct instruction of a teacher."[2] Though the benefits of collaborative learning may have been known for years, they were not articulated until the early and middle 1960s. At the University of London in 1960, M.L.J. Abercrombie published The Anatomy of Judgement, a study describing how peer group discussion was much more effective than traditional instruction in helping medical students learn to make proper judgements and accurate diagnoses. Abercrombie noted that "there are very serious limitations on the extent to which a teacher can help a student to think as distinct from giving him part of an established body of knowledge."[3] Six years later, sociologists Thomas M. Newcomb and Everett K. Wilson described the effects of peer influence on college students in their study, College Peer Groups. In the preface, Newcomb and Wilson hinted at the potential of peer influence in education: "Few students, we suspect, are immune to peer group influence, and we think such influence merits more study than it has received, for both teacher and social scientist have a stake in the matter."[4]

Since students in a collaborative setting learn through communication and interaction with peers rather than only experts, they must have sufficient basic knowledge of a subject to permit discussion, and this knowledge may well be imparted in a traditional classroom situation. In a traditional classroom, however, students can learn to make judgements about their subject only by adopting, imitating, or rejecting their teacher's values. Collaborative learning situations, on the other hand, allow the students to see beyond their own limited perspectives as they express their own ideas and listen to the ideas of fellow students. From this variety of ideas and viewpoints, they develop and express new ideas and make judgements based on a wider perspective than their own or their teacher's. When their formal classroom instruction is supplemented by a collaborative environment, students may expand their narrow view of a subject by "getting outside of themselves" and becoming aware of the different ways of approaching and thinking about the subject.[5]

Since collaborative learning methods are especially effective in making students more conscious of familiar subjects, they are particularly applicable to the teaching of writing.[6]

----

[2] Kenneth A. Bruffee, "The Brooklyn Plan: Attaining Intellectual Growth Through Peer-Group Tutoring," Liberal Education 64 (December 1978), 447.

[3] M.L.J. Abercrombie, The Anatomy of Judgement (London: Hutchinson & Co. Ltd, 1960), p. 77.

[4] Theodore M. Newcomb and Everett K. Wilson, College Peer Groups (Chicago: Aldine Publishing Company, 1966), p. vii.

[5] Kenneth A. Bruffee, A Short Course in Writing (Boston: Little, Brown and Company, 1980), pp. 103-4.

[6] Perhaps the most influential and helpful book describing the use of collaborative techniques in the teaching of writing is Peter Elbow's Writing Without Teachers (New

As Bruffee points out, we are all fluent in our own language, but to write effectively we must become aware of how to use the language. When we write, we constantly make judgements and choices: we select a topic, choose the most effective words, and determine appropriate punctuation.[7] In a collaborative setting, where students' papers are either read aloud or commented on by members of the group, writers will be able to decide exactly how their choices affect readers. When students receive graded papers from an instructor, there is usually an evaluation and perhaps a comment expressing overall approval or disapproval. Evaluative comments, however, do not always indicate the basis of of a paper's success or failure in the way that specific reader responses can. Evaluations may explain what is wrong with a paper, but they rarely show why it is wrong. When peer readers respond to a student's paper, the student can see the consequences of her choices and discuss with classmates ways of making more effective choices in future papers. An evaluation by itself rarely helps a writer improve her approach to writing; it shows her only that her approach did or did not work.

While some professors, particularly those who teach small classes, are able to comment extensively on student prose, others lack the time, willingness, or even the knowledge necessary to comment effectively. Even those who do make extensive comments do not have the peer's advantage of being in the same academic situation as students. Instructors remain separated from the students academically as well as socially and therefore cannot sympathize with a student's writing problem and provide a helpful audience in the same way that another student can. Although peer collaborators invariably do not have the training or the knowledge necessary to make sophisticated comments, they share the same writing process, similar writing problems, and the same goal as students. They provide a sympathetic, responsive audience that can help students develop a sense of audience and voice that will encourage them to write confidently for specific readers.

This personal relationship among collaborating peers also seems to foster more rapid, long-term improvements in student writing. Peer responses do not include grades or formal evaluation, so students are more likely to be concerned with improving their writing skills than with the immediate result of a single paper. In spite of the difficulty involved in measuring how much a student's writing improves as a direct result of a particular type of instruction, studies in recent years have demonstrated that the writing of students who work in peer groups improves as much or more than the writing of students in traditional classrooms. A 1972 study conducted by J.R. Lagana at the University of Pittsburgh showed that although students evaluated by teachers conformed more easily to academic writing conventions, students who received peer responses improved more rapidly in organization, critical thinking, and sentence revision.[8]

Although collaborative learning appeared in some classrooms in the early sixties, it was not widely accepted. But in the middle and late sixties, peer collaboration became a more viable educational alternative as student protest and antagonism towards school

---

York: Oxford University Press, 1973).

7 Kenneth A. Bruffee, "Collaborative Learning: Some Practical Models," College English 34 (February 1973), 640–42, and A Short Course in Writing, pp. 103–5.

8 Studies by Lagana (1972), Ford (1973), and others are summarized by Mary H. Beaven, "Individualized Goal Setting, Self-Evaluation, and Peer Evaluation," in Evaluating Writing, ed. Charles R. Cooper and Lee Odell (Urbana, IL: NCTE, 1977), p. 151.

administrations peaked. Since many students regarded professors as part of the institution that imposed rules on them, the distance between students and their instructors grew even greater. With instructors providing such a distant audience for student writers, traditional teacher-student interaction appeared insufficient as the sole mode of teaching and learning writing.

The political atmosphere and, more importantly, the growing awareness of collaborative learning's potential were largely responsible for its integration into more classrooms and for the establishment of peer tutoring programs based on peer collaboration. By 1970, collaborative learning had found its way into composition courses at many schools, and in the early 1970s, formal peer tutoring programs were introduced at Brooklyn College and the University of California at Berkeley.[9] Since then, peer tutoring programs have appeared in several forms at numerous American colleges and universities in spite of the opposition to student collaboration that still prevails among educators. While some newer peer tutoring programs have strayed from the collaborative learning emphasis, others remain attached to the belief that peers offer a writer a particular kind of assistance that is unavailable in the traditional classroom.

Peer Tutoring: Collaborative Learning Institutionalized

By moving collaborative learning out of the classroom and making it part of a formal program, peer tutoring institutionalized collaborative learning and put it to work in new ways. When peer tutoring programs substitute the tutorial for the larger classroom, they change the relationship between collaborators. Although the peer tutor invariably learns from his tutees, the primary objective in the peer tutorial, unlike the collaborative classroom, is for one participant, the tutee, to learn while the other, the tutor, helps him to learn. The peer tutor is no longer a mere collaborator, but a collaborator who is usually a year or two older than his counterpart, and who presumably possesses a certain amount of knowledge that enables him to give directed responses to fellow students. The one-to-one format also differs from the group or classroom format because it restricts the amount of feedback and therefore the variety of perspectives that the collaborator or tutee is exposed to. At the same time, however, the one-to-one relationship creates greater familiarity between collaborators, and allows the tutor to provide more direct, concentrated criticism. Since it involves only two participants, the peer tutorial is far more flexible than the class or group meeting, and it allows the collaborators to discuss a writing exercise both before and after the final draft is completed.

Peer tutoring programs differ from both traditional and collaborative classrooms since tutors can more easily intervene in the writing process. In most classes, instructors or collaborators focus primarily or exclusively on the students' final written products because their time is limited and their work load is too heavy to permit analysis of each draft for every student, but peer tutors may work with writers as they move through the various stages of the writing process. Whether the tutor comments in writing on a draft or confers with the writer about an outline, a draft, or even unorganized thoughts, he concentrates not only on the product, but also on the steps the writer takes to reach that final product. Like the instructor, the peer tutor will almost always make writers aware of "product errors" in spelling or grammar, but ideally the peer tutor's goal is not merely to

---

9 Joan Putz, "When the Teacher Stops Teaching--An Experiment with Freshman English," College English 32 (October 1970), 50.

proofread or edit, but to help writers learn how to effectively approach writing tasks.

Peer tutoring programs also help provide student writers with what Thom Hawkins, Coordinator of the Writing Center at Berkeley, refers to as "a link between writer and audience which is often missing when students write only for teachers."[10] Hawkins explains that a distant, judgemental audience can create impersonal and timid writing in which students remove themselves from papers, evading responsibility for their assertions and writing in a generic academic voice.[11] Peer tutors create an audience that is more receptive and better able to discuss writing problems "because of the intensely personal characteristics of the social contract between them and their students."[12] Students can learn how to write comfortably and confidently during informal conferences with peer tutors who have written successfully in the eyes of the accepted academic audience. And since peer tutors discuss the writing process from the point of view of peers who are also part of the academic audience, they can help student writers learn to write more powerfully and assume responsibility for their assertions. Bruffee noted that discussions with peer tutors "who are personally sympathetic as well as academically competent" helps students overcome writing problems "caused by the students' inability to imagine an intelligent, sympathetic audience."[13] Though apparently minor, these fundamental differences between peer tutoring and either traditional classroom instruction or classroom collaborative learning are the basis for many of the issues and conflicts that currently confront peer tutoring programs.

In order to become this non-judgemental and personal link between students and their instructors, tutors must avoid assuming only the role of expert. Since their selection or training insures that they have some sort of writing expertise, tutors must avoid becoming distant readers; they must maintain a difficult balance between playing the role of expert and the role of a fellow student who experiences similar writing problems. The tutor must have sufficient expertise to be helpful while appearing to the tutee as a peer in a collaborative environment. In addition, peer tutors must intervene in and focus on the student's writing process to help improve the student's writing skills and, at the same time, remain aware of what Berkeley tutor Gary Lichtenstein calls "the practical realities of the academic setting."[14] In other words, the tutor must account for the fact that the student is concerned with the instructor's expectations and the success of the final product. Peer tutors, therefore, must always be mindful of their roles if they are to be successful; they must attempt to remain peers while being tutors.

---

[10] Thom Hawkins, "Intimacy and Audience: The Relationship Between Revision and the Social Dimension of Peer Tutoring," College English 42 (September 1980), 64.

[11] Richard Lanham calls this type of writing "the school style" and discusses it at length in Revising Prose (New York: Charles Scribner's Sons, 1979), pp. 80–102.

[12] Thom Hawkins, "Intimacy and Audience," p. 64.

[13] Kenneth A. Bruffee, "Staffing and Operating Peer-Tutoring Writing Centers," in Tutoring Writing: A Sourcebook for Writing Labs, ed. Muriel Harris (Glenview, IL: Scott, Foresman, 1981), pp. 141–149.

[14] Gary Lichtenstein, "The Ethics of Peer Tutoring," Writing Center Journal 4 (Fall/Winter 1983), p. 33.

Selecting and Training Peer Tutors

Since peer tutors must maintain this ambiguous position, the process of selecting and, more importantly, training peer tutors is vital to the success of a peer tutoring program. The selection process usually begins with a prospective tutor's self-nomination or nomination by a faculty member. Tutors may be primarily English and humanities majors as in the University of California at Berkeley's program, or, as is the case at Brown University, tutors may major in any discipline, from biology to English to mathematics. Most schools require nominees to undergo an application process that may include letters of recommendation, writing samples, participation in upper level English courses, mock tutoring situations, and interviews. Several program directors have found that the best tutors are usually, though not always, proficient writers. But writing skills are not the sole prerequisite for effective tutoring--tutors must interact well with peers and they must have a strong interest in writing and helping fellow students with writing.

Once tutors are selected, they must be trained to maintain the balance between being an expert and being a peer. In a program that requires no training, tutors may lack adequate understanding of their role or knowledge of how to comment effectively. As a result, tutors will often fail to offer directed, helpful discussion of writing problems or maintain a peer relationship with tutees.

The majority of colleges and universities train their peer tutors through courses within the English or education department curriculum. These courses usually fall somewhere between the the one extreme that focuses on composition theory and the other that teaches the tutor how to create a collaborative environment by maintaining a peer role.

The program at Brooklyn College, for example, requires tutors to enroll in an intermediate composition course that concentrates heavily on role playing, but lightly on composition theory.[15] In their training course, the tutors learn the principles and benefits of collaborative learning by interacting with the other students in the course. According to course director Kenneth A. Bruffee, "The relevant aspects of the students' common environment about which they learn new sets of expectations in the Brooklyn Plan are each other's writing, thought, and judgement, and also the thought and writing of the students they tutor."[16] Students enrolled in the course write four papers, eight critiques of other students' papers, and two responses to student critiques of their own papers. On the day that a paper is due, students read their papers aloud to the class and then exchange them, with each student commenting on two classmates' papers. Finally, all of the papers are handed in to the instructor who evaluates and comments on both the papers and the critiques.

Through this process, peer tutors are subjected to the same situations and pressures that their tutees face when they meet with a tutor--both are writing papers that will be carefully examined and commented on by a peer. By teaching the peer tutors to accept as well as provide criticism, and thereby understand their tutee's situation, Bruffee hopes to make the tutors view their tutees as peers so that it will be easier for the tutees to

---

15 For more detailed description of peer tutoring at Brooklyn College, see Bruffee "The Brooklyn Plan."

16 Bruffee, "The Brooklyn Plan," p. 456.

view the tutors as peers.

The two-semester training course designed by Thom Hawkins and Rondi Gilbert at the University of California at Berkeley emphasizes role playing, but also demands that tutors know how to identify, analyze, and address specific student writing problems. In discussions and readings that stress the benefits of collaboration over evaluation, Hawkins and Gilbert concentrate on the tutor's peer role. Newly selected tutors discuss student papers and watch videotapes of experienced tutors' conferences that demonstrate the tutor's collaborative role and illustrate specific tutoring skills. Later in the course, tutors analyze videotapes of their own conferences so that they can evaluate their own approaches and strategies. Perhaps most importantly, Hawkins and Gilbert use collaborative learning strategies in the training course. They assume the same role of collaborators that they hope the tutors will adopt when they tutor fellow students.

In addition to helping tutors maintain the peer role, Berkeley's training course includes readings on composition theory, such as Linda Flower's "Writer-Based Prose" (College English, September 1979) and selections from various composition handbooks. In addition, certain class meetings are designated for discussion of how to teach grammar and use techniques such as goal setting and effective questioning. In class meetings and at the Student Learning Center where the program is based, tutors discuss their own effective approaches to specific writing and learning problems, thereby using collaborative learning methods among themselves as well as with tutees. At the end of each semester, all tutors in Berkeley's training course must complete the "Tutoring Skills Test," which concentrates primarily on their knowledge of grammar and mechanics. Over half of the test examines the tutor's ability to identify terms, analyze clauses and phrases within a sentence, and locate errors within a paragraph. The remainder asks tutors to determine the strengths and weaknesses of a writing sample and explain how they might structure a conference with the writer of the sample. The test is designed not to give tutors a grade in the course, but rather to show them and the program director where each tutor's strengths are and where he needs work.

Whereas Berkeley and Brooklyn College emphasize the tutor's role in their training courses, the courses at The College of the Holy Cross and Brown University train peer tutors primarily in methods of teaching writing. At Holy Cross, students nominated by faculty and selected to tutor in the Composition Tutorial Workshop enroll in Patricia Bizzell's course, entitled "Composition Theory and Pedagogy." As the title suggests, the main purpose of the course is to introduce tutors to current work in composition studies. Tutors read books such as Erika Lindemann's A Rhetoric for Writing Teachers and Tate and Corbett's anthology The Writing Teacher's Sourcebook in order to familiarize themselves with many of the methods used by writing teachers. Although the tutors do some writing in the course, Bizzell's primary goal is to provide tutors with knowledge that will help them give tutees directed, helpful comments and suggestions.

Only slightly less theory-based is the course used to train peer tutors for Brown University's Undergraduate Writing Fellows Program. Designed and run by Tori Haring-Smith, the course is divided into sections that focus on such topics as the writing process, defining good writing, evaluating writing, analyzing style, curing writer's block, and the teaching of organization, grammar, invention, argumentation, and revision. Tutors study and evaluate the strengths and weaknesses of theories such as Christensen's generative rhetoric and E.D. Hirsch's principle of readability, and they explore recent research on the composing process in books by theorists such as Richard Lanham, Linda Flower, and Peter Elbow. During semi-weekly discussion seminars, tutors translate theory into practice by relating their readings to classroom and tutoring situations and by applying theories and methods to sample papers.

As they study composition theory, tutors also write several papers and exchange comments on these papers. During the discussions, students analyze the tone, validity, and helpfulness of each other's comments, and they experience what it is like to receive peer criticism. Recently, Brown's training course increased its attention to the tutor's peer role by adding a section on conferencing skills.

The differences between the training courses at Brown, Holy Cross, Brooklyn College, and the University of California at Berkeley suggest that the most effective training course for a particular school depends significantly on the size of the school, the nature and goals of the program, and the type of students who attend the school. Yet the basic dilemma remains of whether to emphasize the tutor's role or his knowledge of theory and grammar. As Bruffee points out, to be effective, tutors must be "fairly well-trained. . . . Yet if they're too well-trained or too much older, tutees don't perceive them as peers but as little teachers, and the collaborative effect of peers working together is lost."[17] On the other hand, as Marvin Garrett of the University of Cincinnati notes, if tutors are inadequately trained in theory and mechanics, "tutoring sessions may lack focus and direction, degenerate into 'bull' sessions, and conclude with tutees departing as confused as when they arrived." Training peer tutors only in theory or exclusively in the peer role will, therefore, create tutors whose comments have the qualities of what Garrett called "directiveness" <u>or</u> "responsiveness."[18] Tutors trained only in theory will be able to provide directed criticism that helps students respond to and correct specific problems, but they may not understand their collaborative role. Conversely, tutors instructed only in their peer role will most likely be responsive peers, but they may not be able to offer more than sympathetic but unspecific reactions to student writing.

A general solution, it seems, is to provide tutors with both types of training--to maintain peer tutoring's essential ties to collaborative learning while providing tutors with the knowledge of composition theory and grammar necessary to make them more than just collaborators. Though this solution may be obvious, it is not simple since the question arises of whether a tutor can possibly be a peer while also being an expert. One possible positive answer is that "peerness" is not necessarily a function of knowledge, but rather of institutional role or status. As a student, therefore, the peer tutor is the tutee's peer as long as the tutee does not perceive the tutor as an expert. Some peer tutoring programs have tried to avoid this misperception by eliminating the word "tutor" from their titles (e.g. The Undergraduate Writing Fellows at Brown University and the Writing Consultants at Beaver College and the University of Pennsylvania). The goal of a training course is to assess the school's needs and then train tutors to achieve what Garrett called "a delicate balance" between being purely collaborative and being expert tutors.

---

17 Kenneth A. Bruffee with Paula Beck, Thom Hawkins, and Marcia Silver, "Training and Using Peer Tutors," <u>College English</u>, 40 (December 1978), 446.

18 Marvin Garrett, "Toward a Delicate Balance: The Importance of Role Playing and Peer Criticism in Peer Tutor-Training," in <u>Tutoring Writing: A Sourcebook for Writing Labs</u>, ed. Muriel Harris (Glenview, IL: Scott, Foresman, 1981), p. 95.

Organization

Once tutors are selected and trained, they may be made available to students in any of several different ways, but most programs can be grouped into one of three general categories of organization. The oldest and most common organization is the writing center-based peer tutoring program in which the peer tutors work by themselves or with graduate or faculty tutors in a writing center or any form of student learning center. The tutors generally hold conferences in the center with students who walk in, set up an appointment, or arrange regular meeting times, but in some cases students with writing deficiencies are referred to the peer tutors for assistance. Like all other programs, writing center-based programs may serve all types of students or, like the peer tutors at the University of California at Berkeley, they may provide help exclusively or primarily for students in English or composition courses. The primary advantages of basing a peer tutoring program in a writing center are that a single, central location makes tutors easy to find at all times and fosters communication and collaboration among tutors by keeping them together so that they can learn from each other as well as from students.

Less common than the writing center-based programs are residentially based peer tutors. Residentially based programs operate much like writing center-based programs, but the tutors are distributed throughout campus--in dormitories, libraries, or other areas commonly used by students. At the University of Pennsylvania, for example, Residential Advisors who live in dormitories with the students are also trained as Writing Consultants through a series of lectures and discussions. Though the program has the disadvantage of choosing its tutors not only on basis of their potential as writing tutors, but also on their qualifications as Residential Advisors, it also has the advantage of providing the students with extremely accessible peer tutors. A similar but smaller program at Smith College employs thirteen peer tutors who are selected, trained, and supervised by the professional staff in the writing center, but who work primarily outside the center--in residence halls, the library, and the computer center.

The main advantage of residentially based programs such as these is that they send the tutors out to students rather than asking students to come to them. Though use of the tutors remains voluntary, the fact that a tutor is frequently nearby can encourage more students to seek help. At Smith, for example, the thirteen peer tutors are able to serve over half of the school's 2600 students. But residentially based programs also have the disadvantage of being unable to promote collaboration among tutors as a writing center-based program can; and residentially based tutors usually do not have the abundance of books, periodicals, cassettes, or handouts on writing that are readily available in many writing centers.

The newest and presently the least common form of organization is found in cross-curricular peer tutoring programs, which have become more common with the rising interest in writing across the curriculum. Cross-curricular programs are designed to expose a high percentage of students from all disciplines to peer tutoring in writing by having tutors work in various courses from many departments. At Carleton College, peer Rhetoric Assistants work not only in the writing center, but also in selected courses to help students meet the college's cross-curricular writing requirement, which demands that students take either a required composition course or a writing intensive course in any department that offers one. In these writing intensive courses, professors require more writing from those students taking the course to meet the university's writing requirement. Many of the professors are aided by peer rhetoric assistants who work with these students in conferences or through written comments on drafts. To familiarize themselves with the subject matter of the course in which they are working, Rhetoric Assistants frequently attend the class, and they are often chosen to work in a course because of their familiarity with its content. Since all students except an exempted few must take either the composition course or a writing intensive course, a high percentage of Carleton's students are served by the Rhetoric Assistants.

A very different cross-curricular peer tutoring program is beginning its third year at Brown University. Brown's sixty Undergraduate Writing Fellows work in a wide range of courses in departments as different as history, biology, and environmental studies. Students in these courses submit papers to their assigned Writing Fellow, who makes written comments on the papers before returning them to the students. After the Writing Fellow and the student discuss the paper and the Fellow's written comments, the student revises the paper and submits both the original and the revised copy to the course instructor. Unlike many peer tutoring programs, the Writing Fellows Program requires all students enrolled in a participating course to submit their papers to the Writing Fellow. This requirement encourages all students to revise, and it insures that writing assistance is provided not only for problem writers, but also for skilled writers who are frequently neglected by writing programs.

The advantage of Brown's program and most cross-curricular programs is that the peer tutors are able to assist a very high percentage of the student body. At Brown, the Writing Fellows serve approximately 3000 of the 5300 undergraduates each year, commenting on close to 9000 papers, essays, and lab reports. Cross-curricular programs are able to reach far beyond the English department while other programs often serve primarily English students and writing students, even when they are designed to serve all students. But there are disadvantages to cross-curricular programs as well. Like residentially based programs, cross-curricular programs usually lack a walk-in center to foster collaboration among tutors. And without such a walk-in center, cross-curricular programs may deny peer assistance to students who need or desire it, but who are not enrolled in a course with peer tutors.

Some peer tutoring programs have expanded beyond their formal organization to provide assistance to writers in other ways. Numerous programs have designed workshops or seminars to help interested students or entire classes with specific writing problems or assignments. At Berkeley, the peer tutoring program was awarded a grant to provide training in the teaching of writing for teaching assistants in several departments. And at Brown, Writing Fellows have designed and run workshops for gifted elementary school students from a neighboring town.

Past and Future Challenges

Such expansion and innovation correctly suggest that individual programs as well as the concept of peer tutoring in writing have come a long way since the early 1970s. But each new program, along with the theory behind peer tutoring, faces difficult challenges and problems of doubt, fear, misuse, and opposition among supporters of purely traditional modes of teaching.

The programs established in the early 1970s faced strong skepticism among faculty and administrators because they were an untested novelty based on the unfamiliar and threatening principle of collaborative learning, which undermined prevailing methods of instruction. The notion that peers could assist students as effectively as instructors was bound to encounter strong opposition from instructors and administrators who distrusted the entire concept, knew little about it, or felt threatened by it. The only way these young programs could overcome such opposition was to prove that they were effective by showing that the peer tutors were well-trained and able to make a difference in student writing. The longevity of programs at Brooklyn College, the University of California at Berkeley, and other schools indicates that some programs have convinced faculty and administrators. Although new programs are no longer such a novelty, they still encounter doubt, and at some schools, they are opposed by faculty concerned that peer tutors are "moving in on their territory." Just as the older programs did, the new ones must prove themselves to skeptics by showing that peer tutoring provides a supplement, not a replacement for a classroom writing program.

Like doubt among faculty and administrators, student skepticism represents a recurring problem that can make effective peer tutoring difficult. Although student response to peer tutoring programs has been extremely positive, many programs have suffered from student disuse or misuse. Students are often reluctant to submit their work to a peer, because they regard peer tutors as unqualified, and because peer commenting violates the traditional secrecy between individual students and their instructors. Many more students misuse or resist peer assistance because they do not understand the concept of peer tutoring. Students may mistakenly regard a tutor's suggestions as demands, thereby defeating the tutor's attempt to help the tutee learn how to make judgements while writing. Students may also resist peer advice if the peer's suggestions often contradict the instructor's. Even if the contradiction is little more than a matter of opinion, the student is likely to reject the peer's advice in future instances because it has opposed the word of the instructor, whose position of authority and need to evaluate make him more persuasive. These misunderstandings can usually be avoided if tutors make their purposes clear to students, but there is little peer tutors can do when students use peer assistance as a means to a achieve a better grade rather than to improve their writing skills. In a competitive academic setting, students will frequently regard peer tutors as editors or proofreaders who will help their paper receive a better evaluation. In spite of these possible problems, most students who receive peer assistance respond positively to the program, indicating that students are easier to convince than faculty--perhaps because they can more easily see the benefits of non-judgemental comments made by a sympathetic peer.

Even if peer tutoring programs can eventually overcome skepticism, they still face the threat of mishandling or misuse by administrators and instructors. Peer tutoring represents a relatively inexpensive and attractive alternative for administrators who can not easily afford to hire numerous faculty or build more comprehensive programs. Since peer tutoring is so inexpensive, programs might be used as alternatives rather than supplements to classroom instruction, or faculty might assign tutors inappropriate duties like the grading of papers. Such mishandling neglects the roots of peer tutoring in collaborative learning, causing peer tutors to become little more than mini-teachers. When this situation occurs, the peer tutoring program is reduced to a process described by Harvey Kail, Director of the Writing Lab at the University of Maine at Orono: "a teacher teaches a student to tutor a fellow student to satisfy another teacher."[19]

In the absence of mishandling and skepticism, peer tutoring programs still face the possibility of a gradual move away from emphasis on peer collaboration and towards concentration only on composition theory. This trend is evident in the newer training

----

19 Harvey Kail, "Collaborative Learning in Context: The Problem with Peer Tutoring," College English 45 (October 1983), 596.

courses such as those at Holy Cross and Brown, which are more concerned with composition theory and less concerned with the collaborative role than the older courses at Brooklyn College and Berkeley. If this trend continues too far, then the collaborative aspect that separates peer tutoring from traditional modes may be lost.

The attachment of many educators to purely traditional teaching methods in an academic world that remains overwhelmingly anti-collaborative represents the major challenge to peer tutoring in the near future. But as new programs are established and developed, and continue to receive positive responses, peer tutoring in writing may overcome the difficulties it faces and become an accepted supplement to English curricula. Or, even more optimistically, Harvey Kail's supposition may prove correct: "If the lore of academia comes to include a tradition of student tutors as part of the official audience of other students' writing, it is my guess that we will have fundamentally changed our ideas of what teaching and learning writing actually involves."[20]

Nathaniel Hawkins

----

[20] Kail, p. 599.

BEYOND THE ENGLISH DEPARTMENT: WRITING ACROSS THE CURRICULUM

In the mid-1970's, the news media discovered that Johnny couldn't write, and it was big news. Magazines and newspapers drew the nation's attention to the decline in student writing ability, blaming factors as disparate as television, equal opportunity programs, and parents. But in most cases, the heaviest criticism was leveled at English teachers.

Within colleges and universities, faculty in all disciplines began to complain about students whose writing skills were deficient. Institutions responded to this criticism by raising their entrance requirements, by advising or requiring students to take more English courses, and by instituting competency tests for students and teachers alike. But, except for the competency examinations aimed at faculty, none of these reforms answered the basic criticism that the English department, and more specifically the classical freshman composition course, failed to train students properly. Randall Freisinger, Director of Freshman English at Michigan Technological University, explains, "To many of our colleagues outside of English, one point seems obvious. The responsibility of teaching students to write belongs exclusively to English departments, and these departments have generally failed miserably in meeting this responsibility."[1]

In part, English departments probably were at fault, and their self-examination resulted in movements like "Back to Basics" and the shift to a process paradigm. But the problem also stemmed from the fact that English teachers were fighting the battle single-handedly; their colleagues and students alike perceived writing as an elementary skill divorced from content and thought--an activity of concern only to English teachers. While English teachers were assuring students that competency in writing was a basic skill needed in all disciplines, their colleagues were not commenting on student writing problems since they viewed that activity to be the task of the English department. As a result, English teachers were frequently perceived as preaching an archaic and unreal set of standards. Students discovered from experience that their poor writing skills did not hamper their success in the academic world--or so they thought. The solution to these problems was obvious: involve professors from all disciplines in teaching students to

----

1 Randall Freisinger, "Cross-Disciplinary Writing Workshops: Theory and Practice," College English 42 (October 1980), 154.

write.

This idea is hardly a new one, but rather marks a return to the notion that rhetoric is fundamental to all aspects of a liberal education, a pedagogical assumption still in force at English and Continental universities. The idea is so alien to American teachers that before an American college or university adopts what has come to be called writing across the curriculum, its faculty must be re-educated to recognize that writing is not a specialized skill solely the purview of the English department. They must perceive that all teachers have a responsibility to instruct their students in the language and logic of their discipline.

This recognition is difficult for faculty members who think of good writing as good grammar. Viewing writing from this perspective, faculty outside the English department can claim that they lack the technical expertise to teach writing and that such skill, while useful, bears no relationship to the subjects they must teach. To persuade their colleagues that writing is relevant to the learning and expression of all knowledge, English teachers need to understand how the process of writing drives the process of learning. When students write down ideas that have been presented to them and translate those ideas into their own words, they learn concepts more thoroughly--whether they are studying physics, poetry, or anthropology. In this way, the writing-across-the-curriculum movement has helped fuel the paradigmatic shift within the profession from an emphasis on product to an emphasis on process. The process approach, advocated by researchers and teachers like James Britton (Developmental Writing Abilities (11-18)) and Linda Flower (Problem-Solving Strategies for Writers), gives English teachers a way to discuss writing with their colleagues from other departments. Rather than equating writing with the relatively arcane study of grammar and literary analysis, English faculty can now stress the more universal notions of revision, invention, and writing as learning.

By the late seventies, English faculty at several institutions had convinced their colleagues to experiment with writing-across-the-curriculum programs, and in the last five years or so, the notion of writing across the curriculum has become popular and widespread. In implementing writing across the curriculum, colleges and universities have structured programs in a variety of ways that reflect the curricular structure and educational philosophies of the individual schools.

Writing-Intensive Courses

Many institutions have designated certain courses throughout the curriculum as "writing-intensive." Although instructors in these courses may or may not devote class time to the teaching of writing within their discipline, they usually agree to assign and evaluate a certain amount of student writing. Writing-intensive courses may be proposed by faculty throughout the college, selected by a university-wide committee, or chosen by the English department. In some cases, the administration of the program is handled by the English department, but the program may also be autonomous.

Establishing a program of writing-intensive courses shifts part of the responsibility for teaching writing to departments other than English, even though the teachers involved may be trained or supervised by English faculty. For this reason, it is probably the most prevalent form of writing across the curriculum. Such programs assume that students can best be taught to write within a discipline, that is, when they write to an expert in the field who can judge not only the quality of the writing but also the accuracy of the content and the quality of thought within a discipline-specific essay. This model assumes that all educated readers and writers can discuss and evaluate prose.

The structure of writing-intensive courses is probably best known as it exists at the University of Michigan. Instituted in 1978, the Michigan program requires all students to take an upper-level writing-intensive course in their sophomore or junior year. If possible, students take this course in their area of concentration, or, if no such course is available, they may take the upper-level course in any area. Faculty who teach these courses are offered seminars on the teaching of writing and given the assistance of specially trained graduate assistants. Although these courses may take many forms, most require six substantial pieces of writing.

A program that relies even more heavily on the assistance of graduate students is the "Writing Across the University" program at the University of Pennsylvania. At this school, graduate students from several departments attend colloquia in order to learn how to teach writing, and then work with faculty in various disciplines. The graduate students serve as teaching assistants with special expertise in writing, who may direct discussion groups, evaluate student writing, and hold conferences with students. This program operates upon the premise that scholars in all disciplines have the potential to help students with writing since they, too, are writers. The writing-intensive courses at the University of Pennsylvania explicitly stress the process of writing. Writing and revision are integral parts of these courses, offering students "opportunities for frequent and systematic consultation during the composing process," as the program description states. Much of this consultation is done through classroom discussion of writing. Perhaps because of their emphasis on the basics of the writing process, most courses in the program are offered at the freshman level.

Clark University's program of writing-intensive courses (called Verbal Expression or VE courses) also explicitly stresses the teaching of writing as a learning process. Whereas any course may require writing, the VE courses ask that the instructors review the various stages of composition. An instructor may, for example, assign one long, graded term paper, but require students to submit parts of the paper every week or so, giving them the chance for extensive revision. In revising their papers, students have the opportunity for individual conferences with their instructors, and they meet with each other in "teacherless writing groups" led by a trained undergraduate teaching assistant. These peer editing groups provide students with several different opinions of their writing; the professor no longer has the only word about the quality of a student's prose.

While each of these programs asks some faculty outside the English department to offer specific courses in writing for their discipline, at Beaver College all courses involve formal or informal writing. Faculty at Beaver attend summer training seminars and then integrate the teaching of writing into their courses. They must assume complete responsibility for educating students to write; they cannot rely on the assistance of trained graduate students or peer tutors to grade papers or hold conferences with students. The comprehensiveness of the Beaver College program makes it particularly attractive since it illustrates to students that writing is an important facet of all learning, not just a component of special courses.

Training Seminars

Because faculty need to be re-educated before a school can institute a curriculum change as deep and far-reaching as a program of writing-intensive courses, most colleges and universities first train faculty from all disciplines about alternative ways of teaching writing within content courses. "Curricular change has to be based on scholarly exchange between faculty members," proclaims Elaine Maimon, Director of Writing Programs at Beaver College. Although faculty members' frustration with student writing may make them eager to change the way writing is taught, they need to discuss exactly how they plan to implement these changes. In a brief history of writing across the curriculum, Maimon asserts, "The first schools to establish cross-disciplinary writing programs began by inviting faculty members from all disciplines to become students again, to join in seminars during summer and winter vacations."[2] Inspired by summer rhetoric seminars at Carleton College led by then Dean of the College Harriet Sheridan, Maimon began conducting similar workshops at Beaver College. These workshops give faculty the opportunity for that "scholarly exchange" and teach the underlying principles of cross-disciplinary writing through discussions of teaching techniques, writing assignments, principles of rhetoric, and writing in all disciplines. Through these seminars, teachers explore how to restructure their courses in order to emphasize the twin processes of learning and writing.

Toby Fulwiler, currently the Director of Writing at the University of Vermont, agrees with this strategy for implementing writing-across-the-curriculum.

> We believed that to improve student writing we had to influence the entire academic community in which writing takes place, to make faculty sensitive to the role of writing in learning as well as to the relationship of writing to other communication skills--reading, speaking, and listening.[3]

Before taking his current position at the University of Vermont, Fulwiler spent several years at Michigan Technological University where he led writing workshops affecting more than 200 faculty members. The workshops, which he now offers at Vermont, explore how writing promotes learning in all subject areas, why students sometimes write poorly, and why and how to integrate writing, along with reading, talking, and listening, into the everyday life of the classroom. After teachers discuss principles of teaching and perform exercises designed to expose them to the benefits of a process-orientation, they try to integrate these ideas into their classrooms.

Although Fulwiler, Maimon and others report that faculty seminars are quite successful, establishing them at a given institution is not always easy. Frequently, it is difficult to interest faculty in taking on what many perceive as extra teaching duties--especially when they must devote part of their summer to training seminars. Quite understandably, faculty members who are forced to participate in a training program will resent it and will resist the idea of writing across the curriculum. In conducting his workshops, Toby Fulwiler has realized that "workshops cannot inspire or transform unmotivated, inflexible, or highly suspicious faculty members. Participants must . . . be willing to share ideas, rather than compete with them."[4] In order to entice faculty to participate in training seminars, many colleges and universities offer participants incentives like honoraria. While these incentives may boost attendance, they raise the cost of the program and do not necessarily increase faculty commitment to the idea of

---

2 Elaine P. Maimon, "Writing-Across-the-Curriculum: Past, Present, and Future," in New Directions for Teaching and Learning: Teaching Writing in All Disciplines, no. 12 (San Francisco: Jossey Bass, 1982), p. 67.

3 Toby Fulwiler, "How Well Does Writing Across the Curriculum Work?" College English 46 (February 1984), 113.

4 Fulwiler, p. 115.

writing across the curriculum.

Even those faculty who attend seminars voluntarily may well resent being told by other faculty how to teach, especially if their own methods have seemed satisfactory in the past. Unless carefully designed, training seminars can increase this resistance if participants believe that they are being bullied into teaching a subject that should be solely the concern of the English department. Before the participants are ready to explore how writing can work in their classrooms, they must agree that faculty in all disciplines should share the responsibility for teaching writing. Getting a large number of people to agree to any such proposition is very difficult. For these reasons, training even a small percentage of the faculty takes a great deal of time--"five years of focused, strenuous work is necessary for a small school; ten is a realistic minimum for a large one," according to Joan Graham.[5]

If faculty are not trained in seminars, they may receive informal training through team teaching--usually by being paired with English teachers or by working with specially trained graduate teaching assistants. This system is less likely to cause resentment since teachers are given help in their teaching rather than being asked to devote more time to it, but by fragmenting the training, it weakens the coherence of a program and gives colleagues less opportunity to discuss teaching strategies. In some programs of writing-intensive courses, teachers receive no formal training at all; they simply agree to assign and evaluate more student writing. While this system respects the teacher's "turf" and reinforces the notion that any educated reader can help students improve their writing, it does not give teachers a sense of unified purpose, and it lacks coherence and quality control. Teachers who become frustrated with the time required by the teaching of writing have no easy route to seeking advice. As a result, they may simply abandon the writing component of the course.

Some kind of training, then, seems crucial for any successful program of writing-intensive courses, and the kind of training a school adopts must be determined by the program's goals, the size of the school, and the relative importance of teaching and research at the institution.

Cross-Disciplinary Writing Courses within the English Department

In strong contrast to the writing-intensive model are programs in which the English department is responsible for teaching writing within several different disciplines. This model is most familiar in courses like technical writing and business writing, but such courses may also appear as Writing in the Humanities or Writing Mathematics. Regardless of their titles, discipline-specific writing courses offered by an English department are taught by English faculty who have special expertise or experience in the area. Such programs are attractive because they avoid the problems and costs of training faculty throughout the university. They also answer a criticism commonly leveled at writing-intensive programs: that faculty without extensive training in the teaching of writing do not have the expertise to direct amateur writers. English-based programs make full use of the talents of the English faculty, and, since they are limited to one department, such programs are also easy to administer and to make coherent. On the

---

5 Joan Graham, "What Works: Confronting the Problems and Enjoying the Rewards in Cross-Curriculum Writing Programs," p. 13. Forthcoming in Current Issues in Higher Education (1983-84).

other hand, a writing-across-the-curriculum program that consists solely of English department courses denies some of the fundamental principles of writing across the curriculum. Whereas writing-intensive courses shift part of the responsibility for teaching writing to faculty throughout the university, specialized courses within the English department can perpetuate the idea that the teaching of writing is solely the concern of English teachers. Furthermore, these programs can only teach students how to write about their discipline to a lay reader; they cannot replicate the kind of intellectual community that a writing-intensive course offers. Lil Brannon of New York University and C.H. Knoblauch of SUNY Albany question "whether or not a composition course is really the best vehicle for encouraging writing across the disciplines, precisely because the focus is likely to be on formal shells rather than on modes of thinking and learning in different domains."[6]

The University of Maryland has one of the better known writing-across-the-curriculum programs based in an English department. After taking a standard freshman composition course, Maryland students must take a second writing course during their junior year, this one with a pre-professional emphasis. While the freshman course teaches general writing skills, the junior course concentrates on writing in a specific area like the natural sciences, social sciences, or humanities. Occasionally taught by retired professionals, these courses ask students to explore the kinds of writing they may be doing in a related professional area--law briefs, economic reports, and business proposals, for example. By hiring retired professionals to help teach these courses, Maryland simulates the intellectual community available in most writing-intensive courses. On the other hand, its teachers do not have extensive training in the teaching of writing, an advantage sought by most schools with English-based programs.

In order to take full advantage of the training English teachers receive, some schools have paired writing courses taught by English faculty with content-area courses throughout the curriculum. Students enroll simultaneously in the writing course and the designated content course, and the two teachers coordinate syllabi and writing assignments. The University of Washington at Seattle offers such a program of adjunct courses in which "Writing Labs" are linked to lecture courses in eight different departments. In their Lab, students submit drafts of assignments required for the lecture course and also write papers related to the readings in the lecture course. This system gives both the teacher and the students a chance to concentrate on writing during class time, and the students benefit from receiving the criticism of teachers trained specifically to comment upon student prose. On the other hand, a system of adjunct courses like Washington's clearly reinforces the separation of writing from content, and it may encourage students to adopt the erroneous notion that writing is only of interest to English teachers. The freshman composition courses at Beaver College have a similar structure. At least one of the four major papers required in each semester of this two-semester course must be coordinated with work the student is doing in another freshman course like biology or psychology. Frequently students will work on assignments for other classes within their freshman writing course. Although this system also implies the separation of writing from content, Beaver College students must realize that writing is a concern of the entire faculty since all instructors assign and evaluate writing.

----

6 Lil Brannon and C. H. Knoblauch, "Writing as Learning Through the Curriculum," College English 45 (September 1983), 468.

Vertical Emphasis: Writing Across the Years

As colleges and universities have adopted the basic premises of writing across the curriculum--that the entire faculty should share responsibility for teaching writing and that students must practice writing in many different situations--they have built into their writing programs a vertical emphasis, ensuring that students receive writing instruction throughout their college years. Students in these programs are usually required to take a writing course within the English department during their freshman year, and then to enroll in an upper-level writing course as juniors or seniors. Whether taught outside or within the English department, these upper-level courses usually stress discipline-specific writing skills. At schools like Wittenberg University and Brown University, students' writing is examined in all courses throughout the university, and a student must maintain a certain level of competency in order to graduate. One catalyst for this movement was Derek Bok's well-known study of Harvard students' writing.[7] Bok's work demonstrated that seniors in the natural sciences, who had not practiced their writing during their college years, wrote worse prose than first-year science students who had just completed freshman composition. But senior humanities majors, who were forced to write throughout their college careers, wrote better prose than first-year humanities students fresh from a composition course. Bok's conclusion is clear: students must continually practice writing if they are to maintain their proficiency and improve their writing skills.

One of the new writing-across-the-curriculum programs, recently instituted at Ottawa University in Kansas, is notable in that it insists on discipline-specific writing for both freshmen and seniors. Instead of a freshman English course and then a later writing-intensive or cross-disciplinary writing course, students take courses outside the English Department for both components of their writing requirement. During their freshman year, students enroll in a general philosophy course that requires some form of writing nearly every day of class. Then, after completing the ten general distribution courses, all of which require writing, students enroll in a second writing-intensive course during their senior year. In this class, they explore current social and political issues and work in groups to reach a solution. Because of the amount of writing that they must do during this process, students are led to realize that the process of writing can help them with the thinking and problem-solving processes.

Combined Approaches

Many of the newer writing-across-the-curriculum programs have supplemented traditional writing courses with both writing-intensive courses and English department courses in discipline-specific writing. With this kind of combination, a vertical emphasis is inevitable. Perhaps the most ambitious such program is being proposed by the University of Texas at Austin. Once fully implemented, this program will consist of five required writing courses distributed throughout a student's undergraduate career. Three of the courses will be offered by the English Department: a standard freshman composition course, a sophomore literature course, and a junior cross disciplinary writing course in the social sciences, natural sciences, or the humanities. Students will also take two writing-intensive courses in their area of study, one of which must be at an advanced level. As James Kinneavy points out, such a comprehensive program has all

---

7 Derek Bok, "Report to the Board of Overseers," Harvard Gazette, 17 March 1978, pp. 1-2.

the advantages of both writing-intensive programs and English-based courses.[8] Students will learn the basics of good writing from teachers with extensive training in the teaching of writing, and they will be able to write about their discipline both for their colleagues and for the layman. Furthermore, they will practice writing during every year of their college education.

What Lies Ahead?

Although speculations about the future of such a rapidly growing educational reform must necessarily be tentative, programs like Austin's help us see the direction that writing across the curriculum may take in the near future. Certainly the newer programs will be more comprehensive, offering more courses in more departments and at more levels, so as to take advantage of the benefits of both English-based programs and writing-intensive courses. But the growth of these programs poses many problems as well as promising many rewards.

As new programs grow more and more comprehensive, writing-across-the-curriculum courses will consume an increasingly large percentage of a student's course load. While the ability to write clearly and use language in a persuasive and responsible manner is one of the most important skills a student can learn in college, it is not the only skill. Nor is it the most appropriate means of sparking learning in all disciplines. Schools must not overlook other creative and analytical processes like sketching, constructing mathematical models, or designing experiments. Programs that force writing into all courses for all students overlook the valuable differences in the ways students learn. Extending writing instruction into all classes also forces all instructors to include writing in their syllabi, regardless of the differences in course objectives and teaching methods. An art professor, for example, may want to train her students to analyze the world visually, not verbally, and an introductory psychology professor may determine that his students will best learn the principles of psychology by performing laboratory experiments. Forced participation in a program inevitably generates resistance. And in some cases, this resistance is justified.

Expansion of writing-across-the-curriculum programs will also strain the financial resources of many schools. Most programs require on-going faculty training (sometimes including visits by specialists and consultants), and many will require new courses, new faculty, and new administrators. Those that employ graduate or undergraduate assistants must also consider the cost of training, supervising, and supporting these people. Programs like those at Ottawa, Evergreen, and Beaver were started on so-called "soft money," grants from federal, corporate, or private foundations, and when these sources of funding dry up, their costs must be assumed by the institution. Shifts in funding can eliminate some programs, and they certainly force most to be restructured. Those programs currently funded from within the institution may be curtailed by the school's budget, and with the promise of growing enrollments still a full decade away, few schools are being liberal with their funds.

Finally, as programs age and expand, their administrators must remain aware of the need for constant evaluation. Writing-intensive courses are especially subject to change since they are relatively autonomous. Once a writing-intensive course is established, it must follow the guidelines of the writing program, whether those principles support the

----

[8] James Kinneavy, "Writing Across the Curriculum," <u>Profession 83</u> (1983), pp. 16-18.

teaching of process or simply dictate the number of pages a student will write. Programs based in the English department must re-evaluate frequently how well they are meeting the needs of students and colleagues throughout the university. In either case, it is crucial that writing across the curriculum not be allowed to degenerate into simply a group of courses that include writing assignments, a trend observed by Brannon and Knoblauch in their recent review of high school and college programs.

> Even at their best such programs emphasize "packaging across the curriculum," offering ideal models for the presentation of knowledge in different fields. In either case the main concern of a content course is the mastery of information pertinent to its field of study, while writing is a wholly subordinate activity, at most enabling students to demonstrate the extent of their learning, ceremonially as it were, in a prescribed format.[9]

Despite these potential difficulties, the expansion of writing across the curriculum is promising. With growing programs we should see more research on the subjects of writing and learning within different disciplines. This research will in turn help a larger number of institutions develop writing-across-the-curriculum programs. Soon, more schools should follow the lead of the University of Michigan, Georgetown University, and Brown University by providing workshops for secondary school teachers so that eventually writing across the curriculum can be a standard part of education at all levels.

In time, perhaps, we can even allow ourselves to imagine that if writing across the curriculum is carefully instituted, it will nurture the sense of intellectual community within a college or university. As professors from different disciplines come together to discuss teaching methods and student writing, they will develop a sense of shared purpose. James Kinneavy claims that this "miracle" has already occurred at Beaver College, and Fulwiler reports a similar sense of community at Michigan Technological University."[10] If this trend continues, educational historians will have to interpret writing across the curriculum as more than a fad or a quick-fix created by besieged English departments in the last quarter of the twentieth century. They will have to see it as a fundamental shift in educational philosophy and structure.

Tori Haring-Smith

Lise Stern

---

9 Brannon and Knoblauch, pp. 465-66.

10 Kinneavy, p. 16; Fulwiler, p. 121.

A GUIDE TO WRITING PROGRAMS

AT INDIVIDUAL COLLEGES AND UNIVERSITIES

ADELPHI UNIVERSITY

Garden City, NY 11530

Full-time Students: 1470M/3074W Faculty: 383

Respondent: Philip Greene, Professor, English Department

Writing Requirement: Required freshman English course

Peer Tutoring Program

PROGRAM HAS EXISTED: 2-5 years

ORGANIZATION: Individual conference schedule exclusively

NUMBER OF TUTORS: Fewer than 10

HOURS THEY WORK PER WEEK: Over 20

TUTORS PAID: Yes

TUTOR SELECTION: Appointed by director

TUTORS' TRAINING: No formal training

TUTORS' EVALUATION: Conferences; tutors write reports on their students

PERCENTAGE OF STUDENTS SERVED: Less than 25%

OVER PAST FIVE YEARS THIS PERCENTAGE HAS: Stayed the same

PROGRAM INTENDED TO SERVE: Students in all disciplines

PROGRAM ACTUALLY SERVES: English students and freshmen

STUDENTS SEEK HELP WITH: Remedial English

PERCENTAGE WHO CHOOSE TO USE IT: Less than 25%

MECHANICS OF TUTORING: Tutor and student are required to discuss papers in individual conferences

STUDENT ATTITUDE: Unknown

About five years ago, Adelphi University restored its two-semester freshman English requirement, which serves as the university's primary focus for writing. In addition, several of the faculty teach solely writing and offer courses in journalism, poetry and fiction writing, advanced exposition, and remedial English. Students with writing problems or questions can discuss their papers with peer tutors. Although these tutors receive no formal training, they are appointed to participate in the program based on their scholastic achievements. During the next few years, Philip Greene hopes to expand these innovative writing programs by establishing a writing center or writing lab.

ALBANY STATE COLLEGE

Albany, GA 31705

Full-time Students: 735M/1057W   Faculty: 125

Respondent: James L. Hill, Chairperson, English Department

Writing Requirement: Required freshman English courses and Regent's Examination

Writing Center

CENTER HAS EXISTED: 2-5 years   HOURS OPEN PER WEEK: 20-40

STAFF: Director and 5-20 undergraduate tutors

TUTORS' TRAINING: On-the-job and non-academic course

TUTORS' EVALUATION: Observation and conferences

TUTORS PAID: Yes

PROGRAM DESIGNED TO SERVE: Students in all disciplines

PROGRAM ACTUALLY SERVES: Students in all disciplines, particularly writing students

STUDENTS SEEK HELP WITH: Academic essays, research papers, and resumes or business writing

PERCENTAGE OF STUDENTS SERVED: Less than 25%

OVER PAST FIVE YEARS THIS PERCENTAGE HAS: Increased

STUDENTS USE CENTER: Repeatedly throughout the semester on a walk-in or appointment basis, or by referral

STUDENTS REQUIRED TO USE CENTER: None

MATERIALS AVAILABLE: Handbooks, exercises, educational magazines, and professional books

STUDENT ATTITUDE: Unknown

The basis of Albany State's writing program is its English Department, which includes more than five faculty who teach solely writing. All students must take two composition courses during their freshman year, and pass the Regent's Examination before they graduate. Outside the classroom, Albany State students may seek writing assistance from the peer tutors or the faculty director at the writing center. The center remains open over twenty hours each week and serves a small but increasing percentage of the student body.

ALFRED UNIVERSITY

Alfred, NY 14802

Full-time Students: 984M/895W Faculty: 136

Respondent: Susan Mayberry, Assistant Professor of English

Writing Requirement: Required freshman English course and other English course

Writing Center

CENTER HAS EXISTED: Opened January 1984 HOURS OPEN PER WEEK: 6 or more

STAFF: Fewer than 5 faculty tutors

TUTORS' TRAINING: Academic training course

TUTORS' EVALUATION: Observation and student questionnaires

TUTORS PAID: Yes

PROGRAM DESIGNED TO SERVE: Students in all disciplines

PROGRAM ACTUALLY SERVES: About 80 students per semester

STUDENTS SEEK HELP WITH: Grammar, reports, academic essays, research papers, and theses

PERCENTAGE OF STUDENTS SERVED: 4%

STUDENTS USE CENTER: Throughout the semester on a walk-in basis

STUDENTS REQUIRED TO USE CENTER: None

MATERIALS AVAILABLE: Handbooks, writing exercises, professional books, and a word processor

STUDENT ATTITUDE: Unknown

Peer Tutoring Program

PROGRAM HAS EXISTED: 5-10 years

ORGANIZATION: Curriculum-based

NUMBER OF TUTORS: 10

HOURS THEY WORK PER WEEK: Under 5

TUTORS PAID: Yes

TUTOR SELECTION: Appointed by director, self-nominated, and faculty-nominated

TUTORS' TRAINING: Non-academic training course

TUTORS' EVALUATION: By students, faculty, and administration

PERCENTAGE OF STUDENTS SERVED: 20-25%

OVER THE PAST FIVE YEARS THIS PERCENTAGE HAS: Increased

PROGRAM INTENDED TO SERVE: Students in all disciplines

PROGRAM ACTUALLY SERVES: Students in all disciplines

STUDENTS SEEK HELP WITH: Curriculum areas and study skills

MECHANICS OF TUTORING: Students may choose to discuss any paper with any tutor

STUDENT ATTITUDE: Very positive

Alfred University requires writing of all students, including those in the College of Ceramics. To supplement its well-established and popular peer tutoring program, Alfred introduced a writing center in January 1984. The center is staffed by a small number of faculty members and, like the peer tutoring program, serves any student who seeks help with a writing problem. In the near future Alfred hopes to expand its writing program by encouraging writing across the curriculum and by adding writing classes for students in engineering and nursing programs.

ALLEGHENY COLLEGE

Meadville, PA 16335

Full-time Students: 963M/925W Faculty: 130

Respondents: Rhoda I. Sherwood, Assistant Professor; Ilene Reiner, Instructor, Department of English

Writing Requirement: Required freshman English course; exemption on basis of score on Test of Standard Written English

Writing Center

CENTER HAS EXISTED: 2-5 years HOURS OPEN PER WEEK: 20-40

STAFF: Fewer than 5 undergraduate tutors

TUTORS' TRAINING: On-the-job

TUTORS' EVALUATION: Conferences

TUTORS PAID: Yes

PROGRAM DESIGNED TO SERVE: Students in all disciplines

PROGRAM ACTUALLY SERVES: English and humanities students

STUDENTS SEEK HELP WITH: Academic essays and research papers

PERCENTAGE OF STUDENTS SERVED: Less than 25%

OVER PAST FIVE YEARS THIS PERCENTAGE HAS: Stayed the same

STUDENTS USE CENTER: Repeatedly throughout the semester on a walk-in basis

STUDENTS REQUIRED TO USE CENTER: None

MATERIALS AVAILABLE: Handbooks and exercises

STUDENT ATTITUDE: Somewhat positive

Writing-Across-the-Curriculum Program

PROGRAM HAS EXISTED: 5-10 years

INSTRUCTORS INVOLVED: Faculty in all disciplines

INSTRUCTORS' SELECTION: By appointment and voluntary

INSTRUCTORS' TRAINING: Seminars

PERCENTAGE OF FACULTY INVOLVED: 15%

IN PAST FIVE YEARS THIS PERCENTAGE HAS: Decreased

STUDENTS INVOLVED IN PROGRAM: Students in all disciplines

PERCENTAGE OF STUDENTS INVOLVED: 67%

IN PAST FIVE YEARS THIS PERCENTAGE HAS: Stayed the same

PARTICIPANTS' ATTITUDE: Both positive and negative

Allegheny College's writing-across-the-curriculum program is an expansion of the freshman English requirement. Two-thirds of each entering class are required to take two courses: an English Expository writing class and a writing-intensive course in another discipline. Rhoda Sherwood asserts that "Students aren't crazy about the program their freshman year when they are required to take it, but by their senior year they seem to see the point." Before instituting the two-part requirement, the college tried a similar program without requiring the expository writing course before the section in another discipline. But as Sherwood reports, "Teachers in economics, geology, history, etc., were frustrated by student performance. They asked that we add the English course first, making it a prerequisite for the later course in another discipline." This cross-disciplinary program is supported by a writing center used primarily by students participating in the required freshman sequence. The college has no new plans for the future; Sherwood claims, "We're trying to settle down a bit, having recently gone through changes."

AMHERST COLLEGE

Amherst, MA 01002

Full-time Students: 941M/613W Faculty: 159

Respondent: Susan Snively, Writing Counselor, Dean of Students' Office

Writing Requirement: None

Writing Center

CENTER HAS EXISTED: 5-10 years HOURS OPEN PER WEEK: 20-40

STAFF: One professional writing counselor

PROGRAM DESIGNED TO SERVE: Students in all disciplines

PROGRAM ACTUALLY SERVES: Students in all disciplines

STUDENTS SEEK HELP WITH: Academic essays, research papers, creative writing, and personal essays for graduate school applications

PERCENTAGE OF STUDENTS SERVED: Less than 25%

OVER PAST FIVE YEARS THIS PERCENTAGE HAS: Increased

STUDENTS USE CENTER: Throughout the semester on a walk-in or regular basis, by telephone, or after faculty referral

STUDENTS REQUIRED TO USE CENTER: None

MATERIALS AVAILABLE: Handbooks

STUDENT ATTITUDE: Very positive

At present, Amherst avoids stringent writing requirements and instead relies on the faculty to provide students with individual writing instruction. Consistent with this philosophy, there has never been a formal writing program at Amherst, and the writing requirement for graduation has been discontinued. In place of a writing center, the school provides a writing counselor to discuss writing problems with students. This counseling service has been available on a part-time basis for over five years, and on a full-time basis for the last three years. In the future, a small peer counseling group may be added to supplement the services of the writing counselor, although the office and service are not ready to expand immediately.

ARIZONA STATE UNIVERSITY

Tempe, AZ 85287

Full-time Students: 11,728M/10,132W Faculty: 1687

Respondent: Dorothy M. Guinn, Director of First Year English

Writing Requirement: 2 semesters of required freshman English

Writing Center (English Department)

CENTER HAS EXISTED: 7 years HOURS OPEN PER WEEK: Over 40

STAFF: A part-time faculty director and 5–10 graduate tutors

TUTORS' TRAINING: On-the-job

TUTORS' EVALUATION: Observation, student questionnaire, and faculty evaluation

TUTORS PAID: Yes

PROGRAM DESIGNED TO SERVE: Students in all disciplines, especially writing students

PROGRAM ACTUALLY SERVES: Students in all disciplines, especially writing students

STUDENTS SEEK HELP WITH: Academic essays, research papers, creative writing, and resumes or business writing

PERCENTAGE OF STUDENTS SERVED: Less than 25%

OVER PAST FIVE YEARS THIS PERCENTAGE HAS: Increased

STUDENTS USE CENTER: Throughout the semester on an appointment basis

STUDENTS REQUIRED TO USE CENTER: None

MATERIALS AVAILABLE: Handbooks, exercises, professional books, and videotapes

STUDENT ATTITUDE: Very positive

Arizona State University operates several writing programs in the English, Business, Engineering, and Industrial Technology Departments. The university's writing center offers extensive services: long hours, a large staff, and good resource materials, including videotapes. Although the center is fairly young and not required of students, it attracts a large number of students who are very positive about its services.

AUBURN UNIVERSITY

Auburn, AL 36849

Full-time Students: 9650M/6650W Faculty: 1000

Respondents: H.M. Solomon, Director of Freshman English; Kim Moreland, Director of Writing Center

Writing Requirement: 9 credit hours of required freshman English

Writing Center

CENTER HAS EXISTED: 10 years HOURS OPEN PER WEEK: 27

STAFF: Faculty and graduate teaching assistants

TUTORS' TRAINING: Orientation workshop and on-the-job training

TUTORS' EVALUATION: Observation by director and assistant director

TUTORS PAID: No; part of graduate teaching assistant program and in-service program for new faculty

PROGRAM DESIGNED TO SERVE: Students in all disciplines, especially writing students

PROGRAM ACTUALLY SERVES: Writing students and freshmen

STUDENTS SEEK HELP WITH: Academic essays

PERCENTAGE OF STUDENTS SERVED: Less than 25%

OVER PAST FIVE YEARS THIS PERCENTAGE HAS: Increased

STUDENTS USE CENTER: On both a referral and a walk-in basis

STUDENTS REQUIRED TO USE CENTER: Problem writers referred by composition faculty

MATERIALS AVAILABLE: Handbooks and exercises

STUDENT ATTITUDE: Positive

Auburn University requires that all freshmen undergo a rigorous sequence of composition courses in order to help them "write effective English and appreciate the rhetorical and aesthetic values of written discourse," according to H.M. Solomon. In addition, problem writers must seek help from the writing center, whose primary function is to help students with grammar and mechanics. In conjunction with tutors, students complete appropriate worksheets; the students then correct the errors in their own essays. According to Kim Moreland, "Students suffering from problems with invention and organization are also working at the writing center." A new series of special sessions, focusing on specific issues, has been instituted recently. The center also operates a grammar "hotline" for brief questions.

BAYLOR UNIVERSITY

Waco, TX 76798

Full-time Students: 4015M/4714W Faculty: 500

Respondent: James E. Barcus, Chairperson, Department of English

Writing Requirement: Required freshman English course

Writing Center

CENTER HAS EXISTED: 2-5 years HOURS OPEN PER WEEK: 20-40

STAFF: Fewer than 5 faculty and graduate tutors

TUTORS' TRAINING: On-the-job and non-academic training course

TUTORS' EVALUATION: Observation and conferences

TUTORS PAID: Yes

PROGRAM DESIGNED TO SERVE: Students in all disciplines

PROGRAM ACTUALLY SERVES: Writing students

STUDENTS SEEK HELP WITH: Academic essays, research papers, and resumes or business writing

PERCENTAGE OF STUDENTS SERVED: Less than 25%

OVER PAST FIVE YEARS THIS PERCENTAGE HAS: Increased

STUDENTS USE CENTER: Throughout the semester on an appointment or regular basis

STUDENTS REQUIRED TO USE CENTER: Problem writers

MATERIALS AVAILABLE: Handbooks, writing exercises, and educational magazines

STUDENT ATTITUDE: Somewhat positive

Peer Tutoring Program

PROGRAM HAS EXISTED: Under 2 years

ORGANIZATION: Curriculum-based

NUMBER OF TUTORS: Fewer than 10

HOURS THEY WORK PER WEEK: Under 5

TUTORS PAID: Yes

TUTOR SELECTION: Appointed by the director or nominated by English faculty

TUTORS' TRAINING: On-the-job and non-academic training course

TUTORS' EVALUATION: Observation and conferences

PERCENTAGE OF STUDENTS SERVED: Less than 25%

OVER PAST FIVE YEARS THIS PERCENTAGE HAS: Decreased

PROGRAM INTENDED TO SERVE: English students

PROGRAM ACTUALLY SERVES: English students

STUDENTS SEEK HELP WITH: Academic essays and research papers

MECHANICS OF TUTORING: Students may choose to discuss any paper with a tutor

STUDENT ATTITUDE: Unknown

Over the past few years, Baylor University's writing program has become more structured and has expanded beyond the classroom with the addition of a peer tutoring program and a writing center. In its first year, the writing center served primarily writing students, but the English Department expects the center to serve a greater variety of students in the future. Within the classroom, Baylor's English Department has run successful courses in scientific and technical writing, and advanced expository writing. In addition to a proposed major in professional writing, Baylor hopes to expand the scope of its existing programs, particularly the writing center.

BEAVER COLLEGE

Glenside, PA 19038

Full-time Students: 146M/575W Faculty: 63

Respondents: Elaine Maimon, Associate Dean for Curriculum Research, Director of the Writing Program; Ellen Landau, Assistant Dean of the College; Teresa Petosa, Writing Center Consultant, Departmental Tutor

Writing Requirement: Required freshman English course; 2 semesters for most students, 3 semesters for Basic Writers

Writing Center and Peer Tutoring Program

CENTER HAS EXISTED: 7 years HOURS OPEN PER WEEK: 35

STAFF: 22 undergraduate tutors

TUTORS' TRAINING: A composition course on Advanced Exposition for sophomores or Composition Theory for juniors and seniors; some students undertake independent study with coordinator of Writing Center

TUTORS' EVALUATION: By students' reports; consultants also judged on their presentation of workshop for other consultants and by the head tutor

TUTORS PAID: Yes, after first-semester apprenticeship

PROGRAM DESIGNED TO SERVE: Students in all disciplines

PROGRAM ACTUALLY SERVES: Students in all disciplines, particularly freshmen and writing students

STUDENTS SEEK HELP WITH: Scientific reports, academic essays, research papers, creative writing, theses, and resumes or business writing

STUDENTS USE CENTER: Repeatedly throughout the semester on a walk-in basis

STUDENTS REQUIRED TO USE CENTER: Those required by individual freshman composition instructors

MATERIALS AVAILABLE: Handbooks, exercises, educational magazines, and professional books; consultants and students work primarily from student drafts

STUDENT ATTITUDE: Positive

Writing-Across-the-Curriculum Program

PROGRAM HAS EXISTED: 10 years

INSTRUCTORS INVOLVED: Faculty in all disciplines

INSTRUCTORS' SELECTION: All faculty can participate in the program

INSTRUCTORS' TRAINING: Summer and academic-year seminars

PERCENTAGE OF FACULTY INVOLVED: 100% (over the years)

IN PAST FIVE YEARS THIS PERCENTAGE HAS: Increased

STUDENTS INVOLVED IN PROGRAM: Students in all disciplines

PERCENTAGE OF STUDENTS INVOLVED: 100%

IN PAST FIVE YEARS THIS PERCENTAGE HAS: Increased

PARTICIPANTS' ATTITUDE: Very positive

At Beaver College, composition classes as well as nontraditional writing programs are based on the belief that writing, like learning, is not a subject but a process. All students take at least two required composition courses, which are designed to teach the benefits of collaborative learning, provide practice in the conventions of written English, teach writing as a cross-disciplinary endeavor, and introduce students to writing processes. Beaver stresses writing not only in the English Department but in all disciplines through its highly successful and popular writing-across-the-curriculum program. Over the years, all of Beaver's faculty participate in seminars on the teaching of writing, and all instructors require substantial writing in their courses.

Students who seek additional writing assistance may discuss their papers with the peer Writing Consultants, who staff Beaver's writing center. At the center, students' papers are not edited or proofread; instead students learn collaboratively through interaction with an experienced peer. Although it is open to all students, the center serves primarily freshmen, who are well-acquainted with the Writing Consultants at the beginning of the year. Consultants are initially trained in either an advanced expository writing courses or composition theory courses, and they continue to learn through workshops which they conduct. These workshops, which are offered several times during the year, are run by tutors for tutors and involve discussion and exploration of peer tutoring and the writing process. Faculty are often invited to these workshops, either to lecture on some aspect of writing or teaching, or to join in as workshop participants.

BELOIT COLLEGE

Beloit, WI 53511

Full-time Students: 546M/480W Faculty: 83

Respondent: John Rosenwald, Chairperson, English Department

Writing Requirement: Writing proficiency examination or writing-intensive courses at various levels

Writing Center

CENTER HAS EXISTED: 2-5 years HOURS OPEN PER WEEK: 10-20

STAFF: 5-20 paraprofessionals, paid professional supervisors, peer tutors, and student supervisors.

TUTORS' TRAINING: On-the-job and academic course

TUTORS' EVALUATION: By supervisor

TUTORS PAID: Occasionally (work-study program)

PROGRAM DESIGNED TO SERVE: Students in all disciplines

PROGRAM ACTUALLY SERVES: Students in all disciplines

STUDENTS SEEK HELP WITH: Scientific reports, academic essays, research papers, and resumes or business writing

PERCENTAGE OF STUDENTS SERVED: Less than 25%

OVER PAST FIVE YEARS THIS PERCENTAGE HAS: Increased

STUDENTS USE CENTER: Throughout the semester on an appointment, walk-in, or regular basis

STUDENTS REQUIRED TO USE CENTER: Problem writers

MATERIALS AVAILABLE: Handbooks, exercises, and professional books

STUDENT ATTITUDE: Unknown

Writing-Across-the-Curriculum Program

PROGRAM HAS EXISTED: Over 10 years

INSTRUCTORS INVOLVED: Faculty in all disciplines

INSTRUCTORS' SELECTION: By appointment

INSTRUCTORS' TRAINING: Team teaching, bi-weekly staff meetings, and formal and informal faculty peer counseling

PERCENTAGE OF FACULTY INVOLVED: 25-50%

IN PAST FIVE YEARS THIS PERCENTAGE HAS: Stayed the same

STUDENTS INVOLVED IN PROGRAM: Students in all disciplines

PERCENTAGE OF STUDENTS INVOLVED: More than 75%

IN PAST FIVE YEARS THIS PERCENTAGE HAS: Increased

PARTICIPANTS' ATTITUDE: Generally positive

Beloit College's writing-across-the-curriculum program is unusual in several ways: it is exceptionally well-established, reaches a large percentage of the student body, and relies on the innovative technique of faculty peer counseling, by which faculty meet in small groups to discuss strategies for teaching writing. The faculty are proud of Beloit's college-wide commitment to writing and of cooperation fostered by informal peer tutoring. The writing center has not been quite so successful since, according to John Rosenwald, "the stigma of getting extra help" tends to limit student use of the center. Rosenwald anticipates growth in this new center, however, as well as an expansion in the journalism and fiction writing programs.

BENTLEY COLLEGE

Waltham, MA 02254

Full-time Students: 2070M/1588W Faculty: 165

Respondent: Maureen Goldman, Associate Professor of English, Director of Freshman English

Writing Requirement: Required freshman English courses and other required courses

Writing Center

CENTER HAS EXISTED: 10 years HOURS OPEN PER WEEK: Over 40

STAFF: 5-20 faculty and undergraduate tutors

TUTORS' TRAINING: On-the-job and non-academic course

TUTORS' EVALUATION: Observation, conferences, and student questionnaires

TUTORS PAID: Yes

PROGRAM DESIGNED TO SERVE: Students in all disciplines

PROGRAM ACTUALLY SERVES: Students in all disciplines

STUDENTS SEEK HELP WITH: Scientific reports, creative writing, academic essays, research papers, and resumes or business writing

PERCENTAGE OF STUDENTS SERVED: 25-50%

OVER PAST FIVE YEARS THIS PERCENTAGE HAS: Increased

STUDENTS USE CENTER: Throughout the semester on a walk-in, appointment, or regular basis

STUDENTS REQUIRED TO USE CENTER: Currently none, but this is changing

MATERIALS AVAILABLE: Handbooks, exercises, professional books, and educational magazines

STUDENT ATTITUDE: Very positive

Peer Tutoring Program

PROGRAM HAS EXISTED: 5-10 years

ORGANIZATION: Writing center-based

NUMBER OF TUTORS: 10

HOURS THEY WORK PER WEEK: 10-20

TUTORS PAID: Yes

TUTOR SELECTION: Nominated by English faculty

TUTORS' TRAINING: On-the-job

TUTORS' EVALUATION: Observation, conferences, and student questionnaire

PERCENTAGE OF STUDENTS SERVED: 25-50%

OVER PAST FIVE YEARS THIS PERCENTAGE HAS: Increased

PROGRAM INTENDED TO SERVE: Underclassmen

PROGRAM ACTUALLY SERVES: Underclassmen

STUDENTS SEEK HELP WITH: Scientific reports, academic essays, research papers, creative writing, and resumes or business writing

MECHANICS OF TUTORING: Tutors work with students on any writing problem

STUDENT ATTITUDE: Very positive

Writing-Across-the-Curriculum Program

PROGRAM HAS EXISTED: 2-5 years

INSTRUCTORS INVOLVED: English Department faculty

INSTRUCTORS' SELECTION: Voluntary

INSTRUCTORS' TRAINING: Consulting and interdisciplinary work

PERCENTAGE OF FACULTY INVOLVED: 25-50%

IN PAST FIVE YEARS THIS PERCENTAGE HAS: Increased

STUDENTS INVOLVED IN PROGRAM: Students in all disciplines

PERCENTAGE OF STUDENTS INVOLVED: More than 75%

IN PAST FIVE YEARS THIS PERCENTAGE HAS: Increased

PARTICIPANTS' ATTITUDE: Very positive

Over the past few years, Bentley College has begun to establish several innovative programs in writing. As Maureen Goldman reports, "We have thoroughly revised our program and are now running an experimental, flexible freshman English program." The freshman English courses follow a sequence involving basic communications, research and rhetoric, and critical analysis. Students take a proficiency examination the summer before their freshman year to determine placement into various communications courses. One of the upper-level communications courses offers students a choice of reading and critical analysis in one of three areas: the humanities, science, or business. In whichever area they select, students can use the English Learning Center to "assist in the areas of reading, speaking, or writing . . . to review a draft or improve a variety of communications skills."

BETHEL COLLEGE

North Newton, KS 67117

Full-time Students: 282M/337W Faculty: 78

Respondents: Anna Juhnke, Acting Chairperson, English Department; Sandra Zerger, Director, Learning Resource Center

Writing Requirement: Required freshman English courses and proficiency essay examination

Writing Center

CENTER HAS EXISTED: 5 years HOURS OPEN PER WEEK: 40

STAFF: 18 undergraduate tutors

TUTORS' TRAINING: On-the-job and optional academic training course

TUTORS' EVALUATION: Observation

TUTORS PAID: Yes

PROGRAM DESIGNED TO SERVE: Students in all disciplines

PROGRAM ACTUALLY SERVES: Students in all disciplines

STUDENTS SEEK HELP WITH: Academic essays, research papers, exams, and note-taking

PERCENTAGE OF STUDENTS SERVED: 50%-75%

OVER PAST FIVE YEARS THIS PERCENTAGE HAS: Increased

STUDENTS USE CENTER: Individually or in groups throughout the semester on a walk-in, appointment, or regular basis

STUDENTS REQUIRED TO USE CENTER: Students enrolled in Reading and Study Skills course

MATERIALS AVAILABLE: Handbooks and exercises

STUDENT ATTITUDE: Somewhat positive

Like many schools, Bethel College operates its writing center as part of a larger Learning Resource Center that counsels students in all subjects. The writing section of this center serves a substantial number of students, who come in individually or in groups, seeking help with exams, note-taking, and papers. Many students who use the writing tutors are enrolled in a Reading and Study skills course, which includes work in the center as part of its instruction. The main focus of the Learning Resource Center, however, is the Supplemental Instruction Program, a nontraditional academic support service attached to "high-risk" courses.

BLOOMSBURG UNIVERSITY

Bloomsburg PA 17815

Full-time Students: 1927M/2953W Faculty: 302

Respondent: Louis F. Thompson, Chairperson, English Department

Writing Requirement: Two required freshman English composition courses

Writing Center

CENTER HAS EXISTED: 5-10 years HOURS OPEN PER WEEK: 26

STAFF: 8-10 faculty, graduate, and undergraduate tutors

TUTORS' TRAINING: On-the-job

TUTORS' EVALUATION: Observation, student questionnaires, and by other tutors

TUTORS PAID: Yes

PROGRAM DESIGNED TO SERVE: Students in all disciplines, particularly those requiring remedial help

PROGRAM ACTUALLY SERVES: Remedial students, basic composition students, and some students from other disciplines

STUDENTS SEEK HELP WITH: Academic essays, research papers, resumes or business writing, and skills pertinent to all types of writing

PERCENTAGE OF STUDENTS SERVED: Less than 10%

OVER PAST FIVE YEARS THIS PERCENTAGE HAS: Increased

STUDENTS USE CENTER: Throughout the semester on a walk-in, appointment, or regular basis

STUDENTS REQUIRED TO USE CENTER: Problem writers, usually freshmen

MATERIALS AVAILABLE: Handbooks, writing exercises, professional books, tapes, slides, and computer-assisted instruction

STUDENT ATTITUDE: Somewhat positive

Peer Tutoring Program

PROGRAM HAS EXISTED: 2-5 years

ORGANIZATION: Writing center-based

NUMBER OF TUTORS: 1-3

HOURS THEY WORK PER WEEK: 10-20

TUTORS PAID: Yes

TUTOR SELECTION: Nominated by English faculty

TUTORS' TRAINING: On-the-job

TUTORS' EVALUATION: Observation and student questionnaires

PERCENTAGE OF STUDENTS SERVED: Less than 10%

OVER PAST FIVE YEARS THIS PERCENTAGE HAS: Increased

PROGRAM INTENDED TO SERVE: Primarily writing students, freshmen, and some students in other disciplines

PROGRAM ACTUALLY SERVES: Writing students, freshmen, and a few students from other disciplines

STUDENTS SEEK HELP WITH: Academic essays and resumes or business writing

MECHANICS OF TUTORING: Students may choose to discuss any paper with a tutor

STUDENT ATTITUDE: Somewhat positive

Over the past ten years, Bloomsburg University has developed two programs to help writing students outside of the classroom. The writing center and peer tutors are available to all students, but primarily help students from remedial and standard freshman composition courses. Both of these innovative programs, along with special tutors from Bloomsburg's Writing Proficiency Examination course, are based in a converted classroom and serve students who set up appointments or simply walk in. Bloomsburg also has a heavy writing requirement; all students not selected for the Honors Composition course must take a combination of two composition courses. Bloomsburg has no definite additions or changes planned for the immediate future, but will appoint a composition/rhetoric specialist in September 1984.

BOISE STATE UNIVERSITY

Boise, ID 83725

Full-time Students: 3117M/3513W Faculty: 348

Respondent: Roy F. Fox, Director of Composition

Writing Requirement: Required freshman English course, other required English course, and a minimal competency examination

Writing Center

CENTER HAS EXISTED: 2-5 years HOURS OPEN PER WEEK: Over 40

STAFF: 5-20 faculty, graduate, and undergraduate tutors

TUTORS' TRAINING: On-the-job and non-academic course; also some internships and independent studies

TUTORS' EVALUATION: Observation, student questionnaires, conferences, and by the head tutor

TUTORS PAID: Yes

PROGRAM DESIGNED TO SERVE: Students in all disciplines, particularly English students

PROGRAM ACTUALLY SERVES: Students in all disciplines, particularly English students

STUDENTS SEEK HELP WITH: Scientific reports, academic essays, research papers, and resumes or business writing

PERCENTAGE OF STUDENTS SERVED: 25-50%

OVER PAST FIVE YEARS THIS PERCENTAGE HAS: Increased

STUDENTS USE CENTER: Throughout the semester on a walk-in or appointment basis

STUDENTS REQUIRED TO USE CENTER: None

MATERIALS AVAILABLE: Handbooks, exercises, professional books, educational magazines, computer-assisted instruction, audio tapes, and filmstrips

STUDENT ATTITUDE: Positive

Peer Tutoring Program

PROGRAM HAS EXISTED: Over 10 years

ORGANIZATION: Curriculum-based

NUMBER OF TUTORS: 20-50

HOURS THEY WORK PER WEEK: 5-10

TUTORS PAID: Some paid; some receive academic credit

TUTOR SELECTION: Nominated by themselves and college-wide, then appointed by the director

TUTORS' TRAINING: On-the-job

TUTORS' EVALUATION: Observation, conferences, and student questionnaire

PERCENTAGE OF STUDENTS SERVED: Less than 25%

OVER PAST FIVE YEARS THIS PERCENTAGE HAS: Increased

PROGRAM INTENDED TO SERVE: Writing students, freshmen, and underclassmen

PROGRAM ACTUALLY SERVES: Writing students, freshmen, and underclassmen

STUDENTS SEEK HELP WITH: Academic essays

MECHANICS OF TUTORING: Tutor makes written comments on papers and discusses them with student

STUDENT ATTITUDE: Very positive

Writing-Across-the-Curriculum Program

PROGRAM HAS EXISTED: Less than 2 years

INSTRUCTORS INVOLVED: Faculty in all disciplines

INSTRUCTORS' SELECTION: Instructors apply and submit letters of recommendation from their department chairpersons

INSTRUCTORS' TRAINING: Seminars

PERCENTAGE OF FACULTY INVOLVED: Less than 25%

IN PAST FIVE YEARS THIS PERCENTAGE HAS: Increased

STUDENTS INVOLVED IN PROGRAM: Students in all disciplines

PERCENTAGE OF STUDENTS INVOLVED: 50–75%

IN PAST FIVE YEARS THIS PERCENTAGE HAS: Increased

PARTICIPANTS' ATTITUDE: Very positive

Over the past five years, the English Department at Boise State University has expanded both its traditional and nontraditional writing programs. The required composition courses and upper-level writing courses have been revised, and all students are required to pass the minimal competency exam, which includes an objective test and a writing sample. Outside the English classroom, peer tutoring plays a major role in providing writing instruction. The peer tutoring program, which has been assisting in the basic composition courses for more than ten years, now works out of the writing center as well, to serve students from all disciplines. Within the last two years, Boise State has introduced an NEH-funded "Writing and Learning Across the Curriculum" project to train selected faculty in the teaching of writing. All of these programs, together with Boise State's many creative magazines and journals, provide students with a wide range of writing instruction and opportunities.

BOSTON COLLEGE

Chestnut Hill, MA 02167

Full-time Students: 3666M/4923W Faculty: 558

Respondent: Dennis Taylor, Chairperson of English Department

Writing Requirement: Required freshman English course

Peer Tutoring Program

PROGRAM HAS EXISTED: 5-10 years

ORGANIZATION: Curriculum-based

NUMBER OF TUTORS: Fewer than 10

HOURS THEY WORK PER WEEK: Under 5

TUTORS PAID: Yes

TUTOR SELECTION: Appointed by director

TUTORS' TRAINING: No formal training

TUTORS' EVALUATION: Informal

PERCENTAGE OF STUDENTS SERVED: Less than 25%

OVER PAST FIVE YEARS THIS PERCENTAGE HAS: Stayed the same

PROGRAM INTENDED TO SERVE: English students

PROGRAM ACTUALLY SERVES: English students

STUDENTS SEEK HELP WITH: Writing skills

MECHANICS OF TUTORING: Consultation

STUDENT ATTITUDE: Positive

Boston College considers its two-semester freshman English sequence, which involves writing and literature, to be sufficient writing preparation for its students. The college also has peer tutors who help students in these and other English courses. Most of the students who seek tutoring, however, choose Boston College's more central Learning to Learn Center rather than the peer tutoring program focused specifically on writing.

BOWLING GREEN STATE UNIVERSITY

Bowling Green, OH 43403

Full-time Students: 6059M/8187W Faculty: 737

Respondent: Kathleen Hart, Director, General Studies Writing Program

Writing Requirement: Required freshman English course and other required English course; placement by examination

Writing Center

CENTER HAS EXISTED: Over 10 years HOURS OPEN PER WEEK: Over 40

STAFF: 5-20 graduate and undergraduate tutors

TUTORS' TRAINING: On-the-job or academic course

TUTORS' EVALUATION: Observation, conferences, and student questionnaire

TUTORS PAID: Most are

PROGRAM DESIGNED TO SERVE: Students in all disciplines

PROGRAM ACTUALLY SERVES: Students in all disciplines, especially writing students

STUDENTS SEEK HELP WITH: Scientific reports, academic essays, research papers, and resumes or business writing

PERCENTAGE OF STUDENTS SERVED: Less than 25%

OVER PAST FIVE YEARS THIS PERCENTAGE HAS: Stayed the same

STUDENTS USE CENTER: Once or repeatedly throughout the semester on a walk-in, appointment, or regular basis

STUDENTS REQUIRED TO USE CENTER: None

MATERIALS AVAILABLE: Handbooks and exercises

STUDENT ATTITUDE: Very positive

One of the older writing centers in the nation, the center at Bowling Green State University is a major part of the school's writing program. Open long hours to serve all students in the university, this center is staffed by graduate and undergraduate tutors, many of whom have taken an academic training course and received on-the-job training.

These tutors offer help with many different types of writing, and their work is evaluated through observation, student questionnaires, and conferences with the director of the writing program.

BRENAU COLLEGE

Gainesville, GA 30501

Full-time Students: 821W   Faculty: 60

Respondent: Nancy L. Richardson, Assistant Professor of Humanities and Director of Freshman English

Writing Requirement: Required freshman English course; placement by examination

Writing Center

CENTER HAS EXISTED: Under 2 years   HOURS OPEN PER WEEK: 20–40

STAFF: 5–20 faculty, during office hours

TUTORS PAID: No

PROGRAM DESIGNED TO SERVE: Students in all disciplines

PROGRAM ACTUALLY SERVES: Students in all disciplines

STUDENTS SEEK HELP WITH: Scientific reports, academic essays, research papers, and resumes or business writing

PERCENTAGE OF STUDENTS SERVED: Less than 25%

OVER PAST FIVE YEARS THIS PERCENTAGE HAS: Increased

STUDENTS USE CENTER: Throughout the quarter on a walk-in basis

STUDENTS REQUIRED TO USE CENTER: None

MATERIALS AVAILABLE: Handbooks and exercises

STUDENT ATTITUDE: Somewhat positive

At Brenau, the commitment to writing is college-wide. The staff of the writing center, or Writer's Studio, consists of faculty volunteers from several disciplines who hold office hours during the week to offer help "from commas to coherence," according to Nancy L. Richardson. In the next few years, the Studio plans to install a word processor and hopes this innovation will encourage not only students but also faculty to seek help with writing skills. In general, Brenau's faculty have begun to emphasize practical and traditional skills, including rhetoric and composition. They also plan to create a separate program to teach research skills in different disciplines. As Richardson reports, "We are still looking for workable programs that will help students become more self-motivated, independent thinkers; they are not very confident, at least as freshmen, by and large."

BRIDGEWATER STATE COLLEGE

Bridgewater, MA 02324

Full-time Students: 1627M/2529W Faculty: 224

Respondent: Clifford A. Wood, English Department Chairperson

Writing Requirement: Required freshman English course; placement by SAT

Writing Center

CENTER HAS EXISTED: 5-10 years HOURS OPEN PER WEEK: 20-40

STAFF: Fewer than 5 faculty and undergraduate tutors

TUTORS' TRAINING: On-the-job and non-academic course

TUTORS' EVALUATION: Observation

TUTORS PAID: Yes

PROGRAM DESIGNED TO SERVE: Students in all disciplines

PROGRAM ACTUALLY SERVES: Students in all disciplines

STUDENTS SEEK HELP WITH: Academic essays and research papers

PERCENTAGE OF STUDENTS SERVED: Less than 25%

OVER PAST FIVE YEARS THIS PERCENTAGE HAS: Increased

STUDENTS USE CENTER: Throughout the semester on a walk-in or appointment basis

STUDENTS REQUIRED TO USE CENTER: None

MATERIALS AVAILABLE: Handbooks, exercises, professional books, and educational magazines

STUDENT ATTITUDE: Very positive

The writing center at Bridgewater State College is one of the school's few nontraditional writing programs. This center has remained relatively small over the past five years, serving less than a quarter of the students, but student attitude toward the center has been positive. The school's writing faculty is also small, and specializes in expository composition, technical writing, and journalism. Bridgewater is currently establishing a fifteen to eighteen-hour writing concentration in the English major.

BRIGHAM YOUNG UNIVERSITY

Provo, UT 84602

Full-time Students: 12,874M/11,692W Faculty: 1237

Respondent: Douglas H. Thayer, Coordinator of Composition

Writing Requirement: Freshman English course and an advanced major-oriented composition course

Writing Center and Peer Tutoring Program

CENTER HAS EXISTED: 5-10 years HOURS OPEN PER WEEK: Over 40

STAFF: More than 40 graduate and undergraduate tutors; full-time, non-faculty reading and writing specialists

TUTORS' TRAINING: On-the-job, academic course, and non-academic course

TUTORS' EVALUATION: Observation, conferences, student questionnaires, and by other tutors

TUTORS PAID: Yes, but not while they are interning

PROGRAM DESIGNED TO SERVE: Students in all disciplines

PROGRAM ACTUALLY SERVES: Students in all disciplines

STUDENTS SEEK HELP WITH: Scientific reports, creative writing, academic essays, research papers, and resumes or business writing

PERCENTAGE OF STUDENTS SERVED: Less than 25%

OVER PAST FIVE YEARS THIS PERCENTAGE HAS: Increased

STUDENTS USE CENTER: Throughout the semester on a walk-in or appointment basis; some are referred by faculty

STUDENTS REQUIRED TO USE CENTER: Problem writers

MATERIALS AVAILABLE: Handbooks and exercises

STUDENT ATTITUDE: Generally positive

Writing-Across-the-Curriculum Program

PROGRAM HAS EXISTED: 5 years

INSTRUCTORS INVOLVED: Faculty in all disciplines

INSTRUCTORS' SELECTION: By appointment

INSTRUCTORS' TRAINING: Seminars

PERCENTAGE OF FACULTY INVOLVED: Less than 25%

IN PAST FIVE YEARS THIS PERCENTAGE HAS: Increased

STUDENTS INVOLVED IN PROGRAM: Students in all disciplines

PERCENTAGE OF STUDENTS INVOLVED: Less than 25%

IN PAST FIVE YEARS THIS PERCENTAGE HAS: Increased

PARTICIPANTS' ATTITUDE: Generally positive

Brigham Young University continues to modify and improve its writing program. Instead of the former two-semester freshman English requirement, students now take the freshman course and one advanced composition course chosen from among four courses designed to complement their majors. The composition office has introduced a remedial course and is developing a program that will integrate writing, critical reading, and critical thinking. Other of the office's current projects include offering a pilot computer-assisted instruction composition course for honors freshmen and improving its program for training composition teachers through workshops. The university's successful writing center has existed for nearly ten years and doubles as a peer tutoring program, staffed by more than forty undergraduates each year. This fall, with the addition of new software and IBM personal computers, the center will continue to develop its computer-assisted instruction program for students with writing problems. The writing-across-the-curriculum program is effective in promoting better writing on campus, and as a result, student and faculty support is growing.

BRIGHAM YOUNG UNIVERSITY/HAWAII CAMPUS

Laie, HI 96762

Full-time Students: 865M/1080W Faculty: 78

Respondent: Margaret P. Baker, Coordinator of Freshman Composition

Writing Requirement: Eight semester-hours of writing, including Freshman English, and three semester-hours of literature

Writing Center

CENTER HAS EXISTED: 5-10 years HOURS OPEN PER WEEK: Over 40

STAFF: 5-20 faculty and undergraduate tutors

TUTORS' TRAINING: On-the-job

TUTORS' EVALUATION: Observation and conferences

TUTORS PAID: Yes

PROGRAM DESIGNED TO SERVE: Students in all disciplines, especially writing students, English students, and ESL students

PROGRAM ACTUALLY SERVES: Students in all disciplines, especially writing students, English students, and ESL students

STUDENTS SEEK HELP WITH: Scientific reports, academic essays, research papers, and resumes or business writing

PERCENTAGE OF STUDENTS SERVED: 25-50%

OVER PAST FIVE YEARS THIS PERCENTAGE HAS: Stayed the same

STUDENTS USE CENTER: Repeatedly throughout the semester on a walk-in or regular basis

STUDENTS REQUIRED TO USE CENTER: Problem writers and ESL students

MATERIALS AVAILABLE: Handbooks and exercises

STUDENT ATTITUDE: Somewhat positive

The writing center at Brigham Young University/Hawaii Campus serves a large number of ESL students, who constitute 39 percent of the student population. The center also serves over one quarter of all students. One of BYU's approaches to teaching writing is its portfolio system: the work of each composition student is evaluated by an impartial faculty member, who decides whether the student will pass the course. BYU considers this system advantageous because it standardizes grading throughout the department, circulates new ideas and insights for writing assignments, and raises standards for acceptable writing university-wide.

BROWN UNIVERSITY

Providence, RI 02912

Full-time Students: 2870M/2430W Faculty: 560

Respondent: Tori Haring-Smith, Assistant Professor of English, Director of the Writing Fellows Program

Writing Requirement: Writing competency measured in every course

Writing Center

CENTER HAS EXISTED: 3 years HOURS OPEN PER WEEK: 25

STAFF: 20 graduate tutors

TUTORS' TRAINING: On-the-job

TUTORS' EVALUATION: Observation

TUTORS PAID: Yes

PROGRAM DESIGNED TO SERVE: Students in all disciplines

PROGRAM ACTUALLY SERVES: Students in all disciplines, particularly freshmen and seniors in the humanities

STUDENTS SEEK HELP WITH: Academic essays, scientific reports, research papers, creative writing, and resumes

PERCENTAGE OF STUDENTS SERVED: 15%

OVER PAST FIVE YEARS THIS PERCENTAGE HAS: Increased

STUDENTS USE CENTER: Throughout the semester on a walk-in or appointment basis

STUDENTS REQUIRED TO USE CENTER: Students referred by faculty for severe writing deficiency

MATERIALS AVAILABLE: Handbooks, professional books, and writing exercises

STUDENT ATTITUDE: Very positive

Peer Tutoring Program

PROGRAM HAS EXISTED: 3 years

ORGANIZATION: Curriculum-based

NUMBER OF TUTORS: 60

HOURS THEY WORK: 80–100 hours per semester

TUTORS PAID: Yes

TUTOR SELECTION: Nominated by themselves and by faculty university-wide; selected by program director; application procedure involves interview and writing samples

TUTORS' TRAINING: Academic training course

TUTORS' EVALUATION: Observation, student evaluation, and faculty evaluation

PERCENTAGE OF STUDENTS SERVED: 60% (each year)

OVER PAST FIVE YEARS THIS PERCENTAGE HAS: Increased

PROGRAM INTENDED TO SERVE: Students in all disciplines

PROGRAM ACTUALLY SERVES: Students in all disciplines

STUDENTS SEEK HELP WITH: Academic essays, research papers, and scientific reports

MECHANICS OF TUTORING: Tutors write comments on papers and hold individual conferences with students

STUDENT ATTITUDE: Very positive

Writing-Across-the-Curriculum Program

PROGRAM HAS EXISTED: 3 years

INSTRUCTORS: Faculty in all disciplines

INSTRUCTORS' SELECTION: Voluntary

INSTRUCTORS' TRAINING: Two-day summer seminar

PERCENTAGE OF FACULTY INVOLVED: 3%

IN PAST FIVE YEARS THIS PERCENTAGE HAS: Increased

STUDENTS INVOLVED IN PROGRAM: Students in all disciplines, especially freshmen

PERCENTAGE OF STUDENTS INVOLVED: 10%

IN PAST FIVE YEARS THIS PERCENTAGE HAS: Increased

PARTICIPANTS' ATTITUDE: Somewhat positive

Although new, Brown University's nontraditional writing programs have become important components in the teaching of writing at Brown. The peer tutoring program, staffed by Undergraduate Writing Fellows, now serves about three thousand students each year in over thirty different courses throughout the curriculum. Writing Fellows are each assigned twenty to twenty-five students in a course outside the English Department, and they serve as first readers for those students' papers. Each paper a student writes is submitted to the Writing Fellow, who comments on it in writing and then returns the paper to the student. The student then revises the paper before submitting both versions to the faculty member in charge of the course. All students enrolled in a course participating in this program must submit their work to Fellows and have an individual conference with their Fellows at least once a semester. The writing-across-the-curriculum program trains faculty to integrate writing into courses throughout the curriculum. These trained faculty may work with or without the assistance of a Writing Fellow. Underlying these programs is the basic assumption that all students (regardless of their skills level) need careful comments on their writing at several stages so that they may improve their writing. In addition to implementing these nontraditional programs, Brown has increased the number of expository and creative writing courses it offers. Writing has become a subject of common concern at this university, discussed in dormitories, cafeterias, and faculty meetings as well as in the classroom.

BRYN MAWR COLLEGE

Bryn Mawr, PA 19010

Full-time Students: 1118W Faculty: 177

Respondent: Peter M. Briggs, Associate Professor of English, Director of Freshman English

Writing Requirement: Required freshman English course and upper-level literature course

Although Bryn Mawr College has no nontraditional programs at the present time, its traditional writing program has been quite successful. Peter M. Briggs considers Bryn Mawr's "old-fashioned 'readings and composition' format" to be very effective, especially because of the small classes in the two-semester freshman composition program. The program relies on regular writing, intensive criticism, and regular individual conferences. Although reductions in full-time staff have forced Bryn Mawr to rely more on part-time instructors, the college's composition program is thriving. Bryn Mawr now runs a small experimental section, pairing Freshman English with Introduction to Computing, and Briggs hopes that this program will soon become a standard option in the freshman English sequence.

BUCKNELL UNIVERSITY

Lewisburg, PA 17837

Full-time Students: 1661M/1527W Faculty: 223

Respondent: Catherine F. Smith, Director, University Writing Program and Writing Center

Writing Requirement: 3 writing-emphasis courses

Writing Center

CENTER HAS EXISTED: 2 years HOURS OPEN PER WEEK: Over 40

STAFF: 3 professional tutors and 22 undergraduate tutors

TUTORS' TRAINING: On-the-job and non-credit course for undergraduates

TUTORS' EVALUATION: Observation for undergraduates, student evaluation

TUTORS PAID: Yes

PROGRAM DESIGNED TO SERVE: Students in all disciplines

PROGRAM ACTUALLY SERVES: Students in all disciplines

PERCENTAGE OF STUDENTS SERVED: 25%

OVER PAST FIVE YEARS THIS PERCENTAGE HAS: Increased

STUDENTS USE CENTER: Throughout the semester on an appointment or workshop basis

STUDENTS REQUIRED TO USE CENTER: None; some referred by instructors

MATERIALS AVAILABLE: Professional books, videotapes, and self-help kits.

STUDENT ATTITUDE: Very positive

Peer Tutoring Program

PROGRAM HAS EXISTED: Under 2 years

ORGANIZATION: Curriculum-based and Writing Center-based

NUMBER OF TUTORS: 22

HOURS THEY WORK PER WEEK: 5-10

TUTORS PAID: Yes

TUTORS' SELECTION: Nominated college-wide and self-nominated

TUTORS' TRAINING: On-the-job and non-credit course

TUTORS' EVALUATION: Observation and student evaluations

PERCENTAGE OF STUDENTS SERVED: 25%

OVER PAST FIVE YEARS THIS PERCENTAGE HAS: Increased

PROGRAM INTENDED TO SERVE: Students in all disciplines

PROGRAM ACTUALLY SERVES: Students in all disciplines

MECHANICS OF TUTORING: Students choose to discuss papers with tutor

STUDENT ATTITUDE: Very positive

Writing-Across-the-Curriculum Program

PROGRAM HAS EXISTED: 2 years

INSTRUCTORS SELECTED: Faculty in all disciplines

INSTRUCTORS' SELECTION: Voluntary

INSTRUCTORS' TRAINING: Seminars

PERCENTAGE OF FACULTY INVOLVED: 40%

IN PAST FIVE YEARS THIS PERCENTAGE HAS: Increased

PERCENTAGE OF STUDENTS INVOLVED: 100% (in stages)

IN PAST FIVE YEARS THIS PERCENTAGE HAS: Increased

STUDENTS INVOLVED IN PROGRAM: Students in all disciplines

PARTICIPANTS' ATTITUDE: Positive

Writing across the curriculum is now a requirement at Bucknell University. The program, which is still being phased in and which will affect all students by 1985-86, requires students to complete three writing-intensive courses. These writing emphasis courses are divided into two levels: lower-level "W1" courses, which teach the writing process and several expository skills, and upper-level "W2" courses, which reinforce the process learned in "W1" courses and require substantial and frequent writing. Both "W1" and "W2" courses may be taken in any department. Approximately ninety-seven writing-emphasis courses were offered in 1983-84 in twenty departments across the curriculum. Bucknell also has a well-established writing center that serves over 25 percent of all students and a peer tutoring program in which undergraduate tutors assist faculty in teaching the writing-emphasis courses. Bucknell will increase its writing offerings over the next few years.

CALIFORNIA MARITIME ACADEMY

Vallejo, CA 94590

Full-time Students: 475M/25W Faculty: 32

Respondent: Charles Hartwell, Associate Professor of English

Writing Requirement: Required freshman and other English course; placement by SAT and other examination

Writing-Across-the-Curriculum Program

PROGRAM HAS EXISTED: 2-5 years

INSTRUCTORS INVOLVED: Faculty in all disciplines

INSTRUCTORS' SELECTION: Voluntary and by appointment

INSTRUCTORS' TRAINING: None

PERCENTAGE OF FACULTY INVOLVED: Less than 25%

IN PAST FIVE YEARS THIS PERCENTAGE HAS: Stayed the same

STUDENTS INVOLVED IN PROGRAM: Students in all disciplines

PERCENTAGE OF STUDENTS INVOLVED: More than 75%

IN PAST FIVE YEARS THIS PERCENTAGE HAS: Stayed the same

PARTICIPANTS' ATTITUDE: Generally accepting; occasionally enthusiastic

"Despite the technical nature of this college," says Charles Hartwell, "California Maritime Academy puts a real emphasis on writing for its own sake." While CMA has no formal writing center, the writing faculty office functions as an informal center that serves over 25 percent of students in all fields. The faculty have been fairly satisfied with the standard first-year and upper-level composition sequences, which probably will not undergo major changes in the next few years. All CMA students are required to satisfy a substantial writing requirement as they pursue their degrees in maritime engineering or industrial technology; students generally write a thesis on the industry-internship project they complete in their senior year.

CALIFORNIA POLYTECHNIC INSTITUTE

San Luis Obispo, CA 93407

Full-time Students: 7514M/5643W Faculty: 958

Respondent: David Kann, Professor of English, Director of Writing Programs

Writing Requirement: Required freshman English course, other required English course, and junior writing test or writing course option

Writing Center

CENTER HAS EXISTED: 2-5 years HOURS OPEN PER WEEK: 10-20

STAFF: 5-20 undergraduate tutors

TUTORS' TRAINING: On-the-job

TUTORS' EVALUATION: Observation

TUTORS PAID: Yes

PROGRAM DESIGNED TO SERVE: Writing students

PROGRAM ACTUALLY SERVES: Writing students

STUDENTS SEEK HELP WITH: Academic essays, research papers, and resumes or business writing

PERCENTAGE OF STUDENTS SERVED: Less than 25%

OVER PAST FIVE YEARS THIS PERCENTAGE HAS: Increased

STUDENTS USE CENTER: Throughout the quarter on a walk-in basis

STUDENTS REQUIRED TO USE CENTER: Problem writers

MATERIALS AVAILABLE: Handbooks and exercises

STUDENT ATTITUDE: Somewhat positive

Over the past three years the writing faculty at California Polytechnic have worked to reshape and update existing writing courses and programs. All entering students must take the English Placement Test, a two-part examination consisting of an objective test of vocabulary, syntax, and logic, and an essay that is scored holistically. A student's performance on this test determines placement in one of the three levels within the freshman composition sequence. The faculty have also begun to pay more attention to the needs of foreign students. Any entering foreign students who score below a certain level on the required English Placement Test take a series of three courses taught by staff specially trained in ESL problems. David Kann reports that while "laissez-faire" writing programs work well, common final exams are less successful: the faculty prefer to give individual final exams, and "they don't like to feel their academic freedom has been violated."

CALIFORNIA STATE UNIVERSITY AT FULLERTON

Fullerton, CA 92634

Full-time Students: 11,335M/11,702W Faculty: 1430

Respondent: John White, Professor of English, Composition Coordinator

Writing Requirement: Required freshman English course, upper division writing course in major, and campus-wide examination

Writing Center

CENTER HAS EXISTED: 2 years HOURS OPEN PER WEEK: 45

STAFF: 15 faculty, graduate, and undergraduate tutors

TUTORS' TRAINING: Academic course for peer tutors

TUTORS' EVALUATION: Observation

TUTORS PAID: Yes

PROGRAM DESIGNED TO SERVE: Primarily writing students, also English students

PROGRAM ACTUALLY SERVES: Writing students and English students

STUDENTS SEEK HELP WITH: Academic essays and research papers

PERCENTAGE OF STUDENTS SERVED: Less than 25%

OVER PAST FIVE YEARS THIS PERCENTAGE HAS: Stayed the same

STUDENTS USE CENTER: Throughout the semester on a walk-in, appointment, or regular basis

STUDENTS REQUIRED TO USE CENTER: Problem writers and all students in the remedial class

MATERIALS AVAILABLE: Handbooks, exercises, educational magazines, professional books, computer, and tapes

STUDENT ATTITUDE: Somewhat positive

Peer Tutoring Program

PROGRAM HAS EXISTED: 2 years

ORGANIZATION: Curriculum-based

NUMBER OF TUTORS: 15

HOURS THEY WORK PER WEEK: 5-20

TUTORS PAID: Yes

TUTOR SELECTION: Appointed by director

TUTORS' TRAINING: Academic course

TUTORS' EVALUATION: Observation

PERCENTAGE OF STUDENTS SERVED: Less than 25%

OVER PAST FIVE YEARS THIS PERCENTAGE HAS: Stayed the same

PROGRAM INTENDED TO SERVE: Remedial writing students

PROGRAM ACTUALLY SERVES: Remedial writing students

STUDENTS SEEK HELP WITH: Academic essays and grammar

MECHANICS OF TUTORING: Student may choose to discuss any paper with tutor; remedial students must discuss mechanics with tutor

STUDENT ATTITUDE: Somewhat positive

Writing-Across-the-Curriculum Program

PROGRAM HAS EXISTED: 1 year

INSTRUCTORS INVOLVED: Faculty in all disciplines

INSTRUCTORS' SELECTION: Voluntary

INSTRUCTORS' TRAINING: None

PERCENTAGE OF FACULTY INVOLVED: Less than 25%

IN PAST FIVE YEARS THIS PERCENTAGE HAS: Stayed the same

STUDENTS INVOLVED IN PROGRAM: Students in all disciplines

PERCENTAGE OF STUDENTS INVOLVED: More than 75%

IN PAST FIVE YEARS THIS PERCENTAGE HAS: Stayed the same

PARTICIPANTS' ATTITUDE: Somewhat positive

Though in operation less than two years, the writing-across-the-curriculum program at California State University at Fullerton already involves all departments and all students. The program requires that every department designate a mandatory upper-division writing course that involves substantial writing. Professors in various departments are given help and instruction through continuing workshops in the teaching of writing across the curriculum. In addition, CSUF has two peer tutoring programs. While some undergraduate tutors are trained to work in the writing center along with professional staff and trained graduate tutors, others are assigned to work specifically with a remedial English course. All students in this course are required to work with the peer tutors on both general mechanics and specific papers. In the next few years, the university plans to develop its current programs and, as John White observes, "Anything is possible."

CALIFORNIA STATE UNIVERSITY at LONG BEACH

Long Beach, CA 90840

Full-time Students: 7612M/8836W Faculty: 962

Respondents: David Peck, Composition Coordinator; Charles Pomeroy, Director, Writing Skills Program

Writing Requirement: Required freshman English course and third-year proficiency examination

Writing Center

CENTER HAS EXISTED: 5 years HOURS OPEN PER WEEK: 20-25

STAFF: 5 undergraduate tutors

TUTORS' TRAINING: On-the-job

TUTORS' EVALUATION: Observation and conferences

TUTORS PAID: Yes

PROGRAM DESIGNED TO SERVE: Students in all disciplines, especially writing students

PROGRAM ACTUALLY SERVES: Students in all disciplines, especially writing students

STUDENTS SEEK HELP WITH: Scientific reports, academic essays, and research papers

PERCENTAGE OF STUDENTS SERVED: Less than 10%

OVER PAST FIVE YEARS THIS PERCENTAGE HAS: Increased

STUDENTS USE CENTER: Throughout the semester on a walk-in basis

STUDENTS REQUIRED TO USE CENTER: Problem writers

MATERIALS AVAILABLE: Handbooks, professional books, and workbooks

STUDENT ATTITUDE: Unknown

Despite its modest size, the recently opened writing center at California State University at Long Beach serves an increasing number of students, most notably problem writers and those enrolled in the remedial writing skills program. These remedial writing courses are a new addition to the program at Long Beach, and have been particularly successful during the past three years. Also recently introduced is a new sophomore-level critical thinking course.

CAPITAL UNIVERSITY

Columbus, OH 43209

Full-time Students: 638M/834W Faculty: 119

Respondent: Joyce T. Hathaway, Chairperson, English Department

Writing Requirement: Required freshman English course

Writing Center

CENTER HAS EXISTED: 5-10 years HOURS OPEN PER WEEK: Under 10

STAFF: Fewer than 5 faculty

PROGRAM DESIGNED TO SERVE: Students in all disciplines

PROGRAM ACTUALLY SERVES: Students in all disciplines

STUDENTS SEEK HELP WITH: Academic essays, research papers, resumes or business writing, and legal briefs

PERCENTAGE OF STUDENTS SERVED: Less than 10%

OVER PAST FIVE YEARS THIS PERCENTAGE HAS: Increased

STUDENTS USE CENTER: Mid-semester and throughout the semester on a walk-in, appointment, or regular basis

STUDENTS REQUIRED TO USE CENTER: Problem writers

MATERIALS AVAILABLE: Handbooks, exercises, and professional books

STUDENT ATTITUDE: Very positive

Over the past ten years, Capital University has begun to pay more attention to students with writing problems. The writing workshop has existed for several years, staffed by English Department faculty who help all students with various types of writing. Although only problem writers are required to use the workshop, many others do so voluntarily, and the number of users is increasing. In the future, the school plans to establish a writing-across-the-curriculum program that would involve faculty from various disciplines within the College of Arts and Sciences. The English Department hopes that this program will encourage more attention to writing skills in all courses, not just during freshman year, but throughout a student's college career.

CARLETON COLLEGE

Northfield, MN 55057

Full-time Students: 931M/919W Faculty: 133

Respondents: Robert Tisdale, Professor of English, Coordinator of Writing-Across-the-Curriculum Program; Frank Morral, Chairman of the English Department

Writing Requirement: A course in the Writing Program

Writing Center

CENTER HAS EXISTED: 5-10 years HOURS OPEN PER WEEK: 20-40

STAFF: One part-time English professor and 5 undergraduate tutors

TUTORS' TRAINING: On-the-job and academic course

TUTORS' EVALUATION: Observation and conferences

TUTORS PAID: Yes, after their initial internship term

PROGRAM DESIGNED TO SERVE: Students in all disciplines, especially freshmen and writing students

PROGRAM ACTUALLY SERVES: Students in all disciplines, especially freshmen and writing students

STUDENTS SEEK HELP WITH: Academic essays and research papers

PERCENTAGE OF STUDENTS SERVED: Over 75%

OVER PAST FIVE YEARS THIS PERCENTAGE HAS: Stayed the same

STUDENTS USE CENTER: On a walk-in or regular basis, or by referral from a professor or Rhetoric Assistant

STUDENTS REQUIRED TO USE CENTER: None

MATERIALS AVAILABLE: Handbooks, exercises, and professional books

STUDENT ATTITUDE: Very positive

Peer Tutoring Program (Rhetoric Assistants)

PROGRAM HAS EXISTED: 7 years

ORGANIZATION: Curriculum-based

NUMBER OF TUTORS: 20-25

HOURS THEY WORK PER WEEK: 4-8

TUTORS PAID: Yes, after first semester, during which they receive 3 credits for internship

TUTOR SELECTION: Nominated by themselves and English Department faculty, then appointed by director

TUTORS' TRAINING: 2-hour weekly meetings with director during first semester internship, and on-the-job training

TUTORS' EVALUATION: Observation, conferences, and evaluations by the professors with whom they work

PERCENTAGE OF STUDENTS SERVED: Over 75%

OVER PAST FIVE YEARS THIS PERCENTAGE HAS: Stayed the same

PROGRAM INTENDED TO SERVE: Students in all disciplines, especially freshmen and writing students

PROGRAM ACTUALLY SERVES: Students in all disciplines, especially freshmen and writing students

STUDENTS SEEK HELP WITH: Academic essays and research papers

MECHANICS OF TUTORING: Rhetoric Assistants work in writing-intensive courses

STUDENT ATTITUDE: Positive

Writing-Across-the-Curriculum Program

PROGRAM HAS EXISTED: 5-10 years

INSTRUCTORS INVOLVED: Faculty in all disciplines

INSTRUCTORS' SELECTION: Voluntary

INSTRUCTORS' TRAINING: Seminars

PERCENTAGE OF FACULTY INVOLVED: 25-50%

IN PAST FIVE YEARS THIS PERCENTAGE HAS: Stayed the same

STUDENTS INVOLVED IN PROGRAM: Students in all disciplines

PERCENTAGE OF STUDENTS INVOLVED: 70%

IN PAST FIVE YEARS THIS PERCENTAGE HAS: Increased

PARTICIPANTS' ATTITUDE: Positive

Carleton College's Writing Program encompasses several related programs: a Learning Skills Center, Rhetoric Assistants, a writing requirement, and a writing-across-the-curriculum program. Students who do not score a 5 on the AP English examination or pass the college's entry essay test must take one of several writing-intensive courses offered by a number of departments as part of the Writing Program. Participating faculty members prepare for the program by taking an English Department training seminar. They then agree to accept a certain number of writing students into their courses and require more written assignments from these students than from the rest of the class. Aiding the faculty in the Writing Program, Rhetoric Assistants are usually seniors who have taken advanced rhetoric and who have then been nominated for the position by their instructors. Most also take a semester workshop in the teaching of writing that prepares them to comment on early and final drafts and hold conferences with students. Undergraduate tutors working in the Learning Skills Center are trained through weekly workshops and an internship with a professor. While most students use Rhetoric Assistants for writing help, some Assistants and professors refer students to the Center for more basic help.

CARNEGIE-MELLON UNIVERSITY

Pittsburgh, PA 15213

Full-time Students: 2690M/1301W Faculty: 440

Respondent: David Kaufer, Director of the Freshman Writing Program

Writing Requirement: Placement by SAT examination

Writing Center

CENTER HAS EXISTED: To open in fall 1985 HOURS OPEN PER WEEK: 10

STAFF: Fewer than 5 faculty, graduate, and undergraduate tutors

TUTORS' TRAINING: Non-academic training course

TUTORS' EVALUATION: None

TUTORS PAID: Yes

PROGRAM DESIGNED TO SERVE: Students in all disciplines

MATERIALS AVAILABLE: Computer-assisted instruction

Peer Tutoring Program

PROGRAM HAS EXISTED: Under 2 years

ORGANIZATION: Curriculum-based

NUMBER OF TUTORS: 3

HOURS THEY WORK PER WEEK: Under 5

TUTORS PAID: Yes

TUTOR SELECTION: Self-nominated

TUTORS' TRAINING: Non-academic training course

TUTORS' EVALUATION: Observation

PERCENTAGE OF STUDENTS SERVED: Less than 25%

PROGRAM INTENDED TO SERVE: Students in all disciplines

PROGRAM ACTUALLY SERVES: Students in all disciplines

STUDENTS SEEK HELP WITH: Paper assignments

MECHANICS OF TUTORING: Student may choose to discuss a paper with a tutor

STUDENT ATTITUDE: Positive

In the past two years Carnegie-Mellon has supplemented its wide variety of writing courses with an emphasis on writing outside the classroom. A peer tutoring program designed to serve any student on a voluntary basis was established two years ago. In the fall of 1985 the English Department will open a writing center that will rely primarily on computer-assisted instruction. Among the center's goals are "to integrate computer software into the diagnosis and treatment of students' writing problems" and to develop "general courseware for instruction in reading and writing," according to the center's brochure. This software includes text analysis packages such as Writer's Workbench and Epistle, as well as programs "that can 'walk' a student through the entire writing process" or help instructors diagnose students' problems in generating and revising prose. Carnegie-Mellon hopes to continue its new emphasis on innovative programs by developing a writing-across-the-curriculum program in the near future.

CASE WESTERN RESERVE UNIVERSITY

Cleveland, OH 44106

Full-time Students: 2109M/807W Faculty: 1335

Respondent: William R. Siebenschuh, Director of Composition and the Writing Center

Writing Requirement: Required freshman writing course; exemption by AP or SAT

Writing Center

CENTER HAS EXISTED: 8 years HOURS OPEN PER WEEK: 25

STAFF: Director and 3 full-time graduate fellows assisted occasionally by one or more undergraduate tutors

TUTORS' TRAINING: On-the-job

TUTORS' EVALUATION: Observation, general consultation, and one or two joint grading sessions

TUTORS PAID: Graduates are; undergraduates receive course credit

PROGRAM DESIGNED TO SERVE: Students in all disciplines

PROGRAM ACTUALLY SERVES: Students in all disciplines, with a high percentage of ESL students

STUDENTS SEEK HELP WITH: General writing skills

PERCENTAGE OF STUDENTS SERVED: Less than 25%

OVER PAST FIVE YEARS THIS PERCENTAGE HAS: Stayed the same

STUDENTS USE CENTER: Repeatedly throughout the semester on an appointment or regular basis; some are referred by professors

STUDENTS REQUIRED TO USE CENTER: Problem writers

MATERIALS AVAILABLE: Handbooks, exercises, professional books, and cassettes

STUDENT ATTITUDE: Very positive

Case Western Reserve University involves all faculty in all departments in teaching the required freshman English course by having each faculty member teach a section of the course. Writing is also emphasized beyond the English Department by the eight-year-old writing center. The writing center's staff consists of a director, three graduate fellows, and a small number of peer tutors. Most of the graduate tutors who staff the center have had previous teaching experience and, since a large percentage of those who use the center are foreign students, the graduate tutors are required to have some training in teaching ESL. Tutors at the center work together with students to make a tutoring plan, and the Center also offers two one-credit courses for grades: a writing and a reading tutorial. Students not wishing to take a class or attend a series of tutorial sessions may drop in for assistance, although appointment slots fill up quickly. During the next few years, Case Western plans to expand the writing programs by including the use of word processing and computer-assisted instruction.

CENTRAL MISSOURI STATE UNIVERSITY

Warrensburg, MO 64043

Full-time Students: 4035M/4129W Faculty: 445

Respondent: Allen Ramsey, Associate Professor of English, Director of Freshman Studies

Writing Requirement: Required freshman English course and other required English course

Writing Center

CENTER HAS EXISTED: Over 10 years HOURS OPEN PER WEEK: 20–40

STAFF: 8–12 faculty

TUTORS' TRAINING: Graduate program courses

TUTORS' EVALUATION: By other tutors

TUTORS PAID: Yes

PROGRAM DESIGNED TO SERVE: Writing students

PROGRAM ACTUALLY SERVES: Writing students and underclassmen

STUDENTS SEEK HELP WITH: 80% academic essays, 10% research papers, 5% scientific reports, and 5% resumes or business writing

PERCENTAGE OF STUDENTS SERVED: Less than 25%

OVER PAST FIVE YEARS THIS PERCENTAGE HAS: Increased

STUDENTS USE CENTER: Throughout the semester on a walk-in and regular basis

STUDENTS REQUIRED TO USE CENTER: None

MATERIALS AVAILABLE: Handbooks and exercises

STUDENT ATTITUDE: Somewhat positive

The writing center at Central Missouri State has expanded over the past ten years "from a fledgling unit to a thriving part of the university," according to Allen Ramsey. This Educational Developmental Center offers credit and non-credit tutorials. The College Skills program within the center gives three semester hours of credit and is part of a lecture/tutorial system that teaches basic writing. In these courses, instructors lecture for two days and then hold three days of individual tutorial sessions. The Learning Lab, also part of the writing center, offers non-credit tutorial sessions for students seeking help with basic writing skills. Programs are available in basic writing skills, speed reading, study skills, comprehension, vocabulary, spelling, and grammar.

CENTRAL WESLEYAN COLLEGE

Central, SC 29630

Full-time Students: 178M/198W Faculty: 32

Respondent: Gloria J. Bell, Chairman, Division of Humanities

Writing Requirement: Required freshman English course; exemption by placement exam

Writing Center

CENTER HAS EXISTED: 4 years HOURS OPEN PER WEEK: 20–25

STAFF: Fewer than 5 faculty and undergraduate tutors

TUTORS' TRAINING: On-the-job

TUTORS' EVALUATION: Observation

TUTORS PAID: Yes

PROGRAM DESIGNED TO SERVE: Students in all disciplines

PROGRAM ACTUALLY SERVES: Primarily writing students; some students in other disciplines

STUDENTS SEEK HELP WITH: Academic essays and research papers

PERCENTAGE OF STUDENTS SERVED: 20%

OVER PAST FIVE YEARS THIS PERCENTAGE HAS: Increased

STUDENTS USE CENTER: Throughout the semester on a walk-in, appointment, or regular basis, or over the phone

STUDENTS REQUIRED TO USE CENTER: Problem writers

MATERIALS AVAILABLE: Handbooks, writing exercises, and audio-visual aids

STUDENT ATTITUDE: Somewhat positive

Peer Tutoring Program

PROGRAM HAS EXISTED: 1 year

ORGANIZATION: Auxiliary service of Learning Assistance Center

NUMBER OF TUTORS: 2

HOURS THEY WORK PER WEEK: 6

TUTORS PAID: Yes

TUTOR SELECTION: Nominated by English faculty

TUTORS' TRAINING: On-the-job

TUTORS' EVALUATION: Observation

PERCENTAGE OF STUDENTS SERVED: 20%

OVER PAST FIVE YEARS THIS PERCENTAGE HAS: Increased

PROGRAM INTENDED TO SERVE: Writing students and students in all disciplines

PROGRAM ACTUALLY SERVES: Writing students

STUDENTS SEEK HELP WITH: Academic essays and research papers

MECHANICS OF TUTORING: Tutors sometimes comment in writing but usually discuss exercises in progress with students

STUDENT ATTITUDE: Unknown

In the past five years, Central Wesleyan has raised its writing standards in composition courses while making additional writing instruction available through faculty and peer tutors in the Learning Assistance Center. Though it is open to all students, the center serves under one quarter of the college's small student community, and 90 percent of those students served are writing students. The peer tutors, who began working in the center in 1983, are nominated by English faculty and receive no formal training before they begin working with students. In the next few years, Central Wesleyan hopes to increase its use of peer tutors and place a greater emphasis on writing in classes outside the English Department.

CENTRE COLLEGE

Danville, KY 40422

Full-time Students: 450M/325W Faculty: 65

Respondent: Mark Lucas, Assistant Professor of English, Director of Writing Program

Writing Requirement: Required freshman English course; exemption by proficiency examination

Peer Tutoring Program

PROGRAM HAS EXISTED: 5-10 years

ORGANIZATION: Residentially based

NUMBER OF TUTORS: Fewer than 10

HOURS THEY WORK PER WEEK: 5-10

TUTORS PAID: No

TUTOR SELECTION: Nominated by themselves and by English faculty

TUTORS' TRAINING: No formal training

TUTORS' EVALUATION: Observation

PERCENTAGE OF STUDENTS SERVED: Less than 25%

OVER PAST FIVE YEARS THIS PERCENTAGE HAS: Stayed the same

PROGRAM INTENDED TO SERVE: Students in all disciplines, especially writing students

PROGRAM ACTUALLY SERVES: Students in all disciplines, especially writing students

STUDENTS SEEK HELP WITH: Academic essays

MECHANICS OF TUTORING: Student may choose to discuss any paper with tutor

STUDENT ATTITUDE: Unknown

During the past decade, Centre College has commited itself to the teaching of writing. While ten years ago there were no writing programs, students must now fulfill a proficiency requirement and take a writing course. Mark Lucas considers the traditional expository writing program particularly successful in improving student writing. A peer tutoring program has also been established and, in the next few years, Lucas hopes to create a writing-across-the-curriculum program by involving faculty from disciplines other than English in the teaching of writing.

CHAMINADE UNIVERSITY OF HONOLULU

Honolulu, HI 96816

Full-time Students: 419M/421W Faculty: 51

Respondent: Loretta Petrie, Chairperson, English Department

Writing Requirement: Required freshman English course; exemption by placement examination

Writing Center

CENTER HAS EXISTED: 5-10 years HOURS OPEN PER WEEK: Over 40

STAFF: 5-20 graduate and undergraduate tutors

TUTORS' TRAINING: On-the-job

TUTORS' EVALUATION: Observation and student questionnaires

TUTORS PAID: Yes

PROGRAM DESIGNED TO SERVE: Students in all disciplines, especially writing students and English students

PROGRAM ACTUALLY SERVES: Students in all disciplines, especially writing students and English students

STUDENTS SEEK HELP WITH: Creative writing, academic essays, research papers, and resumes or business writing

PERCENTAGE OF STUDENTS SERVED: 25-50%

OVER PAST FIVE YEARS THIS PERCENTAGE HAS: Stayed the same

STUDENTS USE CENTER: Throughout the semester on a walk-in, appointment, or regular basis

STUDENTS REQUIRED TO USE CENTER: None

MATERIALS AVAILABLE: Handbooks, writing exercises, professional books, and educational magazines

STUDENT ATTITUDE: Very positive

Peer Tutoring Program

PROGRAM HAS EXISTED: 2–5 years

ORGANIZATION: Curriculum–based

NUMBER OF TUTORS: Fewer than 10

HOURS THEY WORK PER WEEK: 5–10

TUTORS PAID: Yes

TUTOR SELECTION: Nominated by English faculty and appointed by the director

TUTORS' TRAINING: On–the–job

TUTORS' EVALUATION: Observation and student questionnaires

PERCENTAGE OF STUDENTS SERVED: 25–50%

OVER PAST FIVE YEARS THIS PERCENTAGE HAS: Stayed the same

PROGRAM INTENDED TO SERVE: Students in all disciplines, primarily writing and English students

PROGRAM ACTUALLY SERVES: Students in all disciplines, primarily writing and English students

STUDENTS SEEK HELP WITH: Academic essays, research papers, creative writing, and resumes or business writing

MECHANICS OF TUTORING: Students may choose to discuss papers with the tutor

STUDENT ATTITUDE: Very positive

With its writing center and peer tutoring program firmly established and serving over 25 percent of all students, Chaminade University is now looking toward writing across the curriculum to supplement its writing classes. In the next few years, the English Department will retain its responsibility for freshman composition and competency, but the advanced freshman composition course will emphasize writing in various disciplines, and each department will demand writing proficiency from its own majors. Emphasis on writing in English classes at Chaminade is also increasing. The English Department is adding upper–level courses in journalism, expository, technical, and professional writing, and is redesigning the freshman composition sequence, shifting it away from its rhetorical model approach. When Chaminade's new programs are developed, all students will have a wide range of courses and tutoring services available to them, and students will be required to write proficiently by both the English Department and the department in which they major.

CHICAGO STATE UNIVERSITY

Chicago, IL 60628

Full-time Students: 1173M/2090W Faculty: 118

Respondent: William Cantrall, Coordinator of Composition, English Department

Writing Requirement: 2 required freshman English courses and English Qualifying Essay Examination

Writing Center

CENTER HAS EXISTED: 5-10 years HOURS OPEN PER WEEK: 20-40

STAFF: One faculty coordinator and 5-20 undergraduate tutors

TUTORS' TRAINING: On-the-job

TUTORS' EVALUATION: Observation

TUTORS PAID: Yes

PROGRAM DESIGNED TO SERVE: Underclassmen, especially writing students

PROGRAM ACTUALLY SERVES: Underclassmen, especially writing students

STUDENTS SEEK HELP WITH: Remedial and freshman composition

PERCENTAGE OF STUDENTS SERVED: Less than 25%

OVER PAST FIVE YEARS THIS PERCENTAGE HAS: Stayed the same

STUDENTS USE CENTER: Throughout the semester on a regular basis

STUDENTS REQUIRED TO USE CENTER: None

MATERIALS AVAILABLE: Handbooks and exercises

STUDENT ATTITUDE: Somewhat positive

Over the past three years, the English faculty at Chicago State University have focused on upgrading the freshman writing program. They have improved the quality of the two required freshman composition courses and have added remedial composition courses for those students who find the pace of the regular courses too difficult. While the remedial courses provide aid to less-prepared students, the exclusion of these students from the freshman composition courses also allows those courses to move more quickly and to provide prepared students with more substantial instruction.

THE CITADEL

Charleston, SC 29409

Full-time Students: 2023M Faculty: 135

Respondent: J.A.W. Reinbert, Professor of English, Chairman of Freshman English Committee

Writing Requirement: Required freshman English course and two sophomore literature courses with writing emphasis

Writing Center

CENTER HAS EXISTED: 2-5 years HOURS OPEN PER WEEK: 10-20

STAFF: 1 graduate tutor and fewer than 5 undergraduates

TUTORS' TRAINING: Academic course

TUTORS' EVALUATION: Observation and conferences

TUTORS PAID: Only graduate tutors

PROGRAM DESIGNED TO SERVE: Students from all disciplines, primarily freshmen and writing students

PROGRAM ACTUALLY SERVES: Primarily freshmen

STUDENTS SEEK HELP WITH: Academic essays and research papers

PERCENTAGE OF STUDENTS SERVED: Less than 25%

OVER PAST FIVE YEARS THIS PERCENTAGE HAS: Increased

STUDENTS USE CENTER: Throughout the semester by appointment or when referred by English professor

STUDENTS REQUIRED TO USE CENTER: Problem writers

MATERIALS AVAILABLE: Handbooks and writing exercises

STUDENT ATTITUDE: Very positive

Peer Tutoring Program

PROGRAM HAS EXISTED: Under 2 years

ORGANIZATION: Conceived and run by English Honor Society

NUMBER OF TUTORS: Fewer than 10

HOURS THEY WORK PER WEEK: Under 5

TUTORS PAID: No

TUTOR SELECTION: Nominated by English faculty

TUTORS' TRAINING: No formal training

TUTORS' EVALUATION: Observation

PERCENTAGE OF STUDENTS SERVED: Less than 25%

OVER PAST FIVE YEARS THIS PERCENTAGE HAS: Stayed the same

PROGRAM INTENDED TO SERVE: Freshmen and writing students

PROGRAM ACTUALLY SERVES: Freshmen and writing students

STUDENTS SEEK HELP WITH: Academic essays and research papers

MECHANICS OF TUTORING: Student may choose to have tutor comment on or discuss any paper

STUDENT ATTITUDE: Unknown

The fairly traditional writing curriculum at The Citadel is supplemented by a writing requirement, a writing center, and a peer tutoring program. All students must take a required freshman composition course and two sophomore literature courses that demand substantial amounts of writing. According to J.A.W. Reinbert, these courses have been very successful, although they do not work for all students. Any student seeking additional writing assistance can use the writing center and the peer tutors. The center's staff is trained in an academic course, and serves primarily freshmen, several of whom are referred to the center by composition professors. The new peer tutoring program, established two years ago and run by the English Honor Society, is comprised of fewer than ten untrained undergraduates and serves under 25 percent of all students. The Citadel has no major changes planned for the next few years.

CITY UNIVERSITY OF NEW YORK/BROOKLYN COLLEGE

Brooklyn, NY 11210

Full-time Students: 5682M/3359W Faculty: 1500

Respondent: Nancy Black, Director of Freshman Composition

Writing Requirement: Two required freshman English courses

Writing Center

CENTER HAS EXISTED: Over 10 years HOURS OPEN PER WEEK: 20–40

STAFF: 5–20 faculty and undergraduate tutors

TUTORS' TRAINING: On-the-job and academic training course

TUTORS' EVALUATION: Observation

TUTORS PAID: Some are

PROGRAM DESIGNED TO SERVE: Students in all disciplines

PROGRAM ACTUALLY SERVES: Students in all disciplines, particularly writing students

STUDENTS SEEK HELP WITH: Academic essays, research papers, and business writing

PERCENTAGE OF STUDENTS SERVED: Less than 25%

OVER PAST FIVE YEARS THIS PERCENTAGE HAS: Stayed the same

STUDENTS USE CENTER: Throughout the semester on a walk-in or appointment basis

STUDENTS REQUIRED TO USE CENTER: None

MATERIALS AVAILABLE: Handbooks and writing exercises

STUDENT ATTITUDE: Very positive

Peer Tutoring Program

PROGRAM HAS EXISTED: Over 10 years

ORGANIZATION: Writing center-based

NUMBER OF TUTORS: 10–20

HOURS THEY WORK PER WEEK: Under 5

TUTORS PAID: No

TUTOR SELECTION: Nominated by English faculty

TUTORS' TRAINING: Academic training course

TUTORS' EVALUATION: Observation

PERCENTAGE OF STUDENTS SERVED: Fewer than 25%

OVER PAST FIVE YEARS THIS PERCENTAGE HAS: Stayed the same

PROGRAM INTENDED TO SERVE: Students in all disciplines, particularly writing students

PROGRAM ACTUALLY SERVES: Students in all disciplines, particularly writing students

STUDENTS SEEK HELP WITH: Academic essays and research papers

MECHANICS OF TUTORING: Student may choose to discuss any paper with a tutor

STUDENT ATTITUDE: Somewhat positive

Writing-Across-the-Curriculum Program

PROGRAM HAS EXISTED: 3 years

INSTRUCTORS: Faculty in all disciplines

INSTRUCTORS' SELECTION: By appointment as a teacher in the core curriculum

INSTRUCTORS' TRAINING: Summer Faculty Development Seminars and workshops during the academic year

PERCENTAGE OF FACULTY INVOLVED: 50%

IN PAST FIVE YEARS THIS PERCENTAGE HAS: Increased

STUDENTS INVOLVED IN PROGRAM: Students in all disciplines

PERCENTAGE OF STUDENTS INVOLVED: More than 75%

IN PAST FIVE YEARS THIS PERCENTAGE HAS: Increased

PARTICIPANTS' ATTITUDE: Very positive

Brooklyn College's peer tutoring program, which was introduced over ten years ago, is one of the oldest in the country. Working out of the writing center, the peer tutors assist any student who seeks help with his or her writing. In the last three years, the peer tutoring program has been supplemented by a writing-across-the-curriculum program that requires writing in all core courses. Brooklyn College has expanded traditional modes of instruction in recent years. Several writing courses have been added, and there are more than ten faculty and twelve graduate students teaching solely writing. The English Department is currently experimenting with computer-assisted instruction, and it plans to expand and strengthen its support of the writing-across-the-curriculum program.

CITY UNIVERSITY OF NEW YORK/THE CITY COLLEGE

New York City, NY 10031

Full-time Students: 5682M/3559W Faculty: 734

Respondent: Allan Danzig, Director of Composition

Writing Requirement: Required freshman English course and other required English course for some programs and schools

Writing Center

CENTER HAS EXISTED: 5-10 years HOURS OPEN PER WEEK: 20-40

STAFF: 2 trained workers and 12 graduate and 12 undergraduate tutors

TUTORS' TRAINING: On-the-job

TUTORS' EVALUATION: Observation

TUTORS PAID: Yes

PROGRAM DESIGNED TO SERVE: Writing students, English students, freshmen, underclassmen, and especially SEEK students

PROGRAM ACTUALLY SERVES: Writing students, English students, freshmen, underclassmen, and especially SEEK students

STUDENTS SEEK HELP WITH: Academic essays and grammar drills

PERCENTAGE OF STUDENTS SERVED: Less than 25%

OVER PAST FIVE YEARS THIS PERCENTAGE HAS: Stayed the same

STUDENTS USE CENTER: Repeatedly on an appointment basis

STUDENTS REQUIRED TO USE CENTER: Problem writers

MATERIALS AVAILABLE: Handbooks and exercises

STUDENT ATTITUDE: Students eager to use center

After undergoing a period of experimentation from 1969 to 1976, The City College writing program has now become more settled and has instituted stricter guidelines. Final examinations are now required in all courses, and grading is done in group sessions. The writing center at City is funded in large part by the SEEK program, which provides financial and academic aid to students with low grades but with strong motivation. Many SEEK students use the center, as do writing students, English students, and freshmen. The center is popular with students, and many are eager to sign up for appointments. A requirement that all teachers of composition courses assign and evaluate 2500 words of writing will be introduced at City College in the fall of 1984.

CITY UNIVERSITY OF NEW YORK/COLLEGE OF STATEN ISLAND

Staten Island, NY 10301

Full-time Students: 5200M/5200W Faculty: 372

Respondent: Joan E. Hartman, Professor and Chairperson, Department of English

Writing Requirement: One semester required freshman English and one semester writing and literature course

Writing Center

CENTER HAS EXISTED: 5-10 years HOURS OPEN PER WEEK: Over 40

STAFF: 5-20 faculty, graduate, and undergraduate tutors

TUTORS' TRAINING: On-the-job and academic course for undergraduates

TUTORS' EVALUATION: Observation, conferences, and student questionnaires

TUTORS PAID: Yes

PROGRAM DESIGNED TO SERVE: Writing students and developmental English students

PROGRAM ACTUALLY SERVES: Writing students and developmental English students

STUDENTS SEEK HELP WITH: Editing, proofreading, ESL conversation, and fluency

PERCENTAGE OF STUDENTS SERVED: Less than 25%

OVER PAST FIVE YEARS THIS PERCENTAGE HAS: Increased

STUDENTS USE CENTER: Repeatedly throughout the semester on an appointment or regular basis

STUDENTS REQUIRED TO USE CENTER: Remedial students

MATERIALS AVAILABLE: Writing exercises

STUDENT ATTITUDE: Very positive

Peer Tutoring Program

PROGRAM HAS EXISTED: 2-5 years

ORGANIZATION: Writing center-based

NUMBER OF TUTORS: 10–20

HOURS THEY WORK PER WEEK: Under 5

TUTORS PAID: Yes

TUTORS' SELECTION: Appointed by director

TUTORS' TRAINING: On-the-job and academic course

TUTORS' EVALUATION: Observation, questionnaire, and conferences

PERCENTAGE OF STUDENTS SERVED: Less than 25%

OVER PAST FIVE YEARS THIS PERCENTAGE HAS: Increased

PROGRAM INTENDED TO SERVE: Writing, reading, and ESL students

PROGRAM ACTUALLY SERVES: Writing, reading, and ESL students

MECHANICS OF TUTORING: Student and tutor work on writing skills

STUDENT ATTITUDE: Very positive

Writing-Across-the-Curriculum Program

PROGRAM HAS EXISTED: Less than 2 years

INSTRUCTORS SELECTED: Faculty in all disciplines

INSTRUCTORS' SELECTION: By appointment

INSTRUCTORS' TRAINING: Seminars

PERCENTAGE OF FACULTY INVOLVED: Less than 25%

STUDENTS INVOLVED IN PROGRAM: Students in all disciplines

PERCENTAGE OF STUDENTS INVOLVED: Less than 25%

IN PAST FIVE YEARS THIS PERCENTAGE HAS: Increased

PARTICIPANTS' ATTITUDE: Somewhat positive

Since the City University of New York/College of Staten Island instituted a more stringent writing requirement in 1978, the college has increased its emphasis on writing skills. In the past six years, the college has established writing-across-the-curriculum and a peer tutoring program based in its English Skills Center. All three of these programs place a special emphasis on serving the developmental and ESL students, who form a growing percentage of the student population. This emphasis is also reflected within the curriculum; Staten Island has expanded its developmental, ESL, and freshman composition offerings in the past five years. Joan E. Hartman hopes that the writing program will be able to continue serving students at all levels, despite the fact that the writing-across-the-curriculum efforts were halted because of insufficient funds.

CITY UNIVERSITY OF NEW YORK/HUNTER COLLEGE

New York, NY 10021

Full-time Students: 2120M/6529W Faculty: 612

Respondent: H. Minkoff, Coordinator, Expository Writing

Writing Requirement: Required freshman English course

Writing Center

CENTER HAS EXISTED: 5-10 years HOURS OPEN PER WEEK: Over 40

STAFF: 5-20 undergraduate tutors

TUTORS' TRAINING: On-the-job and non-academic course

TUTORS' EVALUATION: Observation, conferences, student questionnaires, and evaluation by other tutors

TUTORS PAID: Yes

PROGRAM DESIGNED TO SERVE: Students in all disciplines

PROGRAM ACTUALLY SERVES: Students in all disciplines

STUDENTS SEEK HELP WITH: Academic essays and research papers

PERCENTAGE OF STUDENTS SERVED: Less than 25%

OVER PAST FIVE YEARS THIS PERCENTAGE HAS: Stayed the same

STUDENTS USE CENTER: Throughout the semester on an appointment or walk-in basis

STUDENTS REQUIRED TO USE CENTER: Problem writers

MATERIALS AVAILABLE: Handbooks, exercises, and professional books

STUDENT ATTITUDE: Very positive

Like many institutions, Hunter College established a writing center in the late 1970s. Although this center now serves a cross-section of the college community, it has not managed to reach a large number of students. The center serves less than 25 percent of students, and this percentage has not increased in the past several years. Yet H. Minkoff believes that the writing center is well-received by students and will continue to be a vital part of Hunter College's extracurricular writing program in years to come.

CITY UNIVERSITY OF NEW YORK/LAGUARDIA COMMUNITY COLLEGE

Long Island City, NY 11101

Full-time Students: 6582M&W Faculty: 368

Respondent: Marian Arkin, Director, Writing Center

Writing Requirement: Required freshman English course and other required English course; placement by examination

Writing Center

CENTER HAS EXISTED: Over 10 years HOURS OPEN PER WEEK: Over 40

STAFF: 20-40 faculty, graduate, and undergraduate tutors

TUTORS' TRAINING: On-the-job, non-academic or academic training course

TUTORS' EVALUATION: Observation, student questionnaires, and conferences

TUTORS PAID: Yes

PROGRAM DESIGNED TO SERVE: Students in all disciplines

PROGRAM ACTUALLY SERVES: Students in all disciplines

STUDENTS SEEK HELP WITH: Academic essays, research papers, and resumes or business writing

PERCENTAGE OF STUDENTS SERVED: 25-50%

OVER PAST FIVE YEARS THIS PERCENTAGE HAS: Stayed the same

STUDENTS USE CENTER: Throughout the semester on a walk-in, appointment, or regular basis

STUDENTS REQUIRED TO USE CENTER: None

MATERIALS AVAILABLE: Handbooks, exercises, educational magazines, and professional books

STUDENT ATTITUDE: Somewhat positive

Peer Tutoring Program

PROGRAM HAS EXISTED: 5-10 years

ORGANIZATION: Writing center-based

NUMBER OF TUTORS: 10-20

HOURS THEY WORK PER WEEK: Less than 5

TUTORS PAID: No

TUTOR SELECTION: Nominated college-wide and interviewed by the director

TUTORS' TRAINING: Academic course, including supervised tutoring

TUTORS' EVALUATION: Observation, peer critiques, and essays in the training course

PERCENTAGE OF STUDENTS SERVED: Less than 25%

OVER PAST FIVE YEARS THIS PERCENTAGE HAS: Increased

PROGRAM INTENDED TO SERVE: Writing and English students

PROGRAM ACTUALLY SERVES: Writing and English students

STUDENTS SEEK HELP WITH: Academic essays

MECHANICS OF TUTORING: Student may choose to discuss a paper with a tutor

STUDENT ATTITUDE: Somewhat positive

Writing-Across-the-Curriculum Program

PROGRAM HAS EXISTED: 2-5 years

INSTRUCTORS INVOLVED: English, humanities, and social sciences faculty

INSTRUCTORS' SELECTION: Appointment

INSTRUCTORS' TRAINING: Team-teaching

PERCENTAGE OF FACULTY INVOLVED: Less than 25%

IN PAST FIVE YEARS THIS PERCENTAGE HAS: Increased

STUDENTS INVOLVED IN PROGRAM: Humanities and social sciences students

PERCENTAGE OF STUDENTS INVOLVED: Less than 25%

IN PAST FIVE YEARS THIS PERCENTAGE HAS: Stayed the same

PARTICIPANTS' ATTITUDE: Very positive

Although CUNY/LaGuardia was established as recently as 1971, it has a writing center and a peer tutoring program that are over ten years old. The Writing Center, staffed by faculty, graduate students, and peer tutors, stays open over forty hours each week and serves over 25% of the college's students. Working exclusively with English and writing students, the unpaid peer tutors are trained in an academic course and evaluated by faculty and fellow tutors. In addition to these extracurricular writing programs, CUNY/LaGuardia makes sure that its students receive substantial writing instruction by requiring two English courses, enforcing exit criteria, and emphasizing writing instruction beyond the English Department. The writing-across-the-curriculum program involves certain appointed faculty, who learn about the teaching of writing through team-teaching. Though the program affects less than 25% of all students, it has received very positive responses from participants. In recent years CUNY/LaGuardia has expanded its developmental writing program to include three courses, changed the exit criteria, and instituted a "Writing with the Computer" class. In the next few years, the English Department plans to revise the basic composition courses and expand its use of computers in the teaching and learning of writing.

CITY UNIVERSITY OF NEW YORK/QUEENS COLLEGE

Flushing, NY 11367

Full-time Students: 4888M/5905W Faculty: 1300

Respondent: Nancy R. Comley, Assistant Professor of English, Director of Composition,

Writing Requirement: Two-semester sequence of English composition courses; placement by examination

Writing Center

CENTER HAS EXISTED: Over 10 years HOURS OPEN PER WEEK: Over 40

STAFF: Faculty and 20-40 undergraduate tutors

TUTORS' TRAINING: On-the-job

TUTORS' EVALUATION: Observation

TUTORS PAID: Yes

PROGRAM DESIGNED TO SERVE: Students in all disciplines

PROGRAM ACTUALLY SERVES: Students in all disciplines, particularly underclassmen

STUDENTS SEEK HELP WITH: Academic essays and research papers

PERCENTAGE OF STUDENTS SERVED: 25%

OVER PAST FIVE YEARS THIS PERCENTAGE HAS: Increased

STUDENTS USE CENTER: Throughout the semester on a walk-in, appointment, or regular basis.

STUDENTS REQUIRED TO USE CENTER: Problem writers

MATERIALS AVAILABLE: Handbooks, exercises, and professional books

STUDENT ATTITUDE: Very positive

At Queens College, the faculty carefully consider various writing programs, testing and evaluating them before deciding which to incorporate into the curriculum. A cross-curricular approach, for example, was recently tried in the second semester of freshmen composition but then rejected as ineffective. The school has also recently returned to "literature as a basis for writing," a change that pleased both faculty and students. One program that has remained constant for more than ten years is the writing center, which employs a substantial staff, is well-stocked, and reaches a quarter of the student body.

CLARION UNIVERSITY

Clarion, PA 16214

Full-time Students: 2300M/2800W Faculty: 280

Respondent: Francis G. Greco, Chairperson, English Department

Writing Requirement: Required freshman English course

Writing Center

CENTER HAS EXISTED: 5-10 years HOURS OPEN PER WEEK: 20-40

STAFF: 5-20 faculty, graduate, and undergraduate tutors

TUTORS' TRAINING: On-the-job and academic training course

TUTORS' EVALUATION: Observation, student questionnaires, and training course project

TUTORS PAID: Yes

PROGRAM DESIGNED TO SERVE: Students in all disciplines

PROGRAM ACTUALLY SERVES: Primarily freshmen, writing students, and English students, and some students in other disciplines

STUDENTS SEEK HELP WITH: Scientific reports, creative writing, academic essays, research papers, and resumes or business writing

PERCENTAGE OF STUDENTS SERVED: Less than 25%

OVER PAST FIVE YEARS THIS PERCENTAGE HAS: Increased

STUDENTS USE CENTER: Throughout the semester on an appointment basis

STUDENTS REQUIRED TO USE CENTER: Those referred by instructors

MATERIALS AVAILABLE: Handbooks, writing exercises, and professional books

STUDENT ATTITUDE: Very positive

Peer Tutoring Program

PROGRAM HAS EXISTED: 5-10 years

NUMBER OF TUTORS: Under 10

HOURS THEY WORK PER WEEK: 5-10

TUTORS PAID: Yes

TUTOR SELECTION: Nominated by English faculty

TUTORS' TRAINING: On-the-job and academic training course

TUTORS' EVALUATION: Observation, conferences, and student questionnaires

PERCENTAGE OF STUDENTS SERVED: Less than 25%

OVER PAST FIVE YEARS THIS PERCENTAGE HAS: Stayed the same

PROGRAM INTENDED TO SERVE: Students in all disciplines

PROGRAM ACTUALLY SERVES: Students in all disciplines

STUDENTS SEEK HELP WITH: Academic essays and business writing

MECHANICS OF TUTORING: Tutor and student are required to discuss paper

STUDENT ATTITUDE: Somewhat positive

In addition to its writing courses and freshman English requirement, Clarion University's writing program features a writing center staffed by faculty, graduate students, and peer tutors who are nominated by English faculty and trained in an academic course. Though open to all students, the center serves primarily freshmen, English students, and writing students. Most use the center voluntarily, but some students are referred to the tutors by instructors. The center actively serves less than 25 percent of the entire student body, but those students who have discussed papers with tutors have responded very positively. The English Department plans no major changes in the near future.

CLARK COLLEGE

Atlanta, GA 30314

Full-time Students: 660M/1353W Faculty: 129

Respondent: B. Dilla Buckner, Chairperson, English Department

Writing Requirement: Required freshman English course; placement by examination

Writing Center

CENTER HAS EXISTED: 5 years HOURS OPEN PER WEEK: 40

STAFF: 2 graduate assistants and 2 tutors

TUTORS' TRAINING: On-the-job

TUTORS' EVALUATION: Observation and conferences

TUTORS PAID: Yes

PROGRAM DESIGNED TO SERVE: Freshmen

PROGRAM ACTUALLY SERVES: Freshmen

STUDENTS SEEK HELP WITH: Essays, research papers, grammar, and mechanics

PERCENTAGE OF STUDENTS SERVED: 25%

OVER PAST FIVE YEARS THIS PERCENTAGE HAS: Stayed the same

STUDENTS USE CENTER: Throughout the year on a regular basis

STUDENTS REQUIRED TO USE CENTER: Problem writers referred by instructors

MATERIALS AVAILABLE: Handbooks, exercises, and programmed texts

STUDENT ATTITUDE: Somewhat positive

Peer Tutoring Program

(Special Services Program)

PROGRAM HAS EXISTED: 8-10 years

ORGANIZATION: Curriculum-based

NUMBER OF TUTORS: 4

HOURS THEY WORK PER WEEK: 10-20

TUTORS PAID: Yes

TUTOR SELECTION: Nominated by English faculty

TUTORS' TRAINING: On-the-job

TUTORS' EVALUATION: Observation and conferences

PERCENTAGE OF STUDENTS SERVED: 25%

OVER PAST FIVE YEARS THIS PERCENTAGE HAS: Stayed the same

PROGRAM INTENDED TO SERVE: Special Services underclassmen

PROGRAM ACTUALLY SERVES: Freshmen and Special Services Students

STUDENTS SEEK HELP WITH: Essays, research papers, grammar, and mechanics

MECHANICS OF TUTORING: Tutor and student are required to discuss papers and complete drills

STUDENT ATTITUDE: Somewhat positive

Writing-Across-the-Curriculum Program

PROGRAM HAS EXISTED: 3 years

INSTRUCTORS INVOLVED: Faculty in all disciplines

INSTRUCTORS' SELECTION: All faculty participate

INSTRUCTORS' TRAINING: Seminars and workshops

PERCENTAGE OF FACULTY INVOLVED: 65%

IN PAST FIVE YEARS THIS PERCENTAGE HAS: Increased

STUDENTS INVOLVED IN PROGRAM: Students in all disciplines

PERCENTAGE OF STUDENTS INVOLVED: 65%

IN PAST FIVE YEARS THIS PERCENTAGE HAS: Increased

PARTICIPANTS' ATTITUDE: Somewhat positive

During the past few years, Clark College has added several innovative programs to supplement its traditional freshman English requirement, including a faculty-staffed writing center and a peer tutoring program designed to help first-year students. B. Dilla Buckner believes that the strongest addition has been the writing-across-the-curriculum program, which currently affects over half of all students on all levels and which will ultimately involve all instructors.

CLARK UNIVERSITY

Worcester, MA 01610

Full-time Students: 953M/1077W Faculty: 130

Respondent: Leone Scanlon, Director, Writing Center

Writing Requirement: Required cross-disciplinary writing course

Writing Center

CENTER HAS EXISTED: 5-10 years HOURS OPEN PER WEEK: 20-40

STAFF: Fewer than 5 graduate tutors

TUTORS' TRAINING: On-the-job

TUTORS' EVALUATION: Observation, conferences, and student questionnaire

TUTORS PAID: Yes

PROGRAM DESIGNED TO SERVE: Students in all disciplines

PROGRAM ACTUALLY SERVES: Students in all disciplines

STUDENTS SEEK HELP WITH: Scientific reports, creative writing, academic essays, research papers, and resumes or business writing

PERCENTAGE OF STUDENTS SERVED: Less than 25%

OVER PAST FIVE YEARS THIS PERCENTAGE HAS: Increased

STUDENTS USE CENTER: Throughout the semester on a walk-in, appointment or regular basis, or by phone

STUDENTS REQUIRED TO USE CENTER: None

MATERIALS AVAILABLE: Handbooks, exercises, professional books, and educational magazines

STUDENT ATTITUDE: Very positive

Peer Tutoring Program

PROGRAM HAS EXISTED: 5-10 years

ORGANIZATION: Curriculum-based

NUMBER OF TUTORS: 10–20

HOURS THEY WORK PER WEEK: 5–10

TUTORS PAID: Yes

TUTOR SELECTION: Nominated college-wide

TUTORS' TRAINING: On-the-job and academic course

TUTORS' EVALUATION: Conferences and student questionnaire

PERCENTAGE OF STUDENTS SERVED: 25–50%

OVER PAST FIVE YEARS THIS PERCENTAGE HAS: Increased

PROGRAM INTENDED TO SERVE: Students in all disciplines, especially freshmen

PROGRAM ACTUALLY SERVES: Students in all disciplines, especially freshmen

STUDENTS SEEK HELP WITH: Scientific reports, academic essays, and research papers

MECHANICS OF TUTORING: Tutor runs peer writing groups

STUDENT ATTITUDE: Somewhat positive

Writing-Across-the-Curriculum Program

PROGRAM HAS EXISTED: 5–10 years

INSTRUCTORS INVOLVED: Faculty in all disciplines

INSTRUCTORS' SELECTION: By appointment and voluntary

INSTRUCTORS' TRAINING: Seminars

PERCENTAGE OF FACULTY INVOLVED: Less than 25%

IN PAST FIVE YEARS THIS PERCENTAGE HAS: Stayed the same

STUDENTS INVOLVED IN PROGRAM: Students in all disciplines

PERCENTAGE OF STUDENTS INVOLVED: 25–50%

IN PAST FIVE YEARS THIS PERCENTAGE HAS: Increased

PARTICIPANTS' ATTITUDE: Somewhat positive

Clark University established several innovative writing programs during the past five years. Clark's Verbal Expression program, encompassing both a peer tutoring program and a writing-across-the-curriculum component, emphasizes writing in disciplines other than English. For a course to be included in the program, the faculty member must participate in a colloquium on the teaching of writing, limit the course to twenty students, and require a number of papers that stress the writing process. Each Verbal Expression course is also staffed with a peer tutor, called a Teaching Assistant, who is usually majoring in that particular discipline. The teaching assistants' primary responsibility is to facilitate "Teacherless Writing Groups" of five to seven students in which everyone reads and comments on all papers. According to the Verbal Expression Program handbook, "At the start, the teaching assistants usually have to play a prominent role in the group. . . . As the students gain critical ability and confidence, the teaching assistants should reduce their participation." Leone Scanlon prefaces this handbook with her hopes for the program: "Only if the faculty are all teachers of writing can we insure that our graduates will be able writers. When that happens, the VE program will have achieved its ultimate goal--its disappearance."

THE COLLEGE OF INSURANCE

New York, NY 10038

Full-time Students: 212M/82W Faculty: 42

Respondent: Dr. Charles L. Leavitt, Chairperson, Liberal Arts Department

Writing Requirement: Required freshman English course on the research paper and another required English course

Peer Tutoring Program

PROGRAM HAS EXISTED: 5-10 years

ORGANIZATION: Residentially based

NUMBER OF TUTORS: Fewer than 10

HOURS THEY WORK PER WEEK: Under 5

TUTORS PAID: No

TUTOR SELECTION: Nominated by English faculty and appointed by Director of Student Activities

TUTORS' TRAINING: On-the-job

TUTORS' EVALUATION: Observation

PERCENTAGE OF STUDENTS SERVED: Less than 25%

OVER PAST FIVE YEARS THIS PERCENTAGE HAS: Stayed the same

PROGRAM INTENDED TO SERVE: Students in all disciplines, especially freshmen, writing students, and students of English

PROGRAM ACTUALLY SERVES: Students in all disciplines, especially freshmen

STUDENTS SEEK HELP WITH: Academic essays and research papers

MECHANICS OF TUTORING: Student may choose to discuss any paper with tutor

STUDENT ATTITUDE: Somewhat positive

Charles Leavitt reports that The College of Insurance's more traditional writing programs, such as the two semesters of required composition, are the most successful. In literature courses, some professors ask students to imitate the style of the authors being studied. Writing original poetry has also increased students' knowledge of writing techniques. While the college has offered peer tutoring for over five years, Leavitt finds that students who write for the college newspaper have improved their writing more quickly than students who use the peer tutors. He hopes to see more emphasis on newspaper work in the near future, along with more faculty supervision of the projects.

COLLEGE OF THE HOLY CROSS

Worcester, MA 01610

Full-time Students: 1312M/1182W Faculty: 174

Respondent: Patricia Bizzell, Associate Professor of English, Composition Advisor

Writing Requirement: None

Writing Center

CENTER HAS EXISTED: 2 years HOURS OPEN PER WEEK: 16

STAFF: Faculty supervisor and 15 undergraduate tutors

TUTORS' TRAINING: Academic training course

TUTORS' EVALUATION: Observation and student questionnaires

TUTORS PAID: Some are

PROGRAM DESIGNED TO SERVE: Students in all disciplines

PROGRAM ACTUALLY SERVES: Students in all disciplines, especially freshmen

STUDENTS SEEK HELP WITH: Scientific reports, academic essays, research papers, and resumes

PERCENTAGE OF STUDENTS SERVED: About 25%

OVER PAST FIVE YEARS THIS PERCENTAGE HAS: Increased

STUDENTS USE CENTER: Throughout the semester on an appointment or walk-in basis

STUDENTS REQUIRED TO USE CENTER: Those referred by faculty

MATERIALS AVAILABLE: Handbooks, exercises, professional books, and files on each client

STUDENT ATTITUDE: Very positive

Writing-Across-the-Curriculum Program

PROGRAM HAS EXISTED: 3 years

INSTRUCTORS INVOLVED: Faculty in all disciplines

INSTRUCTORS' SELECTION: Voluntary

INSTRUCTORS' TRAINING: Seminars

PERCENTAGE OF FACULTY INVOLVED: 35%

IN PAST FIVE YEARS THIS PERCENTAGE HAS: Increased

STUDENTS INVOLVED IN PROGRAM: Students in all disciplines

PERCENTAGE OF STUDENTS INVOLVED: 20%

IN PAST FIVE YEARS THIS PERCENTAGE HAS: Increased

PARTICIPANTS' ATTITUDE: Mostly positive

Although relatively new, Holy Cross College's writing program is developing rapidly. Since 1978, Holy Cross has instituted a writing-across-the-curriculum project, a separate workshop for fiction and poetry writers, and a writing center--the Composition Tutorial Workshop. The center's undergraduate tutors participate in an intensive course on composition theory and pedagogy in which they read texts such as Tate and Corbett's Writing Teacher's Sourcebook, design a writing test, and tutor in the Workshop two hours a week. The faculty seminars run by Patricia Bizzell have also worked quite well and have featured outside speakers. Some participants in the faculty seminars have offered writing-intensive courses outside of the English Department. In the future Holy Cross may offer more upper-level writing electives.

COLLEGE OF WILLIAM AND MARY

Williamsburg, VA 23185

Full-time Students: 2122M/2429W   Faculty: 430

Respondent: David Rosenwasser, Director of Writing

Writing Requirement: Required freshman English course; exemption by examination

Writing Center

CENTER HAS EXISTED: Under 2 years   HOURS OPEN PER WEEK: Under 10

STAFF: 5-20 faculty and undergraduate tutors

TUTORS' TRAINING: On-the-job

TUTORS' EVALUATION: Observation

TUTORS PAID: Yes

PROGRAM DESIGNED TO SERVE: Students in all disciplines

PROGRAM ACTUALLY SERVES: Freshmen

STUDENTS SEEK HELP WITH: Academic essays and research papers

PERCENTAGE OF STUDENTS SERVED: Less than 25%

OVER PAST FIVE YEARS THIS PERCENTAGE HAS: Increased

STUDENTS USE CENTER: Throughout the semester on a regular basis

STUDENTS REQUIRED TO USE CENTER: None

MATERIALS AVAILABLE: Handbooks and exercises

STUDENT ATTITUDE: Somewhat positive

Writing-Across-the-Curriculum Program

PROGRAM HAS EXISTED: Under 2 years

INSTRUCTORS INVOLVED: English faculty

INSTRUCTORS' SELECTION: Voluntary

INSTRUCTORS' TRAINING: None

PERCENTAGE OF FACULTY INVOLVED: Less than 25%

IN PAST FIVE YEARS THIS PERCENTAGE HAS: Stayed the same

STUDENTS INVOLVED IN PROGRAM: Students in all disciplines

PARTICIPANTS' ATTITUDE: Neutral to somewhat negative

The College of William and Mary established a new writing requirement in the fall of 1983. According to David Rosenwasser, this new program is "moving rapidly towards greater standardization," yet is moving "across the curriculum at a snail's pace."

COLORADO STATE UNIVERSITY

Fort Collins, CO 80523

Full-time Students: 7110M/7308W Faculty: 1150

Respondent: Jean Wyrick, Director of Composition, English Department

Writing Requirement: Required freshman English course; 6% of all students place out, while 20% place into a pass/fail basic writing course

Writing Center

CENTER HAS EXISTED: 5 years HOURS OPEN PER WEEK: 20

STAFF. Fewer than 5 graduate teaching assistants

TUTORS' TRAINING: On-the-job and academic training course

TUTORS' EVALUATION: Observation

TUTORS PAID: Yes

PROGRAM DESIGNED TO SERVE: Students in all disciplines

PROGRAM ACTUALLY SERVES: Students in all classes and disciplines, especially writing students

STUDENTS SEEK HELP WITH: Academic essays and research papers

PERCENTAGE OF STUDENTS SERVED: Less than 25%

OVER PAST FIVE YEARS THIS PERCENTAGE HAS: Increased

STUDENTS USE CENTER: Throughout the semester on a walk-in or referral basis

STUDENTS REQUIRED TO USE CENTER: Problem writers

MATERIALS AVAILABLE: Handbooks, exercises, and professional books

STUDENT ATTITUDE: Very positive

Over the past ten years, Colorado State University has developed a thorough training program for graduate teaching assistants, who teach all of the basic classes and half of the regular freshman composition courses. These teaching assistants also staff the writing center, which is a popular facility with CSU students. In addition to seeking help from the center's staff, the students can also work with Bell Laboratories' computer-assisted writing package, "The Writer's Workbench," which was specially adapted for CSU. With permission recently granted to add two full-time composition lecturers to the staff, Jean Wyrick writes, "We're feeling more optimistic than in the past several years and hope to expand the services at the Writing Center, to continue improving our fine teacher training program, and to create new computer-assisted instruction programs for our students, especially our basic writers."

COLUMBIA UNIVERSITY

New York, NY 10025

Full-time Students: 2900M/2500W Faculty: 420

Respondent: Linda M. Lemiesz, Assistant Director of College Composition

Writing Requirement: Required freshman English course

Writing Center

CENTER HAS EXISTED: 10 years HOURS OPEN PER WEEK: Over 40

STAFF: 12-15 writing tutors

TUTORS' TRAINING: On-the-job and non-academic course

TUTORS' EVALUATION: Observation

TUTORS PAID: Yes

PROGRAM DESIGNED TO SERVE: Students in all disciplines

PROGRAM ACTUALLY SERVES: Students in all disciplines

STUDENTS SEEK HELP WITH: Academic essays

PERCENTAGE OF STUDENTS SERVED: Unknown

OVER PAST FIVE YEARS THIS PERCENTAGE HAS: Increased

STUDENTS USE CENTER: Repeatedly and on an appointment basis

STUDENTS REQUIRED TO USE CENTER: Problem writers

MATERIALS AVAILABLE: Handbooks, exercises, and professional books

STUDENT ATTITUDE: Positive

Ten years ago, most freshmen were required to take one semester of composition at Columbia College, and some freshmen were exempted from even this requirement on the basis of SAT scores. Since then, the writing requirement has tightened considerably, increasing the number of freshmen required to take two semesters of composition and decreasing the number exempted from composition to less than five a year. The composition faculty have also expanded the size of the Advanced Composition course. Columbia's Learning Center, staffed by over twenty writing tutors, serves a variety of students from all disciplines. In the future, Columbia anticipates using computers to a greater extent in composition courses.

DAKOTA WESLEYAN UNIVERSITY

Mitchell, SD 57301

Full-time Students: 206M/298W Faculty: 37

Respondent: Gloria Smith, English Instructor

Writing Requirement: Freshman English or other English course

Peer Tutoring Program

PROGRAM HAS EXISTED: 2-5 years

ORGANIZATION: Curriculum-based

NUMBER OF TUTORS: 20-50

HOURS THEY WORK PER WEEK: 5-10

TUTORS PAID: Yes

TUTOR SELECTION: Nominated by themselves or by the English faculty and appointed by the director

TUTORS' TRAINING: On-the-job

TUTORS' EVALUATION: Student questionnaire and by other tutors

PERCENTAGE OF STUDENTS SERVED: 25-50%

OVER PAST FIVE YEARS THIS PERCENTAGE HAS: Stayed the same

PROGRAM INTENDED TO SERVE: Students in all disciplines

PROGRAM ACTUALLY SERVES: Students in all disciplines

STUDENTS SEEK HELP WITH: Scientific reports, academic essays, and research papers

MECHANICS OF TUTORING: Tutor and student are required to discuss papers; student may choose to have tutor comment on any paper

STUDENT ATTITUDE: Very positive

During the past decade Dakota Wesleyan University has increasingly emphasized writing by requiring all four-year B.A. students to take composition courses. A few years ago, the university established a peer tutoring program that now serves more than a quarter of the students. The tutors, chosen for their competence in writing, help students in all disciplines with scientific reports, academic essays, and research papers. Dakota's remedial composition and creative writing courses have also been successful additions to the curriculum.

DARTMOUTH COLLEGE

Hanover, NH 03755

Full-time Students: 4000M/1400W   Faculty: 350

Respondent: Louis Renza, Vice Chairperson, Department of English

Writing Requirement: Required freshman English course and freshman seminar

Writing Center

CENTER HAS EXISTED: 9 years   HOURS OPEN PER WEEK: 40

STAFF: 8 undergraduate tutors

TUTORS' TRAINING: One week intensive workshop before fall term and on-the-job training

TUTORS' EVALUATION: By other tutors and by head tutor

TUTORS PAID: Yes

PROGRAM DESIGNED TO SERVE: Students in all disciplines

PROGRAM ACTUALLY SERVES: Students in all disciplines

STUDENTS SEEK HELP WITH: All types of writing

PERCENTAGE OF STUDENTS SERVED: Less than 25%

OVER PAST FIVE YEARS THIS PERCENTAGE HAS: Increased

STUDENTS USE CENTER: Repeatedly throughout the semester on a walk-in or appointment basis

STUDENTS REQUIRED TO USE CENTER: None; some strongly encouraged by professors

MATERIALS AVAILABLE: Handbooks and exercises

STUDENT ATTITUDE: Very positive

Peer Tutoring Program

PROGRAM HAS EXISTED: 7 years

ORGANIZATION: Curriculum-based

NUMBER OF TUTORS: 8, one assigned to each section of Introductory English

HOURS THEY WORK PER WEEK: 40

TUTORS PAID: Yes

TUTOR SELECTION: Recruited and selected by program director and instructors of Introductory English

TUTORS' TRAINING: One-week training program before term starts with in-service training continuing during the term

TUTORS' EVALUATION: Conferences, observation, and student evaluations

PERCENTAGE OF STUDENTS SERVED: 60-65 freshmen per year

OVER PAST FIVE YEARS THIS PERCENTAGE HAS: Stayed the same

PROGRAM INTENDED TO SERVE: English students

PROGRAM ACTUALLY SERVES: English students

STUDENTS SEEK HELP WITH: Academic essays and research papers

MECHANICS OF TUTORING: Tutor and student are required to discuss papers.

STUDENT ATTITUDE: Positive

Dartmouth College's writing program consists of a two-part freshman writing requirement and two peer tutoring programs. The requirement includes one course in Literature and Composition and a second course in a Freshman Seminar (an introductory course across the disciplines which focuses on writing). The peer tutoring programs are the Intensive Academic Support (IAS) Program for underprepared freshmen and the Composition Center. The IAS program includes two English courses designed to develop a student's capacity for clear thinking and good writing across the three academic divisions. Peer tutoring is a major component of this program. Other students, from all classes and disciplines, who need help with writing use the Composition Center, which is staffed by undergraduate tutors.

THE DEFIANCE COLLEGE

Defiance, OH 43512

Full-time Students: 303M/324W Faculty: 52

Respondent: Darnell H. Clevenger, Chairperson, Languages and Literature

Writing Requirement: Two required freshman English courses

Writing Center

CENTER HAS EXISTED: 8-10 years HOURS OPEN PER WEEK: 35-40

STAFF: Fewer than 5 faculty and undergraduate tutors

TUTORS' TRAINING: On-the-job and academic training course

TUTORS' EVALUATION: Observation and conferences

TUTORS PAID: Yes

PROGRAM DESIGNED TO SERVE: Students in all disciplines, especially writing students

PROGRAM ACTUALLY SERVES: Mostly underclassmen, some writing students, and a few students from other disciplines

STUDENTS SEEK HELP WITH: Academic essays and research papers

PERCENTAGE OF STUDENTS SERVED: 25-50%

OVER PAST FIVE YEARS THIS PERCENTAGE HAS: Increased

STUDENTS USE CENTER: Throughout the semester on a walk-in, appointment, or regular basis

STUDENTS REQUIRED TO USE CENTER: Problem writers

MATERIALS AVAILABLE: Handbooks and writing exercises

STUDENT ATTITUDE: Somewhat positive

Peer Tutoring Program

PROGRAM HAS EXISTED: 10-12 years

ORGANIZATION: Curriculum-based

NUMBER OF TUTORS: 4-6 (varies with demand from year to year)

HOURS THEY WORK PER WEEK: 5-10

TUTORS PAID: Yes

TUTOR SELECTION: Appointed by director upon faculty recommendation

TUTORS' TRAINING: On-the-job

TUTORS' EVALUATION: Observation and conferences

PERCENTAGE OF STUDENTS SERVED: Less than 25%

OVER PAST FIVE YEARS THIS PERCENTAGE HAS: Stayed the same

PROGRAM INTENDED TO SERVE: Students in all disciplines

PROGRAM ACTUALLY SERVES: Students in all disciplines

STUDENTS SEEK HELP WITH: Academic essays, research papers, and content area tutoring

MECHANICS OF TUTORING: Students may volunteer or be required to discuss paper with tutor

STUDENT ATTITUDE: Basically positive

Over the past ten years the Defiance College has steadily increased its emphasis on writing. Within the Department of Languages and Literature, successful courses in journalism, creative writing, and business writing have recently been supplemented by courses in advanced and remedial expository writing, a two-semester composition requirement, and an extensive developmental and remedial program. Outside the department, business majors are now required to take business writing, and all students may seek help from the writing center or the peer tutors, both of which are located in the Skills Center. The writing center's small staff serves over 25% of all students, including many students in the remedial program. The Skills Center, which provides tutoring in many subjects, has focused increasingly on writing in recent years. The Languages and Literature Department has no definite plans for change in the next few years.

DE PAUL UNIVERSITY

Chicago, IL 60614

Full-time Students: 2599M/2567W Faculty: 380

Respondents: Kristine Garrigan, Assistant Professor of English and Communications, Coordinator of Common Studies Writing Component; Nancy Freehafer, Director of Writing Program

Writing Requirement: Required freshman English course

Writing Center and Peer Tutoring Program

CENTER HAS EXISTED: 5–10 years HOURS OPEN PER WEEK: 20–40

STAFF: 1–2 faculty, 2–4 graduate tutors, 17–34 undergraduate tutors

TUTORS' TRAINING: On-the-job and academic course

TUTORS' EVALUATION: Observation, conferences, student questionnaire, by other tutors, and a written self-evaluation in the training course

TUTORS PAID: Yes

PROGRAM DESIGNED TO SERVE: Students in all disciplines

PROGRAM ACTUALLY SERVES: Students in all disciplines, especially humanities students, English students, writing students, and freshmen

STUDENTS SEEK HELP WITH: Academic essays, research papers, scientific reports, some creative writing, and resumes or business writing

PERCENTAGE OF STUDENTS SERVED: Less than 25%

OVER PAST FIVE YEARS THIS PERCENTAGE HAS: Increased

STUDENTS USE CENTER: Throughout the semester on a walk-in, appointment, or regular basis, or by phone

STUDENTS REQUIRED TO USE CENTER: Problem writers, freshmen in remedial writing courses

MATERIALS AVAILABLE: Handbooks, exercises, and professional books

STUDENT ATTITUDE: Very positive

Writing-Across-the-Curriculum Program

PROGRAM HAS EXISTED: 4 years

INSTRUCTORS INVOLVED: English and history faculty

INSTRUCTORS' SELECTION: Voluntary and by appointment

INSTRUCTORS' TRAINING: Seminars and regular informal meetings

PERCENTAGE OF FACULTY INVOLVED: 50% of English faculty, 100% of history faculty

IN PAST FIVE YEARS THIS PERCENTAGE HAS: Increased

STUDENTS INVOLVED IN PROGRAM: Students in all disciplines

PERCENTAGE OF STUDENTS INVOLVED: 100%

IN PAST FIVE YEARS THIS PERCENTAGE HAS: Stayed the same

PARTICIPANTS' ATTITUDE: Fairly positive

At De Paul University, students are placed into the interdisciplinary writing program, Common Studies, on the basis of acceptable writing samples and ACT scores or upon satisfactory completion of appropriate developmental writing courses. A two-quarter sequence, the program consists of an eight-hour world civilizations course taught in tandem with a four-hour composition course that incorporates history materials. (Each component is administered and taught by faculty within that department.) During their first quarter in the program, students produce short essays based on subjects covered in their history lectures; during the second quarter, they write research papers on individually chosen historical topics. Common Studies is designed to provide freshmen with a sense of their own place in time while they develop the writing and research capabilities necessary in their future Liberal Studies courses. The program's growing strengths are summed up in this student evaluation: "I've achieved a sense of direction, my history course offering a rich background of knowledge and my writing course coordinating the reaction to it--both were one good influence."

DRAKE UNIVERSITY

Des Moines, IA 50311

Full-time Students: 3182M/3310W Faculty: 340

Respondent: David Foster, Director of Freshman English

Writing Requirement: Required freshman English course

Writing Center

CENTER HAS EXISTED: 9 years HOURS OPEN PER WEEK: 30

STAFF: 5-8 graduate and undergraduate tutors

TUTORS' TRAINING: On-the-job and academic training course

TUTORS' EVALUATION: Observation, conferences, and student questionnaires

TUTORS PAID: Only graduate students

PROGRAM DESIGNED TO SERVE: Students in all disciplines

PROGRAM ACTUALLY SERVES: Students in all disciplines

STUDENTS SEEK HELP WITH: Academic essays and research papers

PERCENTAGE OF STUDENTS SERVED: Less than 25%

OVER PAST FIVE YEARS THIS PERCENTAGE HAS: Increased

STUDENTS USE CENTER: Throughout the semester on a walk-in, appointment, or regular basis

STUDENTS REQUIRED TO USE CENTER: Problem writers

MATERIALS AVAILABLE: Handbooks and writing exercises

STUDENT ATTITUDE: Very positive

The core of Drake University's fairly traditional writing program is the required freshman English course and the Writing Workshop, both of which have worked well in the past. The writing workshop is staffed primarily by graduate tutors together with a small number of peer tutors selected by the English Department. Although only problem writers are required to use the workshop, a gradually increasing number of students from all disciplines have been working with tutors on a voluntary basis over the past three years. In addition to freshman English, Drake also offers courses in expository writing, communications, and creative writing.

DREW UNIVERSITY

Madison, NJ 07298

Full-time Students: 615M/851W Faculty: 100

Respondent: Joan Weimer, English Department Chairperson

Writing Requirement: Required freshman English course; exemption based on Achievement Test score or writing sample

Writing Center and Peer Tutoring Program

CENTER HAS EXISTED: Less than 2 years HOURS OPEN PER WEEK: 20-40

STAFF: Fewer than 5 graduate and undergraduate tutors

TUTOR SELECTION: Nominated by English faculty or by themselves

TUTORS' TRAINING: On-the-job

TUTORS' EVALUATION: Observation, conferences, and student questionnaire

TUTORS PAID: Yes, or they work for Independent Study Credit

PROGRAM DESIGNED TO SERVE: Students in all disciplines

PROGRAM ACTUALLY SERVES: Students in all disciplines, including graduate students

STUDENTS SEEK HELP WITH: Academic essays, research papers, creative writing, and some graduate school application essays

PERCENTAGE OF STUDENTS SERVED: Less than 25%

STUDENTS USE CENTER: Throughout the semester on a walk-in, appointment, or regular basis

STUDENTS REQUIRED TO USE CENTER: None

MATERIALS AVAILABLE: Handbooks, exercises, and professional books

STUDENT ATTITUDE: Very positive

In 1983, Drew University established a small writing center to supplement its writing minor and successful courses in creative writing and intermediate and advanced expository writing. The writing center has fewer than five peer and graduate tutors to help students in all disciplines with academic essays, research papers, some creative writing, and occasional application essays. The tutors are trained on-the-job and help students during appointments or walk-in sessions.

DREXEL UNIVERSITY

Philadelphia, PA 19104

Full-time Students: 5064M/2156W Faculty: 303

Respondent: Judith Scheffler, Acting Director, Developmental Writing Program, Humanities-Communications Department

Writing Requirement: Required freshman English courses

Writing Center

CENTER HAS EXISTED: 5 years HOURS OPEN PER WEEK: By appointment

STAFF: Faculty

PROGRAM DESIGNED TO SERVE: Students in all disciplines

PROGRAM ACTUALLY SERVES: Students in all disciplines

STUDENTS SEEK HELP WITH: All required course writing

PERCENTAGE OF STUDENTS SERVED: Less than 25%

OVER PAST FIVE YEARS THIS PERCENTAGE HAS: Increased

STUDENTS USE CENTER: Throughout the semester on a walk-in or appointment basis

STUDENTS REQUIRED TO USE CENTER: Those recommended by faculty

MATERIALS AVAILABLE: Handbooks, exercises, and videotapes

STUDENT ATTITUDE: Unknown

Drexel University has instituted a developmental writing program for its students. The university has also introduced an honors freshman English program for advanced students, and added a freshman humanities sequence of three courses in composition, reading, research, and literature, with a rigorous writing component. The writing center, which has existed for five years, is staffed by faculty who consult with students during office hours or by appointment. In the next few years, Drexel plans to introduce computer-assisted instruction in composition, since all freshman at the university are required to own micro-computers.

DUKE UNIVERSITY

Durham, NC 27706

Full-time Students: 3093M/2670W Faculty: 1442

Respondent: Ronald R. Butters, Supervisor, Freshman Instruction in English

Writing Requirement: One-semester required freshman English course

Writing Center

CENTER HAS EXISTED: 5-10 years HOURS OPEN PER WEEK: 20-40

STAFF: Fewer than 5 graduate tutors

TUTORS' TRAINING: None

TUTORS' EVALUATION: Self-evaluation

TUTORS PAID: Yes

PROGRAM DESIGNED TO SERVE: Students in all disciplines

PROGRAM ACTUALLY SERVES: Students in all disciplines

STUDENTS SEEK HELP WITH: Scientific reports, academic essays, research papers, and resumes or business writing

PERCENTAGE OF STUDENTS SERVED: Less than 25%

OVER PAST FIVE YEARS THIS PERCENTAGE HAS: Stayed the same

STUDENTS USE CENTER: End of the semester on an appointment or walk-in basis

STUDENTS REQUIRED TO USE CENTER: None

MATERIALS AVAILABLE: Handbooks

STUDENT ATTITUDE: Somewhat positive

Duke University's writing program has remained relatively stable over the past few years and will probably remain stable in the future. The Duke faculty have generally been satisfied with their traditional freshman composition sequence, which includes frequent tutorials. The other introductory courses--which include a wide range of literature, linguistics, and communications courses--have been equally successful and will probably not change dramatically. A similar situation exists with the writing center, which is used only sporadically and does not appear to be growing, although it does serve a wide variety of graduates and undergraduates. The major changes in Duke's writing program have been the discarding of large lectures in freshman composition about ten years ago and an increased emphasis on research skills over the past three years. There is some pressure from the Duke administration to bring computers into the composition program and to adopt a more cross-curricular approach to writing, but most members of the English Department feel that neither change is appropriate for the institution.

EASTERN ILLINOIS UNIVERSITY

Charleston, IL 61920

Full-time Students: 3910M/4869W Faculty: 481

Respondent: James Quivey, English Department Chairperson

Writing Requirement: 2 required freshman English courses and a junior-level writing competency examination

Writing Center

CENTER HAS EXISTED: 3 years in present form, over 10 years as "tutoring room"

HOURS OPEN PER WEEK: 25

STAFF: 1 faculty and 6 graduate tutors

TUTORS' TRAINING: On the-job and non-credit course

TUTORS' EVALUATION: Observation and conferences

TUTORS PAID: Yes

PROGRAM DESIGNED TO SERVE: Students in all disciplines

PROGRAM ACTUALLY SERVES: Students in all disciplines, primarily first-year students

STUDENTS SEEK HELP WITH: Scientific reports, academic essays, research papers, and resumes or business writing

PERCENTAGE OF STUDENTS SERVED: 10%

OVER PAST FIVE YEARS THIS PERCENTAGE HAS: Increased

STUDENTS USE CENTER: Throughout the semester on an appointment or walk-in basis

STUDENTS REQUIRED TO USE CENTER: None

MATERIALS AVAILABLE: Handbooks, rhetorics, style manuals, exercises, professional books, cassettes, and a TRS-80 computer

STUDENT ATTITUDE: Very positive

Writing-Across-the-Curriculum Program

PROGRAM HAS EXISTED: Under 2 years

INSTRUCTORS INVOLVED: Faculty in all disciplines

INSTRUCTORS' SELECTION: Voluntary

INSTRUCTORS' TRAINING: Seminars

PERCENTAGE OF FACULTY INVOLVED: 8-9%

STUDENTS INVOLVED IN PROGRAM: Students in all disciplines

PARTICIPANTS' ATTITUDE: Very positive

Eastern Illinois University's writing programs are growing rapidly. In the past five years, the university's writing center has expanded from a small "tutoring room" to a large center open more than twenty hours a week. Eastern Illinois has also recently begun a writing-across-the-curriculum program in which English faculty hold workshops for faculty in other departments. Graders for the Writing Competency Examination are also selected university-wide and trained by English staff in holistic grading. In the past several years, the university has seen its creative writing program flourish and the emphasis on the process of writing increase. James Quivey suspects that in the next few years, Eastern Illinois will be "paying less attention to process and more attention to reading in an effort to put intellectual ballast back into freshman writing."

EASTERN MONTANA COLLEGE

Billings, MT 59101

Full-time Students: 980M/1585W Faculty: 144

Respondent: Gary Acton, Chairperson, English Department

Writing Requirement: Required freshman English course

Writing Center

CENTER HAS EXISTED: Under 2 years HOURS OPEN PER WEEK: 20-40

STAFF: 5-20 faculty, graduate, and undergraduate tutors

TUTORS' TRAINING: On-the-job and non-academic training course

TUTORS' EVALUATION: Observation and conferences

TUTORS PAID: Only financial aid students

PROGRAM DESIGNED TO SERVE: Students from all disciplines, especially writing and English students, freshmen, and underclassmen

PROGRAM ACTUALLY SERVES: Students from all disciplines, especially English students and freshmen

STUDENTS SEEK HELP WITH: Academic essays and research papers

PERCENTAGE OF STUDENTS SERVED: 25-50%

OVER PAST FIVE YEARS THIS PERCENTAGE HAS: Stayed the same

STUDENTS USE CENTER: Throughout the semester on a walk-in or appointment basis

STUDENTS REQUIRED TO USE CENTER: None

MATERIALS AVAILABLE: Handbooks, exercises, and professional books

STUDENT ATTITUDE: Very positive

The writing program at Eastern Montana College has not changed substantially over the last several years, although new additions are being considered, including a peer tutoring program and an increased emphasis on language, linguistics, and intermediate writing and technical writing skills. The current writing center at Eastern Montana has existed for less than two years; an older center was forced to close due to budget cuts.

EMMANUEL COLLEGE

Boston, MA 02115

Full-time Students: 991W Faculty: 88

Respondent: Sister Ann Daly, SND, Director Freshman Writing Program/Writing Center

Writing Requirement: Required freshman English course and other required English course

Writing Center

CENTER HAS EXISTED: 5-10 years HOURS OPEN PER WEEK: 10-20

STAFF: Fewer than 5 faculty

PROGRAM DESIGNED TO SERVE: Students in all disciplines

PROGRAM ACTUALLY SERVES: Students in all disciplines

STUDENTS SEEK HELP WITH: Academic essays, research papers, dissertations, and theses

PERCENTAGE OF STUDENTS SERVED: 25%-50%

OVER PAST FIVE YEARS THIS PERCENTAGE HAS: Increased

STUDENTS USE CENTER: Throughout the semester, especially during mid-semester, on a walk-in, appointment, or regular basis

STUDENTS REQUIRED TO USE CENTER: Problem writers and students accepted provisionally by the college

MATERIALS AVAILABLE: Handbooks, exercises, and professional books

STUDENT ATTITUDE: Unknown

While Emmanuel College's traditional writing programs have worked well, the college is currently exploring a more innovative interdisciplinary writing program that offers instruction in logic, computer experience, thematic writing, and modes of discourse. This new program has recently replaced some of the more traditional courses, and will need revision over the next few years. Emmanuel is also planning a writing-across-the-curriculum program that will involve faculty volunteers trained through seminars.

EMORY UNIVERSITY

Atlanta, GA 30322

Full-time Students: 1562M/1487W   Faculty: 300

Respondent: Peter W. Dowell, Director of Undergraduate Studies, English Department

Writing Requirement: Required freshman English course and writing requirement in sophomore, junior, and senior years

Writing Center

CENTER HAS EXISTED: 5-10 years   HOURS OPEN PER WEEK: 10-20

STAFF: Fewer than 5 graduate tutors

TUTORS' TRAINING: On-the-job

TUTORS' EVALUATION: Observation and conferences

TUTORS PAID: Yes

PROGRAM DESIGNED TO SERVE: Students in all disciplines

PROGRAM ACTUALLY SERVES: Students in all disciplines; 90% freshmen

STUDENTS SEEK HELP WITH: Academic essays and research papers

PERCENTAGE OF STUDENTS SERVED: Less than 25%

OVER PAST FIVE YEARS THIS PERCENTAGE HAS: Stayed the same

STUDENTS USE CENTER: At the end of the semester and mid-semester on an appointment or regular basis

STUDENTS REQUIRED TO USE CENTER: Those referred by course instructor

MATERIALS AVAILABLE: Handbooks and exercises

STUDENT ATTITUDE: Positive

Emory University's unusual graduation requirement demands that students satisfy a writing requirement in sophomore, junior, and senior years. This writing requirement can be fulfilled by writing papers for any course in which the instructor is willing to grade the work and certify it as a satisfactory writing performance. Although this program ensures that students write throughout their college careers, individual instructor's expectations vary widely and quality control is difficult. More successful programs include the required freshman courses, and elective courses in creative writing, advanced writing workshop, journalism, and modes of practical writing.

EMPORIA STATE UNIVERSITY

Emporia, KS 66801

Full-time Students: 1727M/2085W Faculty: 245

Respondent: Faye Vowell, Director of the Writing Lab

Writing Requirement: 2 required freshman English courses and Junior Writing Competency Examination

Writing Center

CENTER HAS EXISTED: Over 10 years HOURS OPEN PER WEEK: 23

STAFF: 4 graduate and 6 undergraduate tutors and one faculty assistant

TUTORS' TRAINING: On-the-job, academic training course, and non-academic training course

TUTORS' EVALUATION: Observation, conferences, student questionnaires, and by other tutors

TUTORS PAID: Yes

PROGRAM DESIGNED TO SERVE: Students in all disciplines

PROGRAM ACTUALLY SERVES: Students in all disciplines; 49% freshmen

STUDENTS SEEK HELP WITH: Scientific reports, academic essays, research papers, and resumes or business writing

PERCENTAGE OF STUDENTS SERVED: Less than 25%

OVER PAST FIVE YEARS THIS PERCENTAGE HAS: Increased

STUDENTS USE CENTER: Throughout the semester on a walk-in, appointment, or regular basis, or in course offered by the center

STUDENTS REQUIRED TO USE CENTER: Those referred by instructors

MATERIALS AVAILABLE: Handbooks, writing exercises, professional books, and educational magazines

STUDENT ATTITUDE: Very positive

Peer Tutoring Program

PROGRAM HAS EXISTED: 5-10 years

ORGANIZATION: Writing center-based

NUMBER OF TUTORS: 6

HOURS THEY WORK PER WEEK: 10

TUTORS PAID: Yes

TUTOR SELECTION: Appointed by the director

TUTORS' TRAINING: On-the-job and academic training course

TUTORS' EVALUATION: Observation, conferences, student questionnaires, and by other tutors

PERCENTAGE OF STUDENTS SERVED: Less than 25%

OVER PAST FIVE YEARS THIS PERCENTAGE HAS: Increased

PROGRAM INTENDED TO SERVE: Students in all disciplines

PROGRAM ACTUALLY SERVES: Students in all disciplines

STUDENTS SEEK HELP WITH: Scientific reports, academic essays, research papers, and resumes or business writing

MECHANICS OF TUTORING: Tutor and student are required to discuss papers

STUDENT ATTITUDE: Very positive

Innovative writing programs are well-established at Emporia State University, whose writing center was established over ten years ago. The center's staff of highly trained graduate and peer tutors, assisted by English faculty, helps students individually and in special classes. Although the center serves many freshmen, students from all classes and disciplines seek help with different types of writing. Emporia State also offers several writing courses taught by faculty and graduate students, and requires all students to take freshman English and pass a junior year writing competency test.

EUREKA COLLEGE

Eureka, IL 61530

Full-time Students: 250M/240W Faculty: 38

Respondent: Mary Tookey, Coordinator of Freshman Composition

Writing Requirement: Two required freshman English courses; exemption by examination

Writing Center and Peer Tutoring Program

CENTER HAS EXISTED: 2-5 years HOURS OPEN PER WEEK: 10-20

STAFF: 10-20 undergraduate tutors and a faculty director

TUTOR SELECTION: Nominated by English faculty and appointed by the director

TUTORS' TRAINING: On the job and non academic training course

TUTORS' EVALUATION: Student questionnaires

TUTORS PAID: Yes

HOURS THEY WORK PER WEEK: Under 5

PROGRAM DESIGNED TO SERVE: Students in all disciplines

PROGRAM ACTUALLY SERVES: Writing students, many math students, and some students from other disciplines

STUDENTS SEEK HELP WITH: Scientific reports, academic essays, and research papers

PERCENTAGE OF STUDENTS SERVED: Less than 25%

OVER PAST FIVE YEARS THIS PERCENTAGE HAS: Increased

STUDENTS USE CENTER: Throughout the semester on an appointment or regular basis

STUDENTS REQUIRED TO USE CENTER: None

MATERIALS AVAILABLE: Handbooks, audio-visual and computer materials, writing exercises, and professional books

STUDENT ATTITUDE: Somewhat positive

In addition to its standard writing courses and majors in English and journalism, Eureka College offers its students writing instruction from peer tutors in the Learning Center. Under the supervision of a faculty director, the trained peer tutors help students from all disciplines with any type of writing problem or question. Although no students are required to use the Learning Center, all students are required to pass or place out of the two required freshman English courses. Students who show weaknesses in freshman English or continue to have writing problems after freshman year are strongly urged to seek help from the peer tutors. Apart from the establishment of the Learning Center, Eureka has made no major changes in its writing program in the last ten years and has no plans for changes in the near future.

THE EVERGREEN STATE COLLEGE

Olympia, WA 98505

Full-time Students: 1093M/1190W Faculty: 127

Respondent: Barbara Smith, Academic Dean

Writing Requirement: No writing requirement, but a freshman cross-curricular requirement

Writing Center and Peer Tutoring Program

CENTER HAS EXISTED: 10 years HOURS OPEN PER WEEK: Over 40

STAFF: 2 staff instructors and 10-12 undergraduate tutors

TUTOR SELECTION: Recommended by faculty, self-nominated if intern, then hired by director

TUTORS' TRAINING: On-the-job and pre-quarter and weekly training sessions

TUTORS' EVALUATION: Observation and conferences

TUTORS PAID: Most are; some intern for academic credit

HOURS THEY WORK PER WEEK: 10-20

PROGRAM DESIGNED TO SERVE: Students in all disciplines

PROGRAM ACTUALLY SERVES: Students in all disciplines

STUDENTS SEEK HELP WITH: Scientific reports academic essays, research papers, resumes or business writing, and reading or study skills

PERCENTAGE OF STUDENTS SERVED: Less than 25%

OVER PAST FIVE YEARS THIS PERCENTAGE HAS: Increased

STUDENTS USE CENTER: Throughout the quarter on a walk-in, appointment, or regular basis, by attending workshops, or by arranging a conference with instructor

MECHANICS OF TUTORING: Students may choose to have tutor comment on any paper; process varies since students work with both instructor and tutor

STUDENTS REQUIRED TO USE CENTER: Problem writers recommended

MATERIALS AVAILABLE: Handbooks, exercises, professional books, self-programmed texts, and some computer software

STUDENT ATTITUDE: Positive

Writing-Across-the-Curriculum Program

PROGRAM HAS EXISTED: 10 years

INSTRUCTORS INVOLVED: Faculty in all disciplines

INSTRUCTORS' SELECTION: All faculty participate

INSTRUCTORS' TRAINING: Monthly Teaching Strategy Seminars and team teaching

PERCENTAGE OF FACULTY INVOLVED: 100%

IN PAST FIVE YEARS THIS PERCENTAGE HAS: Increased

STUDENTS INVOLVED IN PROGRAM: Students in all disciplines

PERCENTAGE OF STUDENTS INVOLVED: More than 75%

IN PAST FIVE YEARS THIS PERCENTAGE HAS: Increased

PARTICIPANTS' ATTITUDE: Very positive

The Evergreen State College has no formal writing requirement for graduation, but almost all courses stress writing. Barbara Smith feels that "what works best is ongoing writing on a weekly basis throughout the student's career." If students have any writing problems or questions, instructors and peer tutors are available to help them at the Learning Resource Center. Those students needing extensive help work on a diagnostic basis, designing a study plan and meeting regularly with an instructor; some students can receive credit for work they do at the writing center. In the next few years, Evergreen hopes to develop more specialized services for ESL students and for students with skill deficiencies or learning disabilities.

FITCHBURG STATE COLLEGE

Fitchburg, MA 01420

Full-time Students: 1396M/2260W Faculty: 225

Respondent: Terry Grabar, Chairperson, English Department

Writing Requirement: Required 2-semester freshman English course

Writing Center and Peer Tutoring Program

CENTER HAS EXISTED: 5-10 years HOURS OPEN PER WEEK: 20-40

STAFF: Faculty and 5-8 undergraduate tutors

TUTOR' SELECTION: Appointed by director

TUTORS' TRAINING. On-the-job

TUTORS' EVALUATION: Observation

TUTORS PAID: Yes

HOURS THEY WORK PER WEEK: More than 20

PROGRAM DESIGNED TO SERVE: Students in all disciplines, especially writing students, freshmen, and underclassmen

PROGRAM ACTUALLY SERVES: Students in all disciplines, especially writing students, freshmen, and underclassmen

STUDENTS SEEK HELP WITH: Academic essays and research papers

PERCENTAGE OF STUDENTS SERVED: Less than 25%

OVER PAST FIVE YEARS THIS PERCENTAGE HAS: Stayed the same

STUDENTS USE CENTER: 10% once, 30% repeatedly, 50% mid-semester, 50% throughout the semester on a walk-in or regular basis

STUDENTS REQUIRED TO USE CENTER: Problem writers

MATERIALS AVAILABLE: Handbooks, exercises, and guides to report and research paper writing

STUDENT ATTITUDE: Unknown

The writing program at Fitchburg State College has recently been very active. In addition to maintaining a long-standing writing center and a peer tutoring program, the school now plans to start a writing-across-the-curriculum program. Fitchburg also recently introduced a professional writing track to the English major and added several new courses. The English Department has developed special composition courses for problem writers and introduced courses such as Advanced Expository Writing, Writing for Natural and Social Sciences, and Business and Technical Writing. In the future, the writing program will be further expanded with the addition of new upper-level writing courses throughout the curriculum.

FLORIDA INSTITUTE OF TECHNOLOGY

Melbourne, FL 32901

Full-time Students: 2369M/790W   Faculty: 209

Respondent: Jane LeMoine, Head of Humanities, Director of Individualized Learning Center **Writing Requirement:** Two required freshman English courses

Writing Center

CENTER HAS EXISTED: 2-5 years   HOURS OPEN PER WEEK: Over 40

STAFF: 5-20 faculty and undergraduate tutors

TUTORS' TRAINING: Academic training course

TUTORS' EVALUATION: Observation

TUTORS PAID: Yes

PROGRAM DESIGNED TO SERVE: Students in all disciplines

PROGRAM ACTUALLY SERVES: Students in all disciplines

STUDENTS SEEK HELP WITH: Academic essays, research papers, and resumes or business writing

PERCENTAGE OF STUDENTS SERVED: Less than 25%

OVER PAST FIVE YEARS THIS PERCENTAGE HAS: Increased

STUDENTS USE CENTER: Throughout the semester on a walk-in or appointment basis

STUDENTS REQUIRED TO USE CENTER: None

MATERIALS AVAILABLE: Handbooks and writing exercises

STUDENT ATTITUDE: Very positive

Although Florida Institute of Technology specializes in engineering and the sciences and has no English major, it does emphasize writing skills. Students in all disciplines are required to pass the freshman English sequence and they may elect to take any of twenty-one other English courses, seven of which are writing courses. The majors in business communications and technical communications also demand that students write proficiently. Students with writing problems or questions may volunteer or be required to seek help from the tutors at the Individualized Learning Center, which provides tutoring in many skills, including writing. Although there are several peer tutors in the center, students with writing problems generally meet with faculty tutors to discuss papers.

FROSTBURG STATE COLLEGE

Frostburg, MD 21532

Full-time Students: 1372M/1353W Faculty: 184

Respondent: Alan M. Rose, Head of Department of English

Writing Requirement: Required freshman English course and junior-level composition

Writing Center

CENTER HAS EXISTED: 6-10 years HOURS OPEN PER WEEK: 20-40

STAFF: 10-15 undergraduate tutors and Writing Center professionals

TUTORS' TRAINING: Non-academic course

TUTORS' EVALUATION: Observation and student questionnaire

TUTORS PAID: Yes

PROGRAM DESIGNED TO SERVE: Freshmen

PROGRAM ACTUALLY SERVES: Students in all disciplines

STUDENTS SEEK HELP WITH: Scientific reports, academic essays, research papers, and remedial writing skills

PERCENTAGE OF STUDENTS SERVED: Less than 25%

OVER PAST FIVE YEARS THIS PERCENTAGE HAS: Increased

STUDENTS USE CENTER: Throughout the semester on a walk-in, appointment, or regular basis

STUDENTS REQUIRED TO USE CENTER: Problem writers

MATERIALS AVAILABLE: Handbooks and exercises

STUDENT ATTITUDE: Somewhat positive

Over the past three years, Frostburg State College has moved from product-oriented to process-oriented writing instruction. The college has also changed the writing requirement to include a freshman and junior course in order to ensure that students continue to write throughout their academic careers. In keeping with this philosophy, Frostburg plans to add writing-intensive sections to several general studies courses over the next few years. Alan M. Rose believes good writing programs depend on well-trained, concerned faculty. By involving faculty from different disciplines in the planned writing-across-the-curriculum program, the college hopes to encourage better writing in many fields.

GENEVA COLLEGE

Beaver Falls, PA 15010

Full-time Students: 651M/511W Faculty: 58

Respondent: P. Smith, Head of English Department

Writing Requirement: Required freshman English course

Writing Center

CENTER HAS EXISTED: 5-10 years HOURS OPEN PER WEEK: Under 10

STAFF: Fewer than 5 undergraduate tutors

TUTORS' TRAINING: On-the-job and academic course

TUTORS' EVALUATION: Observation and conferences

TUTORS PAID: Yes

PROGRAM DESIGNED TO SERVE: Students in all disciplines, especially writing students, freshmen, and underclassmen

PROGRAM ACTUALLY SERVES: Students in all disciplines, especially writing students, freshmen, and underclassmen

STUDENTS SEEK HELP WITH: Academic essays or business writing

PERCENTAGE OF STUDENTS SERVED: Less than 25%

OVER PAST FIVE YEARS THIS PERCENTAGE HAS: Stayed the same

STUDENTS USE CENTER: Repeatedly, at mid-semester, on appointment or regular basis

STUDENTS REQUIRED TO USE CENTER: Problem writers

MATERIALS AVAILABLE: Handbooks, exercises, and professional books

STUDENT ATTITUDE: Somewhat positive

The writing center at Geneva College relies primarily on well-trained undergraduates. Undergraduate teaching assistants play a large part in remedial writing programs and help grade in freshman composition courses, and the writing center is staffed by peer tutors, who receive academic and on-the-job training. Some of the changes at Geneva over the past ten years include the introduction of remedial writing and language courses, the establishment of a writing major, and the administration of an entry-level English proficiency examination to determine which students will be assigned remedial work and which will be exempted from the college-wide writing requirement. In the next few years, students may have to take a junior-level proficiency examination, and those who fail may be required to take an additional composition course.

GEORGE MASON UNIVERSITY

Fairfax, VA 22030

Full-time Students: 2866M/3460W (and 7000 part time) Faculty: 462

Respondent: Chris Thaiss, Director of Composition

Writing Requirement: Required freshman and other English course; proficiency examination

Writing Center

CENTER HAS EXISTED: 5–10 years HOURS OPEN PER WEEK: Over 40

STAFF: 8–10 graduate tutors

TUTORS' TRAINING: On-the-job and academic course

TUTORS' EVALUATION: Observation, conferences, by other tutors, and by maintaining logs

TUTORS PAID: Yes

PROGRAM DESIGNED TO SERVE: Students in all disciplines

PROGRAM ACTUALLY SERVES: Students in all disciplines

STUDENTS SEEK HELP WITH: Scientific reports, creative writing, academic essays, research papers, and resumes or business writing

PERCENTAGE OF STUDENTS SERVED: Less than 25%

OVER PAST FIVE YEARS THIS PERCENTAGE HAS: Increased

STUDENTS USE CENTER: Throughout the semester, usually on an appointment basis

STUDENTS REQUIRED TO USE CENTER: Problem writers

MATERIALS AVAILABLE: Handbooks, exercises, professional books, and anthologies

STUDENT ATTITUDE: Very positive

Writing-Across-the-Curriculum Program

PROGRAM HAS EXISTED: 6 years

INSTRUCTORS INVOLVED: Faculty in all disciplines

INSTRUCTORS' SELECTION: Voluntary

INSTRUCTORS' TRAINING: Seminars and workshops

PERCENTAGE OF FACULTY INVOLVED: 20%

IN PAST FIVE YEARS THIS PERCENTAGE HAS: Greatly increased

STUDENTS INVOLVED IN PROGRAM: Students in all disciplines

PERCENTAGE OF STUDENTS INVOLVED: 25-50%

IN PAST FIVE YEARS THIS PERCENTAGE HAS: Increased

PARTICIPANTS' ATTITUDE: Very positive

George Mason University is one of the few schools with two writing centers--one that serves all students, and one that tutors potential problem writers. Chris Thaiss believes that students have sought help at these centers because of "increased faculty committment to writing" during the past several years. The faculty's committment to writing is integral to some of George Mason's other writing programs as well. Increasing numbers of faculty from all disciplines participate in George Mason's Plan for Alternative General Education (PAGE), a cross-curricular program that integrates writing with interdisciplinary humanities, social science, and natural science courses. This new program has greatly increased faculty training in the teaching of writing. In the more standard writing courses, the English faculty continue to emphasize the writing process, integrating freewriting and journal writing into composition courses while avoiding "skills" approaches such as computerized skills programs. This emphasis on process has apparently been highly successful: Thaiss anticipates that the number of majors and graduate students in writing programs will continue to increase in the next few years.

GEORGETOWN UNIVERSITY

Washington, DC 20057

Full-time Students: 2553M/2877W Faculty: 384

Respondent: James F. Slevin, Associate Professor, Chairperson, English Department

Writing Requirement: Required freshman English course

Writing Center and Peer Tutoring Program

CENTER HAS EXISTED: 5-10 years HOURS OPEN PER WEEK: 40

STAFF: 7-10 graduate and 20-25 undergraduate tutors

PEER TUTOR SELECTION: Self-nominated with faculty recommendations; appointed by director

TUTORS' TRAINING: Academic course

TUTORS' EVALUATION: Observation, conferences, and by other tutors

TUTORS PAID: In spring semester only; in the fall they receive college credit for their work

PROGRAM DESIGNED TO SERVE: Primarily English students, with some students in other disciplines

PROGRAM ACTUALLY SERVES: Primarily English students, with some students in other disciplines

STUDENTS SEEK HELP WITH: Scientific reports, academic essays, and research papers

PERCENTAGE OF STUDENTS SERVED: Less than 25%

STUDENTS USE CENTER: Repeatedly throughout the semester on an appointment or regular basis

STUDENTS REQUIRED TO USE CENTER: Some required, some "strongly advised," others come in voluntarily

MATERIALS AVAILABLE: Handbooks, exercises, professional books, and educational magazines

STUDENT ATTITUDE: Very positive

Writing-Across-the-Curriculum Program

PROGRAM HAS EXISTED: 3 years

INSTRUCTORS INVOLVED: Faculty in all disciplines and graduate students

INSTRUCTORS' SELECTION: By appointment

INSTRUCTORS' TRAINING: Seminars, team teaching, and a special training program for graduate teaching assistants

PERCENTAGE OF FACULTY INVOLVED: Less than 25%

IN PAST FIVE YEARS THIS PERCENTAGE HAS: Increased

STUDENTS INVOLVED IN PROGRAM: Students in all disciplines

PARTICIPANTS' ATTITUDE: Very positive

Georgetown University's Writing Center sponsors several writing-related activities, including a strong interaction with the D.C. community and secondary schools, dormitory-based seminars on writing-related topics, and panels on writing careers. In the same vein, the center publishes Critical Literacy, a journal for high school and college writing teachers. In conjunction with the English Department, the center sponsors a graduate Writing Center Associate's Program, which combines a Master's degree in English and American Literature with an emphasis on the teaching of writing. Graduate Associates help manage the center, and both they and the peer tutors who staff the center are trained in an academic course. The undergraduate tutors take a fall semester seminar, "Approaches to Composition," in which they discuss practices and theories of teaching writing, while the graduates' training is part of the Associates Program. Funded through 1987 by a grant from the National Endowment for the Humanities, the writing-across-the-curriculum program at Georgetown is still very new. Less than 25 percent of all faculty are currently involved, but that number is expected to exceed 40 percent during the next three years. During that time, 50 percent of the English Department faculty will participate in a special training program designed to introduce them to new ways of teaching writing. Approximately 35 percent of the faculty from other departments will participate in a similar program.

GEORGIA SOUTHERN COLLEGE

Statesboro, GA 30460

Full-time Students: 2498M/2780W Faculty: 375

Respondent: Sandra Robitsil, Assistant Professor of English

Writing Requirement: Two required freshman composition courses and Regent's Examination

Writing Center -- Learning Resource Center

CENTER HAS EXISTED: 2-5 years HOURS OPEN PER WEEK: Over 40

STAFF: 5-20 graduate and peer tutors

TUTORS' TRAINING: On-the-job and academic training course

TUTORS' EVALUATION: Observation, conferences, and by other tutors

TUTORS PAID: Yes

PROGRAM DESIGNED TO SERVE: Students in all disciplines

PROGRAM ACTUALLY SERVES: Students in all disciplines

STUDENTS SEEK HELP WITH: Academic essays, research papers, scientific reports, and resumes or business writing

PERCENTAGE OF STUDENTS SERVED: Less than 25%

OVER PAST FIVE YEARS THIS PERCENTAGE HAS: Increased

STUDENTS USE CENTER: Throughout the quarter on a walk-in basis

STUDENTS REQUIRED TO USE CENTER: Problem writers

MATERIALS AVAILABLE: Handbooks, writing exercises, computer programs, and taped lessons

STUDENT ATTITUDE: Somewhat positive

Writing Center -- Conference Program

CENTER HAS EXISTED: 2-5 years HOURS OPEN PER WEEK: 20-40

STAFF: Fewer than 5 graduate tutors

TUTORS' TRAINING: On-the-job and academic training course

TUTORS' EVALUATION: Observation, conferences, and by other tutors

TUTORS PAID: Yes

PROGRAM DESIGNED TO SERVE: English students, writing students, freshmen, and underclassmen

PROGRAM ACTUALLY SERVES: English students, writing students, freshmen, and underclassmen

STUDENTS SEEK HELP WITH: Academic essays and research papers

PERCENTAGE OF STUDENTS SERVED: Less than 25%

OVER PAST FIVE YEARS THIS PERCENTAGE HAS: Increased

STUDENTS USE CENTER: Throughout the quarter on an appointment or regular basis

STUDENTS REQUIRED TO USE CENTER: Problem writers

MATERIALS AVAILABLE: Handbooks and writing exercises

STUDENT ATTITUDE: Somewhat positive

In the last five years, Georgia Southern College has introduced two nontraditional writing programs: the Learning Resource Center and the Conference Program. The former is a campus-wide facility that began to employ peer tutors in 1973. Together with graduate tutors, the peer tutors offer assistance to all students with writing problems or questions. Though currently trained on-the-job, the peer tutors will soon be required to undergo formal training. The Conference Program consists of five graduate tutors who hold individual conferences with English students after every essay the students write. Both of these programs have been fairly successful, but Georgia Southern's English Department continues to look for new ideas by reviewing programs from other schools.

GEORGIA STATE UNIVERSITY

Atlanta, GA 30303

Full-time Students: 9387M/11,948W Faculty: 926

Respondents: A. Leslie Harris, Director, Lower Division Studies; Dabney Hart, Director, Writing Center, English Department

Writing Requirement: Required freshman English course, other required English course, and state-wide Regents' Examination

Writing Center

CENTER HAS EXISTED: 5 years HOURS OPEN PER WEEK: 40

STAFF: 35 faculty and 8-10 graduate tutors

TUTORS' TRAINING: On-the job

TUTORS' EVALUATION: Observation and conferences

TUTORS PAID: Yes

PROGRAM DESIGNED TO SERVE: Students in all disciplines

PROGRAM ACTUALLY SERVES: 75% writing students, 60% freshmen, 85% underclassmen, and 5% students in all disciplines

STUDENTS SEEK HELP WITH: 90% academic essays, 8% research papers, 1% creative writing, and 1% resumes or business writing

PERCENTAGE OF STUDENTS SERVED: Less than 25%

OVER PAST FIVE YEARS THIS PERCENTAGE HAS: Stayed the same

STUDENTS USE CENTER: Throughout semester on walk-in or appointment basis

STUDENTS REQUIRED TO USE CENTER: None

MATERIALS AVAILABLE: Handbooks, exercises, professional books, and audio-cassette programs

STUDENT ATTITUDE: Positive

While all official remedial work is handled by the Division of Developmental Studies, writing instructors at Georgia State University must do a great deal of unofficial remedial work with students who are ill-prepared for courses for which they are technically eligible. Many of these students are referred to the Writing Center for additional assistance. To meet the need of all students for college-level writing skills, Georgia State has also established a departmental proficiency examination for the first freshman course and has placed more emphasis on writing in the sophomore English course. The school has introduced several new advanced writing courses, one particularly designed for and required of accounting majors. In the future, Georgia State plans to introduce an M.A. with a concentration in writing.

GOLDEY BEACOM COLLEGE

Wilmington, DE 19808

Full-time Students: 199M/699W Faculty: 41

Respondent: Kay W. Rickard, Assistant Professor of English

Writing Requirement: Four required English courses with a writing/communications emphasis

Writing Center

CENTER HAS EXISTED: 2 years HOURS OPEN PER WEEK: 20-40

STAFF: 2 part-time faculty

TUTORS' TRAINING: On-the-job

TUTORS' EVALUATION: Observation

TUTORS PAID: Yes

PROGRAM DESIGNED TO SERVE: Writing students, English students, freshmen, underclassmen, and others from all disciplines

PROGRAM ACTUALLY SERVES: Writing students, English students, freshmen, underclassmen, and others from all disciplines

STUDENTS SEEK HELP WITH: Academic essays, resumes or business writing, basic grammar, and coursework from all disciplines

PERCENTAGE OF STUDENTS SERVED: Less than 25%

STUDENTS USE CENTER: On a walk-in or referral basis, primarily at mid-semester and the end of the semester

STUDENTS REQUIRED TO USE CENTER: Problem writers

MATERIALS AVAILABLE: Handbooks, writing exercises, audiovisual and multi-media aids, and computer-assisted instruction

STUDENT ATTITUDE: Generally positive

Peer Tutoring Program

PROGRAM HAS EXISTED: 1 year

ORGANIZATION: Curriculum-based

NUMBER OF TUTORS: 10-20

HOURS THEY WORK PER WEEK: Under 5

TUTORS PAID: No

TUTOR SELECTION: Self-nominated

TUTORS' TRAINING: No formal training (tutor must have "A" or "B" average in the course tutored)

TUTORS' EVALUATION: Observation and student questionnaires

PERCENTAGE OF STUDENTS SERVED: Less than 25%

PROGRAM INTENDED TO SERVE: Writing students, English students, freshmen, underclassmen, and students from all disciplines

PROGRAM ACTUALLY SERVES: Writing students, English students, freshmen, underclassmen, and students in all disciplines

STUDENTS SEEK HELP WITH: Academic essays, grammar, and any course material

MECHANICS OF TUTORING: Students may choose to discuss any paper with a tutor

STUDENT ATTITUDE: Generally positive

Until recently Goldey Beacom's writing program consisted of two required courses in grammar and English principles, which were generally ineffective in increasing overall writing skills, according to Kay W. Rickard. But in the past few years, new programs and requirements have been introduced. A total of four courses in writing and communication are now required for graduation: English Principles, Composition, Written Communications, and Oral Communications. After completing these four courses, students are expected to be proficient communicators and should seek additional assistance on their own initiative. Goldey Beacom has also recently hired faculty with interest and expertise in composition to teach expository writing and communications. The Learning Center and a peer tutoring program, both introduced within the past two years, will assist all types of students with writing problems and questions. The college is currently revising its writing curriculum to emphasize the writing process and to establish high standards for communication.

GRAND CANYON COLLEGE

Phoenix, AZ 85061

Full-time Students: 445M/469W Faculty: 35

Respondent: Ralph T. Bryan, Humanities Chairperson

Writing Requirement: Required freshman English course and a junior year proficiency examination; students may fulfill examination requirement through writing courses

Peer Tutoring Program

PROGRAM HAS EXISTED: 2-5 years

ORGANIZATION: Curriculum-based

NUMBER OF TUTORS: 10-20

HOURS THEY WORK PER WEEK: Under 5

TUTORS PAID: Yes

TUTOR SELECTION: Nominated by English faculty and appointed by the director

TUTORS' TRAINING: Non-academic training course

TUTORS' EVALUATION: Observation and conferences

PERCENTAGE OF STUDENTS SERVED: Less than 25%

OVER PAST FIVE YEARS THIS PERCENTAGE HAS: Increased

PROGRAM INTENDED TO SERVE: Students in all disciplines

PROGRAM ACTUALLY SERVES: Students in all disciplines, especially writing students

STUDENTS SEEK HELP WITH: Academic essays and research papers

MECHANICS OF TUTORING: Students may choose to have tutor comment in writing on papers, or discuss the paper in a conference

STUDENT ATTITUDE: Unknown

At Grand Canyon College ten years ago, the humanities division's course offerings in English focused primarily on literature. But since then, new programs have created a strong emphasis on writing skills. In the mid-seventies, the college established a writing major that now accounts for one-third of all English majors. More recently, the peer tutoring program has been introduced to help any student with a writing problem. The tutors are trained in a non-academic course and discuss papers with students who choose to seek help. The college's only unsuccessful program was a limited writing laboratory that few students used. In the next few years, Grand Canyon College plans to expand its course offerings in journalism and technical writing.

GRINNELL COLLEGE

Grinnell, IA 50112

Full-time Students: 623M/553W Faculty: 117

Respondent: Mathilda Liberman, Director, Writing Lab

Writing Requirement: One-semester freshman tutorial

Writing Center

CENTER HAS EXISTED: 12 years HOURS OPEN PER WEEK: 35-40

STAFF: 5 adjunct faculty

TUTORS' TRAINING: On-the job

TUTORS' EVALUATION: Observation

TUTORS PAID: Yes

PROGRAM DESIGNED TO SERVE: Students in all disciplines

PROGRAM ACTUALLY SERVES: Students in all disciplines

STUDENTS SEEK HELP WITH: 2% scientific reports, 86% academic essays, 10% research papers, and 2% resumes or business writing

PERCENTAGE OF STUDENTS SERVED: Less than 25% per semester

OVER PAST FIVE YEARS THIS PERCENTAGE HAS: Stayed the same

STUDENTS USE CENTER: Throughout semester, on walk-in, appointment, or regular basis

STUDENTS REQUIRED TO USE CENTER: None

MATERIALS AVAILABLE: Handbooks and exercises

STUDENT ATTITUDE: Very positive

Writing-Across-the-Curriculum Program

PROGRAM HAS EXISTED: 12 years

INSTRUCTORS INVOLVED: Faculty in all disciplines

INSTRUCTORS' SELECTION: By Dean and specific departments

INSTRUCTORS' TRAINING: Seminars

PERCENTAGE OF FACULTY INVOLVED: Over 75%

IN PAST FIVE YEARS THIS PERCENTAGE HAS: Stayed the same

STUDENTS INVOLVED IN PROGRAM: From all disciplines

PERCENTAGE OF STUDENTS INVOLVED: Over 75%

IN PAST FIVE YEARS THIS PERCENTAGE HAS: Stayed the same

The Writing Center at Grinnell College works in conjunction with the freshman tutorial and other writing courses to address students' writing difficulties. Students enrolled in writing courses come to the center once a week or as needed to discuss problems with current class assignments. In addition to the lecturers who staff the center, a few students assist in the lab as part of an independent study in the teaching of writing. In addition to the very successful writing center, Grinnell operates faculty training seminars during the summer to help instructors teach writing and plan assignments. Mathilda Liberman writes, "The system of writing across the curriculum is effective or ineffective, depending on the number of papers assigned each semester and on the quality of the teaching. Not everyone, no matter how competent in his or her particular field, can teach composition effectively. Perhaps writing across the curriculum will soon undergo evaluation throughout the country."

GUILFORD COLLEGE

Greensboro, NC 27410

Full-time Students: 578M/507W   Faculty: 85

Respondent: Ellen O'Brien, Chairperson, English Department

Writing Requirement: Required freshman English course

Writing Center

CENTER HAS EXISTED: 2-5 years   HOURS OPEN PER WEEK: Over 40

STAFF: Fewer than 5 faculty and 20-40 undergraduate tutors in all subjects

TUTORS' TRAINING: No formal training

TUTORS' EVALUATION: Conferences and student questionnaires

TUTORS PAID: Yes

PROGRAM DESIGNED TO SERVE: Students in all disciplines

PROGRAM ACTUALLY SERVES: Students in all disciplines

STUDENTS SEEK HELP WITH: Scientific reports, academic essays, business writing, research papers, and some creative writing

PERCENTAGE OF STUDENTS SERVED: 25-50%

OVER PAST FIVE YEARS THIS PERCENTAGE HAS: Stayed the same

STUDENTS USE CENTER: Throughout the semester on a walk-in, appointment, or regular basis, in small workshops, or in class visits

STUDENTS REQUIRED TO USE CENTER: None

MATERIALS AVAILABLE: Handbooks, educational magazines, writing exercises, professional books, audio-visual programs, and computer programs

STUDENT ATTITUDE: Unknown

Peer Tutoring Program

PROGRAM HAS EXISTED: 2-5 years

ORGANIZATION: Writing center-based

NUMBER OF TUTORS: 20-40

HOURS THEY WORK PER WEEK: Varies widely

TUTORS PAID: Yes

TUTOR SELECTION: Nominated college-wide

TUTORS' TRAINING: No formal training

TUTORS' EVALUATION: Conferences and student questionnaires

PERCENTAGE OF STUDENTS SERVED: 25-50%

OVER PAST FIVE YEARS THIS PERCENTAGE HAS: Stayed the same

PROGRAM INTENDED TO SERVE: Students in all disciplines

PROGRAM ACTUALLY SERVES: Students in all disciplines

STUDENTS SEEK HELP WITH: Scientific reports, creative writing, academic essays, business writing, and research papers

STUDENT ATTITUDE: Somewhat positive

The most significant change in Guilford College's writing program over the past five years was the establishment of the Academic Skills Center. Staffed by a few faculty members and several untrained peer tutors, the Center offers students assistance in various subjects, including writing. The Center is open over forty hours each week, and is able to serve over 25 percent of Guilford's students. Inside the classroom, Guilford has changed its freshman-sophomore composition requirement to a two-semester freshman sequence. Although the English Department concentrates on expository writing in its courses, other types of writing, such as journalism, are also offered. In the near future, the department may introduce a developmental writing course for students not prepared for the freshman sequence, and one English professor is currently experimenting with word processor-based instruction.

HAMILTON COLLEGE

Clinton, NY 13323

Full-time Students: 978M/669W Faculty: 132

Respondent: John H. O'Neill, Professor of English

Writing Requirement: None

Writing-Across-the-Curriculum Program

PROGRAM HAS EXISTED: Less than 2 years

INSTRUCTORS INVOLVED: Faculty in all disciplines

INSTRUCTORS' SELECTION: Voluntary

INSTRUCTORS' TRAINING: Seminars

PERCENTAGE OF FACULTY INVOLVED: Less than 25%

STUDENTS INVOLVED IN PROGRAM: Students in all disciplines

PARTICIPANTS' ATTITUDE: Unknown

At Hamilton College, the English Department is turning to innovative writing programs as an answer to students' writing problems. Although the traditional writing program has worked well for almost forty years, according to John O'Neill, "Many members of the English Department are increasingly uncertain that English 120 is getting as many students as need it. . . . Courses in the freshman year do not meet all the needs of the kinds of students we now get." To better meet these needs, Hamilton began a writing-across-the-curriculum program two years ago and plans to open a writing center soon. Mr. O'Neill says, "We believe that in a small institution with a favorable student-faculty ratio, we can maintain a high degree of awareness of writing for both students and faculty." In keeping with this philosophy, Hamilton discontinued its graduation writing requirement in 1968, but the school's advising system is strong and most students elect a freshman English course.

HARDING UNIVERSITY

Searcy, AR 72143

Full-time Students: 1336M/1473W Faculty: 111

Respondent: Larry R. Long, Associate Professor of English, Director of Writing Lab

Writing Requirement: Required freshman English course and Junior English Proficiency (earned by examination or course work)

Writing Center

CENTER HAS EXISTED: 2-5 years HOURS OPEN PER WEEK: 20-40

STAFF: Director, 2 graduate tutors, and 20 undergraduate tutors

TUTORS' TRAINING: On-the-job

TUTORS' EVALUATION: Observation and by other tutors

TUTORS PAID: Only graduate tutors

PROGRAM DESIGNED TO SERVE: Students in all disciplines

PROGRAM ACTUALLY SERVES: Students in all disciplines, primarily freshman English students

STUDENTS SEEK HELP WITH: All types of writing, particularly academic essays and research papers

PERCENTAGE OF STUDENTS SERVED: Less than 25%

OVER PAST FIVE YEARS THIS PERCENTAGE HAS: Increased

STUDENTS USE CENTER: Throughout the semester on an appointment or walk-in basis

STUDENTS REQUIRED TO USE CENTER: Freshmen in the basic grammar and composition course

MATERIALS AVAILABLE: Handbooks and writing exercises

STUDENT ATTITUDE: Somewhat positive

In the past few years, Harding University has twice updated its curriculum, redesigning and adding courses to focus more on the process of writing. The required composition course, for example, involves extensive discussion of writing strategies, stages of the writing process, style, and especially revision. Harding also offers basic composition courses for underprepared students and more advanced courses that emphasize sophisticated rhetorical strategies. Students from the Advanced Composition course tutor in Harding's Writing Lab, which serves primarily students who need help with basic writing skills. In addition to these peer tutors, the lab is staffed by a faculty director and two graduate tutors. According to Larry Long, the English Department plans to continue the trend toward teaching writing as a process by offering more advanced composition courses and instruction in rhetorical theory.

HARVARD UNIVERSITY

Cambridge, MA 02138

Full-time Students: 4062M/2434W Faculty: 568

Respondent: Sheila Reindl, Director of the Writing Center

Writing Requirement: Required freshman English course

Writing Center and Peer Tutoring Program

CENTER HAS EXISTED: 5 years HOURS OPEN PER WEEK: 20–40

STAFF: 10 undergraduate tutors

TUTORS' SELECTION: Self-nominated and appointed by director, who is advised by veteran tutors

TUTORS' TRAINING: On-the-job and month-long non-academic course

TUTORS' EVALUATION: Observation, conferences, student questionnaires, and by other tutors

TUTORS PAID: Yes

HOURS THEY WORK PER WEEK: 10

PROGRAM DESIGNED TO SERVE: Students in all disciplines

PROGRAM ACTUALLY SERVES: Students in all disciplines

STUDENTS SEEK HELP WITH: Scientific reports, academic essays, research papers, theses, and applications for fellowships

PERCENTAGE OF STUDENTS SERVED: Less than 25%

OVER PAST FIVE YEARS THIS PERCENTAGE HAS: Increased

STUDENTS USE CENTER: Repeatedly on an appointment basis

STUDENTS REQUIRED TO USE CENTER: None

MATERIALS AVAILABLE: Handbooks, exercises, and model papers

MECHANICS OF TUTORING: Student chooses to discuss papers with consultant; student determines focus of conference

STUDENT ATTITUDE: Very positive

Writing-Across-the-Curriculum Program

PROGRAM HAS EXISTED: 3 years

INSTRUCTORS SELECTED: Faculty in the core curriculum

INSTRUCTORS' SELECTION: Voluntary

INSTRUCTORS' TRAINING: Luncheon meetings

PERCENTAGE OF FACULTY INVOLVED: Less than 25%

IN PAST FIVE YEARS THIS PERCENTAGE HAS: Stayed the same

STUDENTS INVOLVED IN PROGRAM: Students in all disciplines

PARTICIPANTS' ATTITUDE: Positive

Harvard University's writing program is diverse. The university's writing center, staffed by undergraduate peer consultants, attracts a faithful following of tutees who use the center repeatedly. The center also sponsors discussions for faculty as well as helping teaching fellows with assigning and evaluating student writing. The writing-across-the-curriculum program is almost as popular as the writing center among students and faculty. The program affects over 75 percent of the student body, an unusually large proportion even for a cross-curricular program. In existence for over three years, the program brings in professional writers to lead various seminars on the teaching of writing. Richard Marius, who has chaired Harvard's Expository Writing Department for over three years, is confident that Harvard's well-established writing program will continue to expand and develop in years to come.

HAWAII PACIFIC COLLEGE

Honolulu, HI 96813

Full-time Students: 413M/297W Faculty: 24

Respondent: Jean Coffman, Chairperson, Language Arts

Writing Requirement: None

Many of Hawaii Pacific College's programs, including its writing program, are growing rapidly. Since the college's student body doubled several years ago, the administration has re-examined student writing. Although the college has no real writing center, it does have a course known as the Writing Skills Lab where ESL students meet regularly with faculty tutors. This course may eventually develop into a full-fledged writing center that serves students in all disciplines. In the next few years, Hawaii Pacific will probably approach writing more as a process and may even establish a peer tutoring program.

HOPE COLLEGE

Holland, MI 49423

Full-time Students: 1077M/1119W Faculty: 148

Respondent: William Reynolds, Associate Professor of English

Writing Requirement: Required freshman English course; exemption based on ACT English test

Writing Center

CENTER HAS EXISTED: 10-12 years HOURS OPEN PER WEEK: 45

STAFF: Director and 5-9 undergraduate tutors

TUTORS' TRAINING: 5-6 hours of bi-weekly seminars, staff meetings, and observation

TUTORS' EVALUATION: Student evaluations

TUTORS PAID: Yes

PROGRAM DESIGNED TO SERVE: Students from all disciplines

PROGRAM ACTUALLY SERVES: Primarily freshmen English students; also humanities students

STUDENTS SEEK HELP WITH: Academic essays, research papers, brainstorming and organizing thoughts, developing ideas, proofreading, documenting, and improving style

PERCENTAGE OF STUDENTS SERVED: 15%

OVER PAST FIVE YEARS THIS PERCENTAGE HAS: Increased

STUDENTS USE THE CENTER: Throughout the semester, some on a weekly appointment basis

STUDENTS REQUIRED TO USE CENTER: 25-45 freshmen in special support program for conditionally accepted freshmen

MATERIALS AVAILABLE: Handbooks, writing exercises, and professional books

STUDENT ATTITUDE: Very positive

Peer Tutoring Program

PROGRAM HAS EXISTED: Less than 2 years

ORGANIZATION: Curriculum-based

NUMBER OF TUTORS: 55

HOURS THEY WORK PER WEEK: 3-6

TUTORS PAID: Yes

TUTOR SELECTION: Appointed by tutoring coordinator upon departmental recommendation

TUTORS' TRAINING: Non-academic training workshops

TUTORS' EVALUATION: Observation and student questionnaires

PERCENTAGE OF STUDENTS SERVED: 10%

OVER PAST FIVE YEARS THIS PERCENTAGE HAS: Increased

PROGRAM INTENDED TO SERVE: Students in all disciplines

PROGRAM ACTUALLY SERVES: Students in all disciplines

STUDENTS SEEK HELP WITH: Learning strategies

MECHANICS OF TUTORING: Students meet with tutor once or twice a week on a regular basis

STUDENT ATTITUDE: Very positive

Hope College's English Department has tried different innovative programs but has found that one-on-one peer tutoring is the most effective. Both the Academic Support Center and the Peer Tutoring Center have succeeded because of the dedication of the program directors and the tutors, according to William Reynolds. Students have responded very positively to the peer tutors, who help students from all disciplines with all types of writing problems. The English Department also offers a wide range of courses from "Writing Workshop," which focuses on the different stages of the writing process, to courses that integrate literature and composition. The department has no definite plans for new programs or courses in the next few years.

HUSSON COLLEGE

Bangor, ME 04401

Full-time Students: 306M/345W Faculty: 35

Respondent: Wayne Westbrook, Coordinator, Freshman English

Writing Requirement: Required freshman English course and other required English courses

Writing Center

CENTER HAS EXISTED: 9 years HOURS OPEN PER WEEK: 40

STAFF: 5-20 instructors and undergraduate tutors

TUTORS' TRAINING: Academic training course and training in interpersonal communications skills

TUTORS' EVALUATION: By students, faculty, and supervisors

TUTORS PAID: Yes

PROGRAM DESIGNED TO SERVE: Primarily freshmen English students; also underclassman writing students

PROGRAM ACTUALLY SERVES: English students, writing students, and underclassmen

STUDENTS SEEK HELP WITH: Academic essays and research papers

PERCENTAGE OF STUDENTS SERVED: 25-50%

OVER PAST FIVE YEARS THIS PERCENTAGE HAS: Increased

STUDENTS USE CENTER: Throughout the semester on a walk-in, appointment, or regular basis

STUDENTS REQUIRED TO USE CENTER: Problem writers and students with learning disabilities

MATERIALS AVAILABLE: Handbooks, writing exercises, and professional books

STUDENT ATTITUDE: Very positive

Peer Tutoring Program

PROGRAM HAS EXISTED: 6 years

ORGANIZATION: Writing center-based

NUMBER OF TUTORS: 5

HOURS THEY WORK PER WEEK: 6

TUTORS PAID: Yes

TUTOR SELECTION: Nominated by themselves or English faculty

TUTORS' TRAINING: On-the-job, academic, and interpersonal training

TUTORS' EVALUATION: Observation and formal assessment

PERCENTAGE OF STUDENTS SERVED: 25-50%

OVER PAST FIVE YEARS THIS PERCENTAGE HAS: Increased

PROGRAM INTENDED TO SERVE: Underclassmen, writing students, and English students

PROGRAM ACTUALLY SERVES: Primarily freshmen writing students and also underclassmen English students

STUDENTS SEEK HELP WITH: Academic essays and research papers

MECHANICS OF TUTORING: Student may volunteer or be required to discuss a paper with a tutor or have a tutor comment in writing on the paper

STUDENT ATTITUDE: Very positive

Through its innovative programs and writing courses, Husson College is able to expose an unusually high percentage of its students to some form of writing instruction. The writing center, which serves as a base for the peer tutoring program, is run by a federally funded Special Services Staff comprised of professional instructors. The instructors and peer tutors help between 25 and 50 percent of all students with their academic essays and research papers. In the near future Husson will continue to innovate by using word processing equipment in the teaching of composition.

ILLINOIS INSTITUTE OF TECHNOLOGY

Chicago, IL 60616

Full-time Students: 2299M/494W Faculty: 269

Respondent: Henry Knepler, Professor of English, Department of Humanities

Writing Requirement: Required freshman English course

Writing Center

CENTER HAS EXISTED: 2-5 years HOURS OPEN PER WEEK: 20

STAFF: Fewer than 5 part-time faculty

TUTORS' TRAINING: None; tutors are part-time instructors with advanced degrees

TUTORS' EVALUATION: Observation and conferences

TUTORS PAID: Yes

PROGRAM DESIGNED TO SERVE: Students in all disciplines

PROGRAM ACTUALLY SERVES: Students in all disciplines

STUDENTS SEEK HELP WITH: Grammatical and syntactical problems

PERCENTAGE OF STUDENTS SERVED: Less than 25%

OVER PAST FIVE YEARS THIS PERCENTAGE HAS: Stayed the same

STUDENTS USE CENTER: Repeatedly throughout the semester on an appointment or regular basis.

STUDENTS REQUIRED TO USE CENTER: Problem writers

An institution long committed to student writing, Illinois Institute of Technology has recently made significant advances in computer-aided composition instruction. The Computers and Writing Project is IIT's newest addition to the existing writing program. This project, funded in part by the Paul V. Galvin Venture Fund award, is described as a "long-term development commitment." Located in the school's Educational Technology Center, the project offers students software tutorial programs designed at IIT, with instruction in punctuation, subject-verb agreement, grammar, organization, report writing, and more. In 1983, IIT conducted a community-wide seminar to introduce Bell Laboratories' "Writer's Workbench" program and the ways it could enhance composition instruction. In the future IIT will expand its technical communications program and continue to emphasize word processing and computer-assisted instruction.

ILLINOIS STATE UNIVERSITY

Normal, IL 61761

Full-time Students: 7055M/9028W Faculty: 955

Respondent: Elizabeth McMahan, Director of Writing Programs

Writing Requirement: Required freshman English course; junior-level competency examination

Writing Center

CENTER HAS EXISTED: 8 years HOURS OPEN PER WEEK: Over 40

STAFF: 2 faculty supervisors, 3 graduate tutors, and 10 undergraduate tutors

TUTORS' TRAINING: On-the-job, academic training course, and non-academic training course

TUTORS' EVALUATION: Observation, student questionnaires; also each tutor writes a case study and keeps a journal

TUTORS PAID: Yes

PROGRAM DESIGNED TO SERVE: Students in all disciplines, especially writing students

PROGRAM ACTUALLY SERVES: Students in all disciplines, especially writing students

STUDENTS SEEK HELP WITH: Scientific reports, academic essays, research papers, resumes or business writing, theses, and dissertations

PERCENTAGE OF STUDENTS SERVED: Less than 25%

OVER PAST FIVE YEARS THIS PERCENTAGE HAS: Stayed the same

STUDENTS USE CENTER: Throughout the semester--mid-semester is the heaviest time--on an appointment or regular basis; grammar hotline also available

STUDENTS REQUIRED TO USE CENTER: None

MATERIALS AVAILABLE: Handbooks, exercises, professional books, and educational magazines

STUDENT ATTITUDE: Very positive

Peer Tutoring Program

PROGRAM HAS EXISTED: 1 year

ORGANIZATION: Curriculum-based

NUMBER OF TUTORS: 35

HOURS THEY WORK PER WEEK: 10

TUTORS PAID: Yes

TUTOR SELECTION: Nominated by English faculty and appointed by director; any competent student may serve--need not be an English major

TUTORS' TRAINING: On-the-job and academic course

TUTORS' EVALUATION: Observation, student questionnaire; also each tutor does a case study and keeps a journal

PERCENTAGE OF STUDENTS SERVED: Less than 25%

PROGRAM INTENDED TO SERVE: Freshmen

PROGRAM ACTUALLY SERVES: Freshmen

STUDENTS SEEK HELP WITH: Academic essays, research papers, and resumes or business writing

MECHANICS OF TUTORING: Tutor and student discuss drafts of papers

STUDENT ATTITUDE: Positive

Writing-Across-the-Curriculum Program

PROGRAM HAS EXISTED: Less than 2 years

INSTRUCTORS INVOLVED: Arts and Sciences Faculty

INSTRUCTORS' SELECTION: Voluntary

INSTRUCTORS' TRAINING: Seminars conducted by writing faculty

PERCENTAGE OF FACULTY INVOLVED: 5%

STUDENTS INVOLVED IN PROGRAM: Humanities, social sciences, and natural sciences students

PARTICIPANTS' ATTITUDE: Unknown

During the past two years, Illinois State University has established innovative writing programs in peer tutoring and writing across the curriculum. Programs in technical and creative writing have been operating successfully for many years. A writing center, which includes a Grammar Hotline, has been serving students for eight years. This emphasis on writing is also being extended beyond the university; according to Elizabeth McMahan, "We are becoming increasingly involved in articulation programs for high schools, community colleges, and four-year state universities." Illinois State offers a Doctor of Arts degree with primary emphasis on the teaching of composition and language. By 1985 the department expects to offer a master's degree in writing as well.

INDIANA STATE UNIVERSITY at TERRE HAUTE

Terre Haute, IN 47809

Full-time Students: 5261M/5232W Faculty: 636

Respondent: James S. Mullican, Director of Writing Programs, English Department

Writing Requirement: 2 required freshman English courses and 2 semester hours of junior composition; exemption by SAT examination

Writing Center

CENTER HAS EXISTED: 5 years HOURS OPEN PER WEEK: 20–40

STAFF: 2–6 faculty, 2 graduate, and 5 undergraduate tutors

TUTORS' TRAINING: On-the-job, observation of experienced tutors, and briefing from Director

TUTORS' EVALUATION: None

TUTORS PAID: Graduates and some undergraduates

PROGRAM DESIGNED TO SERVE: Freshmen, ESL students, and students in all disciplines, especially writing and English students

PROGRAM ACTUALLY SERVES: Freshmen, writing and English students, ESL students, and students in all disciplines

STUDENTS SEEK HELP WITH: Academic essays, research papers, and ESL instruction

PERCENTAGE OF STUDENTS SERVED: 2%

OVER PAST FIVE YEARS THIS PERCENTAGE HAS: Increased

STUDENTS USE CENTER: Throughout the semester on an appointment or regular basis

STUDENTS REQUIRED TO USE CENTER: None

MATERIALS AVAILABLE: Exercises and a limited library

STUDENT ATTITUDE: Positive

The English Department at Indiana State University has a firm commitment to student writing. "We believe we should assist students to develop writing skills that will serve them well in the university and in their careers, but we also believe we should contribute to their development as human beings," states the program brochure, "We owe it to all students to provide the writing and related reading experiences that give them opportunities to broaden themselves and thus gain a liberal education." Indiana State offers a program especially designed for international students. International students who score below a certain level on a placement exam take one or two ESL courses before entering the regular composition program. ISU also offers remedial composition courses required of students with verbal SAT scores below 280; both ESL and remedial students may find additional help in the writing center, as may any other student on campus.

ITHACA COLLEGE

Ithaca, NY 14850

Full-time Students: 2070M/2650W Faculty: 293

Respondent: Mary Lynch Kennedy, Chairperson, Writing and Reading

Writing Requirement: Placement by SAT, other writing examination, and a reading test

Writing Center

CENTER HAS EXISTED: Over 10 years HOURS OPEN PER WEEK: Over 50

STAFF: 8 faculty tutors and 8 undergraduate tutors

TUTORS' TRAINING: On-the job and pre-service workshops

TUTORS' EVALUATION: Observation, conferences, and student questionnaires

TUTORS PAID: Yes

PROGRAM DESIGNED TO SERVE: Students in all disciplines

PROGRAM ACTUALLY SERVES: Students in all disciplines

STUDENTS SEEK HELP WITH: Scientific reports, creative writing, academic essays, research papers, resumes or business writing, reading comprehension, test-taking skills, and study skills.

PERCENTAGE OF STUDENTS SERVED: Less than 25%

OVER PAST FIVE YEARS PERCENTAGE HAS: Increased

STUDENTS USE CENTER: Throughout the semester on an appointment, walk-in, or regular basis

STUDENTS REQUIRED TO USE CENTER: None

MATERIALS AVAILABLE: Handbooks, exercises, professional books, and educational magazines

STUDENT ATTITUDE: Very positive

Writing-Across-the-Curriculum Program

PROGRAM HAS EXISTED: 2-5 years

INSTRUCTORS INVOLVED: Humanities faculty

INSTRUCTORS' SELECTION: Voluntary

INSTRUCTORS' TRAINING: Seminars

PERCENTAGE OF FACULTY INVOLVED: Less than 25%

IN PAST FIVE YEARS THIS PERCENTAGE HAS: Increased

STUDENTS INVOLVED IN PROGRAM: Students in all disciplines

PERCENTAGE OF STUDENTS INVOLVED: Less than 25%

IN PAST FIVE YEARS THIS PERCENTAGE HAS: Increased

PARTICIPANTS' ATTITUDE: Somewhat positive

Three years ago, Ithaca College's Applied Writing Program consisted of seventeen part-time faculty. Today, ten full-time and twelve part-time faculty work in the program, which merged with the Reading and Academic Skills program two years ago. The college's writing programs are growing in other areas as well. The unusually large writing center, for example, has increased its hours of business over the past ten years to forty hours a week. Mary Lynch Kennedy hopes that Ithaca College's writing program will continue to grow and gain departmental status within the next few years.

JAMESTOWN COLLEGE

Jamestown, ND 58401

Full-time Students: 275M/250W Faculty: 37

Respondent: James Blake, Chairperson, English Department

Writing Requirement: Required freshman English course, other required English course, and proficiency examination

Writing Center

CENTER HAS EXISTED: 2 years HOURS OPEN PER WEEK: Under 10

STAFF: 5-20 faculty and undergraduate tutors

TUTORS' TRAINING: On-the-job and academic

TUTORS' EVALUATION: Observation and conferences

TUTORS PAID: Yes

PROGRAM DESIGNED TO SERVE: Students in all disciplines

PROGRAM ACTUALLY SERVES: 90% writing and English students, 10% students in other disciplines

STUDENTS SEEK HELP WITH: Academic essays and research papers

PERCENTAGE OF STUDENTS SERVED: Less than 25%

STUDENTS USE CENTER: Throughout the semester on a walk-in or appointment basis

STUDENTS REQUIRED TO USE CENTER: Problem writers

MATERIALS AVAILABLE: Handbooks, exercises, and handouts

STUDENT ATTITUDE: Unknown

Jamestown College has recently developed a new rigorous writing program for its students. Introduced three or four years ago, this sequence of writing classes involves a composition course that familiarizes students with rhetoric, critical thinking, and college survival skills. The subsequent composition and literature course expands the instruction to include a term paper, introduction to library skills, and analysis of fiction. Other English courses require extensive writing of essays, papers, and examinations. In addition to the traditional course offerings, Jamestown has opened a small writing center to provide further help for students.

JOHNSON STATE COLLEGE

Johnson, VT 05686

Full-time Students: 450M/450W Faculty: 47

Respondent: Brent Sargent, Learning Resource Coordinator

Writing Requirement: Required freshman English course, one other required English course, and a Writing Competency Examination

Writing Center

CENTER HAS EXISTED: 5-10 years HOURS OPEN PER WEEK: Over 40

STAFF: More than 40 graduate and undergraduate tutors

TUTORS' TRAINING: On-the-job and academic training course

TUTORS' EVALUATION: Observation, conferences, and student questionnaires

TUTORS PAID: Yes

PROGRAM DESIGNED TO SERVE: Students in all disciplines

PROGRAM ACTUALLY SERVES: Students in all disciplines

STUDENTS SEEK HELP WITH: Scientific reports, academic essays, research papers, and other writing exercises

PERCENTAGE OF STUDENTS SERVED: 25-50%

OVER PAST FIVE YEARS THIS PERCENTAGE HAS: Increased

STUDENTS USE CENTER: Throughout the semester on a walk-in, appointment, or regular basis

STUDENTS REQUIRED TO USE CENTER: Students referred by faculty or administrative staff

MATERIALS AVAILABLE: Handbooks, writing exercises, and professional books

STUDENT ATTITUDE: Very positive

Peer Tutoring Program

PROGRAM HAS EXISTED: 5-10 years

ORGANIZATION: Curriculum-based

NUMBER OF TUTORS: 30-40

HOURS THEY WORK PER WEEK: 5-10

TUTORS PAID: Yes

TUTOR SELECTION: Nominated by English faculty and appointed by the director

TUTORS' TRAINING: On-the-job and academic training course

TUTORS' EVALUATION: Observation, conferences, and student questionnaires

PERCENTAGE OF STUDENTS SERVED: 25-50%

OVER PAST FIVE YEARS THIS PERCENTAGE HAS: Increased

PROGRAM INTENDED TO SERVE: Students in all disciplines

PROGRAM ACTUALLY SERVES: Students in all disciplines

STUDENTS SEEK HELP WITH: Scientific reports, academic essays, research papers, and all writing and English assignments

MECHANICS OF TUTORING: Students discuss papers with tutors

STUDENT ATTITUDE: Somewhat positive

Johnson State College's substantial writing requirement and extensive tutoring services ensure that each student is exposed to intense writing instruction before graduating. Since the college employs some forty peer tutors, nearly half of the student body receives individualized tutoring in addition to classroom instruction. These students are often referred to the writing center by their professors, and receive help from peer tutors who are carefully selected, trained in an academic course, and thoroughly evaluated. Since the writing program at Johnson State College is so extensive, the school has no plans for further expansion in the near future.

KANSAS STATE UNIVERSITY

Manhattan, KS 66506

Full-time Students: 8636M/6470W Faculty: 2500

Respondent: Lucien L. Agosta, Director of Composition

Writing Requirement: 2 required freshman English courses

Writing Center

CENTER HAS EXISTED: Over 10 years HOURS OPEN PER WEEK: 20-40

STAFF: 5-10 faculty, adjunct faculty, and graduate tutors

TUTORS' TRAINING: On-the-job

TUTORS' EVALUATION: Observation and student questionnaires

TUTORS PAID: Yes

PROGRAM DESIGNED TO SERVE: Students in all disciplines

PROGRAM ACTUALLY SERVES: Students in all disciplines, especially writing students

STUDENTS SEEK HELP WITH: Scientific reports, academic essays, research papers, and resumes or business writing

PERCENTAGE OF STUDENTS SERVED: Less than 25%

OVER PAST FIVE YEARS THIS PERCENTAGE HAS: Stayed the same

STUDENTS USE CENTER: Throughout the semester on a walk-in or regular basis

STUDENTS REQUIRED TO USE CENTER: Problem writers

MATERIALS AVAILABLE: Handbooks, exercises, professional books, and model essays

STUDENT ATTITUDE: Very positive

Kansas State University has shifted in the past few years from a "highly formulaic, form-oriented approach" to a process approach in the teaching of writing, according to L.L. Agosta. The freshman composition program aims at helping students become versatile writers able to respond effectively in a variety of writing situations. The writing center, its growth limited only by funding, offers one-on-one tutoring on a regular or walk-in basis to students needing additional help with their writing tasks. In addition, the department is building a strong teacher apprenticeship program to prepare graduate instructors to enter composition and technical writing classrooms. Kansas State is also exploring the services that computers can provide for students in the writing center and general writing programs.

KNOX COLLEGE

Galesburg, IL 61401

Full-time Students: 447M/369W Faculty: 86

Respondent: Michael Crowell, Chairperson, English Department

Writing Requirement: A 2-term core course with required writing

Writing Center

CENTER HAS EXISTED: 5–10 years HOURS OPEN PER WEEK: 20–40

STAFF: Fewer than 5 faculty and undergraduate tutors

TUTORS' TRAINING: On-the-job

TUTORS' EVALUATION: Observation

TUTORS PAID: Yes

PROGRAM DESIGNED TO SERVE: Students from all disciplines, especially English students and underclassmen

PROGRAM ACTUALLY SERVES: Students from all disciplines, especially English students and underclassmen

STUDENTS SEEK HELP WITH: Scientific reports, academic essays, and research papers

PERCENTAGE OF STUDENTS SERVED: Less than 25%

OVER PAST FIVE YEARS THIS PERCENTAGE HAS: Stayed the same

STUDENTS USE CENTER: Repeatedly throughout the semester on an appointment basis

STUDENTS REQUIRED TO USE CENTER: None

MATERIALS AVAILABLE: Handbooks, exercises, educational magazines, and professional books

STUDENT ATTITUDE: Unknown

Writing-Across-the-Curriculum Program

PROGRAM HAS EXISTED: 6 years

INSTRUCTORS INVOLVED: Faculty in all disciplines

INSTRUCTORS' SELECTION: Selected by faculty involved

INSTRUCTORS' TRAINING: Week-long workshops

PERCENTAGE OF FACULTY INVOLVED: 50% teach in program; 70% participate in faculty workshops

IN PAST FIVE YEARS THIS PERCENTAGE HAS: Increased

STUDENTS INVOLVED IN PROGRAM: All freshmen

PERCENTAGE OF STUDENTS INVOLVED: 25% (100% over four years)

IN PAST FIVE YEARS THIS PERCENTAGE HAS: Stayed the same

PARTICIPANTS' ATTITUDE: Positive

Instead of enforcing a rigid writing requirement, the faculty at Knox College try to encourage students to work on writing skills. Entering freshmen take a placement examination and are then advised whether to take the introductory freshman composition course, depending on the examination's results. In addition, all freshmen enroll in the Freshman Preceptorial, a course taught by faculty from all departments, which has a heavy reading list and requires some writing. About 70 percent or more of the faculty at Knox also participate in week-long workshops to help them identify and work with students' writing difficulties, and each faculty member is expected to work individually with students on writing. Aside from these programs, Knox operates a modest writing center, but Michael Crowell admits, "It is hard to get all students who need help into the center."

LA ROCHE COLLEGE

Pittsburgh, PA 15237

Full-time Students: 278M/403W   Faculty: 32

Respondent: Rita Yeasted, Assistant Professor of English

Writing Requirement: Required freshman English courses

Writing Center

CENTER HAS EXISTED: 5 years   HOURS OPEN PER WEEK: 20-40

STAFF: Faculty (part-time) and fewer than 5 undergraduate tutors

TUTORS' TRAINING: On-the-job

TUTORS' EVALUATION: Observation and conferences

TUTORS PAID: Yes

PROGRAM DESIGNED TO SERVE: Students in all disciplines

PROGRAM ACTUALLY SERVES: Students in all disciplines

STUDENTS SEEK HELP WITH: Academic essays, research papers, and business writing

PERCENTAGE OF STUDENTS SERVED: Less than 25%

OVER PAST FIVE YEARS THIS PERCENTAGE HAS: Increased

STUDENTS USE CENTER: Throughout the semester on a walk-in or appointment basis

STUDENTS REQUIRED TO USE CENTER: None

MATERIALS AVAILABLE: Handbooks, writing exercises, and computer exercises

STUDENT ATTITUDE: Somewhat positive

Peer Tutoring Program

PROGRAM HAS EXISTED: 5 years

ORGANIZATION: Curriculum-based

NUMBER OF TUTORS: 20-50

HOURS THEY WORK PER WEEK: 5-10

TUTORS PAID: Yes

TUTOR SELECTION: Nominated college-wide

TUTORS' TRAINING: On-the-job

TUTORS' EVALUATION: Observation and conferences

PERCENTAGE OF STUDENTS SERVED: 25-50%

OVER PAST FIVE YEARS THIS PERCENTAGE HAS: Increased

PROGRAM INTENDED TO SERVE: Students in all disciplines

PROGRAM ACTUALLY SERVES: Students in all disciplines

STUDENTS SEEK HELP WITH: Academic essays, research papers, and resumes or business writing

MECHANICS OF TUTORING: Student may choose to discuss a paper with tutor

STUDENT ATTITUDE: Somewhat positive

Writing-Across-the-Curriculum Program

PROGRAM HAS EXISTED: 4 years

INSTRUCTORS INVOLVED: Faculty in all disciplines

INSTRUCTORS' SELECTION: Voluntary

INSTRUCTORS' TRAINING: Summer seminars

PERCENTAGE OF FACULTY INVOLVED: 33%

IN PAST FIVE YEARS THIS PERCENTAGE HAS: Increased

STUDENTS INVOLVED IN PROGRAM: Students in all disciplines

PERCENTAGE OF STUDENTS INVOLVED: 100%

IN PAST FIVE YEARS THIS PERCENTAGE HAS: Increased

PARTICIPANTS' ATTITUDE: Very positive

In the early seventies La Roche College had little success with its non-required composition courses and its open curriculum, but in the past six years the school has changed its writing curriculum three times and has added a writing center, the peer tutoring program, and a writing-across-the-curriculum program. The new required freshman composition sequence and the three successful, innovative programs expose all of La Roche's students to intensive writing instruction and offer individualized tutoring to any student seeking additional help. The large peer tutoring program and the small writing center have served increasing numbers of students since they were opened, and both have received fairly positive responses from students. The writing-across-the-curriculum program, which emphasizes basic skills, has also been very successful. Trained in the teaching of writing during summer seminars, faculty from all disciplines are able to help all of La Roche's students with their writing. During the past three summers, La Roche has had a grant to study the teaching of reading, writing, and composition skills in lower-level courses in every discipline. In the past three years the English Department has been able to adapt the writing program to student needs.

LAWRENCE UNIVERSITY

Appleton, WI 54912

Full-time Students: 571M/572W Faculty: 102

Respondent: Linda Stanley, Director, Writing Lab

Writing Requirement: Freshman core program involving all departments

Writing Center

CENTER HAS EXISTED: 2 years HOURS OPEN PER WEEK: 10–20

STAFF: Director, undergraduate tutors, and community volunteers

TUTORS' TRAINING: On-the-job and pre-tutoring training by the Writing Lab director

TUTORS' EVALUATION: Observation and student questionnaires

TUTORS PAID: Yes

PROGRAM DESIGNED TO SERVE: Students in all disciplines

PROGRAM ACTUALLY SERVES: Students in all disciplines

STUDENTS SEEK HELP WITH: Academic essays and research papers

PERCENTAGE OF STUDENTS SERVED: Less than 25%

OVER PAST FIVE YEARS THIS PERCENTAGE HAS: Increased

STUDENTS USE CENTER: Throughout the semester on a weekly appointment basis

STUDENTS REQUIRED TO USE CENTER: None

MATERIALS AVAILABLE: Handbooks, writing exercises, professional books, and educational magazines

STUDENT ATTITUDE: Very positive

Peer Tutoring Program

PROGRAM HAS EXISTED: 2 years

ORGANIZATION: Writing center-based

NUMBER OF TUTORS: 10–15

HOURS THEY WORK PER WEEK: Under 5

TUTORS PAID: Yes

TUTOR SELECTION: Nominated college-wide, then selected by director

TUTORS' TRAINING: Instruction by the Writing Lab Director

TUTORS' EVALUATION: Observation and student questionnaires

PERCENTAGE OF STUDENTS SERVED: Less than 25%

PROGRAM INTENDED TO SERVE: Students in all disciplines

PROGRAM ACTUALLY SERVES: Students in all disciplines

STUDENTS SEEK HELP WITH: Academic essays and research papers

MECHANICS OF TUTORING: Weekly 45-minute tutorial sessions and additional sessions upon request

STUDENT ATTITUDE: Very positive

Lawrence University instituted a writing center for the first time in 1982. The center augments the regular freshman writing program, which requires that all freshmen take a standard core course taught by faculty from various disciplines. When the course is completed, those students identified as deficient in writing skills are advised to complete a non-credit remedial course taught by the Writing Lab director. During their second or third term, all freshmen take a seminar requiring substantial writing. Those students previously advised to take the remedial course work with a Writing Lab tutor during the seminar. The Writing Lab is also open to all students who desire assistance in writing.

LE MOYNE COLLEGE

Syracuse, NY 13214

Full-time Students: 897M/897W Faculty: 110

Respondent: Roger Lund, Chairperson, English Department

Writing Requirement: Required freshman English course and other required English course

Writing Center

CENTER HAS EXISTED: 2-5 years HOURS OPEN PER WEEK: 20-40

STAFF: 1 faculty and 5 undergraduate tutors

TUTORS' TRAINING: On-the-job and non-academic course

TUTORS' EVALUATION: Observation and conferences

TUTORS PAID: Yes

PROGRAM DESIGNED TO SERVE: Students in all disciplines

PROGRAM ACTUALLY SERVES: Mostly freshmen

STUDENTS SEEK HELP WITH: Academic essays and research papers

PERCENTAGE OF STUDENTS SERVED: Less than 25%

OVER PAST FIVE YEARS THIS PERCENTAGE HAS: Increased

STUDENTS USE CENTER: Throughout the semester on a regular basis, by faculty recommendation

STUDENTS REQUIRED TO USE CENTER: Problem writers

MATERIALS AVAILABLE: Programmed instruction and audio-visual tapes

STUDENT ATTITUDE: Somewhat positive

Although the writing center at Le Moyne College is designed to serve the entire student body, most patrons are freshmen. Still, the center serves 25 percent of all students on campus. The center also provides programmed instruction and audio-visual tapes for the students who seek help with their writing.

LEWIS AND CLARK COLLEGE

Portland, OR 97219

Full-time Students: 775M/916W Faculty: 117

Respondent: Susan M. Hubbuch, Director, Writing Skills Center

Writing requirement: Writing in core courses

Writing Center

CENTER HAS EXISTED: 7 years HOURS OPEN PER WEEK: 40

STAFF: 2 professional non-faculty tutors and 5–10 undergraduate tutors

TUTORS' TRAINING: On-the-job and in seminars run by the director

TUTORS' EVALUATION: Informally by the director

TUTORS PAID: Yes

PROGRAM DESIGNED TO SERVE: Students in all disciplines

PROGRAM ACTUALLY SERVES: Students in all disciplines

STUDENTS SEEK HELP WITH: All writing except creative writing

PERCENTAGE OF STUDENTS SERVED: Less than 25% each year

OVER PAST FIVE YEARS THIS PERCENTAGE HAS: Increased

STUDENTS USE CENTER: Throughout the term by appointment with a specific tutor

STUDENTS REQUIRED TO USE CENTER: None

MATERIALS AVAILABLE: Handbooks, handouts, writing exercises, and professional books

STUDENT ATTITUDE: Very positive

Writing-Across-the-Curriculum Program

PROGRAM HAS EXISTED: 6 years

INSTRUCTORS INVOLVED: Faculty in all disciplines

INSTRUCTORS' SELECTION: Voluntary

INSTRUCTORS' TRAINING: Workshops

PERCENTAGE OF FACULTY INVOLVED: 75%

IN PAST FIVE YEARS THIS PERCENTAGE HAS: Increased

STUDENTS INVOLVED IN PROGRAM: Students in all disciplines

PERCENTAGE OF STUDENTS INVOLVED: 90-100%

IN PAST FIVE YEARS THIS PERCENTAGE HAS: Increased

PARTICIPANTS' ATTITUDE: Very positive

Lewis and Clark has no faculty who teach only writing courses, but the college recently started to develop a writing program with the establishment of the Writing Skills Center and a writing-across-the-curriculum program. The Center is staffed by professional and peer tutors who assist students in all disciplines with writing. The two experienced tutors are evaluated through the college's staff review process, while the peer tutors are chosen, trained, and evaluated by the director of the center. The Writing Skills Center serves the college in another way as well: it provides workshops and informal consultation for faculty who want assistance with developing assignments, evaluating prose, and using writing in their courses. In the next few years, Lewis and Clark plans to expand the present program; current college-wide proposals for revisions in programs and curriculum may result in changes in the writing requirement

LINCOLN UNIVERSITY

Jefferson City, MO 65101

Full-time Students: 917M/788W   Faculty: 146

Respondent: Linda Wyman, Professor of English in the English, Foreign Languages, and Philosophy Department

Writing Requirement: Required freshman English courses

Writing Center

CENTER HAS EXISTED: 5 years   HOURS OPEN PER WEEK: Over 40

STAFF: 2 full-time professional (B.A. or M.A.) tutors

TUTORS' TRAINING: On-the-job

TUTORS' EVALUATION: Observation and conferences

TUTORS PAID: Yes

PROGRAM DESIGNED TO SERVE: Freshman writing students

PROGRAM ACTUALLY SERVES: Freshman writing students

STUDENTS SEEK HELP WITH: Academic essays, research papers, basic skills, and other writing assignments for freshman English

PERCENTAGE OF STUDENTS SERVED: 50-75%

OVER PAST FIVE YEARS THIS PERCENTAGE HAS: Increased

STUDENTS USE CENTER: Throughout the semester on a walk-in or appointment basis, or when referred by instructor

STUDENTS REQUIRED TO USE CENTER: Students in remedial English course

MATERIALS AVAILABLE: Handbooks, exercises, and filmstrip/cassette presentations

STUDENT ATTITUDE: Very positive

Peer Tutoring Program

PROGRAM HAS EXISTED: 5 years

ORGANIZATION: Curriculum-based

NUMBER OF TUTORS: Fewer than 10

HOURS THEY WORK PER WEEK: 5-10

TUTORS PAID: No

TUTOR SELECTION: Nominated by English faculty, then appointed by the director

TUTORS' TRAINING: On-the-job and academic course

TUTORS' EVALUATION: Observation, conferences, by instructor with whom they work daily, by professional tutors in lab, by director of peer tutoring course, and by themselves

PERCENTAGE OF STUDENTS SERVED: 25-50%

OVER PAST FIVE YEARS THIS PERCENTAGE HAS: Stayed the same

PROGRAM INTENDED TO SERVE: Freshmen writing students and English students

PROGRAM ACTUALLY SERVES: Freshmen writing students and English students

STUDENTS SEEK HELP WITH: Academic essays, research papers, basic skills, and other writing assignments for freshman courses

MECHANICS OF TUTORING: Student may choose to discuss or to have tutor comment in writing on any paper

STUDENT ATTITUDE: Very positive

Writing-Across-the-Curriculum Program

INSTRUCTORS INVOLVED: English faculty and faculty in all disciplines

INSTRUCTORS' SELECTION: Voluntary

INSTRUCTORS' TRAINING: Seminars

STUDENTS INVOLVED IN PROGRAM: Students in all disciplines

According to Linda Wyman, the writing programs at Lincoln University have "become process-oriented, student-centered, and competency-based" during the past decade, a shift evident in the successful establishment of both a writing center and a peer tutoring program five years ago. The peer tutors, who work exclusively with freshman English courses, serve more than a quarter of the students, while over half of the university's students use the center. In January 1984, Lincoln expanded its writing center to help students from all disciplines. Peer tutors still work with freshman English courses, but the writing center is being geared towards all students, and a cross-disciplinary program has recently been started.

LINCOLN UNIVERSITY

Lincoln, PA 19352

Full-time Students: 535M/479W Faculty: 70

Respondent: J. K. Van Dover, Assistant Professor of English, Director of Freshman English

Writing Requirement: Required freshman English course, sophomore World Literature course, and upperclass writing proficiency examination

Writing Center

CENTER HAS EXISTED: 5-10 years HOURS OPEN PER WEEK: Over 40

STAFF: 5-10 professional tutors and some faculty

TUTORS' TRAINING: On-the-job and academic course

TUTORS' EVALUATION: Observation and conferences

TUTORS PAID: Yes

PROGRAM DESIGNED TO SERVE: Students in all disciplines

PROGRAM ACTUALLY SERVES: Students in all disciplines

STUDENTS SEEK HELP WITH: Academic essays, research papers, resumes or business writing

PERCENTAGE OF STUDENTS SERVED: 25-35%

OVER PAST FIVE YEARS THIS PERCENTAGE HAS: Increased

STUDENTS USE CENTER: Throughout the semester on a walk-in basis

STUDENTS REQUIRED TO USE CENTER: Freshmen and problem writers

MATERIALS AVAILABLE: Handbooks, exercises, professional books, and tapes

STUDENT ATTITUDE: Very positive

In keeping with a national trend, Lincoln University has gradually shifted its writing program over the past ten years from heavy use of literature to an emphasis on writing skills. English 101 and 102, the required freshman English courses, are "almost entirely devoted to the essay and the research paper," according to J.K. Van Dover. Lincoln's

English Department has worked steadily on refining the required English course sequence and has tried to define more clearly "the enabling and terminal objectives" of the required English sequence. In the future, Lincoln will continue its commitment to writing, possibly adding a writing-across-the-curriculum program and a program for ESL students.

LOUISIANA COLLEGE

Pineville, LA 71359

Full-time Students: 406M/440W Faculty: 81

Respondent: Rosanne Osborne, Chairperson, English, Journalism, and Language Department

Writing Requirement: Two 3-hour freshman English courses

Writing Center

CENTER HAS EXISTED: 6 years HOURS OPEN PER WEEK: Under 10

STAFF: Fewer than 5 undergraduate tutors

TUTORS' TRAINING: No formal training

TUTORS' EVALUATION: Observation

TUTORS PAID: Yes

PROGRAM DESIGNED TO SERVE: Freshman English students

PROGRAM ACTUALLY SERVES: Writing students and freshmen

STUDENTS SEEK HELP WITH: Academic essays

PERCENTAGE OF STUDENTS SERVED: Less than 25%

OVER PAST FIVE YEARS THIS PERCENTAGE HAS: Decreased

STUDENTS USE CENTER: Throughout the semester on a walk-in basis

STUDENTS REQUIRED TO USE CENTER: Problem writers

MATERIALS AVAILABLE: Handbooks and writing exercises

STUDENT ATTITUDE: Somewhat positive

Peer Tutoring Program

PROGRAM HAS EXISTED: 6 years

ORGANIZATION: Curriculum-based

NUMBER OF TUTORS: Fewer than 10

HOURS THEY WORK PER WEEK: Under 5

TUTORS PAID: Yes

TUTOR SELECTION: Nominated by the English faculty

TUTORS' TRAINING: Academic training course

TUTORS' EVALUATION: Observation

PERCENTAGE OF STUDENTS SERVED: Less than 25%

OVER PAST FIVE YEARS THIS PERCENTAGE HAS: Decreased

PROGRAM INTENDED TO SERVE: Freshman English students

PROGRAM ACTUALLY SERVES: Freshman English students

STUDENTS SEEK HELP WITH: Academic essays

MECHANICS OF TUTORING: Student and tutor are required to discuss papers

STUDENT ATTITUDE: Somewhat positive

The English Department at Louisiana College has found individual conferences to be the most effective way of helping students overcome writing problems. One-on-one conferences are emphasized, therefore, in writing courses and in both of the tutoring programs. The writing center, which is staffed by fewer than five untrained peer tutors, assists students enrolled in freshman composition. The trained tutors in the peer tutoring program discuss papers with English and writing students in individual conferences. For unknown reasons, the number of students using Louisiana's tutoring programs has decreased in the past five years. Currently the writing center is being equipped with Commodore computers for usage drills and word processing. In the fall of 1984, the center will be the basis for a pilot freshman course using word processors for composition, grading, and rewriting.

LYNCHBURG COLLEGE

Lynchburg, VA 24501

Full-time Students: 689M/965W Faculty: 125

Respondent: Kenneth Alrutz, Director of Freshman English

Writing Requirement: Required freshman English course and other required English course

Writing Center

CENTER HAS EXISTED: 2-5 years HOURS OPEN PER WEEK: 10-20

STAFF: Fewer than 5 faculty

TUTORS' TRAINING: Academic course

TUTORS' EVALUATION: Observation

TUTORS PAID: No

PROGRAM DESIGNED TO SERVE: Students in all disciplines

PROGRAM ACTUALLY SERVES: Students in all disciplines

STUDENTS SEEK HELP WITH: Academic essays, research papers, and resumes or business writing

PERCENTAGE OF STUDENTS SERVED: Less than 25%

OVER PAST FIVE YEARS THIS PERCENTAGE HAS: Stayed the same

STUDENTS USE CENTER: Throughout the semester on a walk-in or appointment basis

STUDENTS REQUIRED TO USE CENTER: None

MATERIALS AVAILABLE: Handbooks, exercises, professional books, tape recorders, filmstrips, and typewriters

STUDENT ATTITUDE: Very positive

Peer Tutoring Program

PROGRAM HAS EXISTED: 5-10 years

ORGANIZATION: Curriculum-based

NUMBER OF TUTORS: 10-20

HOURS THEY WORK PER WEEK: Under 5

TUTORS PAID: Yes

TUTOR SELECTION: Self-nominated

TUTORS' TRAINING: Academic training course

TUTORS' EVALUATION: Observation and student questionnaire

PERCENTAGE OF STUDENTS SERVED: Less than 25%

OVER PAST FIVE YEARS THIS PERCENTAGE HAS: Stayed the same

PROGRAM INTENDED TO SERVE: Students in all disciplines

PROGRAM ACTUALLY SERVES: Students in all disciplines

STUDENTS SEEK HELP WITH: Scientific reports, academic essays, research papers, and resumes or business writing

MECHANICS OF TUTORING: Tutor and student are required to discuss papers

STUDENT ATTITUDE: Very positive

Writing-Across-the-Curriculum Program

PROGRAM HAS EXISTED: 2-5 years

INSTRUCTORS INVOLVED: Faculty in all disciplines

INSTRUCTORS' SELECTION: Voluntary

INSTRUCTORS' TRAINING: None

PERCENTAGE OF FACULTY INVOLVED: Less than 25%

IN PAST FIVE YEARS THIS PERCENTAGE HAS: Stayed the same

STUDENTS INVOLVED IN PROGRAM: Students in all disciplines

PERCENTAGE OF STUDENTS INVOLVED: 50-75%

IN PAST FIVE YEARS THIS PERCENTAGE HAS: Stayed the same

PARTICIPANTS' ATTITUDE: Very positive

Lynchburg College has added several innovative programs to its curriculum during the past few years, each designed to serve students in all disciplines. Both the peer tutoring program and the writing center have been successful in helping students with writing problems, and Kenneth Alrutz is very pleased with writing across the curriculum, which became part of the freshman English program three years ago. In the next few years, Alrutz hopes to standardize the freshman course and to encourage additional writing assignments in other disciplines.

MACALESTER COLLEGE

St. Paul, MN 55105

Full-time Students: 826M/743W Faculty: 125

Respondent: Michael Keenan, Associate Professor in English

Writing Requirement: Placement by SAT or other examination

Writing Center

CENTER HAS EXISTED: 2-5 years HOURS OPEN PER WEEK: 20-40

STAFF: 5-20 undergraduate tutors

TUTORS' TRAINING: On-the-job and academic training course

TUTORS' EVALUATION: Observation and conferences

TUTORS PAID: No

PROGRAM DESIGNED TO SERVE: Students in all disciplines

PROGRAM ACTUALLY SERVES: Students in all disciplines

STUDENTS SEEK HELP WITH: Academic essays and research papers

PERCENTAGE OF STUDENTS SERVED: Less than 25%

OVER PAST FIVE YEARS THIS PERCENTAGE HAS: Stayed the same

STUDENTS USE CENTER: Repeatedly throughout the semester on a walk-in, appointment, or regular basis, or by phone

STUDENTS REQUIRED TO USE CENTER: None

MATERIALS AVAILABLE: Handbooks, exercises, and professional books

STUDENT ATTITUDE: Somewhat positive

Peer Tutoring Program

PROGRAM HAS EXISTED: 2-5 years

ORGANIZATION: Freelance

NUMBER OF TUTORS: Fewer than 10

HOURS THEY WORK PER WEEK: 10-20

TUTORS PAID: No

TUTOR SELECTION: Self-nominated

TUTORS' TRAINING: On-the-job and academic training course

TUTORS' EVALUATION: Observation and conferences

PERCENTAGE OF STUDENTS SERVED: Less than 25%

OVER PAST FIVE YEARS THIS PERCENTAGE HAS: Stayed the same

PROGRAM INTENDED TO SERVE: Students in all disciplines

PROGRAM ACTUALLY SERVES: Students in all disciplines

STUDENTS SEEK HELP WITH: Scientific reports, academic essays, and research papers

MECHANICS OF TUTORING: Tutor and student are required to discuss papers; student may choose to have tutor comment in writing on any paper

STUDENT ATTITUDE: Somewhat positive

Writing-Across-the-Curriculum Program

PROGRAM HAS EXISTED: 2-5 years

INSTRUCTORS INVOLVED: Faculty in all disciplines

INSTRUCTORS' SELECTION: Voluntary

INSTRUCTORS' TRAINING: Seminars

PERCENTAGE OF FACULTY INVOLVED: Less than 25%

IN PAST FIVE YEARS THIS PERCENTAGE HAS: Stayed the same

STUDENTS INVOLVED IN PROGRAM: Students in all disciplines

PERCENTAGE OF STUDENTS INVOLVED: 25-50%

IN PAST FIVE YEARS THIS PERCENTAGE HAS: Stayed the same

PARTICIPANTS' ATTITUDE: Somewhat positive

Over the past three years, Macalester College has developed several innovative writing programs. According to Michael Keenan, "Writing-across-the-curriculum consciousness has come into being" during this short time, and "increased numbers of students and teachers have voluntarily been seeking more help for writing problems." The Learning Skills Center and peer tutors have been helpful in this respect, along with non–English faculty who have taken workshops on how to teach writing. In the near future, Keenan hopes to involve more faculty and to increase attention given to technology, computers, and writing.

MANKATO STATE UNIVERSITY

Mankato, MN 56001

Full-time Students: 4697M/4925W Faculty: 487

Respondent: Suzanne Bunkers, Chairperson, Freshman English Committee

Writing Requirement: Required freshman English course

Writing Center

CENTER HAS EXISTED: Under 2 years HOURS OPEN PER WEEK: 30

STAFF: 1 graduate and 4 undergraduate tutors

TUTORS' TRAINING: 2-week simulation workshops, on-the-job training, and follow-up meetings with faculty advisor

TUTORS' EVALUATION: Observation, written reports, and conferences

TUTORS PAID: No

PROGRAM DESIGNED TO SERVE: Students in all disciplines

PROGRAM ACTUALLY SERVES: Students in all disciplines

STUDENTS SEEK HELP WITH: Academic essays and review of basic grammar and usage

PERCENTAGE OF STUDENTS SERVED: Less than 25%

OVER PAST FIVE YEARS THIS PERCENTAGE HAS: Increased

STUDENTS USE CENTER: Throughout the quarter on an appointment, walk-in, or regular basis

STUDENTS REQUIRED TO USE CENTER: None

MATERIALS AVAILABLE: Handbooks and exercises

STUDENT ATTITUDE: Positive

Writing-Across-the-Curriculum Program

PROGRAM HAS EXISTED: 4 years

INSTRUCTORS INVOLVED: Faculty in a variety of disciplines

INSTRUCTORS' SELECTION: Voluntary

INSTRUCTORS' TRAINING: Seminars and workshops

PERCENTAGE OF FACULTY INVOLVED: Less than 25%

IN PAST FIVE YEARS THIS PERCENTAGE HAS: Increased

STUDENTS INVOLVED IN PROGRAM: Students in all disciplines

PERCENTAGE OF STUDENTS INVOLVED: 25-50%

IN PAST FIVE YEARS THIS PERCENTAGE HAS: Increased

PARTICIPANTS' ATTITUDE: Positive

Among Mankato State's more innovative writing programs are its Valley Writing Project (a writing-across-the-curriculum program) and its new writing laboratory. Funded by a Bush Foundation Grant, the Valley Writing Project is co-directed by one English and one political science faculty member. Additional faculty representing each of the five colleges make up the Valley Writing Project staff. During the academic year, in-service seminars are offered for university faculty from all disciplines, and each summer a week-long workshop in writing is also offered. Faculty indicate strong interest and support for the Project, and a number of faculty members incorporate writing into their content-area courses. Continuing this trend toward flexibility and growth in other areas as well, Mankato State has recently expanded its remedial and freshman composition sequences. Suzanne Bunkers hopes that in the next few years the one required semester of freshman English will be increased to two. According to Bunkers, flexible writing programs that accommodate a variety of instructors and students work more effectively than programs centered on grammar, usage, and mechanics.

MARQUETTE UNIVERSITY

Milwaukee, WI 53233

Full-time Students: 4321M/3610W Faculty: 568

Respondent: Clinton Luckett, Director of Writing Lab

Writing Requirement: None

Writing Center

CENTER HAS EXISTED: 5-10 years HOURS OPEN PER WEEK: 35-40

STAFF: 1 full-time and 2 part-time staff

TUTORS' TRAINING: On-the-job

TUTORS' EVALUATION: Student questionnaires

TUTORS PAID: Yes

PROGRAM DESIGNED TO SERVE: Writing students, English students, and freshmen

PROGRAM ACTUALLY SERVES: Writing students, English students, and freshmen

STUDENTS SEEK HELP WITH: Academic essays and resumes or business writing

PERCENTAGE OF STUDENTS SERVED: Unknown

OVER PAST FIVE YEARS THIS PERCENTAGE HAS: Increased

STUDENTS USE CENTER: Throughout the semester on a walk-in or regular basis

STUDENTS REQUIRED TO USE CENTER: None

MATERIALS AVAILABLE: Handbooks and exercises

STUDENT ATTITUDE: Very positive

Nearly ten years ago, Marquette University established its writing center, a facility that continues to grow each year. This center serves primarily freshmen, writing students, and English students who seek help with a variety of writing assignments. Aside from the writing center, very little has changed in the format of Marquette's writing program, and little is expected to change within the next few years.

MASSACHUSETTS INSTITUTE OF TECHNOLOGY

Cambridge, MA 02139

Full-time Students: 3549M/951W Faculty: 1294

Respondent: James Paradis, Associate Professor of Technical Communication

Writing Requirement: Required English course; placement by ACH or other examination

Writing Center

CENTER HAS EXISTED: 2-5 years HOURS OPEN PER WEEK: 20-40

STAFF: Fewer than 5 faculty, undergraduate, and professional tutors

TUTORS' TRAINING: On-the-job and non-academic course

TUTORS' EVALUATION: Observation

TUTORS PAID: Yes

PROGRAM DESIGNED TO SERVE: Students in all disciplines

PROGRAM ACTUALLY SERVES: Students in all disciplines

STUDENTS SEEK HELP WITH: Scientific reports, creative writing, academic essays, research papers, and resumes or business writing

PERCENTAGE OF STUDENTS SERVED: Less than 25%

OVER PAST FIVE YEARS THIS PERCENTAGE HAS: Increased

STUDENTS USE CENTER: Usually once at the middle or end of the semester on a walk-in basis

STUDENTS REQUIRED TO USE CENTER: Problem writers

MATERIALS AVAILABLE: Handbooks and exercises

STUDENT ATTITUDE: Unknown

Writing-Across-the-Curriculum Program

PROGRAM HAS EXISTED: Over 10 years

INSTRUCTORS INVOLVED: Faculty in all disciplines

INSTRUCTORS' SELECTION: Voluntary

INSTRUCTORS' TRAINING: None

PERCENTAGE OF FACULTY INVOLVED: Less than 25%

IN PAST FIVE YEARS THIS PERCENTAGE HAS: Increased

STUDENTS INVOLVED IN PROGRAM: Students in all disciplines

PERCENTAGE OF STUDENTS INVOLVED: 50–75% in School of Engineering

IN PAST FIVE YEARS THIS PERCENTAGE HAS: Increased

PARTICIPANTS' ATTITUDE: Unknown

In the past three years, Massachusetts Institute of Technology's writing program has expanded significantly. The school has recently established a writing requirement and has enlarged its Interdepartmental Cooperative Writing Programs. These ten-year-old interdisciplinary programs focus on science writing and technical communication, although well-grounded programs do exist in expository and creative writing. Offering such courses as "Science and Engineering Writing," the cross-disciplinary programs teach writing for science, engineering, management, and urban studies students. The MIT faculty have found that these diverse programs tend to fit their needs most effectively.

MERCER UNIVERSITY

Atlanta, GA 30341

Full-time Students: 1181M/1178W   Faculty: 109

Respondent: Mary E. Willingham, Director of English Lab

Writing Requirement: Required freshman English course sequence

Writing Center

CENTER HAS EXISTED: 2 years   HOURS OPEN PER WEEK: 30-40

STAFF: Fewer than 5 faculty and 10-15 undergraduate tutors

TUTORS' TRAINING: On-the-job and academic training course

TUTORS' EVALUATION: Observation, conferences, and student questionnaires

TUTORS PAID: Some are

PROGRAM DESIGNED TO SERVE: Faculty and students in all disciplines

PROGRAM ACTUALLY SERVES: Faculty and students in all disciplines

STUDENTS SEEK HELP WITH: Scientific reports, academic essays, research papers, business writing, and study skills

PERCENTAGE OF STUDENTS SERVED: Less than 25%

STUDENTS USE CENTER: Throughout the semester on a walk-in or regular basis

STUDENTS REQUIRED TO USE CENTER: Problem writers

MATERIALS AVAILABLE: Handbooks, writing exercises, professional books, and handouts on reading, writing, and speaking techniques

STUDENT ATTITUDE: Very positive

Mercer University emphasizes writing as a process in the English Department and in all disciplines. The English Lab is staffed by faculty and undergraduate tutors, and is well stocked with professional books, writing exercises, and handouts. The Lab serves faculty and students in all disciplines and tries to provide the atmosphere necessary for a true community of scholars. Mercer hopes to expand its program in the next few years to include additional work with international students and increased involvement with the local community.

MIAMI UNIVERSITY

Oxford, OH 45056

Full-time Students: 6667M/7830W Faculty: 788

Respondent: Mary F. Hayes, Director, Freshman Composition

Writing Requirement: Required freshman English course

Writing Center

CENTER HAS EXISTED: 5-10 years HOURS OPEN PER WEEK: Over 40

STAFF: 20-40 faculty, graduate, and undergraduate tutors

TUTORS' TRAINING: Academic training course

TUTORS' EVALUATION: Observation, conferences, and student questionnaires

TUTORS PAID: Yes

PROGRAM DESIGNED TO SERVE: Students in all disciplines

PROGRAM ACTUALLY SERVES: Students in all disciplines

STUDENTS SEEK HELP WITH: Academic essays, research papers, scientific reports, creative writing, and resumes or business writing

PERCENTAGE OF STUDENTS SERVED: Less than 25%

OVER PAST FIVE YEARS THIS PERCENTAGE HAS: Decreased

STUDENTS USE CENTER: Throughout the semester on a walk-in or regular basis

STUDENTS REQUIRED TO USE CENTER: None

MATERIALS AVAILABLE: Handbooks, writing exercises, educational magazines, and professional books

STUDENT ATTITUDE: Very positive

Peer Tutoring Program

PROGRAM HAS EXISTED: 5-10 years

ORGANIZATION: Residentially based

NUMBER OF TUTORS: 50-100

HOURS THEY WORK PER WEEK: 10–20

TUTORS PAID: Yes

TUTOR SELECTION: Appointed by the director

TUTORS' TRAINING: Academic training course

TUTORS' EVALUATION: Observation, conferences, and student questionnaires

PERCENTAGE OF STUDENTS SERVED: Less than 25%

OVER PAST FIVE YEARS THIS PERCENTAGE HAS: Stayed the same

PROGRAM INTENDED TO SERVE: Students in all disciplines

PROGRAM ACTUALLY SERVES: Students in all disciplines

STUDENTS SEEK HELP WITH: All types of writing

MECHANICS OF TUTORING: Student may choose to discuss a paper with tutor

STUDENT ATTITUDE: Very positive

Miami University strongly emphasizes collaborative learning and peer tutoring in teaching writing. The freshman writing program uses workshops in which students spend over 85 percent of their class time writing, discussing writing, and working in peer groups that discuss student writing. To help divide Miami's fourteen thousand students into manageable groups, the university employs fifty graduate students and several faculty to teach solely writing. Outside the classroom, Miami offers an unusually large peer tutoring program and a writing center. More than fifty trained peer tutors work over ten hours each week, helping students from all disciplines with a variety of writing problems. The enormous peer tutoring network, the readily accessible writing center, and the number of instructors all demonstrate Miami's dedication to individualized instruction for its large student body.

MILLS COLLEGE

Oakland, CA 94613

Full-time Students: 737W Faculty: 60

Respondent: Ruth Saxton, Director of Freshman Writing

Writing Requirement: Required freshman English course; exemption by placement examination

Writing Center

CENTER HAS EXISTED: 5-10 years HOURS OPEN PER WEEK: 10-20

STAFF: 5-20 graduate tutors

TUTORS' TRAINING: On-the-job and academic courses

TUTORS' EVALUATION: Observation, conferences, student questionnaire, and by other tutors

TUTORS PAID: Yes

PROGRAM DESIGNED TO SERVE: Freshmen and students in all disciplines

PROGRAM ACTUALLY SERVES: Freshmen and students in all disciplines

STUDENTS SEEK HELP WITH: Academic essays and research papers

PERCENTAGE OF STUDENTS SERVED: 25-50%

OVER PAST FIVE YEARS THIS PERCENTAGE HAS: Increased

STUDENTS USE CENTER: Throughout the semester on an appointment or regular basis

STUDENTS REQUIRED TO USE CENTER: None

STUDENT ATTITUDE: Somewhat positive

Although the writing center at Mills College has existed for several years, it has remained fairly small and Ruth Saxton reports that it may become part of a large general tutoring center. This merger may help the center reach more students, since it currently serves mostly freshmen. The center's graduate tutor staff is carefully trained and their required academic course includes an ESL section, to help them assist international students.

MISSISSIPPI COLLEGE

Clinton, MS 39058

Full-time Students: 931M/702W Faculty: 120

Respondent: Wanda Clay, Chairperson, Freshman English

Writing Requirement: Required freshman English course

Peer Tutoring Program

PROGRAM HAS EXISTED: 2-5 years

ORGANIZATION: Informal

NUMBER OF TUTORS: 10-20

HOURS THEY WORK PER WEEK: Fewer than 5

TUTORS PAID: No

TUTOR SELECTION: Volunteers

TUTORS' TRAINING: No formal training

TUTORS' EVALUATION: Conferences

PERCENTAGE OF STUDENTS SERVED: Less than 25%

OVER PAST FIVE YEARS THIS PERCENTAGE HAS: Increased

PROGRAM INTENDED TO SERVE: Students in all disciplines

PROGRAM ACTUALLY SERVES: Students in all disciplines

STUDENTS SEEK HELP WITH: Academic essays and research papers

MECHANICS OF TUTORING: Student may choose to have tutor comment on a paper in writing or discuss it in a conference

STUDENT ATTITUDE: Somewhat positive

In the past five years Mississippi College has expanded its small writing program by adding courses in creative and technical writing, and by developing a peer tutoring program. The untrained and unpaid peer tutors serve any student who chooses to discuss a paper. Though less than 25 percent of all students make use of the tutors, those who do respond favorably. Beginning in Fall 1984, Mississippi College will start a Writing Laboratory, a referral center where teachers in all disciplines can send students with writing problems. The lab will be non-credit and oriented toward solving individual problems, complementing the programmed remedial course already available. The laboratory will be under the direction of a full-time professor trained in linguistics and grammar, who will be aided by teaching assistants and faculty.

MUHLENBURG COLLEGE

Allentown, PA 18104

Full-time Students: 826M/707W Faculty: 122

Respondent: Jay H. Hartman, Associate Professor of English

Writing Requirement: Required freshman English course; exemption by placement examination

Writing Center

CENTER HAS EXISTED: 2 years HOURS OPEN PER WEEK: 10-20

STAFF: 5-20 undergraduate tutors

TUTORS' TRAINING: No formal training

TUTORS' EVALUATION: Observation and conferences

TUTORS PAID: Yes

PROGRAM DESIGNED TO SERVE: Freshmen

PROGRAM ACTUALLY SERVES: Writing students

STUDENTS SEEK HELP WITH: Academic essays and research papers

PERCENTAGE OF STUDENTS SERVED: Less than 25%

STUDENTS USE CENTER: Throughout the semester on a walk-in and appointment basis

STUDENTS REQUIRED TO USE CENTER: Freshmen and problem writers

MATERIALS AVAILABLE: Handbooks and exercises

STUDENT ATTITUDE: Very positive

The writing program at Muhlenburg College focuses on freshmen, who are required to pass a semester English course and who are strongly encouraged--sometimes required--to use the writing center. Instructors read and comment extensively on freshman essays, often returning papers for revision, and urging students to seek help in conferences. This careful attention to writing skills by all faculty is a new and positive development. According to Jay Hartman, "To show a student how a sentence can be improved works better than merely writing 'awk' in the margin. Students produce . . . when they see evidence of faculty effort and concern." The school's concern about writing has paid off--writing courses work well, and students are very positive about the center. In response, the English Department is considering extending the freshman English course to two-semesters.

NATIONAL COLLEGE OF EDUCATION

Evanston, IL 60201

Full-time Students: 300M/750W   Faculty: 75

Respondent: Lee C. Ramsey, Chairperson, English Department

Writing Requirement: Required freshman English course, English competency test

Writing Center

CENTER HAS EXISTED: 2-5 years   HOURS OPEN PER WEEK: 20-40

STAFF: Fewer than 5 faculty tutors

TUTORS' TRAINING: On-the-job

TUTORS' EVALUATION: None

TUTORS PAID: Yes

PROGRAM DESIGNED TO SERVE: Students in all disciplines

PROGRAM ACTUALLY SERVES: Students in all disciplines

STUDENTS SEEK HELP WITH: Academic essays and research papers

PERCENTAGE OF STUDENTS SERVED: Less than 25%

OVER PAST FIVE YEARS THIS PERCENTAGE HAS: Stayed the same

STUDENTS USE CENTER: Throughout the semester on an appointment basis

STUDENTS REQUIRED TO USE CENTER: Problem writers

MATERIALS AVAILABLE: Handbooks

STUDENT ATTITUDE: Very positive

Writing-Across-the-Curriculum Program

PROGRAM HAS EXISTED: 5-10 years

INSTRUCTORS INVOLVED: English faculty

INSTRUCTORS' TRAINING: None

PERCENTAGE OF FACULTY INVOLVED: 100% of English faculty

IN PAST FIVE YEARS THIS PERCENTAGE HAS: Stayed the same

STUDENTS INVOLVED IN PROGRAM: Students in all disciplines

PERCENTAGE OF STUDENTS INVOLVED: 25-50%

IN PAST FIVE YEARS THIS PERCENTAGE HAS: Stayed the same

PARTICIPANTS' ATTITUDE: Somewhat positive

The National College of Education's writing program has undergone some changes in the past decade, adding remedial writing courses and an English Competency Test, both of which have been successful. A more recent addition is the writing center, a small but thriving program that serves students from all disciplines. The college's cross-curricular program is not entirely cross-disciplinary in nature since it caters exclusively to English faculty, yet it has been an effective new program. Despite these new developments, Lee Ramsey does not anticipate that the college's writing program will change significantly in the near future.

NEW COLLEGE OF CALIFORNIA

San Francisco, CA 94110

Full-time Students: 100M/200W Faculty: 20

Respondent: Linda Martin, Director of the Humanities Program

Writing Requirement: None

Writing Center

CENTER HAS EXISTED: Under 2 years HOURS OPEN PER WEEK: 20-40

STAFF: 5 faculty and 6 undergraduate tutors

TUTORS' TRAINING: On-the-job and non-academic training course

TUTORS' EVALUATION: Conferences and student questionnaires

TUTORS PAID: No

PROGRAM DESIGNED TO SERVE: Students in all disciplines

PROGRAM ACTUALLY SERVES: Students in all disciplines

STUDENTS SEEK HELP WITH: Essays and basic skills

PERCENTAGE OF STUDENTS SERVED: 40%

OVER PAST FIVE YEARS THIS PERCENTAGE HAS: Increased

STUDENTS USE CENTER: Throughout the semester by appointment with any tutor

STUDENTS REQUIRED TO USE CENTER: None

MATERIALS AVAILABLE: Handbooks and computer-assisted instruction

STUDENT ATTITUDE: Very positive

Peer Tutoring Program

PROGRAM HAS EXISTED: Under 2 years

ORGANIZATION: Writing center-based

NUMBER OF TUTORS: Fewer than 6

HOURS THEY WORK PER WEEK: 5-10

TUTORS PAID: No

TUTOR SELECTION: Appointed by the director

TUTORS' TRAINING: On-the-job and non-academic training course

TUTORS' EVALUATION: Conference and student questionnaires

PERCENTAGE OF STUDENTS SERVED: Fewer than 25%

OVER PAST FIVE YEARS THIS PERCENTAGE HAS: Increased

PROGRAM INTENDED TO SERVE: English students

PROGRAM ACTUALLY SERVES: Students in all disciplines

STUDENTS SEEK HELP WITH: Essays and basic skills

MECHANICS OF TUTORING: Student may choose to discuss any paper with a tutor

STUDENT ATTITUDE: Very positive

In the past three years, the writing program at New College of California has "grown from nothing" into a program that involves one third of the school's student body, according to Linda Martin. New College now has a small number of faculty who teach solely writing and offer instruction in expository writing, journalism, creative writing, communications and English as a second language. In addition, the writing center has successfully combined computer-assisted instruction (which was found to be "too alienating" when used by itself) with peer tutoring. The center has reached a much more extensive clientele than originally intended, serving students in all disciplines rather than just English students.

NEW HAMPSHIRE COLLEGE

Manchester, NH 03104

Full-time Students: 820M/707W   Faculty: 52

Respondent: Don W. Sieker, Chairperson, Humanities/Social Sciences

Writing Requirement: Required freshman English course, other required English course, and proficiency examination

Writing Center

CENTER HAS EXISTED: 2-5 years   HOURS OPEN PER WEEK: Over 40

STAFF: 2 faculty and 20 undergraduate tutors

TUTORS' TRAINING: On-the-job and non-academic course

TUTORS' EVALUATION: Student questionnaire

TUTORS PAID: Yes

PROGRAM DESIGNED TO SERVE: Students in all disciplines

PROGRAM ACTUALLY SERVES: Students in all disciplines, especially freshmen, underclassmen, and writing students

STUDENTS SEEK HELP WITH: Academic essays, research papers, and resumes or business writing

PERCENTAGE OF STUDENTS SERVED: 25-50%

OVER PAST FIVE YEARS THIS PERCENTAGE HAS: Increased

STUDENTS USE CENTER: Throughout the semester on a walk-in or appointment basis

STUDENTS REQUIRED TO USE CENTER: Problem writers

MATERIALS AVAILABLE: Handbooks and exercises

STUDENT ATTITUDE: Very positive

Like several other schools, New Hampshire College operates its writing center as part of a general skills center. While the writing section of the Learning Center is popular among students, it is small and understaffed, unable to meet an increasing demand for writing help. To address this need, the college plans to start a peer tutoring program.

Operating out of the Learning Center, these tutors will be business and communications majors who will help ESL students and those students with serious writing problems.

NEW YORK UNIVERSITY

New York, NY 10003

Full-time Students: 5500M/5500W Faculty: 1300

Respondent: Lil Brannon, Assistant Director of Expository Writing, English Department

Writing Requirement: Two-semester required freshman English course

Writing Center

CENTER HAS EXISTED: 2–5 years HOURS OPEN PER WEEK: 20–40

STAFF: 3 undergraduate tutors and 12 graduate tutors

TUTORS' TRAINING: Graduate tutors take a non-academic training course; peer tutors take an academic training course

TUTORS' EVALUATION: Observation and conferences

TUTORS PAID: Only graduate tutors

PROGRAM DESIGNED TO SERVE: Students in all disciplines

PROGRAM ACTUALLY SERVES: Students in all disciplines

STUDENTS SEEK HELP WITH: Scientific reports, creative writing, academic essays, research papers, and resumes or business writing

PERCENTAGE OF STUDENTS SERVED: Less than 25%

OVER PAST FIVE YEARS THIS PERCENTAGE HAS: Increased

STUDENTS USE CENTER: Throughout the semester by appointment with a specific tutor

STUDENTS REQUIRED TO USE CENTER: None

MATERIALS AVAILABLE: Professional books

STUDENT ATTITUDE: Very positive

Peer Tutoring Program

PROGRAM HAS EXISTED: 2–5 years

ORGANIZATION: Writing center-based

NUMBER OF TUTORS: Fewer than 10

HOURS THEY WORK PER WEEK: Under 5

TUTORS PAID: No

TUTOR SELECTION: Appointed by the director

TUTORS' TRAINING: Academic training course

TUTORS' EVALUATION: Observation and conferences

PERCENTAGE OF STUDENTS SERVED: Less than 25%

OVER PAST FIVE YEARS THIS PERCENTAGE HAS: Increased

PROGRAM INTENDED TO SERVE: Freshmen

PROGRAM ACTUALLY SERVES: Freshmen

STUDENTS SEEK HELP WITH: Academic essays, research papers, and resumes or business writing

MECHANICS OF TUTORING: Student may choose to discuss any paper with tutor

STUDENT ATTITUDE: Very positive

Ten years ago, New York University's writing program was primarily product-oriented, but by the late 1970s it began to emphasize the process approach. More recently, the program shifted its focus to group-oriented, collaborative teaching methods, and then to the current critical reading focus. In the past five years, the English Department has introduced both a writing center and a peer tutoring program. The writing center, staffed primarily by graduate tutors, offers writing assistance to students in all disciplines, while the small peer tutoring program is designed specifically to help freshman. New York University will continue with its present programs, but Lil Brannon is not certain what changes might be made in years to come.

NORTH CAROLINA STATE UNIVERSITY

Raleigh, NC 27650

Full-time Students: 9694M/4448W Faculty: 1337

Respondent: Lucinda MacKethan, Assistant Director, Freshman Composition

Writing Requirement: Required freshman English course

Writing Center

CENTER HAS EXISTED: 5–10 years

HOURS OPEN PER WEEK: 8

STAFF: 5 graduate tutors

TUTORS' TRAINING: No formal training

TUTORS' EVALUATION: Student questionnaires

TUTORS PAID: Yes

PROGRAM DESIGNED TO SERVE: Underclassmen, especially freshmen

PROGRAM ACTUALLY SERVES: Underclassmen, especially freshmen and writing students

STUDENTS SEEK HELP WITH: Academic essays and research papers

PERCENTAGE OF STUDENTS SERVED: Less than 25%

OVER PAST FIVE YEARS THIS PERCENTAGE HAS: Increased

STUDENTS USE CENTER: Primarily at the middle and end of the semester on an appointment, walk-in, or regular basis

STUDENTS REQUIRED TO USE CENTER: Problem writers

MATERIALS AVAILABLE: Handbooks

STUDENT ATTITUDE: Unknown

North Carolina State University's Writing Lab works well but is "very limited" in size and scope, as Lucinda MacKethan reports. But the lab is growing, as are the university's more traditional programs. The composition program, for instance, has shifted its focus from reading to writing, and now includes a remedial course and more tutorials. Freshman English students write regular in-class themes that they prepare with outlines, revise, and resubmit. North Carolina State anticipates, however, that freshman composition will include less in-class writing in the future.

NORTHEASTERN UNIVERSITY

Boston, MA 02115

Full-time Students: 11,548M/6891W Faculty: 832

Respondent: Timothy R. Donovan, Coordinator of Composition, English Department

Writing Requirement: Required English course, other required English course, and upper-level writing course

Writing Center and Peer Tutoring Program

CENTER HAS EXISTED: 5-10 years HOURS OPEN PER WEEK: 20-40

STAFF: 5-20 graduate and undergraduate tutors

TUTORS' TRAINING: On-the-job, academic course, and non-academic course

TUTORS' EVALUATION: Observation, student questionnaire, and faculty questionnaire

TUTORS PAID: Yes

PROGRAM DESIGNED TO SERVE: Students in all disciplines

PROGRAM ACTUALLY SERVES: Students in all disciplines, especially writing students

STUDENTS SEEK HELP WITH: Primarily academic essays

PERCENTAGE OF STUDENTS SERVED: Less than 25%

OVER PAST FIVE YEARS THIS PERCENTAGE HAS: Increased

STUDENTS USE CENTER: Repeatedly at the middle and end of semester on a walk-in and appointment basis

STUDENTS REQUIRED TO USE CENTER: Problem writers

MATERIALS AVAILABLE: None

STUDENT ATTITUDE: Very positive

Over the past three years the writing program at Northeastern University has expanded significantly: the school has added new courses, hired new faculty, and re-structured the entire framework of the program. The English Department believes that these changes will help faculty better address students' needs and meet the growing demand for writing instruction. In addition to its two extra-curricular programs, the peer tutoring program and the writing center, Northeastern offers several traditional writing courses including remedial, technical, graduate and undergraduate business writing, and a seminar on the teaching of writing. The university also confers Master of Sciences and Master of Arts degrees in writing, and runs various courses geared toward writing for specific professions including health services, business administration, and criminal justice. As part of its general expansion, Northeastern is also planning a writing-across-the-curriculum program that will enlist volunteers from the English Department to be trained to serve 100 percent of the student body.

NORTH TEXAS STATE UNIVERSITY

Denton, TX 76203

Full-time Students: 4821M/5227W   Faculty: 690

Respondent: William Warde, Director of Writing Center

Writing Requirement: Required freshman English course, three other required English courses, and proficiency examination for any student earning a "D" in one or more of the four required English courses; placement by SAT examination

Writing Center

CENTER HAS EXISTED: 2–5 years   HOURS OPEN PER WEEK: 20–40

STAFF: Usually graduate tutors

TUTORS' TRAINING: Informal discussion and workshops

TUTORS' EVALUATION: Observation, conferences, and student comments

TUTORS PAID: Yes

PROGRAM DESIGNED TO SERVE: Students in all disciplines

PROGRAM ACTUALLY SERVES: Students in all disciplines

STUDENTS SEEK HELP WITH: Formal exposition; no class work

PERCENTAGE OF STUDENTS SERVED: Less than 25%

OVER PAST FIVE YEARS THIS PERCENTAGE HAS: Increased slightly

STUDENTS USE CENTER: Throughout the semester on an appointment or regular basis; workshops also offered

STUDENTS REQUIRED TO USE CENTER: Students failing proficiency examination and problem writers referred by faculty

MATERIALS AVAILABLE: Handbooks, exercises, educational magazines, and professional books

STUDENT ATTITUDE: Very positive

An interesting blend of rigidity and flexibility characterizes North Texas State University's writing program. While all students must pass four composition courses, none are required to use the writing center or the peer tutors. The four composition courses follow a standard sequence and emphasize traditional composition skills. Outside the classroom, however, the writing center offers regular workshops on writing skills, and the tutors develop individual teaching programs. This blend of structured classroom instruction and flexible tutoring has been successful, and demand for tutoring assistance is increasing.

OKLAHOMA CITY UNIVERSITY

Oklahoma City, OK 73111

Full-time Students: 471M/491W Faculty: 97

Respondent: Terry Phelps, Director, Writing Center

Writing Requirement: Required freshman English course

Writing Center

CENTER HAS EXISTED: Less than 2 years HOURS OPEN PER WEEK: 20-40

STAFF: One faculty director and undergraduate tutors

TUTORS' TRAINING: On-the-job and academic course

TUTORS' EVALUATION: Observation, conferences

TUTORS PAID: Some receive work/study salary; others receive credit

PROGRAM DESIGNED TO SERVE: Students in all disciplines

PROGRAM ACTUALLY SERVES: Students in all disciplines

STUDENTS SEEK HELP WITH: Academic essays, research papers, creative writing, legal briefs, and resumes or business writing

PERCENTAGE OF STUDENTS SERVED: Less than 25%

OVER PAST FIVE YEARS THIS PERCENTAGE HAS: Increased

STUDENTS USE CENTER: Repeatedly throughout the semester on a walk-in, appointment, or regular basis

STUDENTS REQUIRED TO USE CENTER: None

MATERIALS AVAILABLE: Handbooks and exercises

STUDENT ATTITUDE: Very positive

Writing-Across-the-Curriculum Program

PROGRAM HAS EXISTED: 2 years

INSTRUCTORS INVOLVED: English faculty

INSTRUCTORS' SELECTION: All English faculty participate

INSTRUCTORS' TRAINING: Bi-weekly composition colloquia

PERCENTAGE OF FACULTY INVOLVED: 100% of English faculty

IN PAST FIVE YEARS THIS PERCENTAGE HAS: Stayed the same

STUDENTS INVOLVED IN PROGRAM: All freshmen

PERCENTAGE OF STUDENTS INVOLVED: 25%

IN PAST FIVE YEARS THIS PERCENTAGE HAS: Stayed the same

PARTICIPANTS' ATTITUDE: Ambivalent

The writing center at Oklahoma City University has successfully provided tutorial assistance for the past two years, generating student enthusiasm for writing. One of the programs developed during this wave of enthusiasm is the series of bi-weekly colloquia on composition, in which English faculty discuss teaching strategies, tutoring techniques, and teaching goals. Terry Phelps believes that the center is one of Oklahoma City's more successful programs, and has positive plans for the next few years. "Use of the Center should expand," writes Phelps, "offering a greater variety of materials, services, and equipment," including computers to be used in teaching, writing, and research.

OAKLAND UNIVERSITY

Rochester, MI 48603

Full-time Students: 2700M/3500W   Faculty: 527

Respondent: Ronald A. Sudol, Associate Professor of Rhetoric, Director of Rhetoric Program

Writing Requirement: Required sequences of courses; exemption based on evidence of superior writing skill

Writing Center

CENTER HAS EXISTED: 5-10 years   HOURS OPEN PER WEEK: 10-20

STAFF: Fewer than 5 undergraduate tutors

TUTORS' TRAINING: On the job and academic course

TUTORS' EVALUATION: Observation and conferences

TUTORS PAID: Yes, except when enrolled in credit course

PROGRAM DESIGNED TO SERVE: Students in all disciplines

PROGRAM ACTUALLY SERVES: Students in all disciplines

STUDENTS SEEK HELP WITH: Scientific reports, academic essays, and research papers

PERCENTAGE OF STUDENTS SERVED: Less than 25%

OVER PAST FIVE YEARS THIS PERCENTAGE HAS: Stayed the same

STUDENTS USE CENTER: Throughout the semester on a walk-in, appointment, or regular basis

STUDENTS REQUIRED TO USE CENTER: None

MATERIALS AVAILABLE: Handbooks and exercises

STUDENT ATTITUDE: Unknown

Peer Tutoring Program

PROGRAM HAS EXISTED: Under 2 years

ORGANIZATION: Curriculum-based

NUMBER OF TUTORS: Fewer than 10

HOURS THEY WORK PER WEEK: Under 5

TUTORS PAID: No

TUTOR SELECTION: Self-nominated

TUTORS' TRAINING: Academic training course

TUTORS' EVALUATION: Observation and conferences

PERCENTAGE OF STUDENTS SERVED: Less than 25%

OVER PAST FIVE YEARS THIS PERCENTAGE HAS: Increased

PROGRAM INTENDED TO SERVE: Students in all disciplines

PROGRAM ACTUALLY SERVES: Students in all disciplines

STUDENTS SEEK HELP WITH: Scientific reports, academic essays, and research papers

STUDENT ATTITUDE: Unknown

Writing-Across-the-Curriculum Program

PROGRAM HAS EXISTED: Less than 2 years

INSTRUCTORS INVOLVED: Faculty in all disciplines

INSTRUCTORS' SELECTION: Voluntary

INSTRUCTORS' TRAINING: Seminars

PERCENTAGE OF FACULTY INVOLVED: Less than 25%

IN PAST FIVE YEARS THIS PERCENTAGE HAS: Increased

STUDENTS INVOLVED IN PROGRAM: Students in all disciplines

PERCENTAGE OF STUDENTS INVOLVED: Less than 25%

IN PAST FIVE YEARS THIS PERCENTAGE HAS: Increased

PARTICIPANTS' ATTITUDE: Very positive

Oakland University's oldest writing program is its writing center, staffed by undergraduate tutors who take a course in peer tutoring to help them respond to student needs. Along with the help offered by the center, the university has begun to use computers in its composition curriculum. In January 1984, the university began offering eight composition sections in which students do all their work on Apple IIe computers.

Ronald Sudol asserts that "the use of word processing is the most promising development in the teaching of writing," and plans to expand this program over the next few years.

OREGON STATE UNIVERSITY

Corvallis, OR 97331

Full-time Students: 8120M/5895W Faculty: 1075

Respondent: Lisa Ede, Director of the Communication Skills Center

Writing Requirement: Required freshman English and other communications courses

Writing Center

CENTER HAS EXISTED: 8 years HOURS OPEN PER WEEK: 40

STAFF: 3 faculty, 17 undergraduate tutors

TUTORS' TRAINING: Training manuals provided; tutors read articles and a book on writing and tutoring and attend weekly meetings

TUTORS' EVALUATION: Observation, conferences, and student questionnaires

TUTORS PAID: Some are; others tutors for credit

PROGRAM DESIGNED TO SERVE: Students in all disciplines

PROGRAM ACTUALLY SERVES: Students in all disciplines

STUDENTS SEEK HELP WITH: Scientific reports, creative writing, academic essays, research papers, resumes or business writing, and personal letters

PERCENTAGE OF STUDENTS SERVED: Unknown (5,000 contacts in 1982-83)

OVER PAST FIVE YEARS THIS PERCENTAGE HAS: Increased

STUDENTS USE CENTER: Throughout the semester on an appointment or drop-in basis

STUDENTS REQUIRED TO USE CENTER: Basic Writers and ESL freshmen

MATERIALS AVAILABLE: Handbooks, exercises, professional books, and Educulture cassettes

STUDENT ATTITUDE: Very positive

Oregon State University's major nontraditional program is its writing lab. The undergraduates who tutor in the lab receive training and support through frequent training meetings, conferences with faculty instructors, and quarterly observation of their work. Students have options as well as structure in their writing curriculum, including a wide variety of creative and expository writing courses. In the future, Oregon State may place more emphasis on ESL and develop a writing-across-the-curriculum program and various computer-assisted instruction programs.

OTTAWA UNIVERSITY

Box 59, Ottawa, KS 66067

Full-time Students: 248M/179W   Faculty: 36

Respondent: Ina K. Reiter, Head of English Department

Writing Requirement: Required freshman course or transfer General Education Requirement course with emphasis on writing; exemption or placement by ACT examination

Writing Center

CENTER HAS EXISTED: 2-5 years   HOURS OPEN PER WEEK: 20-40

STAFF: Fewer than 5 faculty members

TUTORS PAID: Yes

PROGRAM DESIGNED TO SERVE: Students in all disciplines, especially freshmen

PROGRAM ACTUALLY SERVES: Students in all disciplines

STUDENTS SEEK HELP WITH: Academic writing, which includes all but creative writing

PERCENTAGE OF STUDENTS SERVED: Less than 25%

OVER PAST FIVE YEARS THIS PERCENTAGE HAS: Decreased

STUDENTS USE CENTER: Throughout the semester on a walk-in basis or when assigned by professors

STUDENTS REQUIRED TO USE CENTER: All students are encouraged to use the center

MATERIALS AVAILABLE: Exercises, tapes, modules, and film strips

STUDENT ATTITUDE: Unknown

Peer Tutoring Program

PROGRAM HAS EXISTED: 3 years

ORGANIZATION: Based in composition courses

NUMBER OF TUTORS: 1-2

HOURS THEY WORK PER WEEK: 2

TUTORS PAID: Yes

TUTOR SELECTION: Selected by composition faculty

TUTORS' TRAINING: On-the-job and previous composition course

TUTORS' EVALUATION: Student questionnaire

PERCENTAGE OF STUDENTS SERVED: Approximately 4%

OVER PAST FIVE YEARS THIS PERCENTAGE HAS: Decreased

PROGRAM INTENDED TO SERVE: Students in freshman composition

PROGRAM ACTUALLY SERVES: Students in freshman composition

STUDENTS SEEK HELP WITH: Academic writing

MECHANICS OF TUTORING: Peer tutors work with content and mechanics in composition courses; students volunteer to work with tutor

STUDENT ATTITUDE: Mixed

Writing-Across-the-Curriculum Program

PROGRAM HAS EXISTED: 2-5 years

INSTRUCTORS INVOLVED: All faculty

INSTRUCTORS' SELECTION: All faculty participate

INSTRUCTORS' TRAINING: Workshops with consultants from other schools

PERCENTAGE OF FACULTY INVOLVED: 100%

IN PAST FIVE YEARS THIS PERCENTAGE HAS: Increased

STUDENTS INVOLVED IN PROGRAM: Students in all disciplines

PERCENTAGE OF STUDENTS INVOLVED: More than 75%

IN PAST FIVE YEARS THIS PERCENTAGE HAS: Increased

PARTICIPANTS' ATTITUDE: Very positive

During the past five years, Ottawa University experimented with a number of writing-across-the-curriculum programs before settling on the one currently in practice. Ina Reiter states, "We originally had concentrated on developing critical thinking skills in a cluster of general distribution courses." This method was difficult to "control or evaluate, so we decided to approach developing systematic thinking skills through writing (as a medium) in all courses." The resulting program involves all of the university's faculty, who participate in developmental workshops and discussions. Faculty then incorporate "a systematic thinking component into all general distribution courses" through "writing instructional strategies." The program is supplemented with an IAP grant that allows for four more years of development, during which Reiter hopes "to incorporate reasoning skills through writing into a full-fledged writing-across-the-curriculum program."

PENNSYLVANIA STATE UNIVERSITY

University Park, PA 16802

Full-time Students: 28,101M/18,719W Faculty: 3026

Respondent: Lewis Ulman, Composition Assistant

Writing Requirement: Required freshman English course and another required English course

Writing Center

CENTER HAS EXISTED: 5-10 years HOURS OPEN PER WEEK: 20-40

STAFF: 5-20 graduate and undergraduate tutors

TUTORS' TRAINING: On-the-job, academic, and non-academic training course

TUTORS' EVALUATION: Observation, conferences, and student questionnaires

TUTORS PAID: Yes

PROGRAM DESIGNED TO SERVE: Students in all disciplines

PROGRAM ACTUALLY SERVES: Students in all disciplines, primarily writing students

STUDENTS SEEK HELP WITH: Primarily academic essays, with occasional research papers, resumes or business writing

PERCENTAGE OF STUDENTS SERVED: Less than 25%

OVER PAST FIVE YEARS THIS PERCENTAGE HAS: Increased

STUDENTS USE CENTER: Throughout the semester on an appointment basis

STUDENTS REQUIRED TO USE CENTER: Problem writers

MATERIALS AVAILABLE: Handbooks, writing exercises, professional books, and computer-assisted instruction

STUDENT ATTITUDE: Very positive

Peer Tutoring Program

PROGRAM HAS EXISTED FOR: 2 years

ORGANIZATION: Writing center-based

NUMBER OF TUTORS: 15-20

HOURS THEY WORK PER WEEK: 5-10

TUTORS PAID: Yes, except for those enrolled in peer tutoring course

TUTOR SELECTION: Self-nominated and appointed by the director and the instructor of the peer tutoring course

TUTORS' TRAINING: Academic training course, which includes an internship at the writing center

TUTORS' EVALUATION: Observation, conferences, and student and faculty questionnaires

PERCENTAGE OF STUDENTS SERVED: Less than 25%

OVER PAST FIVE YEARS THIS PERCENTAGE HAS: Increased

PROGRAM INTENDED TO SERVE: Students in all disciplines, especially writing students and freshmen

PROGRAM ACTUALLY SERVES: Writing students and freshmen

STUDENTS SEEK HELP WITH: Academic essays; some research papers and resumes

MECHANICS OF TUTORING: Students discuss papers in conference with tutors; conferences by appointment or on a drop-in basis

STUDENT ATTITUDE: Very positive

Pennsylvania State University has made several changes in its writing program over the past ten years, including the addition of a second course to the composition requirement, and the introduction of both a writing center and a peer tutoring program. The writing center is staffed by five to twenty thoroughly trained tutors, many of whom are undergraduates. This program has received very positive response from students, but it serves primarily writing students and only a small percentage of Pennsylvania State's enormous student body. Therefore, the university must rely primarily on its required English courses (taught by faculty and seventy-five graduate students) to provide composition instruction.

PINE MANOR COLLEGE

Chestnut Hill, MA 02167

Full-time Students: 530W Faculty: 29

Respondent: Patricia Macvaugh, Director of Freshman Composition

Writing Requirement: 2-3 required freshman English courses

Writing Center

CENTER HAS EXISTED: 2-5 years HOURS OPEN PER WEEK: 68

STAFF: Fewer than 5 adjunct faculty

TUTORS' TRAINING: On-the-job

TUTORS' EVALUATION: Observation and conferences

TUTORS PAID: Yes

PROGRAM DESIGNED TO SERVE: Students in all disciplines

PROGRAM ACTUALLY SERVES: Students in all disciplines

STUDENTS SEEK HELP WITH: Scientific reports, creative writing, academic essays, research papers, and resumes or business writing

PERCENTAGE OF STUDENTS SERVED: 50%

STUDENTS USE CENTER: Throughout the semester on an appointment, workshop, or regular basis

STUDENTS REQUIRED TO USE CENTER: None

MATERIALS AVAILABLE: Handbooks, exercises, professional books, and educational magazines

STUDENT ATTITUDE: Very positive

Writing-Across-the-Curriculum Program

PROGRAM HAS EXISTED: 12 years

INSTRUCTORS INVOLVED: Faculty in all disciplines

INSTRUCTORS' SELECTION: Voluntary

INSTRUCTORS' TRAINING: Seminars

PERCENTAGE OF FACULTY INVOLVED: 35%

IN PAST FIVE YEARS THIS PERCENTAGE HAS: Stayed the same

STUDENTS INVOLVED IN PROGRAM: Students in all disciplines

PERCENTAGE OF STUDENTS INVOLVED: 100% of freshmen

IN PAST FIVE YEARS THIS PERCENTAGE HAS: Increased

PARTICIPANTS' ATTITUDE: Very positive

Pine Manor College's writing center has been unusually successful. Although no students are required to use the three-year-old center, 50 percent of all students elect to do so. As a result, the center is now open sixty-eight hours every week. Faculty response to the cross-curricular program has been as favorable as student response to the writing center. Over 25 percent of Pine Manor faculty in all disciplines volunteer to teach content-related sections of the required Freshman Composition course. After participating in training seminars, these faculty assign reading from the work of "historians, biologists, psychologists, journalists, literary artists, and sociologists, just to name a few," as Patricia Macvaugh reports. Pine Manor's Freshman Composition sections focus on both technical and rhetorical aspects of writing and are aimed at sharpening "critical thinking and writing skills." In addition to this interdisciplinary program, Pine Manor offers courses in practical, persuasive, creative, and journalistic writing.

PITZER COLLEGE

Claremont, CA 91711

Full-time Students: 317M/346W Faculty: 61

Respondent: William Pietz, Assistant Professor, History and Literature

Writing Requirement: None

Peer Tutoring Program

PROGRAM HAS EXISTED: Under 2 years

ORGANIZATION: Residentially based

NUMBER OF TUTORS: Fewer than 10

HOURS THEY WORK PER WEEK: Less than 5

TUTORS PAID: Yes

TUTOR SELECTION: Appointed by the director

TUTORS' TRAINING: Non-academic training course

TUTORS' EVALUATION: Conferences

PERCENTAGE OF STUDENTS SERVED: Less than 25%

OVER PAST FIVE YEARS THIS PERCENTAGE HAS: Increased

PROGRAM INTENDED TO SERVE: Students in all disciplines

STUDENTS SEEK HELP WITH: Academic essays

MECHANICS OF TUTORING: Student may choose to have tutor comment on or discuss a paper

STUDENT ATTITUDE: Unknown

Writing-Across-the-Curriculum Program

(Still in planning stages)

PROGRAM HAS EXISTED: Not yet in operation

INSTRUCTORS INVOLVED: Faculty in all disciplines

INSTRUCTORS' SELECTION: Voluntary

INSTRUCTORS' TRAINING: Seminars

PERCENTAGE OF FACULTY INVOLVED: Less than 25%

STUDENTS INVOLVED IN PROGRAM: Students in all disciplines

Pitzer College's small writing program has only recently started to expand. Students are offered two standard composition courses and one advanced course in writing and argument, but no writing courses are required. Pitzer recently introduced a residentially based peer tutoring program that assists any student seeking help with a writing problem. In order to provide additional writing instruction to students in all disciplines, the school is currently working on a writing-across-the-curriculum program that will offer seminars on the teaching of composition for faculty who volunteer for the program.

POLYTECHNIC INSTITUTE OF NEW YORK

Brooklyn, NY 11201

Full-time Students: 1836M/251W   Faculty: 220

Respondent: Duane DeVries, Administrative Officer

Writing Requirement: Freshman English and other English course

Writing-Across-the-Curriculum Program

PROGRAM HAS EXISTED: 3 years

INSTRUCTORS INVOLVED: Humanities faculty

INSTRUCTORS' SELECTION: Voluntary

INSTRUCTORS' TRAINING: Weekly staff meetings

PERCENTAGE OF FACULTY INVOLVED: 25%

IN PAST FIVE YEARS THIS PERCENTAGE HAS: Increased

STUDENTS INVOLVED IN PROGRAM: Students in all disciplines

PERCENTAGE OF STUDENTS INVOLVED: 50%

IN PAST FIVE YEARS THIS PERCENTAGE HAS: Increased

PARTICIPANTS' ATTITUDE: Very positive

Three years ago, the Polytechnic Institute of New York instituted a writing across-the-curriculum program that emphasizes writing in the humanities. Funded by a pilot grant from NEH, Writing and the Humanities combines expository writing instruction with humanities coursework. Students explore the relationship between content, style, and form through freewriting, drafting, editing, and keeping a writing journal. One of the course's more recent innovative assignments asked students to prepare a report to the NEH on the course. Writing and the Humanities is now being phased in as the standard freshman sequence. In addition to this program, the journalism and technical writing degree programs at the institute have been working well.

POMONA COLLEGE

Claremont, CA 91711

Full-time Students: 698M/678W Faculty: 132

Respondent: Thomas Pinney, Acting Chairperson, English Department

Writing Requirement: None

Peer Tutoring Program

PROGRAM HAS EXISTED: Over 10 years

ORGANIZATION: Curriculum-based

NUMBER OF TUTORS: 10–20

HOURS THEY WORK PER WEEK: Under 5

TUTORS PAID: Yes

TUTOR SELECTION: Nominated by English faculty

TUTORS' TRAINING: On-the-job and in workshops

TUTORS' EVALUATION: Observation and conferences

PERCENTAGE OF STUDENTS SERVED: Less than 25%

OVER PAST FIVE YEARS THIS PERCENTAGE HAS: Increased

PROGRAM INTENDED TO SERVE: Students in all disciplines

PROGRAM ACTUALLY SERVES: Students in all disciplines

STUDENTS SEEK HELP WITH: All types of writing

MECHANICS OF TUTORING: Student may choose to discuss any paper with a tutor

STUDENT ATTITUDE: Unknown

Pomona College's writing courses have worked well, but according to Thomas Pinney, too few students have enrolled in these courses since the college dropped its writing requirement. Pomona's peer tutoring program has been more successful, serving an increasing percentage of the college's students. In operation for over ten years, the program offers students in all disciplines assistance with all types of writing. Pomona's faculty recently voted to hire a specialist in remedial writing and to establish a program of writing-intensive courses in all departments, to be initiated in the 1985–86 school year. Two of these courses will be required of all students.

PROVIDENCE COLLEGE

Providence, RI 02918

Full-time Students: 1775M/1850W Faculty: 220

Respondent: Ellen Goodman, Chairperson, English Department

Writing Requirement: Required English courses; exemption by examination or AP

Writing Center

CENTER HAS EXISTED: Over 2 years HOURS OPEN PER WEEK: 20-40

STAFF: 10-12 undergraduate tutors

TUTORS' TRAINING: On-the-job

TUTORS' EVALUATION: Observation and conferences

TUTORS PAID: Yes

PROGRAM DESIGNED TO SERVE: Students in all disciplines, especially writing students

PROGRAM ACTUALLY SERVES: Students in all disciplines, especially writing students

STUDENTS SEEK HELP WITH: Academic essays

STUDENTS USE CENTER: Throughout the semester on an appointment or regular basis

STUDENTS REQUIRED TO USE CENTER: None

MATERIALS AVAILABLE: Handbooks and exercises

STUDENT ATTITUDE: Unknown

Providence College is currently experimenting with several different approaches to writing, including a writing program for athletes, a peer tutoring program, and a writing program that is part of a more general Learning Resource Center. The college also offers its students computer-assisted instruction and may soon establish a writing-across the curriculum program. More traditional writing offerings include courses in creative writing, composition, journalism, and scientific writing. Ellen Goodman believes that the different writing programs need to be centralized, a change that will take effect in the near future.

PURDUE UNIVERSITY

West Lafayette, IN 47906

Full-time Students: 15,513M/10,950W Faculty: 1800

Respondent: Irwin Weiser, Acting Director of Composition

Writing Requirement: Required freshman English course

Writing Center

CENTER HAS EXISTED: 5-10 years HOURS OPEN PER WEEK: Over 40

STAFF: 1 faculty, 10 graduate, and 15 undergraduate tutors

TUTORS' TRAINING: On-the-job for graduate tutors and academic training course for undergraduate tutors

TUTORS' EVALUATION: Observation and student questionnaires

TUTORS PAID: Yes

PROGRAM DESIGNED TO SERVE: Students in all disciplines

PROGRAM ACTUALLY SERVES: Students in all disciplines

STUDENTS SEEK HELP WITH: Scientific reports, creative writing, academic essays, research papers, and resumes or business writing

PERCENTAGE OF STUDENTS SERVED: 25-50%

OVER PAST FIVE YEARS THIS PERCENTAGE HAS: Increased

STUDENTS USE CENTER: Throughout the semester on a walk-in basis

STUDENTS REQUIRED TO USE CENTER: Students in the Developmental Writing course (about 350 students)

MATERIALS AVAILABLE: Handbooks, writing exercises, professional books, audio-tutorial tapes, handouts, and educational magazines

STUDENT ATTITUDE: Very positive

Peer Tutoring Program

PROGRAM HAS EXISTED: Under 2 years

ORGANIZATION: Writing center-based

NUMBER OF TUTORS: Approximately 15

HOURS THEY WORK PER WEEK: 5–10

TUTORS PAID: Some are paid; others receive course credit

TUTOR SELECTION: Appointed by the director after application

TUTORS' TRAINING: Academic training course

TUTORS' EVALUATION: Observation

PERCENTAGE OF STUDENTS SERVED: Less than 25%

PROGRAM INTENDED TO SERVE: Freshmen in developmental writing course

PROGRAM ACTUALLY SERVES: Freshmen in developmental writing course

STUDENTS SEEK HELP WITH: Grammar and mechanics

MECHANICS OF TUTORING: Tutors evaluate and discuss exercises with students

STUDENT ATTITUDE: Somewhat negative

Throughout Purdue University's writing program, faculty have increased the emphasis on the process approach to writing. Instructors and tutors are now more concerned with invention and revision, and less dependent on professional models. All of Purdue's students may use the writing center, which stays open for over forty hours each week and serves students on a walk-in basis. While ten graduate tutors and numerous books, tapes, and handouts are available to all students, the center's peer tutors help only students enrolled in the Developmental Writing course with grammar and mechanics problems. Within the writing curriculum, the small number of faculty who teach only writing are responsible for the extremely successful and popular upper-level Business and Technical Writing courses. The less popular but still effective freshman composition courses are taught by 140 graduate writing instructors. The English Department is currently exploring a more integrated writing-across-the-curriculum approach for the near future.

RAMAPO COLLEGE

Mahwah, NJ 07430

Full-time Students: 1383M/1230W Faculty: 147

Respondent: Donald Fucci, Director, Division of Basic Studies

Writing Requirement: 1-3 writing courses; placement by examination

Writing Center and Peer Tutoring Program

CENTER HAS EXISTED: 5 years HOURS OPEN PER WEEK: Over 40

STAFF: 1 Developmental Educational Specialist and 8-10 undergraduate tutors

TUTOR SELECTION: Appointed by director or discipline coordinator after application and interview

TUTORS' TRAINING: On-the-job, non-academic course, and training sessions

TUTORS' EVALUATION: Observation and conferences with discipline coordinator

TUTORS PAID: Yes

HOURS THEY WORK PER WEEK: 15

PROGRAM DESIGNED TO SERVE: Students in all disciplines

PROGRAM ACTUALLY SERVES: Students in all disciplines, especially freshmen and writing students

STUDENTS SEEK HELP WITH: Scientific reports, academic essays, research papers, and resumes or business writing

PERCENTAGE OF STUDENTS SERVED: 25-50%

OVER PAST FIVE YEARS THIS PERCENTAGE HAS: Increased

STUDENTS USE CENTER: Throughout the semester on an appointment basis

STUDENTS REQUIRED TO USE CENTER: Remedial students

MATERIALS AVAILABLE: Handbooks, exercises, professional books, and educational magazines

MECHANICS OF TUTORING: Tutor and student discuss papers individually

STUDENT ATTITUDE: Very positive

Writing-Across-the-Curriculum Program

PROGRAM HAS EXISTED: More than 10 years

INSTRUCTORS INVOLVED: Faculty in all disciplines

INSTRUCTORS' SELECTION: Voluntary

INSTRUCTORS' TRAINING: Summer seminars

PERCENTAGE OF FACULTY INVOLVED: 25%

IN PAST FIVE YEARS THIS PERCENTAGE HAS: Stayed the same

STUDENTS INVOLVED IN PROGRAM: Students needing writing courses

PERCENTAGE OF STUDENTS INVOLVED: 25%

IN PAST FIVE YEARS THIS PERCENTAGE HAS: Stayed the same

PARTICIPANTS' ATTITUDE: Very positive

Since its founding in 1969, Ramapo College has demonstrated a strong commitment to writing instruction college-wide. Its writing-across-the-curriculum program is over ten years old and involves faculty in all disciplines. Five years ago, Ramapo established a writing center as part of an Academic Skills Center that addresses students' needs in reading, writing, and mathematics. Between five and ten full-time faculty members teach exclusively writing courses, from remedial to advanced level. Business writing instruction has been particularly successful. Ramapo's plans for the future include restructuring the developmental reading/writing courses and encouraging more professors from disciplines outside of English to teach writing courses.

RANDOLPH-MACON COLLEGE

Ashland, VA 23005

Full-time Students: 542M/367W Faculty: 60

Respondent: Theodore F. Sheckels, Assistant Professor of English

Writing Requirement: Required freshman English course

Writing Center and Peer Tutoring Program

CENTER HAS EXISTED: 5-10 years HOURS OPEN PER WEEK: 10-20

STAFF: A faculty member and a few undergraduate tutors

TUTOR SELECTION: Appointed by director

HOURS THEY WORK PER WEEK: Under 5 hours

TUTORS' TRAINING: On-the-job

TUTORS' EVALUATION: Observation and conferences

TUTORS PAID: Yes

PROGRAM DESIGNED TO SERVE: Students in all disciplines

PROGRAM ACTUALLY SERVES: Students in all disciplines, especially freshmen composition students and humanities underclassmen

STUDENTS SEEK HELP WITH: Academic essays and research papers

PERCENTAGE OF STUDENTS SERVED: Less than 25%

OVER PAST FIVE YEARS THIS PERCENTAGE HAS: Increased

STUDENTS USE CENTER: Repeatedly throughout the semester on a walk-in or appointment basis

MECHANICS OF TUTORING: Student may choose to discuss drafts or specific writing problems with tutor

STUDENTS REQUIRED TO USE CENTER: None

MATERIALS AVAILABLE: Handbooks, exercises, computer programs, and cassettes

STUDENT ATTITUDE: Positive

Writing-Across-the-Curriculum Program

PROGRAM HAS EXISTED: 2-5 years

INSTRUCTORS INVOLVED: English faculty

INSTRUCTORS' SELECTION: Voluntary

INSTRUCTORS' TRAINING: None

PERCENTAGE OF FACULTY INVOLVED: Less than 25%

IN PAST FIVE YEARS THIS PERCENTAGE HAS: Stayed the same

STUDENTS INVOLVED IN PROGRAM: Students in all disciplines

PERCENTAGE OF STUDENTS INVOLVED: Less than 25%

IN PAST FIVE YEARS THIS PERCENTAGE HAS: Stayed the same

PARTICIPANTS' ATTITUDE: Positive

Over the past few years, Randolph-Macon College has considered different types of writing programs. According to Theodore Sheckels, a cross-curricular freshman program was not attempted because of the English Department's "lack of total enthusiasm for the approach." The proposed writing requirement for freshmen and juniors with a cross-curricular component was finally abandoned "because of the inability to staff the required extra courses." The English Department then developed a cross-curricular writing minor, which features writing courses serving the needs of science, social science, and business majors. This minor and a traditional freshman composition course sequence promise to help upgrade student writing. During the next few years, Sheckels plans to expand the writing minor so that more students from other majors will elect courses in that program. Thus he hopes to establish a "de facto" junior writing requirement.

REED COLLEGE

Portland, OR 97207

Full-time Students: 3380M/2904W Faculty: 477

Respondent: Gail Berkeley, Assistant Professor, English and Humanities

Writing Requirement: Required freshman humanities course and senior thesis

Writing Center

CENTER HAS EXISTED: 2 years HOURS OPEN PER WEEK: 5

STAFF: 10–12 undergraduate tutors

TUTORS' TRAINING: On-the-job

TUTORS' EVALUATION: Observation and student questionnaires

TUTORS PAID: Yes

PROGRAM DESIGNED TO SERVE: Students in all disciplines, especially freshmen

PROGRAM ACTUALLY SERVES: Students in all disciplines, especially freshmen

STUDENTS SEEK HELP WITH: Academic essays

PERCENTAGE OF STUDENTS SERVED: 25–50% of freshman class

STUDENTS USE CENTER: Throughout the semester on a walk-in or appointment basis

STUDENTS REQUIRED TO USE CENTER: A few required by individual professors

MATERIALS AVAILABLE: Handbooks and exercises

STUDENT ATTITUDE: Unknown

Peer Tutoring Program

PROGRAM HAS EXISTED: 5–10 years

ORGANIZATION: Located in the writing center and funded through the Dean's office

NUMBER OF TUTORS: Fewer than 10

HOURS THEY WORK PER WEEK: Under 5

TUTORS PAID: Yes

TUTOR SELECTION: Self-nominated and nominated by the English faculty

TUTORS' TRAINING: No formal training

TUTORS' EVALUATION: None

PERCENTAGE OF STUDENTS SERVED: 10%

OVER PAST FIVE YEARS THIS PERCENTAGE HAS: Stayed the same

PROGRAM INTENDED TO SERVE: Students in all disciplines

PROGRAM ACTUALLY SERVES: Few students--most use writing center instead

STUDENTS SEEK HELP WITH: Academic essays

MECHANICS OF TUTORING: Tutors make long-term commitment to help individual students with their academic work

STUDENT ATTITUDE: Very positive

The most significant change in Reed College's writing program in recent years was the addition of the writing center in 1982. Although it is open only five hours each week, the center is quite successful and serves 25 to 50 percent of the freshman class. The undergraduate tutors who work at the center also train other students in Peer Editing Groups. These small groups of students work informally with other students on editing, revising, and composition skills. The peer tutors who work out of the writing center make a long-term commitment to work with individual students on academic skills. Reed previously operated Dormitory Writing Groups, but this program was recently discontinued. Now, most students seek help with their writing through the writing center.

RENSSELAER POLYTECHNIC INSTITUTE

Troy, NY 12181

Full-time Students: 3503M/831W Faculty: 353

Respondent: Karen Burke LeFevre, Director, Writing Center

Writing Requirement: None

Writing Center

CENTER HAS EXISTED: 5-10 years HOURS OPEN PER WEEK: 36-40

STAFF: 1-2 adjunct faculty and 2 graduate tutors

TUTORS' TRAINING: On-the-job and academic course

TUTORS' EVALUATION: Observation and student questionnaires

TUTORS PAID: Yes

PROGRAM DESIGNED TO SERVE: Students in all disciplines

PROGRAM ACTUALLY SERVES: Students in all disciplines

STUDENTS SEEK HELP WITH: Scientific reports, creative writing, academic essays, research papers, and resumes or business writing

PERCENTAGE OF STUDENTS SERVED: Less than 25%

OVER PAST FIVE YEARS THIS PERCENTAGE HAS: Increased

STUDENTS USE CENTER: Throughout the semester on a walk-in basis

STUDENTS REQUIRED TO USE CENTER: None

MATERIALS AVAILABLE: Handbooks, exercises, professional books, and a computer resume program

STUDENT ATTITUDE: Unknown

Rensselaer Polytechnic Institute's Writing Center is an active and successful program. Attracting between 1500 and 2000 visits per year, the Center serves the entire university community, including faculty, staff, and many international graduate students. Among the Center's innovative approaches are its computer program that guides students in writing resumes; its occasional writing workshops, and its tutoring program. The tutors are graduate assistants who work in selected engineering courses as writing adjuncts. Karen Burke LeFevre predicts that in the future the Center will "reach more individual students, .

. . become a center for research in writing as well as a teaching center, and . . . possibly assist faculty to a greater extent with their writing." Aside from its Writing Center, RPI also offers M.A. and Ph.D. programs in Technical Writing, Communication, and Rhetoric.

ROCHESTER INSTITUTE OF TECHNOLOGY

Rochester, NY 14623

Full-time Students: 3503M/831W Faculty: 650

Respondent: Joseph Nassar, Writing Coordinator and Chairperson, Language Faculty

Writing Requirement: Required freshman English courses and third-year competency examination

Writing Center

CENTER HAS EXISTED: Over 10 years HOURS OPEN PER WEEK: 20-40

STAFF: 5 faculty and fewer than 5 undergraduate tutors

TUTORS' TRAINING: Non-academic training course

TUTORS' EVALUATION: Observation, student questionnaire, and conferences

TUTORS PAID: Yes

PROGRAM DESIGNED TO SERVE: Students in all disciplines, especially writing students

PROGRAM ACTUALLY SERVES: Students in all disciplines, especially writing students

STUDENTS SEEK HELP WITH: Scientific and technical reports, academic essays, research papers, creative writing, and resumes or business writing

PERCENTAGE OF STUDENTS SERVED: 15-20%

OVER PAST FIVE YEARS THIS PERCENTAGE HAS: Increased

STUDENTS USE CENTER: Repeatedly throughout the quarter on a walk-in basis

STUDENTS REQUIRED TO USE CENTER: None

MATERIALS AVAILABLE: Handbooks, exercises, magazines, and professional books

STUDENT ATTITUDE: Very positive

Peer Tutoring Program

PROGRAM HAS EXISTED: Over 10 years

ORGANIZATION: Writing Center-based

NUMBER OF TUTORS: 5

HOURS THEY WORK PER WEEK: Under 5

TUTORS PAID: Yes

TUTORS' SELECTION: Nominated college-wide and self-nominated

TUTORS' TRAINING: Non-academic training course

TUTORS' EVALUATION: Observation, student questionnaire, and conferences

PERCENTAGE OF STUDENTS SERVED: 2%

OVER PAST FIVE YEARS THIS PERCENTAGE HAS: Increased

PROGRAM INTENDED TO SERVE: Students in all disciplines

PROGRAM ACTUALLY SERVES: Students in all disciplines

STUDENTS SEEK HELP WITH: Scientific and technical reports, academic essays, and research papers

MECHANICS OF TUTORING: Students may choose to discuss papers with tutor

STUDENT ATTITUDE: Very positive

Rochester Institute of Technology has long attended to writing skills; today it continues to review and revise writing programs to meet students' needs. Like many schools across the country, the institute has begun to focus on the process of writing rather than emphasizing the written product. And according to Joseph Nassar, RIT has required greater writing competency over the past few years. Most of its programs are well-established; both the writing center and the peer tutoring program have existed over ten years. The undergraduate peer writing tutors are part of a larger peer tutoring program, and the writing center is well-equipped. The writing center and the current English composition course are successful because they "identify and respond to student needs," according to Joseph Nassar. While RIT operates longstanding programs, it is also considering innovations like computer-assisted instruction and word processing.

ROOSEVELT UNIVERSITY

Chicago, IL 60605

Full-time Students: 740M/995W Faculty: 420

Respondent: Priscilla Davidson, Director of Composition

Writing Requirement: Required freshman English course, qualifying examination for transfers

Writing Center

CENTER HAS EXISTED: 5-10 years HOURS OPEN PER WEEK: 20-40

STAFF: 5-10 faculty, graduate, and undergraduate tutors

TUTORS' TRAINING: On-the-job; academic course for some

TUTORS' EVALUATION: Observation, conferences, and by writing center director

TUTORS PAID: Yes

PROGRAM DESIGNED TO SERVE: Students in all disciplines

PROGRAM ACTUALLY SERVES: Students in all disciplines

STUDENTS SEEK HELP WITH: Scientific reports, creative writing, academic essays, research papers, and resumes or business writing

PERCENTAGE OF STUDENTS SERVED: 25-50%

OVER PAST FIVE YEARS THIS PERCENTAGE HAS: Increased

STUDENTS USE CENTER: Throughout the semester on an appointment basis

STUDENTS REQUIRED TO USE CENTER: Some problem writers

MATERIALS AVAILABLE: Handbooks, exercises, and professional books

STUDENT ATTITUDE: Positive

Writing-Across-the-Curriculum Program

PROGRAM HAS EXISTED: 5 years

INSTRUCTORS INVOLVED: Faculty in all disciplines

INSTRUCTORS' SELECTION: By appointment

INSTRUCTORS' TRAINING: None

PERCENTAGE OF FACULTY INVOLVED: 1%

IN PAST FIVE YEARS THIS PERCENTAGE HAS: Decreased

STUDENTS INVOLVED IN PROGRAM: Students in various disciplines, depending on where writing intensive courses are offered

PERCENTAGE OF STUDENTS INVOLVED: Approximately 5%

PARTICIPANTS' ATTITUDE: Positive

Since participating in the University of Iowa Institute on Writing several years ago, Roosevelt University has updated many of its principles and pedagogies. The university has improved course designs, restructured staff training programs, and established the University Writing Committee, a board that makes recommendations for cross-curricular writing activities. In an effort to keep its services up-to-date, this board constantly evaluates its programs and makes changes when needed. Perhaps because of such flexibility, Roosevelt's writing faculty have generally been satisfied with programs such as the two-semester freshman composition program, and with the remedial and advanced writing programs. Roosevelt's Writing Lab has been equally successful, serving 25-50 percent of students in all disciplines, who seek help from the center voluntarily. The Writing Lab houses a collection of over 500 workbooks, reference works, and pedagogical materials on the teaching of college writing. Slightly less successful is the writing-across-the-curriculum program, which has suffered from lack of faculty involvement.

RUTGERS UNIVERSITY/COOK COLLEGE

New Brunswick, NJ 08903

Full-time Students: 1425M/1253W Faculty: 122

Respondent: Barbara M. Goff, Assistant Dean of Instruction and Director of Composition, Department of Humanities and Communication

Writing Requirement: 2 courses in writing or public speaking

Writing Center

CENTER HAS EXISTED: 5-10 years HOURS OPEN PER WEEK: 20-40

STAFF: 1 faculty administrator, 20 undergraduate tutors, and several part-time professionals

TUTORS' TRAINING: On-the-job and academic course

TUTORS PAID: No

PROGRAM DESIGNED TO SERVE: Students in all disciplines, including graduate students

PROGRAM ACTUALLY SERVES: Students in all disciplines, including graduate students

STUDENTS SEEK HELP WITH: Scientific reports, creative writing, academic essays, research papers, and essays for professional schools

PERCENTAGE OF STUDENTS SERVED: Less than 25%

OVER PAST FIVE YEARS THIS PERCENTAGE HAS: Stayed the same

STUDENTS USE CENTER: Throughout the semester on a walk-in or regular basis

STUDENTS REQUIRED TO USE CENTER: Problem writers

MATERIALS AVAILABLE: Handbooks, exercises, and professional books for tutor use

STUDENT ATTITUDE: Neutral to somewhat negative

Peer Tutoring Program

PROGRAM HAS EXISTED: 5-10 years

ORGANIZATION: Writing center-based

NUMBER OF TUTORS: 20

HOURS THEY WORK PER WEEK: Under 5

TUTORS PAID: No

TUTOR SELECTION: Nominated by themselves, English faculty, and faculty college-wide, then appointed by the director

TUTORS' TRAINING: On-the-job and academic course

PERCENTAGE OF STUDENTS SERVED: Less than 25%

OVER PAST FIVE YEARS THIS PERCENTAGE HAS: Stayed the same

PROGRAM INTENDED TO SERVE: Students in all disciplines, especially writing students and freshmen

PROGRAM ACTUALLY SERVES: Students in all disciplines, especially writing students, freshmen, and foreign students

STUDENTS SEEK HELP WITH: Scientific reports, academic essays, creative writing, research papers, and essays for professional schools

MECHANICS OF TUTORING: Student may choose to discuss with tutor any paper except those for composition courses

STUDENT ATTITUDE: Neutral to somewhat negative

Writing-Across-the-Curriculum Program

PROGRAM HAS EXISTED: Over 10 years

INSTRUCTORS INVOLVED: Graduate students

INSTRUCTORS' SELECTION: By appointment

INSTRUCTORS' TRAINING: Seminars

PERCENTAGE OF FACULTY INVOLVED: Less than 25%

IN PAST FIVE YEARS THIS PERCENTAGE HAS: Stayed the same

STUDENTS INVOLVED IN PROGRAM: Students in all disciplines

PERCENTAGE OF STUDENTS INVOLVED: More than 75%

IN PAST FIVE YEARS THIS PERCENTAGE HAS: Stayed the same

PARTICIPANTS' ATTITUDE: Somewhat positive

The programs at Cook College, the former agriculture school of Rutgers University, "are exclusively those in agriculture, the environment, the life sciences, and human ecology," according to Barbara Goff. She reports that the school's writing-across-the-curriculum emphasis is "threatened by the 'liberal-arts' orientation of Rutger's other undergraduate colleges and the English Department's desire to standardize the courses at all colleges." If students are having particular difficulties in grammar or essay writing, they must register for a supplementary tutorial mini-course offered at the Writing Center. Students have reacted less than favorably to the writing center and these tutorials because they resent the extra work.

RUTGERS UNIVERSITY/ RUTGERS COLLEGE

New Brunswick, N.J. 08903

Full-time Students: 4298M/3812W Faculty: 492

Respondent: George Kearns, Director of Expository Writing, English Department

Writing Requirement: Required freshmen English courses

Writing Center

CENTER HAS EXISTED: 5-10 years HOURS OPEN PER WEEK: 20-40

STAFF: Over 40 graduate tutors and a few undergraduate tutors

TUTORS' TRAINING: On-the-job

TUTORS' EVALUATION: Observation and conferences

TUTORS PAID: Yes

PROGRAM DESIGNED TO SERVE: Freshmen and students in all disciplines, especially writing students

PROGRAM ACTUALLY SERVES: Freshmen and students in all disciplines, especially writing students

STUDENTS SEEK HELP WITH: Academic essays

PERCENTAGE OF STUDENTS SERVED: Less than 25%

OVER PAST FIVE YEARS THIS PERCENTAGE HAS: Increased

STUDENTS USE CENTER: Throughout semester on an appointment or regular basis

STUDENTS REQUIRED TO USE CENTER: None; some students strongly encouraged

MATERIALS AVAILABLE: Exercises

STUDENT ATTITUDE: Very positive

Over the past few years, Rutgers College has pulled its writing program together, developing closer supervision over student writing and creating a common syllabus and goals for composition instructors. Writing courses at the college are now more demanding and stress expository writing because as George Kearns says, "Personal experience or opinions writing classes work less well and allow instructors to pass along problem writers." In the future Rutgers will continue to tighten its standards and the English Department plans to continue revising its curriculum of writing courses.

ST. JOHN'S UNIVERSITY

Collegeville, MN 56321

Full-time Students: 1807M Faculty: 93

Respondent: Dr. Janet McNew, Director of Colloquium, Assistant Professor of English

Writing Requirement: Freshman cross-disciplinary colloquium

Writing Center

CENTER HAS EXISTED: 2-5 years HOURS OPEN PER WEEK: 40

STAFF: 5-20 undergraduate tutors

TUTORS' TRAINING: On-the-job and academic or non-academic course

TUTORS' EVALUATION: Observation, conferences, student questionnaires, and by other tutors

TUTORS PAID: Some are; others receive credit

PROGRAM DESIGNED TO SERVE: Students in all disciplines, faculty, and graduate students

PROGRAM ACTUALLY SERVES: Students in all disciplines, faculty and graduate students

STUDENTS SEEK HELP WITH: Academic essays, research papers, some resumes or business writing, and some faculty research and journal articles

PERCENTAGE OF STUDENTS SERVED: 10-15%

OVER PAST FIVE YEARS THIS PERCENTAGE HAS: Stayed the same

STUDENTS USE CENTER: Throughout the semester on an appointment basis

STUDENTS REQUIRED TO USE CENTER: None

MATERIALS AVAILABLE: Handbooks, exercises, educational magazines, professional books, and specific topic handouts

STUDENT ATTITUDE: Very positive

Peer Tutoring Program

PROGRAM HAS EXISTED: 5-10 years

ORGANIZATION: Curriculum-based

NUMBER OF TUTORS: 20-50 in areas other than writing; 5 writing tutors

HOURS THEY WORK PER WEEK: 10

TUTORS PAID: Yes

TUTOR SELECTION: Self-nominated

TUTORS' TRAINING: Academic course

TUTORS' EVALUATION: Student questionnaire

PROGRAM INTENDED TO SERVE: Students in all disciplines

PROGRAM ACTUALLY SERVES: Students in all disciplines

STUDENTS SEEK HELP WITH: Academic essays and research papers

MECHANICS OF TUTORING: Tutor and student are required to discuss papers

STUDENT ATTITUDE: Very positive

Writing-Across-the-Curriculum Program

PROGRAM HAS EXISTED: 9 years

INSTRUCTORS INVOLVED: Faculty in all disciplines

INSTRUCTORS' SELECTION: Voluntary

INSTRUCTORS' TRAINING: Week-long summer seminars and three seminars during the academic year

PERCENTAGE OF FACULTY INVOLVED: 21%

IN PAST FIVE YEARS THIS PERCENTAGE HAS: Stayed the same

STUDENTS INVOLVED IN PROGRAM: Students in all disciplines

PERCENTAGE OF STUDENTS INVOLVED: 100% of freshmen

IN PAST FIVE YEARS THIS PERCENTAGE HAS: Stayed the same

PARTICIPANTS' ATTITUDE: Somewhat positive

The writing requirement for graduation at St. John's University is a cross-disciplinary course. This emphasis on writing across the curriculum has been in practice at the university for over five years, affecting almost all students. Janet McNew believes that "purely 'expository' writing" has been less successful in promoting good prose than the broader requirement now in practice, including areas such as "liberal studies and critical reading, writing, and discussion skills combined." In addition to this program, a writing center was established a few years ago. At least a third of those who use the center are freshmen and a number are English and writing students, but the center is designed to serve all faculty and students.

ST. JOSEPH'S UNIVERSITY

Philadelphia, PA 19131

Full-time Students: 1274M/1056W Faculty: 173

Respondent: Robert Dunn, Associate Professor of English

Writing Requirement: Required composition course

Peer Tutoring Program

PROGRAM HAS EXISTED: 5–10 years

ORGANIZATION: Academic Support Service

NUMBER OF TUTORS: 7

HOURS THEY WORK PER WEEK: 3

TUTORS PAID: Yes

TUTOR SELECTION: Self-nominated and supported by faculty recommendation

TUTORS' TRAINING: 5-hour training session, then on-the-job

TUTORS' EVALUATION: Observation by tutoring coordinator

PERCENTAGE OF STUDENTS SERVED: 1–2%

OVER PAST FIVE YEARS THIS PERCENTAGE HAS: Increased

PROGRAM INTENDED TO SERVE: Students in all disciplines

PROGRAM ACTUALLY SERVES: Primarily freshmen

STUDENTS SEEK HELP WITH: Academic essays, research papers, and creative writing

MECHANICS OF TUTORING: Student may choose to discuss any paper with tutor; tutor does not comment in writing

STUDENT ATTITUDE: Very positive

Robert Dunn claims that St. Joseph's University "does not have a writing 'program,' but there is much writing across the curriculum as a consequence of faculty workshops." This past fall, the university began a two-year NEH project to introduce more expository writing into its General Education Requirements (GER). In the workshops connected to this project, faculty "design expository writing assignments that will encourage students to integrate their learning in each GER course and, whenever possible, to make cognitive connections between and among studies in the required curriculum." Dunn hopes to improve students' analytical, integrative, and composing skills through this project.

ST. MARY'S COLLEGE

Notre Dame, IN 46556

Full-time Students: 17M/1802W Faculty: 117

Respondent: Ann Kimble Loux, Director, Writing Proficiency Program

Writing Requirement: Certification of proficiency in writing

Writing Center

CENTER HAS EXISTED: 5–10 years HOURS OPEN PER WEEK: 10–20

STAFF: 5–20 undergraduate tutors

TUTORS' TRAINING: On-the-job and non-academic course

TUTORS' EVALUATION: Observation, conferences, and student questionnaires

TUTORS PAID: Yes

PROGRAM DESIGNED TO SERVE: Students in all disciplines

PROGRAM ACTUALLY SERVES: Students in all disciplines

STUDENTS SEEK HELP WITH: Academic essays

PERCENTAGE OF STUDENTS SERVED: Less than 25%

OVER PAST FIVE YEARS THIS PERCENTAGE HAS: Stayed the same

STUDENTS USE CENTER: Throughout the semester on a walk-in or appointment basis

STUDENTS REQUIRED TO USE CENTER: None

MATERIALS AVAILABLE: Handbooks and exercises

STUDENT ATTITUDE: Somewhat positive

Peer Tutoring Program

PROGRAM HAS EXISTED: 2–5 years

ORGANIZATION: Curriculum-based

NUMBER OF TUTORS: Fewer than 10

HOURS THEY WORK PER WEEK: 5–10

TUTORS PAID: Yes

TUTOR SELECTION: Nominated college-wide and appointed by director

TUTORS' TRAINING: On-the-job and non-academic course

TUTORS' EVALUATION: Observation and student questionnaire

PERCENTAGE OF STUDENTS SERVED: Less than 25%

OVER PAST FIVE YEARS THIS PERCENTAGE HAS: Stayed the same

PROGRAM INTENDED TO SERVE: Students in all disciplines

PROGRAM ACTUALLY SERVES: Students in all disciplines

STUDENTS SEEK HELP WITH: Academic essays

MECHANICS OF TUTORING: Tutor comments in writing on all papers; student may choose to discuss any paper with tutor

STUDENT ATTITUDE: Somewhat positive

Writing-Across-the-Curriculum Program

PROGRAM HAS EXISTED: 5-10 years

INSTRUCTORS INVOLVED: Faculty in all disciplines

INSTRUCTORS' SELECTION: Voluntary

INSTRUCTORS' TRAINING: Seminars and team teaching

PERCENTAGE OF FACULTY INVOLVED: 25-50%

IN PAST FIVE YEARS THIS PERCENTAGE HAS: Increased

STUDENTS INVOLVED IN PROGRAM: Students in all disciplines

PERCENTAGE OF STUDENTS INVOLVED: More than 75%

IN PAST FIVE YEARS THIS PERCENTAGE HAS: Increased

PARTICIPANTS' ATTITUDE: Very positive

Over the past five years, the writing-across-the-curriculum program at St. Mary's College has grown, demonstrating the increasing trend toward more collaboration between departments at the college. In particular, tandems, or team-taught courses in writing and two thematically linked disciplines, have been successful. During the next few years, Anne Kimble Loux hopes to strengthen and add to the current writing programs.

ST. OLAF COLLEGE

Northfield, MN 55057

Full-time Students: 1310M/1565W Faculty: 222

Respondent: Lowell E. Johnson, Chairperson, English Department

Writing Requirement: Required freshman English course; a cross-disciplinary writing component taken after freshman English

Writing Center and Peer Tutoring Program

CENTER HAS EXISTED: 7 years HOURS OPEN PER WEEK: 22

STAFF: 15 faculty and undergraduate tutors

TUTORS' TRAINING: On-the-job, academic course, non-academic course, and tutors' handbook

TUTOR SELECTION: Nominated by themselves, the English faculty and college-wide; then interviewed and appointed by the director

TUTORS' EVALUATION: Observation, conferences, and student questionnaires

TUTORS PAID: Yes

PROGRAM DESIGNED TO SERVE: Students in all disciplines

PROGRAM ACTUALLY SERVES: Students in all disciplines, primarily freshmen

STUDENTS SEEK HELP WITH: Academic essays and research papers

PERCENTAGE OF STUDENTS SERVED: 15%

OVER PAST FIVE YEARS THIS PERCENTAGE HAS: Increased

STUDENTS USE CENTER: Repeatedly throughout the semester on a walk-in or appointment basis

STUDENTS REQUIRED TO USE CENTER: None

MATERIALS AVAILABLE: Handbooks, exercises, professional books, and educational magazines

STUDENT ATTITUDE: Very positive

Writing-Across-the-Curriculum Program

PROGRAM HAS EXISTED: 7 years

INSTRUCTORS INVOLVED: Faculty in all disciplines

INSTRUCTORS' SELECTION: Voluntary

INSTRUCTORS' TRAINING: Seminars

PERCENTAGE OF FACULTY INVOLVED: 33%

IN PAST FIVE YEARS THIS PERCENTAGE HAS: Increased slightly

STUDENTS INVOLVED IN PROGRAM: Students in all disciplines

PERCENTAGE OF STUDENTS INVOLVED: 100%

IN PAST FIVE YEARS THIS PERCENTAGE HAS: Stayed the same

PARTICIPANTS' ATTITUDE: Very positive to somewhat positive

St. Olaf College instituted several programs and curricular changes to improve student writing in the late 1970's. In addition to the one-semester required course in Freshman English, several new writing courses were added to the curriculum and the number of expository writing classes increased. In 1977, St. Olaf developed the "Advanced Writing Component" (AWC) program, which currently involves all the students at St. Olaf and nearly one-third of the faculty from all disciplines. The faculty attend a series of meetings, short workshops, and a week-long summer writing workshop currently run by the director of the Writing Program. All students are required to complete an AWC course for graduation. The AWC requires students to write three 1,000 word essays that instructors not only evaluate for form and content, but also discuss in classes. Lowell Johnson encourages "greater emphasis on teachers planning sequences of writing together and on teaching the process of writing." He notes that the amount of writing required of students throughout the college has increased dramatically and that students are writing better as a result. St. Olaf receives external and institutional grants to support the Writing Place, the Academic Support Center, cross-disciplinary writing programs, research projects on writing, teaching released time, funding for Director of the Writing Program, and summer workshops.

SALEM STATE COLLEGE

Salem, MA 01970

Full-time Students: 2078M/3205W   Faculty: 297

Respondent: Frank Devlin, Associate Professor of English

Writing Requirement: Two-semester required freshman English course

Writing Center

CENTER HAS EXISTED: 8 years   HOURS OPEN PER WEEK: 35-40

STAFF: Faculty and 13-15 undergraduate tutors

TUTORS' TRAINING: On-the-job and academic course

TUTORS' EVALUATION: Observation, conferences, and tutoring reports

TUTORS PAID: Yes

PROGRAM DESIGNED TO SERVE: Students in all disciplines

PROGRAM ACTUALLY SERVES: Primarily freshmen composition students, with some students in all disciplines

STUDENTS SEEK HELP WITH: Academic essays, research papers, scientific reports, creative writing, and resumes or business writing

PERCENTAGE OF STUDENTS SERVED: Less than 15%

OVER PAST FIVE YEARS THIS PERCENTAGE HAS: Stayed the same

STUDENTS USE CENTER: Throughout the semester on a walk-in or appointment basis

STUDENTS REQUIRED TO USE CENTER: None

MATERIALS AVAILABLE: Handbooks and exercises

STUDENT ATTITUDE: Very positive

Salem State College's writing center is open to all students, though the majority come from freshmen writing courses. The center's tutors are prepared through on-the-job training and an academic course. Though use of the center is completely voluntary, attendance is high among freshmen, who are enthusiastic about its services. In addition to creative writing, Salem State offers writing courses for various disciplines including business, public relations, and technical writing. The school hopes to introduce a major in communications that will involve new writing courses, such as advertising writing for the media.

SALVE REGINA COLLEGE

Newport, RI 02840

Full-time Students: 186M/1042W Faculty: 81

Respondent: Diane M. Caplin, Director, Academic Resource Center

Writing Requirement: Required freshman English course

Peer Tutoring Program

PROGRAM HAS EXISTED: 7 years

NUMBER OF TUTORS: 15

HOURS THEY WORK PER WEEK: 10–20

TUTORS PAID: Yes

TUTOR SELECTION: Nominated by department chairpersons

TUTORS' TRAINING: On-the-job

PERCENTAGE OF STUDENTS SERVED: Less than 25%

OVER PAST FIVE YEARS THIS PERCENTAGE HAS: Increased

PROGRAM INTENDED TO SERVE: Students in all disciplines

PROGRAM ACTUALLY SERVES: Students in all disciplines

STUDENTS SEEK HELP WITH: Academic essays and research papers

MECHANICS OF TUTORING: Student may choose to discuss any paper with tutor

STUDENT ATTITUDE: Somewhat positive

Salve Regina College offers a variety of writing courses, including Creative Writing, Composition, and Journalism. Recently, the English Department established a composition course for underprepared students, allowing these students to study composition five days a week throughout the semester. Better prepared students can enroll in the new Honors English course. As part of the general Academic Resource Center, Salve Regina's peer tutoring program does not focus exclusively on writing skills. Instead, the peer tutors offer help with all academic skills, including mathematics, accounting, and economics, as well as writing. The staff at Salve Regina is satisfied with the college's present system and has no plans for change in the near future.

SAN FRANCISCO STATE UNIVERSITY

San Francisco, CA 94132

Full-time Students: 5168M/6042W Faculty: 1400

Respondent: William S. Robinson, Coordinator of Composition

Writing Requirement: Required freshman and other English courses, junior essay test; placement by California State English test

Writing Center

CENTER HAS EXISTED: 5-10 years HOURS OPEN PER WEEK: Over 40

STAFF: 20-40 graduate tutors

TUTORS' TRAINING: Academic course

TUTORS' EVALUATION: Conferences and student questionnaires

TUTORS PAID: A few are

PROGRAM DESIGNED TO SERVE: Writing and English students, all but seniors

PROGRAM ACTUALLY SERVES: Writing and English students, all but seniors

STUDENTS SEEK HELP WITH: Academic essays

PERCENTAGE OF STUDENTS SERVED: Less than 25%

OVER PAST FIVE YEARS THIS PERCENTAGE HAS: Stayed the same

STUDENTS USE CENTER: Throughout the semester on an appointment or regular basis

STUDENTS REQUIRED TO USE CENTER: None

MATERIALS AVAILABLE: Handbooks, exercises, reading and spelling materials

STUDENT ATTITUDE: Very positive

Writing-Across-the-Curriculum Program

PROGRAM HAS EXISTED: 2-5 years

INSTRUCTORS INVOLVED: Faculty in all disciplines

INSTRUCTORS' SELECTION: Voluntary

INSTRUCTORS' TRAINING: Seminars

PERCENTAGE OF FACULTY INVOLVED: Less than 25%

IN PAST FIVE YEARS THIS PERCENTAGE HAS: Increased

STUDENTS INVOLVED IN PROGRAM: Students in all disciplines

PERCENTAGE OF STUDENTS INVOLVED: 25-50%

IN PAST FIVE YEARS THIS PERCENTAGE HAS: Increased

PARTICIPANTS' ATTITUDE: Somewhat positive

San Francisco State University has tried various new programs, the most successful of which have been teacher-training, remedial composition, freshman English, the junior essay examination, and junior composition. In the teacher-training program, San Francisco State hires part-time teachers from among its graduate students, who are trained through four courses to teach writing. The remedial program relies on journal writing, sentence combining, and formal writing exercises for its success. The university has fared less well with its cross-curricular faculty training program, which requires participating faculty to complete a full graduate course in the teaching of writing with a grade of "B" or better and is considering either increasing the rigor of this training or abandoning the program altogether. William S. Robinson is not sure how San Francisco State's writing program will change in the next few years; in the past decade the program has returned "to required composition after the laissez-faire of the 60's."

SCRIPPS COLLEGE

Claremont, CA 91711

Full-time Students: 575W　　　　Faculty: 51

Respondent: Cheryl Walker, Chairperson, Department of British and American Literature

Writing Requirement: Required freshman English course

Writing Center

CENTER HAS EXISTED: 4 years　　　　HOURS OPEN PER WEEK: Under 10

STAFF: Fewer than 5 graduate tutors

TUTORS' TRAINING: Non-academic course

TUTORS' EVALUATION: Informal

TUTORS PAID: Yes

PROGRAM DESIGNED TO SERVE: Students in all disciplines

PROGRAM ACTUALLY SERVES: Students in all disciplines

STUDENTS SEEK HELP WITH: Academic essays and research papers

PERCENTAGE OF STUDENTS SERVED: Less than 25%

OVER PAST FIVE YEARS THIS PERCENTAGE HAS: Increased

STUDENTS USE CENTER: Throughout the semester on an appointment basis

STUDENTS REQUIRED TO USE CENTER: None

MATERIALS AVAILABLE: Handbooks

STUDENT ATTITUDE: Positive

Peer Tutoring Program

PROGRAM HAS EXISTED: 2–5 years

ORGANIZATION: Curriculum-based

NUMBER OF TUTORS: 10–20

HOURS THEY WORK PER WEEK: Approximately 3–6 hours

TUTORS PAID: Yes

TUTOR SELECTION: Nominated by themselves and by faculty college-wide

TUTORS' TRAINING: No formal training

TUTORS' EVALUATION: By tutees and their professors

PERCENTAGE OF STUDENTS SERVED: Less than 25%

OVER PAST FIVE YEARS THIS PERCENTAGE HAS: Increased

PROGRAM INTENDED TO SERVE: Students in all disciplines

PROGRAM ACTUALLY SERVES: Students in all disciplines

STUDENTS SEEK HELP WITH: All types of writing

MECHANICS OF TUTORING: Students may choose to discuss papers, have tutors comment in writing on any paper, and may also participate in group tutoring sessions

STUDENT ATTITUDE: Somewhat positive

Writing-Across-the-Curriculum Program

PROGRAM HAS EXISTED: 2-5 years

INSTRUCTORS INVOLVED: Faculty in all disciplines

INSTRUCTORS' SELECTION: Voluntary

INSTRUCTORS' TRAINING: Seminars

PERCENTAGE OF FACULTY INVOLVED: Less than 25%

IN PAST FIVE YEARS THIS PERCENTAGE HAS: Stayed the same

PARTICIPANTS' ATTITUDE: Very positive

Scripps College recently implemented several innovative writing programs. In its writing-across-the-curriculum program, faculty from all disciplines participate in workshops that prepare them to teach writing in non-English courses. Cheryl Walker believes that the college's freshman writing program, "Reading, Writing, and Thinking," is very successful. "It combines training in essay composition with reading and analysis, revision, self and peer criticism. This is supplemented by a half-credit grammar course for those who need it." Having also recently established a writing center and general peer tutoring program, Scripps has no immediate plans, but Walker feels that change is "always possible."

SETON HALL UNIVERSITY

South Orange, NJ 07079

Full-time Students: 2756M/2937W Faculty: 365

Respondent: Alexander J. Butrym, Associate Professor of English

Writing Requirement: Required freshman English course

Writing Center

CENTER HAS EXISTED: 2-5 years HOURS OPEN PER WEEK: 20-40

STAFF: 5-20 graduate tutors

TUTORS' TRAINING: On-the-job and non-academic training course

TUTORS' EVALUATION: Observation and conferences

TUTORS PAID: Yes

PROGRAM DESIGNED TO SERVE: Students in all disciplines, especially freshmen, writing students, and developmental students

PROGRAM ACTUALLY SERVES: Students in all disciplines, especially freshmen, writing students, and developmental students

STUDENTS SEEK HELP WITH: Academic essays and research papers

PERCENTAGE OF STUDENTS SERVED: 25-50%

OVER PAST FIVE YEARS THIS PERCENTAGE HAS: Stayed the same

STUDENTS USE CENTER: Repeatedly throughout the semester on a walk-in or regular basis

STUDENTS REQUIRED TO USE CENTER: Problem writers

MATERIALS AVAILABLE: Exercises

STUDENT ATTITUDE: Very positive

Peer Tutoring Program

PROGRAM HAS EXISTED: 2-5 years

ORGANIZATION: Curriculum-based; supplements the remedial program

NUMBER OF TUTORS: Fewer than 10

HOURS THEY WORK PER WEEK: 5-10

TUTORS PAID: Yes

TUTOR SELECTION: Self-nominated and appointed by the director

TUTORS' TRAINING: On-the-job and non-academic course

TUTORS' EVALUATION: Observation and conferences

PERCENTAGE OF STUDENTS SERVED: Less than 25%

OVER PAST FIVE YEARS THIS PERCENTAGE HAS: Stayed the same

PROGRAM INTENDED TO SERVE: Freshmen problem writers

PROGRAM ACTUALLY SERVES: Freshmen problem writers

STUDENTS SEEK HELP WITH: Academic essays, research papers, and resumes or business writing

MECHANICS OF TUTORING: Tutor and student are required to discuss paper, or student may choose to have tutor comment in writing on any paper

STUDENT ATTITUDE: Very positive

Writing-Across-the-Curriculum Program

PROGRAM HAS EXISTED: 2-5 years

INSTRUCTORS INVOLVED: Faculty in all disciplines

INSTRUCTORS' SELECTION: Voluntary

INSTRUCTORS' TRAINING: Seminars

PERCENTAGE OF FACULTY INVOLVED: Less than 25%

IN PAST FIVE YEARS THIS PERCENTAGE HAS: Stayed the same

STUDENTS INVOLVED IN PROGRAM: Students in all disciplines

PERCENTAGE OF STUDENTS INVOLVED: 25-50%

IN PAST FIVE YEARS THIS PERCENTAGE HAS: Stayed the same

PARTICIPANTS' ATTITUDE: Somewhat positive

Over the past three years, Seton Hall University has made several changes in its writing programs. For example, students can now obtain a Writing Certificate in English in addition to their given major. To qualify for the certification, students must complete one general composition course and three courses emphasizing language, rhetoric, and specialized writing. They must maintain a "B" average these courses. In addition, students may complete an M.A. with a concentration in writing. To help implement these programs, the university received a FIPSE grant to train college English teachers to teach technical writing and it sponsors a graduate summer institute for technical writers. The department plans to build upon these existing programs during the next few years.

SHIMER COLLEGE

Waukegan, IL 60085

Full-time Students: 80M&W Faculty: 12

Respondent: Jack Sigel, Humanities Faculty

Writing Requirement: Required General Studies Writing Project

Writing-Across-the-Curriculum Program

PROGRAM HAS EXISTED: Over 10 years

INSTRUCTORS INVOLVED: All faculty

INSTRUCTORS' TRAINING: One faculty member trained in the teaching of writing

PERCENTAGE OF FACULTY INVOLVED: 100%

IN PAST FIVE YEARS THIS PERCENTAGE HAS: Stayed the same

STUDENTS INVOLVED IN PROGRAM: Students in all disciplines

PERCENTAGE OF STUDENTS INVOLVED: 100%

IN PAST FIVE YEARS THIS PERCENTAGE HAS: Stayed the same

PARTICIPANTS' ATTITUDE: Very positive

Shimer College's longstanding writing-across-the-curriculum program guides students through the planning, drafting, and editing of their writing by teaching these students to criticize and edit their own work. Within the General Studies Writing Project, students elect courses in which the Great Books are read and regular writing is assigned. Each student also writes a General Studies Paper, completes comprehensive writing examinations, and writes a senior thesis; some of these writing projects are completed as a part of Shimer's annual Writing Week and Writing Weekends. According to Jack Sigel, programs that do not enable writers to become their own editors generally do not work well. Shimer also promotes this philosophy of self-help in the Writing Workshop, which provides additional tutoring for students who desire it.

SIMON'S ROCK OF BARD COLLEGE

Great Barrington, MA 01230

Full-time Students: 132M/161W Faculty: 26

Respondent: John Paskus, Associate Academic Dean, Head of English Department

Writing Requirement: Required freshman English course and week-long intensive writing program incoming students prior to fall term

Writing Center

CENTER HAS EXISTED: Under 2 years HOURS OPEN PER WEEK: Under 10

STAFF: Fewer than 5 faculty

TUTORS' TRAINING: On-the-job and academic training course

TUTORS' EVALUATION: Observation; success based on student response

TUTORS PAID: Yes

PROGRAM DESIGNED TO SERVE: Students in all disciplines

PROGRAM ACTUALLY SERVES: Students in all disciplines, especially freshmen

STUDENTS SEEK HELP WITH: Academic essays and research papers

PERCENTAGE OF STUDENTS SERVED: Less than 25%

OVER PAST FIVE YEARS THIS PERCENTAGE HAS: Increased

STUDENTS USE CENTER: Throughout the semester on a walk-in or appointment basis

STUDENTS REQUIRED TO USE CENTER: None

MATERIALS AVAILABLE: Handbooks, exercises, and professional books

STUDENT ATTITUDE: Very positive

Peer Tutoring Program

PROGRAM HAS EXISTED: Under 2 years

ORGANIZATION: Residentially based; not a formal program

NUMBER OF TUTORS: Fewer than 10

HOURS THEY WORK PER WEEK: Under 5

TUTORS PAID: No

TUTOR SELECTION: Self-nominated

TUTORS' TRAINING: No formal training; tutors work with faculty periodically

TUTORS' EVALUATION: No formal evaluation

PERCENTAGE OF STUDENTS SERVED: Less than 25%

OVER PAST FIVE YEARS THIS PERCENTAGE HAS: Stayed the same

PROGRAM INTENDED TO SERVE: Students in all disciplines

PROGRAM ACTUALLY SERVES: Humanities students

STUDENTS SEEK HELP WITH: Academic essays and creative writing

MECHANICS OF TUTORING: Student may choose to discuss any paper with tutor

STUDENT ATTITUDE: Somewhat positive

Writing-Across-the-Curriculum Program

PROGRAM HAS EXISTED: 2-5 years

INSTRUCTORS INVOLVED: Faculty in all disciplines

INSTRUCTORS' SELECTION: Voluntary

INSTRUCTORS' TRAINING: Seminars

PERCENTAGE OF FACULTY INVOLVED: 50-75%

IN PAST FIVE YEARS THIS PERCENTAGE HAS: Increased

STUDENTS INVOLVED IN PROGRAM: Students in all disciplines, especially humanities and social sciences students

PERCENTAGE OF STUDENTS INVOLVED: 50-75%

IN PAST FIVE YEARS THIS PERCENTAGE HAS: Increased

PARTICIPANTS' ATTITUDE: Very positive

Simon's Rock of Bard College accepts as freshmen not only high school graduates, but also students who have just finished ninth, tenth, or eleventh grade. Like many of the faculty, John Paskus, believes that all entering students need to "strengthen their powers of verbal communication, for college depends on verbal communication." Simon's Rock focuses on writing even before the academic year begins: All students are required to participate in a three-week Workshop in Language and Thinking the summer before their freshman year. During this summer session, students spend nearly six hours a day in intensive writing workshops. Paskus claims that the amount of writing students do during this time is equivalent to a semester of work and that students will easily be prepared for college writing after such an intensive experience. In accordance with the summer training, the general education courses taken during the school year all emphasize writing. During the next few years, Paskus hopes for a "refinement of strategies of our present program. We are working for full faculty involvement and are now consulting and offering out-reach programs for high schools."

SKIDMORE COLLEGE

Saratoga Springs, NY 12866

Full-time Students: 562M/1622W   Faculty: 224

Respondent: Phil Boshoff, Coordinator of Composition

Writing Requirement: Proficiency examination

Writing Center

CENTER HAS EXISTED: 4 years   HOURS OPEN PER WEEK: 25

STAFF: 3 undergraduate tutors

TUTORS' TRAINING: Academic course for undergraduates

TUTORS' EVALUATION: Observation

TUTORS PAID: Yes

PROGRAM DESIGNED TO SERVE: The college community

PROGRAM ACTUALLY SERVES: Students in all disciplines

STUDENTS SEEK HELP WITH: Academic essays and some business writing

PERCENTAGE OF STUDENTS SERVED: Less than 25%

OVER PAST FIVE YEARS THIS PERCENTAGE HAS: Increased

STUDENTS USE CENTER: Throughout the semester on an appointment or walk-in basis

STUDENTS REQUIRED TO USE CENTER: Problem writers and some freshmen

MATERIALS AVAILABLE: Handbooks, exercises, professional books, and cassettes

STUDENT ATTITUDE: Very positive

Peer Tutoring Program

PROGRAM HAS EXISTED: 6 years

ORGANIZATION: Curriculum-based

NUMBER OF TUTORS: 15

HOURS THEY WORK PER WEEK: 2

TUTORS PAID: Yes

TUTORS' SELECTION: Nominated by faculty in all disciplines

TUTORS' TRAINING: Academic course

TUTORS' EVALUATION: Observation

PERCENTAGE OF STUDENTS SERVED: Less than 25%

OVER PAST FIVE YEARS THIS PERCENTAGE HAS: Stayed the same

PROGRAM INTENDED TO SERVE: Students in all disciplines

PROGRAM ACTUALLY SERVES: English students

STUDENTS SEEK HELP WITH: Academic essays, creative writing, scientific reports, research papers, and resumes or business writing

MECHANICS OF TUTORING: Student and tutor discuss papers twice a week

STUDENT ATTITUDE: Very positive

Writing-Across-the-Curriculum Program

PROGRAM HAS EXISTED: 3 years

INSTRUCTORS INVOLVED: Faculty in all disciplines

INSTRUCTORS' SELECTION: Voluntary

INSTRUCTORS' TRAINING: Seminars

PERCENTAGE OF FACULTY INVOLVED: 25-50%

IN PAST FIVE YEARS THIS PERCENTAGE HAS: Increased

STUDENTS INVOLVED IN PROGRAM: Students in all disciplines

PERCENTAGE OF STUDENTS INVOLVED: 25-50%

IN PAST FIVE YEARS THIS PERCENTAGE HAS: Increased

PARTICIPANTS' ATTITUDE: Mostly positive

Skidmore's three-year-old writing-across-the-curriculum program of faculty training seminars has been highly successful. This success may be attributed to the fact that the program works in moderation: faculty are not required to attend lengthy follow-up workshops or frequently asked to overhaul their courses. Skidmore's writing center and peer tutoring programs, which use challenging academic courses to train the peer tutors, are also beginning to work well. Skidmore's faculty are confident that in the next few years the writing center, as well as the cross-curricular program, will continue to grow.

SLIPPERY ROCK UNIVERSITY

Slippery Rock, PA 16057

Full-time Students: 2655M/2629W Faculty: 341

Respondent: Barbara M. Williams, Freshman Coordinator

Writing Requirement: Required 2-semester freshman English course

Writing Center

CENTER HAS EXISTED: Over 10 years HOURS OPEN PER WEEK: 40

STAFF: 6 graduate tutors

TUTORS' TRAINING: On-the-job and optional academic course

TUTORS' EVALUATION: Observation and conferences

TUTORS PAID: Yes

PROGRAM DESIGNED TO SERVE: Students in all disciplines

PROGRAM ACTUALLY SERVES: Freshmen

STUDENTS SEEK HELP WITH: Scientific reports, creative writing, academic essays, research papers, and resumes or business writing

PERCENTAGE OF STUDENTS SERVED: Less than 25%

OVER PAST FIVE YEARS THIS PERCENTAGE HAS: Increased

STUDENTS USE CENTER: Throughout the semester on a walk-in basis

STUDENTS REQUIRED TO USE CENTER: Developmental students

MATERIALS AVAILABLE: Handbooks, exercises, professional books, cassettes, and film clips

STUDENT ATTITUDE: Somewhat positive

Writing-Across-the-Curriculum Program

(Planned for Fall 1984)

INSTRUCTORS INVOLVED: Faculty in all disciplines

INSTRUCTORS' SELECTION: Voluntary

INSTRUCTORS' TRAINING: Seminars

PERCENTAGE OF FACULTY INVOLVED: At least 25%

STUDENTS INVOLVED IN PROGRAM: Students in all disciplines

PERCENTAGE OF STUDENTS INVOLVED: 100%

Slippery Rock University is beginning to view writing as a concern for all academic disciplines. To expand on its longstanding writing program, which includes a university-wide writing center, the university is developing a writing-across-the-curriculum program. Beginning in the fall of 1984, all incoming students will participate in this program. Among Slippery Rock's other innovative programs is a new B.S. degree in English that is based on writing. Students in this new program may study technical, creative, expository, and journalistic writing, as well as literature, a foreign language, and computer programming. Students must also undertake a complementary minor in another department as part of this program.

SMITH COLLEGE

Northampton, MA 01063

Full-time Students: 2660W Faculty: 260

Respondent: Jefferson Hunter, Associate Professor of English

Writing Requirement: None

Writing Center

CENTER HAS EXISTED: 5-10 years HOURS OPEN PER WEEK: Over 40

STAFF: 6 professional staff members and 13 peer tutors who work primarily outside the center

TUTORS' TRAINING: On-the-job

TUTORS' EVALUATION: Observation and conferences

TUTORS PAID: Yes

PROGRAM DESIGNED TO SERVE: Students in all disciplines

PROGRAM ACTUALLY SERVES: Students in all disciplines

STUDENTS SEEK HELP WITH: All types of writing

PERCENTAGE OF STUDENTS SERVED: 50-75%

OVER PAST FIVE YEARS THIS PERCENTAGE HAS: Increased

STUDENTS USE CENTER: Throughout the semester on a walk-in, appointment, or regular basis, individually or in groups, or by phone

STUDENTS REQUIRED TO USE CENTER: Students in classes working with the center

MATERIALS AVAILABLE: Handbooks

STUDENT ATTITUDE: Positive

Peer Tutoring Program

PROGRAM HAS EXISTED: 2-5 years

ORGANIZATION: Residentially based

NUMBER OF TUTORS: 13

HOURS THEY WORK PER WEEK: 5-10

TUTORS PAID: Yes

TUTOR SELECTION: Nominated college-wide on the basis of grades, a writing sample, and an interview

TUTORS' TRAINING: Non-academic training course

TUTORS' EVALUATION: Conferences

PERCENTAGE OF STUDENTS SERVED: 50-75%

OVER PAST FIVE YEARS THIS PERCENTAGE HAS: Increased

PROGRAM INTENDED TO SERVE: Students in all disciplines

PROGRAM ACTUALLY SERVES: Students in all disciplines

STUDENTS SEEK HELP WITH: All types of writing

MECHANICS OF TUTORING: Student may choose to discuss any paper with a tutor

STUDENT ATTITUDE: Positive

Nontraditional writing programs at Smith College play an important role in the college's strong emphasis on writing skills. The peer tutors and the writing center serve an exceptionally high number of all students--half to three-quarters. In addition to tutoring duties, the writing center's permanent, six-member staff selects, trains, and supervises the undergraduate tutors. These peer tutors work primarily outside the center--in dormitories, the library, and even the computer center. To provide even more widespread writing instruction, Smith has been promoting writing awareness among faculty in all departments. During the past three years, a series of workshops funded by outside grants has brought together faculty from different disciplines to discuss the teaching of writing.

SOUTHWESTERN AT MEMPHIS

Memphis, TN 38112

Full-time Students: 528M/527W Faculty: 86

Respondent: Bernice W. Dicks, Director of Writing Center, Associate Professor of English

Writing Requirement: Required freshman English course; exemption by AP examination

Writing Center

CENTER HAS EXISTED: 3 years HOURS OPEN PER WEEK: 10–20

STAFF: 1 faculty tutor/director and 7 undergraduate tutors

TUTORS' TRAINING: On-the-job

TUTORS' EVALUATION: Observation and student questionnaire

TUTORS PAID: Yes

PROGRAM DESIGNED TO SERVE: Students in all disciplines, especially foreign students

PROGRAM ACTUALLY SERVES: Students in all disciplines especially foreign students

STUDENTS SEEK HELP WITH: Scientific reports, academic essays, and research papers

PERCENTAGE OF STUDENTS SERVED: Less than 25%

OVER PAST FIVE YEARS THIS PERCENTAGE HAS: Decreased

STUDENTS USE CENTER: Throughout the semester, primarily at mid-semester and the end of the semester, on a walk-in basis

STUDENTS REQUIRED TO USE CENTER: Those referred by faculty members

MATERIALS AVAILABLE: Handbooks, exercises, educational magazines, professional books, and texts for ESL students

STUDENT ATTITUDE: Very positive

At Southwestern at Memphis, the English Department is attempting to emphasize writing throughout the college. At present, the department has suggested several changes in the writing program, including requirement of an ESL course for some foreign students; standardization of the one-term required composition course; introduction of writing-intensive courses as the first step towards a writing-across-the-curriculum-program; and expansion of the creative writing program. Bernice Dicks reports that the writing program at Southwestern has not changed over the past three years, although previously, in 1973-74, the freshman writing requirement was re-instated. She indicates that changes may be forthcoming once the department reaches consensus on the various programs.

SPRINGFIELD COLLEGE

Springfield, MA 01109

Full-time Students: 928M/1077W Faculty: 175

Respondent: Allan D. Austin, Head, English Department

Writing Requirement: Required freshman English course and another required English course

Writing Center and Peer Tutoring Program

CENTER HAS EXISTED: 2-5 years HOURS OPEN PER WEEK: 41

STAFF: 20 faculty and undergraduate tutors

TUTOR SELECTION: Self-nominated, nominated by English faculty, nominated college-wide, and appointed by the director

TUTORS' TRAINING: Academic course

TUTORS' EVALUATION: Observation and feedback from students

TUTORS PAID: Yes

PROGRAM DESIGNED TO SERVE: Students in all disciplines

PROGRAM ACTUALLY SERVES: Students in all disciplines

STUDENTS SEEK HELP WITH: Scientific reports, academic essays, research papers, and resumes or business writing

PERCENTAGE OF STUDENTS SERVED: 25-50%

OVER PAST FIVE YEARS THIS PERCENTAGE HAS: Increased

STUDENTS USE CENTER: 25% at mid-semester, 25% at the end of the semester, and 50% throughout the semester, on a walk-in or regular basis, or by phone

STUDENTS REQUIRED TO USE CENTER: Problem writers

MATERIALS AVAILABLE: Handbooks, exercises, and professional books

STUDENT ATTITUDE: Positive

Springfield College's writing program consists primarily of ten full-time English faculty and a writing center staffed by faculty and several peer tutors. Open forty-one hours each week, the center provides students with assistance in areas such as editing, organization, and various modes of writing. The center also sponsors short seminars on study skills and specific writing problems. Some of these seminars are designed for faculty outside the English Department who are interested in learning how to comment more effectively on student prose. In the past few years, Springfield has expanded its writing program by adding business, scientific, and technical writing courses, enlarging the advanced composition course, and moving towards a writing-across-the-curriculum program with the writing center seminars. In the near future, the English Department plans to add more writing courses, refine the writing center's programs, add computer software and other materials, and demand a greater attention to writing outside of English classes.

STANFORD UNIVERSITY

Stanford, CA 94305

Full-time Students: 3726M/2864W Faculty: 1219

Respondent: Dagmar Logie, Administrative Assistant

Writing Requirement: Required two-quarter freshman English course; exemption by AP

Writing Center

CENTER HAS EXISTED: 5–10 years HOURS OPEN PER WEEK: 16

STAFF: 1 graduate tutor

TUTORS' TRAINING: On-the-job

TUTORS' EVALUATION: None

TUTORS PAID: Yes

PROGRAM DESIGNED TO SERVE: Students in all disciplines

PROGRAM ACTUALLY SERVES: Students in all disciplines

STUDENTS SEEK HELP WITH: Essays, research papers, and resumes or business writing

PERCENTAGE OF STUDENTS SERVED: Less than 25%

OVER PAST FIVE YEARS THIS PERCENTAGE HAS: Increased

STUDENTS USE CENTER: Throughout semester on a sign-up basis

STUDENTS REQUIRED TO USE CENTER: A few problem writers

MATERIALS AVAILABLE: None

STUDENT ATTITUDE: Positive

Writing-Across-the-Curriculum Program

PROGRAM HAS EXISTED: 2–5 years

INSTRUCTORS INVOLVED: Two graduate students from English Department

INSTRUCTORS' SELECTION: Appointed by Director of Freshman English

INSTRUCTORS' TRAINING: English Department pedagogy course and teaching experience

PERCENTAGE OF STUDENTS INVOLVED: 25%

PARTICIPANTS' ATTITUDE: Very positive

Stanford University's writing-across-the-curriculum program relies on graduate students from departments other than English who grade and comment on undergraduate writing. Offered a monetary incentive for completion a series of workshops and assignments, these graduate teaching assistants participate in a series of three two-hour workshops. Stanford's Freshman English program also emphasizes intensive writing instruction. Most freshman English courses are writing workshops that focus on particular themes, bringing small groups together twice a week. The English Department also offers a few innovative small-group tutorials where students meet once a week as a class and once a week in individual conferences with the instructor. Stanford considers large lectures on writing unsatisfactory and incompatible with its philosophy of careful, individualized instruction in writing.

STATE UNIVERSITY OF NEW YORK at ALBANY

Albany, NY 12222

Full-time Students: 4980M/4990W Faculty: 700

Respondent: C. H. Knoblauch, Associate Professor of English and Director of Writing

Writing Requirement: Required freshman composition course, 300-level writing course, or cross-disciplinary writing course

Writing Center

CENTER HAS EXISTED: 5-10 years HOURS OPEN PER WEEK: 20-40

STAFF: 10-20: faculty director, graduate tutors (50-60%), and undergraduate tutors (40-50%)

TUTORS' TRAINING: On-the-job; graduates take a non-academic course and undergraduates take an academic course

TUTORS' EVALUATION: Conferences

TUTORS PAID: Graduates are; some undergraduates receive course credit, others are paid

PROGRAM DESIGNED TO SERVE: Students in all disciplines

PROGRAM ACTUALLY SERVES: Humanities students (50%) and students in other disciplines (50%)

STUDENTS SEEK HELP WITH: Academic essays, research papers, creative writing, resumes or business writing, scientific reports, graduate school applications, dissertations, and examination writing, at all planning and draft levels

PERCENTAGE OF STUDENTS SERVED: Approximately 25%

OVER PAST FIVE YEARS THIS PERCENTAGE HAS: Increased

STUDENTS USE CENTER: Repeatedly on an appointment basis, some on a walk-in or regular basis

STUDENTS REQUIRED TO USE CENTER: None

MATERIALS AVAILABLE: Professional books

STUDENT ATTITUDE: Very positive

Writing-Across-the-Curriculum Program

PROGRAM HAS EXISTED: 2 years

INSTRUCTORS INVOLVED: Faculty in all disciplines and some graduate students

INSTRUCTORS' SELECTION: Voluntary

INSTRUCTORS' TRAINING: Seminars

PERCENTAGE OF FACULTY INVOLVED: Less than 25%

IN PAST FIVE YEARS THIS PERCENTAGE HAS: Increased

STUDENTS INVOLVED IN PROGRAM: Students in all disciplines, especially humanities and social sciences students

PERCENTAGE OF STUDENTS INVOLVED: 25-50%

IN PAST FIVE YEARS THIS PERCENTAGE HAS: Increased

PARTICIPANTS' ATTITUDE: Somewhat positive to neutral

The writing center at SUNY Albany has been very successful. Opened only five years ago, the center now serves more than 1700 students, and the demand for service often exceeds the available number of appointment slots. Extensive attention is given to student writing in writing classes, however, and as a consequence few of these students use the center. Instead, the students who do visit the center come from a variety of disciplines. The center's tutors attend weekly staff meetings on collaborative learning and other conceptual issues, and keep tutorial journals, which the director reads and remarks upon. C.H. Knoblauch claims that a "growing concern for rhetoric and composition as a professional discipline culminated recently in our graduate concentration in the area." At the undergraduate level, the writing-across-the-curriculum program is still working for acceptance, as "faculty and students still have questions about workload, and other obligations and feelings vary quite a bit right now." Knoblauch hopes for only positive reactions in the future and, at the same time, greater faculty participation.

STATE UNIVERSITY OF NEW YORK at BINGHAMTON

Binghamton, NY 13901

Full-time Students: 3539M/4235W Faculty: 489

Respondent: Elizabeth Tricomi, Adjunct Instructor, Writing Center

Writing Requirement: 2-course interdisciplinary requirement

Writing Center

CENTER HAS EXISTED: 2-5 years HOURS OPEN PER WEEK: 20-40

STAFF: 5-20 adjunct faculty and graduate tutors

TUTORS' TRAINING: On-the-job

TUTORS' EVALUATION: Observation and staff meetings

TUTORS PAID: Yes

PROGRAM DESIGNED TO SERVE: Students in all disciplines

PROGRAM ACTUALLY SERVES: Students in all disciplines, especially undergraduates in English

STUDENTS SEEK HELP WITH: Academic essays, research papers, and resumes or business writing

PERCENTAGE OF STUDENTS SERVED: Less than 25%

OVER PAST FIVE YEARS THIS PERCENTAGE HAS: Increased

STUDENTS USE CENTER: Throughout the semester on an appointment basis

STUDENTS REQUIRED TO USE CENTER: None

MATERIALS AVAILABLE: Handbooks, professional books, and handouts

STUDENT ATTITUDE: Very positive

Writing-Across-the-Curriculum Program

PROGRAM HAS EXISTED: 2-5 years

INSTRUCTORS INVOLVED: Faculty in all disciplines

INSTRUCTORS' SELECTION: Voluntary

INSTRUCTORS' TRAINING: None

PERCENTAGE OF FACULTY INVOLVED: Less than 25%

IN PAST FIVE YEARS THIS PERCENTAGE HAS: Increased

STUDENTS INVOLVED IN PROGRAM: Students in all disciplines

PERCENTAGE OF STUDENTS INVOLVED: More than 75%

IN PAST FIVE YEARS THIS PERCENTAGE HAS: Increased

PARTICIPANTS' ATTITUDE: Unknown; to be evaluated in 1984-85

Part of SUNY Binghamton's writing requirement is an interdisciplinary writing-across-the-curriculum program for all students in Harpur College, Binghamton's arts and sciences division. In this relatively new program, instructors pay special attention to student writing in various content courses throughout the curriculum. SUNY Binghamton's writing center and its courses combining literature and composition have worked well. Some of the expository courses have been less successful, however, due to inexperienced teaching assistants and "exercise-like" writing assignments; an English Department task force is presently studying all freshman English courses and will make recommendations for their improvement. In the future, SUNY Binghamton may increase its offerings in both composition and literature.

STATE UNIVERSITY OF NEW YORK at BUFFALO

Buffalo, NY 14260

Full-time Students: 8682M/5912W Faculty: 1404

Respondents: Robert Edwards, Associate Chairperson of English; Denise David, Writing Place Coordinator

Writing Requirement: Required freshman English course; placement or exemption by examination

Writing Center and Peer Tutoring Program

CENTER HAS EXISTED: 5–10 years HOURS OPEN PER WEEK: Over 40

STAFF: More than 40 undergraduate and graduate tutors

TUTORS' TRAINING: Academic training course

TUTORS' EVALUATION: Observation and student questionnaires

TUTORS PAID: No

PROGRAM DESIGNED TO SERVE: Students in all disciplines

PROGRAM ACTUALLY SERVES: Students in all disciplines, particularly underclassmen enrolled in humanities courses

STUDENTS SEEK HELP WITH: Primarily academic essays, research papers, resumes, some business writing, and scientific reports

PERCENTAGE OF STUDENTS SERVED: Less than 25%

OVER PAST FIVE YEARS THIS PERCENTAGE HAS: Increased

STUDENTS USE CENTER: Throughout the semester only on a walk-in basis

STUDENTS REQUIRED TO USE CENTER: Those students or classes referred by a professor

MATERIALS AVAILABLE: Handbooks, exercises, professional books, and educational magazines

STUDENT ATTITUDE: Very positive

SUNY Buffalo's major nontraditional program is its large writing center, which is staffed by more than forty graduate and peer tutors. These tutors are trained in an academic course and carefully evaluated through observation and student questionnaires. Open over forty hours each week, the center is available to all students, but it is used primarily by underclassmen in humanities courses.

STATE UNIVERSITY OF NEW YORK AT STONY BROOK

Stony Brook, NY 11794

Full-time Students: 5259M/4668W Faculty: 1030

Respondents: Peter Elbow and Pat Belanoff, Directors, Writing Program

Writing Requirement: 'C' or higher in one-semester freshman writing course

Writing Center

CENTER HAS EXISTED: 7-8 years HOURS OPEN PER WEEK: 30-40

STAFF: 15-20 graduate and undergraduate tutors

TUTORS' TRAINING: Academic course

TUTORS' EVALUATION: Conferences and student questionnaires

TUTORS PAID: Some are

PROGRAM DESIGNED TO SERVE: Students in all disciplines

PROGRAM ACTUALLY SERVES: Students in all disciplines

STUDENTS SEEK HELP WITH: Scientific reports, creative writing, academic essays, research papers, and resumes or business writing

PERCENTAGE OF STUDENTS SERVED: 25%

OVER PAST FIVE YEARS THIS PERCENTAGE HAS: Increased

STUDENTS USE CENTER: Throughout the semester on an appointment, walk-in, or regular basis, or by phone

STUDENTS REQUIRED TO USE CENTER: A few problem writers

MATERIALS AVAILABLE: A few handbooks

STUDENT ATTITUDE: Mostly positive

Over the past several years, SUNY Stony Brook has increased its emphasis on writing. Stony Brook's writing center is unusual in that it does not serve primarily writing students: its clients are a blend of students in all disciplines and classes. Many of the center's tutors are undergraduates who tutor in the center several hours a week as part of an advanced course on writing. Peter Elbow, Director of Stony Brook's writing program, hopes that all students will soon be required to take cross-curricular core courses and will have to be certified in writing skills by the departments in which they are majoring.

STATE UNIVERSITY OF NEW YORK/COLLEGE AT BUFFALO

Buffalo, NY 14222

Full-time Students: 3787M/4739W Faculty: 40

Respondent: John E. Reedy, Director, Freshman Writing

Writing Requirement: Writing competency examination

The State University of New York/College at Buffalo stresses writing in its competency-based writing program. The summer before they enter school, students must write a placement essay, on the basis of which they either pass the writing requirement or are placed in one of three levels of writing courses: English 99 (Developmental Writing), English 101 (College Writing I), or English 102 (College Writing II). At the end of each course, the student must pass the English Department writing examination in order to advance to the next course in the program. Over the next few years, John Reedy believes "that we will continue to refine our writing competencies and evaluation criteria for each course level to improve the writing literacy of our students."

STATE UNIVERSITY OF NEW YORK/COLLEGE AT FREDONIA

Fredonia, NY 14063

Full-time Students: 2400M/2460W Faculty: 258

Respondents: Theodore Steinberg, Associate Chairperson, English; Penelope Deakin, Head of Learning Center

Writing Requirement: Required freshman English course

Writing Center

CENTER HAS EXISTED: 2-5 years HOURS OPEN PER WEEK: 20-40

STAFF: 3 undergraduate tutors

TUTORS' TRAINING: On-the-job and non-academic course

TUTORS' EVALUATION: Observation and student questionnaires

TUTORS PAID: Yes

PROGRAM DESIGNED TO SERVE: Students in all disciplines

PROGRAM ACTUALLY SERVES: Students in all disciplines

STUDENTS SEEK HELP WITH: Scientific reports, essays, research papers, and resumes or business writing

PERCENTAGE OF STUDENTS SERVED: Less than 25%

OVER PAST FIVE YEARS THIS PERCENTAGE HAS: Decreased

STUDENTS USE CENTER: Throughout the semester on a walk-in basis

STUDENTS REQUIRED TO USE CENTER: None

MATERIALS AVAILABLE: Handbooks and exercises

STUDENT ATTITUDE: Very positive

Writing-Across-the-Curriculum Program

PROGRAM HAS EXISTED: Less than 2 years

INSTRUCTORS INVOLVED: Faculty in all disciplines

INSTRUCTORS' SELECTION: Voluntary

INSTRUCTORS' TRAINING: Seminars

PERCENTAGE OF FACULTY INVOLVED: Less than 25%

STUDENTS INVOLVED IN PROGRAM: Students in all disciplines

PERCENTAGE OF STUDENTS INVOLVED: More than 75%

PARTICIPANTS' ATTITUDE: Unknown

SUNY Fredonia's writing program is changing in interesting ways. This year, for example, Fredonia is launching a new cross-curricular program that requires a year of composition and intensive writing in non-English courses. Although many faculty outside of the English Department have evaluated student prose in the past, this is the first time that many will be required to do so, and Theodore Steinberg eagerly anticipates the outcome of this venture. In addition to this new program, Fredonia employs three undergraduates to tutor writing in the Learning Center. Requests for help with writing dropped as the need for math, computer science, and business tutors increased, but recently this trend has reversed, with an increase in requests for writing tutors.

STATE UNIVERSITY OF NEW YORK/EMPIRE STATE COLLEGE

Saratoga Springs, NY 12866

Full-time Students: 3000M/2300W Faculty: 207

Respondent: Ellen B. Blake, Assessment Specialist

Writing Requirement: None

Writing-Across-the-Curriculum Program

PROGRAM HAS EXISTED: Under 2 years

INSTRUCTORS INVOLVED: Faculty in all disciplines

INSTRUCTORS' SELECTION: Voluntary

INSTRUCTORS' TRAINING: Seminars

PERCENTAGE OF FACULTY INVOLVED: Less than 25%

IN PAST FIVE YEARS THIS PERCENTAGE HAS: Increased

STUDENTS INVOLVED IN PROGRAM: Students in all disciplines

PERCENTAGE OF STUDENTS INVOLVED: 25%

IN PAST FIVE YEARS THIS PERCENTAGE HAS: Increased

PARTICIPANTS' ATTITUDE: Very positive

A non-residential arts and sciences college serving many adult students, Empire State College has modelled its writing program after an adult writing program developed at the Genesee Valley Regional Center in Rochester. The program's objectives include combining group and individual work, using computer-assisted instruction, pairing students with faculty advisors in all disciplines, and training participating faculty in the teaching of writing. As Ellen B. Blake describes it, this "individualized, learner-centered, cross-disciplinary effort to improve adult writing skills" has worked well in the two years that it has existed. Empire State has also established a writing-across-the-curriculum program at one of its branch colleges.

STONEHILL COLLEGE

North Easton, MA 02356

Full-time Students: 785M/921W   Faculty: 130

Respondent: Eugene Green, Director of the Writing Program

Writing Requirement: Placement by SAT examination

Writing Center

CENTER HAS EXISTED: 2-5 years   HOURS OPEN PER WEEK: 20-40

STAFF: 1-4 faculty and 4-16 undergraduate tutors

TUTORS' TRAINING: Academic course

TUTORS' EVALUATION: Conferences

TUTORS PAID: Yes; some are work-study, others volunteer

PROGRAM DESIGNED TO SERVE: Students in all disciplines

PROGRAM ACTUALLY SERVES: Students in all disciplines, especially freshmen and writing students

STUDENTS SEEK HELP WITH: Academic essays, research papers, and resumes or business writing

PERCENTAGE OF STUDENTS SERVED: Less than 25%

OVER PAST FIVE YEARS THIS PERCENTAGE HAS: Increased

STUDENTS USE CENTER: Primarily at mid-semester on a walk-in or appointment basis

STUDENTS REQUIRED TO USE CENTER: Problem writers

MATERIALS AVAILABLE: Handbooks, professional books, in-house handouts on grammar and the writing process

STUDENT ATTITUDE: Somewhat positive

Peer Tutoring Program

PROGRAM HAS EXISTED: 2-5 years

ORGANIZATION: Writing center-based

NUMBER OF TUTORS: 10-20

HOURS THEY WORK PER WEEK: Less than 5

TUTORS PAID: Yes; some are work-study, others volunteer

TUTOR SELECTION: Self-nominated and appointed by the director

TUTORS' TRAINING: Academic course

TUTORS' EVALUATION: Conferences

PERCENTAGE OF STUDENTS SERVED: Less than 25%

OVER PAST FIVE YEARS THIS PERCENTAGE HAS: Increased

PROGRAM INTENDED TO SERVE: Students in all disciplines

PROGRAM ACTUALLY SERVES: Students in all disciplines, especially freshmen and writing students

STUDENTS SEEK HELP WITH: Academic essays, research papers, and resumes or business writing

MECHANICS OF TUTORING: Tutor and student are required to discuss papers; student may choose to have tutor comment in writing on any paper

STUDENT ATTITUDE: Somewhat positive

Writing-Across-the-Curriculum Program

PROGRAM HAS EXISTED: 2-5 years

INSTRUCTORS INVOLVED: Faculty in all disciplines

INSTRUCTORS' SELECTION: Voluntary

INSTRUCTORS' TRAINING: Seminars

PERCENTAGE OF FACULTY INVOLVED: 50-75%

IN PAST FIVE YEARS THIS PERCENTAGE HAS: Increased

STUDENTS INVOLVED IN PROGRAM: Students in all disciplines

PERCENTAGE OF STUDENTS INVOLVED: 50-75%

IN PAST FIVE YEARS THIS PERCENTAGE HAS: Increased

PARTICIPANTS' ATTITUDE: Somewhat positive

During the past five years, Stonehill College has placed a strong emphasis on writing, an emphasis strengthened by the separation of the Writing Program from the English Department and demonstrated in the developing cross-disciplinary programs. As Eugene Green points out, having an independent Writing Program makes writing-across-the-curriculum more feasible, and "all core courses have writing as a required item on their agenda." As part of the emphasis on writing, Stonehill now requires students to use word-processing. Green believes that this has particularly "helped in teaching revision in the writing courses."

SWEET BRIAR COLLEGE

Sweet Briar, VA 24595

Full-time Students: 1M/668W Faculty: 65

Respondent: Elizabeth R. Baer, Assistant Professor of English

Writing Requirement: Required freshman English course

Writing Center and Peer Tutoring Program

CENTER HAS EXISTED: 2–5 years HOURS OPEN PER WEEK: Under 10

STAFF: Director and 20–40 peer tutors in all academic areas

TUTOR SELECTION: Nominated by departmental chairpersons

TUTORS' TRAINING: One tutor orientation session

TUTORS' EVALUATION: Student questionnaire

TUTORS PAID: Yes

HOURS THEY WORK PER WEEK: Under 5

PROGRAM DESIGNED TO SERVE: Students in all disciplines

PROGRAM ACTUALLY SERVES: Students in all disciplines

STUDENTS SEEK HELP WITH: Academic essays, research papers, and study skills

PERCENTAGE OF STUDENTS SERVED: 25–50%

OVER PAST FIVE YEARS THIS PERCENTAGE HAS: Increased

STUDENTS USE CENTER: Throughout the semester on a walk-in basis

STUDENTS REQUIRED TO USE CENTER: Academic probation students

MATERIALS AVAILABLE: Handbooks, professional books, and word processing equipment

STUDENT ATTITUDE: Very positive

Sweet Briar College offers its students writing assistance outside of the English classroom in the Academic Resource Center. Staffed by over twenty peer tutors who are nominated by department heads, the Center offers students help in all subjects, including writing. The tutors often work outside the Center, but students seeking writing assistance usually use the staff, handbooks, professional books, and word processing equipment in the Center.

TEMPLE UNIVERSITY

Philadelphia, PA 19122

Full-time Students: 7270M/7037W   Faculty: 1781

Respondent: Dr. Stephen Zelnick, Associate Professor of English, Director of College Composition

Writing Requirement: Required freshman English course and other required English course; placement by examination

Writing Center

CENTER HAS EXISTED: 10 years   HOURS OPEN PER WEEK: 40

STAFF: 12–15 graduate teaching assistants

TUTORS' TRAINING: Academic course and on-the-job

TUTORS' EVALUATION: Observation

TUTORS PAID: Yes

PROGRAM DESIGNED TO SERVE: Writing students

PROGRAM ACTUALLY SERVES: Writing students

STUDENTS SEEK HELP WITH: Academic essays

PERCENTAGE OF STUDENTS SERVED: Less than 25%

OVER PAST FIVE YEARS THIS PERCENTAGE HAS: Increased

STUDENTS USE CENTER: Throughout the semester on a walk-in or appointment basis

STUDENTS REQUIRED TO USE CENTER: Problem writers

MATERIALS AVAILABLE: Writing exercises and computer-assisted instruction

STUDENT ATTITUDE: Somewhat positive

Part of one of the older writing programs in the country, Temple's writing center often serves as a model for schools opening new centers. The center is open all week and employs over twelve graduate tutors who have undergone academic and on-the-job training. Students are usually assigned to a specific tutor, and only problem writers are required to use the center. One of the more unusual aspects of Temple's center is that it is designed especially to serve writing students. The writing program has also developed a writing-across-the-curriculum emphasis over the past three years.

TEXAS A & M UNIVERSITY

College Station, TX 77843

Full-time Students: 16,939M/10,277W Faculty: 2093

Respondent: Claude Gibson, Director of Freshman English, English Department

Writing Requirement: 2 terms of required freshman English course; exemption by AP, ACH, or essay examination; and other requirements set by individual departments and colleges

Writing Center

CENTER HAS EXISTED: Over 10 years HOURS OPEN PER WEEK: Over 40

STAFF: Faculty and 5-20 graduate teaching assistants

TUTORS' TRAINING: Academic course

TUTORS' EVALUATION: Observation, conferences, and student questionnaire

TUTORS PAID: Yes

PROGRAM DESIGNED TO SERVE: Students in all disciplines

PROGRAM ACTUALLY SERVES: Students in all disciplines

STUDENTS SEEK HELP WITH: Scientific reports, academic essays, research papers, and resumes or business writing

PERCENTAGE OF STUDENTS SERVED: Less than 25%

OVER PAST FIVE YEARS THIS PERCENTAGE HAS: Increased

STUDENTS USE CENTER: Repeatedly throughout the semester on a regular basis

STUDENTS REQUIRED TO USE CENTER: Problem writers

MATERIALS AVAILABLE: Handbooks, exercises, professional books, tapes, and films

STUDENT ATTITUDE: Very positive

At Texas A & M, instructors stress the importance of the writing process because, as one syllabus notes, "students need a systematic approach to all writing tasks. . . . By participating in the process, teachers can often pinpoint student writing problems when they occur." Consistent with this philosophy, students at Texas A & M must practice pre–writing, brainstorming, organizational skills, and considerable revision and editing. Instructors assign specific "workshop days" when groups of students examine rhetorical strategies, discuss writing problems, and receive immediate feedback on and individual attention to their writing. Students are very enthusiastic about the Writing Specialization Program, which is comprised of five writing–intensive courses that offer training in technical writing, argumentation, and composition.

TOUGALOO COLLEGE

Tougaloo, MS 39174

Full-time Students: 215M/348W   Faculty: 50

Respondents: N. J. Townsend, Director, Basic Studies Division; Ruth Johnson, Director of Composition

Writing Requirement: Required freshman English course, other required English courses, and a proficiency examination

Writing Center

CENTER HAS EXISTED: 10 years   HOURS OPEN PER WEEK: Over 40

STAFF: Fewer than 5 faculty and undergraduate tutors

TUTORS' TRAINING: On-the-job and non-academic training course

TUTORS' EVALUATION: Observation, conferences, and student questionnaire

TUTORS PAID: Yes

PROGRAM DESIGNED TO SERVE: Students in all disciplines, especially freshmen and English students

PROGRAM ACTUALLY SERVES: Students in all disciplines, especially freshmen and English students

STUDENTS SEEK HELP WITH: Academic essays, special assignments, and special tests

PERCENTAGE OF STUDENTS SERVED: 40%

OVER PAST FIVE YEARS THIS PERCENTAGE HAS: Increased

STUDENTS USE CENTER: Throughout the semester on a walk-in or regular basis, or by referral

STUDENTS REQUIRED TO USE CENTER: Freshman and problem writers

MATERIALS AVAILABLE: Handbooks, exercises, magazines, tests, commercial modules, audio-visual materials, computer terminals, and student writing samples

STUDENT ATTITUDE: Very positive

Peer Tutoring Program

PROGRAM HAS EXISTED: 5 years

ORGANIZATION: Curriculum-based and residentially based

NUMBER OF TUTORS: Fewer than 10

HOURS THEY WORK PER WEEK: 5-10

TUTORS PAID: Yes

TUTOR SELECTION: Nominated by themselves, the English faculty, and faculty college-wide, then selected by the director

TUTORS' TRAINING: On-the-job and non-academic course

TUTORS' EVALUATION: Observation, conferences, student questionnaires, and by other tutors

PERCENTAGE OF STUDENTS SERVED: 50-75%

OVER PAST FIVE YEARS THIS PERCENTAGE HAS: Increased

PROGRAM INTENDED TO SERVE: Students in all disciplines, especially freshmen

PROGRAM ACTUALLY SERVES: Students in all disciplines, especially freshmen

STUDENTS SEEK HELP WITH: Academic essays and research papers

MECHANICS OF TUTORING: Tutor and student discuss papers; student may choose to have tutor comment on any paper

STUDENT ATTITUDE: Very positive

Writing-Across-the-Curriculum Program

PROGRAM HAS EXISTED: 7 years

INSTRUCTORS INVOLVED: Faculty in all disciplines

INSTRUCTORS' SELECTION: Voluntary

INSTRUCTORS' TRAINING: Seminars and faculty development workshops

PERCENTAGE OF FACULTY INVOLVED: 25-50%

IN PAST FIVE YEARS THIS PERCENTAGE HAS: Increased

STUDENTS INVOLVED IN PROGRAM: Students in all disciplines

PERCENTAGE OF STUDENTS INVOLVED: 25–50%

IN PAST FIVE YEARS THIS PERCENTAGE HAS: Increased

PARTICIPANTS' ATTITUDE: Somewhat positive

Tougaloo College's "vertical" writing requirement requires that students enroll in a two-semester freshman English course and later pass a writing proficiency examination before graduating. A writing center is open daily to help students with any writing problems they may have, and students assigned to tutors meet with them at least once a week. In addition to tutoring aid and written material, the Center provides tapes of basic grammar and writing skills reviews, filmstrips, and instructional modules. There are two peer tutoring programs in writing at Tougaloo. The curriculum-based program is supervised by the Department of English, while the residentially based program is managed by the Office of the Dean of Students. The two programs overlap, and tutors may serve in both. The writing-across-the-curriculum program, which involved 55% of the faculty in the spring of 1983, has resulted in "marked improvement in style and content" in the writing of seniors. Within writing courses, instructors have attempted to stress more innovative methods of teaching. These include the "use of freewriting and journals, team taught modules (writing, reading, and speech), and compositions based on experience and a few short readings," according to N.J. Townsend.

TRINITY COLLEGE

Hartford, CT 06106

Full-time Students: 850M/791W Faculty: 130

Respondent: Peter A. Lyons, Lecturer in Composition, Director of Writing Center

Writing Requirement: None

Writing Center

CENTER HAS EXISTED: 5 years HOURS OPEN PER WEEK: 34

STAFF: 1 faculty member, 10 undergraduate and graduate tutors

TUTORS' TRAINING: Non-academic and on-the-job; extensive pre-semester orientation

TUTORS' EVALUATION: Observation and review of tutor's reports

TUTORS PAID: Work-study or 3 hours course credit

PROGRAM DESIGNED TO SERVE: Students in all disciplines

PROGRAM ACTUALLY SERVES: Primarily freshmen, writing, and English students; some students in other disciplines

STUDENTS SEEK HELP WITH: Academic essays, research papers, scientific reports, and resumes or business writing

PERCENTAGE OF STUDENTS SERVED: 24%

OVER PAST FIVE YEARS THIS PERCENTAGE HAS: Increased

STUDENTS USE CENTER: Throughout the semester on a walk-in or appointment basis, or by phone

STUDENTS REQUIRED TO USE CENTER: None; some strongly urged by faculty

MATERIALS AVAILABLE: Handbooks and exercises

STUDENT ATTITUDE: Positive

Although relatively young, the Writing Center at Trinity College is quite successful, providing students with help during all stages of the writing process. The number of students using the Center has increased substantially over the past few years; 35 percent of these users are not English concentrators, and all seek help voluntarily. Many students use the Center to supplement the instruction of Trinity's popular basic expository writing courses. Although handbooks and writing exercises are available at the center, these resources are not frequently used. More popular is the "Grammar Hotline," staffed by the Center's undergraduate tutors, and designed to answer simple questions on grammar and construction.

TRINITY COLLEGE

Burlington, VT 05401

Full-time Students: 164M/434W Faculty: 63

Respondent: Mary H. Dickson, Associate Professor, Humanities, and Coordinator of Writing Center

Writing Requirement: Successful completion of a Writing Competency Examination or vouchers for competency

Writing Center

CENTER HAS EXISTED: 2–5 years HOURS OPEN PER WEEK: 10–20

STAFF: Director and fewer than 5 undergraduate tutors

TUTORS' TRAINING: Academic training course

TUTORS' EVALUATION: Observation, conferences, and student questionnaires

TUTORS PAID: No

PROGRAM DESIGNED TO SERVE: Students in all disciplines

PROGRAM ACTUALLY SERVES: Primarily writing students, English students, freshmen, and underclassmen

STUDENTS SEEK HELP WITH: Academic essays and research papers

PERCENTAGE OF STUDENTS SERVED: Less than 25%

OVER PAST FIVE YEARS THIS PERCENTAGE HAS: Increased

STUDENTS USE CENTER: Throughout the semester on a walk-in, appointment, or regular basis

STUDENTS REQUIRED TO USE CENTER: Problem writers

MATERIALS AVAILABLE: Handbooks, writing exercises, and professional books

STUDENT ATTITUDE: Unknown

Peer Tutoring Program

PROGRAM HAS EXISTED: 2–5 years

ORGANIZATION: Writing center–based

NUMBER OF TUTORS: Fewer than 10

HOURS THEY WORK PER WEEK: 5–10

TUTORS PAID: No

TUTOR SELECTION: Based on prerequisites

TUTORS' TRAINING: Academic training course

TUTORS' EVALUATION: Observation and student questionnaires

PERCENTAGE OF STUDENTS SERVED: Fewer than 25%

OVER PAST FIVE YEARS THIS PERCENTAGE HAS: Stayed the same

PROGRAM INTENDED TO SERVE: Students in all disciplines

PROGRAM ACTUALLY SERVES: Writing students, English students, freshmen, and underclassmen

STUDENTS SEEK HELP WITH: Academic essays and research papers

MECHANICS OF TUTORING: Tutor and student discuss papers

STUDENT ATTITUDE: Somewhat positive

A small school with approximately six hundred full–time students, Trinity College in Vermont has just started to develop an organized writing curriculum. The "Advanced Composition: Peer Tutoring" course was recently introduced, and the writing center and peer tutoring program, both created within the last five years, assist students seeking help outside the classroom. Though the number of peer tutors has decreased, those who now work serve a small but steady percentage of Trinity's students.

UNITY COLLEGE

Unity, ME 04988

Full-time Students: 200M/100W Faculty: 23

Respondent: Donald Mortland, Chairperson, Center of Arts and Humanities

Writing Requirement: Required freshman English course

At the present time, Unity College's writing program is fairly traditional, with two required semesters of freshman composition and a workshop for ill-prepared students. Unity College may achieve more faculty-wide cooperation in teaching writing during the next several years; Donald Mortland hopes that Unity will begin a writing-across-the-curriculum program sometime during the next few years.

UNIVERSITY OF ALBUQUERQUE

Albuquerque NM 87140

Full-time Students: 521M/536W   Faculty: 87

Respondent: N. C. Martinez, Associate Dean, College of General Studies

Writing Requirement: Two required freshman English courses

Writing Center

CENTER HAS EXISTED: 5-10 years   HOURS OPEN PER WEEK: Over 40

STAFF: 8-12 faculty, graduate, and undergraduate tutors

TUTORS' TRAINING: On-the-job

TUTORS' EVALUATION: Observation and conferences

TUTORS PAID: Yes

PROGRAM DESIGNED TO SERVE: Students in all disciplines

PROGRAM ACTUALLY SERVES: Students in all disciplines

STUDENTS SEEK HELP WITH: Scientific reports, academic essays, research papers, and resumes or business writing

PERCENTAGE OF STUDENTS SERVED: 25-50%

OVER PAST FIVE YEARS THIS PERCENTAGE HAS: Increased

STUDENTS USE CENTER: Throughout the semester on a walk-in or appointment basis, or in workshops on specific course assignments

STUDENTS REQUIRED TO USE CENTER: Problem writers and all developmental English students

MATERIALS AVAILABLE: Handbooks, educational magazines, writing exercises, professional books, paperbacks, cassettes, and filmstrips

STUDENT ATTITUDE: Very positive

Peer Tutoring Program

PROGRAM HAS EXISTED: 5–10 years

ORGANIZATION: Curriculum-based

NUMBER OF TUTORS: Fewer than 10

HOURS THEY WORK PER WEEK: 5–10

TUTORS PAID: Yes

TUTOR SELECTION: Self-nominated and appointed by the director

TUTORS' TRAINING: On-the-job and in workshops

TUTORS' EVALUATION: Observation, conferences, and student questionnaires

PERCENTAGE OF STUDENTS SERVED: Less than 25%

OVER PAST FIVE YEARS THIS PERCENTAGE HAS: Increased

PROGRAM INTENDED TO SERVE: Academically disadvantaged students

PROGRAM ACTUALLY SERVES: Academically disadvantaged students

STUDENTS SEEK HELP WITH: Academic essays

MECHANICS OF TUTORING: Students may choose to discuss any paper with a tutor, or they may be referred to a tutor for work on any language or writing problem

STUDENT ATTITUDE: Very positive

The University of Albuquerque's writing program has recently become more goal-oriented and has tightened its standards by demanding more work from students. According to Dean N.C. Martinez, courses in business and technical writing, developmental courses, and ESL instruction for native Americans, Hispanics, and immigrants have been particularly successful. Students have responded positively to the peer tutoring program, which is aimed at academically disadvantaged writers, and to the writing center, which is used both by developmental English students and other students with writing problems. Unfortunately, at the end of the 1983–84 school year all developmental courses and ESL courses for American students who speak English as a second language will be discontinued, so students with deficiencies will have to rely solely upon tutors for help.

UNIVERSITY OF CALIFORNIA at BERKELEY

Berkeley, CA 94720

Full-time Students: 11,490M/8600W Faculty: 1880

Respondents: Thom Hawkins and Rondi Gilbert, Co-coordinators, Tutoring Services in Writing, Student Learning Center

Writing Requirement: Required freshman English courses

Writing Center

CENTER HAS EXISTED: 12 years HOURS OPEN PER WEEK: 50 STAFF: More than 40 undergraduate tutors and 4 professional non-faculty writing specialists

TUTORS' TRAINING: On-the-job, and academic training courses

TUTORS' EVALUATION: Observation, conferences, student questionnaires, by other tutors, videotape, and skills test

TUTORS PAID: Yes, but a few volunteer and many tutor for credit

PROGRAM DESIGNED TO SERVE: Primarily freshman writing students; Educational Opportunity Program and Affirmative Action students and athletes receive high priority

PROGRAM ACTUALLY SERVES: Primarily freshman writing students; Educational Opportunity Program and Affirmative Action students and athletes receive high priority

STUDENTS SEEK HELP WITH: Academic essays

PERCENTAGE OF STUDENTS SERVED: Less than 25%

OVER PAST FIVE YEARS THIS PERCENTAGE HAS: Increased

STUDENTS USE CENTER: Throughout the semester on an appointment or regular basis

STUDENTS REQUIRED TO USE CENTER: None, but some are strongly encouraged

MATERIALS AVAILABLE: Handbooks, writing exercises, professional books, and computer-assisted instruction in grammar

STUDENT ATTITUDE: Very positive

Peer Tutoring Program

PROGRAM HAS EXISTED: 12 years

ORGANIZATION: Learning center-based

NUMBER OF TUTORS: 20-50

HOURS THEY WORK PER WEEK: 2-20

TUTORS PAID: Yes, or they receive credit or volunteer

TUTOR SELECTION: Appointed by the coordinators

TUTORS' TRAINING: On-the-job and academic training course

TUTORS' EVALUATION: Observation, conferences, by other tutors, student questionnaires, videotape, and skills test

PERCENTAGE OF STUDENTS SERVED: Less than 25%

OVER PAST FIVE YEARS THIS PERCENTAGE HAS: Increased

PROGRAM INTENDED TO SERVE: Primarily freshman writing students; Educational Opportunity Program and Affirmative Action students and athletes are first priority

PROGRAM ACTUALLY SERVES: Primarily freshman writing students; Educational Opportunity Program and Affirmative Action students and athletes are first priority

STUDENTS SEEK HELP WITH: Academic essays

MECHANICS OF TUTORING: Students may choose to discuss any paper with a tutor, and the tutor may intervene at any stage of the writing process

STUDENT ATTITUDE: Very positive

The University of California at Berkeley has had success with peer tutoring, both one-on-one and in small groups. Based in the Student Learning Center, the peer tutoring program is comprised of nearly fifty carefully selected undergraduates who are trained in an intensive course. These tutors meet with students in one-hour sessions to help them with assignments at any stage in the writing process. Students see the same tutor once or twice a week on a regular basis, and some meet in small groups of five to eight Educational Opportunity Program and Affirmative Action students; attendance is high although all tutorials are voluntary and non-credit. The Student Learning Center also hires non-faculty professionals as trainers and supervisors, and has been expanding its services since its conception in 1973. The center's professional staff has been reaching out to teaching assistants and instructors from many departments with workshops on teaching writing, and hopes to further expand this program over the next few years.

UNIVERSITY OF CALIFORNIA at DAVIS

Davis, CA 95616

Full-time Students: 6574M/7206W   Faculty: 1040

Respondent: Timothy Lulofs, Assistant Director of Composition and Campus Writing Center

Writing Requirement: Required freshman English course; placement by examination

Writing Center

CENTER HAS EXISTED: 4 years   HOURS OPEN PER WEEK: 40

STAFF: 8–9 visiting lecturers

TUTORS PAID: Yes

PROGRAM DESIGNED TO SERVE: Undergraduate students in all disciplines, especially those enrolled in adjunct writing courses

PROGRAM ACTUALLY SERVES: Undergraduate students in all disciplines and some graduate students

STUDENTS SEEK HELP WITH: Academic essays, research papers, scientific reports, and papers assigned for adjunct writing courses

PERCENTAGE OF STUDENTS SERVED: 10%

OVER PAST FIVE YEARS THIS PERCENTAGE HAS: Increased

STUDENTS USE CENTER: During regular meeting times

STUDENTS REQUIRED TO USE CENTER: Those enrolled in adjunct writing courses

MATERIALS AVAILABLE: Computer-assisted instruction; handbooks and professional books available for visiting lecturers

STUDENT ATTITUDE: Very positive

Writing-Across-the-Curriculum Program

PROGRAM HAS EXISTED: 4 years

INSTRUCTORS INVOLVED: 8–9 visiting lecturers

INSTRUCTORS' SELECTION: Hired specifically for position or chosen from the composition program

STUDENTS INVOLVED IN PROGRAM: Students in all disciplines

PERCENTAGE OF STUDENTS INVOLVED: 10%

IN PAST FIVE YEARS THIS PERCENTAGE HAS: Increased

PARTICIPANTS' ATTITUDE: Very positive

To supplement its traditional and successful composition sequence, the University of California at Davis set up a unique writing-across-the-curriculum program four years ago. Based in the writing center, this program consists of adjunct composition courses taught by visiting lecturers. The adjunct courses are linked mostly to upper division courses in several departments, though some are linked to lower division or graduate courses. Not all students in the subject course enroll in the adjunct course, but those who do are assigned extra writing by the adjunct lecturer. Consultation between the adjunct lecturer and the course professor is done on an informal basis, but participants in the program have responded enthusiastically to it. Although the writing center staff focuses primarily on the writing-across-the-curriculum program, they also conduct workshops of one to three sessions for students in different fields, and provide computer-assisted instruction for all students in the adjunct courses. In the next few years the English Department hopes to continue emphasizing writing in various disciplines.

UNIVERSITY OF CALIFORNIA at LOS ANGELES

Los Angeles, CA 90024

Full-time Students: 11,202M/11,406W Faculty: 3000

Respondents: Carol P. Hartzog, Director UCLA Writing Programs; Judy Collas, Supervisor, Composition Tutoring Lab

Writing Requirement: Required freshman English course

Writing Center and Peer Tutoring Program

CENTER HAS EXISTED: 2-5 years HOURS OPEN PER WEEK: 20-40

STAFF: 20-40 undergraduate tutors

TUTORS' TRAINING: On-the-job and non-academic training course

TUTORS' EVALUATION: Observation, conferences, student questionnaires, and by other tutors

TUTORS PAID: Yes

HOURS TUTORS WORK PER WEEK: 5-10

PROGRAM DESIGNED TO SERVE: Writing students, freshmen, and students in all disciplines

PROGRAM ACTUALLY SERVES: Primarily freshman and sophomore English and writing students, and some students from other disciplines

STUDENTS SEEK HELP WITH: Primarily academic essays and research papers, and some resumes, business writing, creative writing, and scientific reports

PERCENTAGE OF STUDENTS SERVED: Less than 25% of student body, but between 25% and 50% of all composition students

OVER PAST FIVE YEARS THIS PERCENTAGE HAS: Increased

STUDENTS USE CENTER: Throughout the semester on an appointment or regular basis

STUDENTS REQUIRED TO USE CENTER: None

MATERIALS AVAILABLE: Handbooks, writing exercises, professional books, and handouts on various writing tasks

STUDENT ATTITUDE: Very positive

UCLA's Writing Program began its rapid, innovative expansion five years ago, when a series of faculty-wide conferences led to major administrative and curricular changes. In 1979 the Writing Program had only eight staff members to serve UCLA's twenty-two thousand full-time students, but since the establishment of the Composition Section within the English Department, the staff has grown to include fifty lecturers and thirty teaching assistants. Several new programs have also been added. One of UCLA's most successful new programs is its writing center, the Composition Tutoring Lab, which is staffed by trained peer tutors. The tutors offer writing assistance primarily for basic composition students, but also for any undergraduate or graduate student with writing problems or questions. In addition to individual assistance, the Lab offers computer and video teaching materials to both students and writing instructors. The Lab is now supplemented by two new basic skills programs for underprepared writers: the Freshman Summer Program and the Freshman Preparatory Program, both of which offer interdisciplinary writing instruction, additional in-class hours, workshops, tutorials, and computer-assisted instruction. UCLA has no formal writing-across-the-curriculum program, but offers teaching assistants in several disciplines instruction in the evaluation of student writing. Over the next few years, UCLA plans to expand its upper-division and graduate writing programs.

UNIVERSITY OF CALIFORNIA at SAN DIEGO

La Jolla, CA 92093

Full-time Students: 1250M/1300W Faculty: 170

Respondent: Charles Cooper, Professor of Literature and Coordinator of Writing Programs

Writing Requirement: Required freshman English course

Writing Center

CENTER HAS EXISTED: 5 years HOURS OPEN PER WEEK: 30

STAFF: 20 upper division undergraduate tutors trained by staff

TUTORS' TRAINING: On-the-job and academic course

TUTORS' EVALUATION: Observation

TUTORS PAID: Yes

PROGRAM DESIGNED TO SERVE: Students in all disciplines

PROGRAM ACTUALLY SERVES: Students in all disciplines

STUDENTS SEEK HELP WITH: Academic essays, research papers, scientific reports, creative writing, and resumes or business writing

PERCENTAGE OF STUDENTS SERVED: 10%

OVER PAST FIVE YEARS THIS PERCENTAGE HAS: Stayed the same

STUDENTS USE CENTER: Throughout the semester on a walk-in or appointment basis

STUDENTS REQUIRED TO USE CENTER: Problem writers

MATERIALS AVAILABLE: Center operates on a strictly tutorial/conference basis

STUDENT ATTITUDE: Very positive

Peer Tutoring Program

PROGRAM HAS EXISTED: 6 years

ORGANIZATION: Exists only in Muir College Writing Program; curriculum-based

NUMBER OF TUTORS: 15

HOURS THEY WORK PER WEEK: 10

TUTORS PAID: Yes, or they receive academic credit

TUTOR SELECTION: Based on performance in the course, "Teaching of Writing"

TUTORS' TRAINING: Academic course

TUTORS' EVALUATION: Observation by instructor

PERCENTAGE OF STUDENTS SERVED: 100% of students in Muir College over the course of 4 years

OVER PAST FIVE YEARS THIS PERCENTAGE HAS: Stayed the same

PROGRAM INTENDED TO SERVE: Freshmen

PROGRAM ACTUALLY SERVES: Freshmen

STUDENTS SEEK HELP WITH: Expository writing and analysis

MECHANICS OF TUTORING: Tutor and student are required to discuss papers

STUDENT ATTITUDE: Very positive

The writing center at the University of California at San Diego serves the entire university, which is divided into four residential colleges. As part of its writing program, the university's Muir College offers a peer tutoring program. In this program, upper division students are chosen to work with instructors of selected freshman courses and to tutor the students of these courses. This program is mandatory for all freshmen enrolled in these courses. Over the past ten years, San Diego has become more interested in innovative writing programs, as illustrated by the development of the university's writing center and peer tutoring program. Charles Cooper feels, however, that San Diego may witness a return to more conventional writing programs in the future.

UNIVERSITY OF COLORADO at COLORADO SPRINGS

Colorado Springs, CO 80907

Full-time Students: 986M/983W   Faculty: 148

Respondent: Janice N. Hays, Director of Composition, English Department

Writing Requirement: Required freshman and other English courses

Writing Center

CENTER HAS EXISTED: 4 years   HOURS OPEN PER WEEK: 40

STAFF: 1 faculty member and 8–10 undergraduate and graduate tutors

TUTORS' TRAINING: On-the-job and academic course

TUTORS' EVALUATION: Observation and student questionnaires

TUTORS PAID: Yes

PROGRAM DESIGNED TO SERVE: Students in all disciplines

PROGRAM ACTUALLY SERVES: Writing students and freshmen

STUDENTS SEEK HELP WITH: Academic essays, research papers, and skills problems

PERCENTAGE OF STUDENTS SERVED: Less than 25%

OVER PAST FIVE YEARS THIS PERCENTAGE HAS: Increased

STUDENTS USE CENTER: Throughout the semester on an appointment or regular basis

STUDENTS REQUIRED TO USE CENTER: Problem writers

MATERIALS AVAILABLE: Handbooks, exercises, and taped and tutorial programs

STUDENT ATTITUDE: Very positive

Peer Tutoring Program

PROGRAM HAS EXISTED: 4 years

ORGANIZATION: Curriculum-based

NUMBER OF TUTORS: 10–20

HOURS THEY WORK PER WEEK: Under 5

TUTORS PAID: Some are

TUTORS' SELECTION: Nominated by English faculty or self-nominated, and appointed by director

TUTORS' TRAINING: On-the-job and academic course

TUTORS' EVALUATION: Observation and questionnaire

PERCENTAGE OF STUDENTS SERVED: Less than 25%

OVER PAST FIVE YEARS THIS PERCENTAGE HAS: Increased

PROGRAM INTENDED TO SERVE: Students in all disciplines

PROGRAM ACTUALLY SERVES: Students in all disciplines

STUDENTS SEEK HELP WITH: Academic essays, research papers, and skills problems

MECHANICS OF TUTORING: Tutor comments in writing on all papers; student chooses to discuss papers with tutor

STUDENT ATTITUDE: Very positive

Writing-Across-the-Curriculum Program

PROGRAM HAS EXISTED: Less than 2 years

INSTRUCTORS INVOLVED: Humanities faculty

INSTRUCTORS' SELECTION: Voluntary

INSTRUCTORS' TRAINING: Seminars

PERCENTAGE OF FACULTY INVOLVED: Less than 25%

IN PAST FIVE YEARS THIS PERCENTAGE HAS: Stayed the same

STUDENTS INVOLVED IN PROGRAM: Humanities and social science students

PERCENTAGE OF STUDENTS INVOLVED: Less than 25%

IN PAST FIVE YEARS THIS PERCENTAGE HAS: Increased

PARTICIPANTS' ATTITUDE: Somewhat positive

"Well rounded" is an accurate description of the writing program at the University of Colorado at Colorado Springs. In addition to a writing center, a peer tutoring program, and a faculty training program, the university has recently developed new composition courses, a competency test for freshman English, a writing requirement, and a Basic Writing program. Trained intensively in an academic course on the teaching of writing, peer tutors assist small groups of Basic Writers and tutor students from all disciplines on a one-on-one basis. The university has tried and rejected programs that train English faculty and recruit faculty outside the English Department to give writing-intensive courses. Although cooperative, faculty in other departments have neither the time nor the interest to devote to writing. In the future, the University of Colorado hopes to develop its business and technical writing programs and add a graduate degree in rhetoric and composition.

UNIVERSITY OF DELAWARE

Newark, DE 19716

Full-time Students: 5441M/6917W Faculty: 800

Respondent: George Miller, Director, Lower-Division Program in English

Writing Requirement: Required freshman English course

Writing Center

CENTER HAS EXISTED: Over 10 years HOURS OPEN PER WEEK: Over 40

STAFF: 10–20 part-time faculty and 10–20 graduate tutors

TUTORS' TRAINING: On-the-job and non-academic workshops

TUTORS' EVALUATION: Observation and conferences

TUTORS PAID: Yes

PROGRAM DESIGNED TO SERVE: Students in all disciplines

PROGRAM ACTUALLY SERVES: Students in all disciplines

STUDENTS SEEK HELP WITH: Scientific reports, academic essays, research papers, resumes or business writing, dissertations, theses, and applications to graduate schools

PERCENTAGE OF STUDENTS SERVED: Less than 25%

OVER PAST FIVE YEARS THIS PERCENTAGE HAS: Increased

STUDENTS USE CENTER: Throughout the semester on a walk-in, appointment, or regular basis, or by phone

STUDENTS REQUIRED TO USE CENTER: Problem writers

MATERIALS AVAILABLE: Handbooks, exercises, professional books, and material developed by tutors

STUDENT ATTITUDE: Very positive

To accommodate night owls, University of Delaware's writing center is open twelve hours a week at night in addition to its thirty-five daytime hours. Students with serious writing problems are required to visit the center regularly as part of a "communications condition system" and may not graduate without fulfilling certain requirements. Writing courses at Delaware, many of which are part of the journalism and business technical writing majors, are popular but unfortunately always over-subscribed.

UNIVERSITY OF FLORIDA

Gainesville, FL 32611

Full-time Students: 13,129M/9777W Faculty: 2802

Respondent: Wayne Losano, Director of Freshman English

Writing Requirement: Required freshman English course, other English course, and two courses with writing components

Writing Center

CENTER HAS EXISTED: 5-10 HOURS OPEN PER WEEK: 20-40

STAFF: 1-4 faculty and 4-16 graduate tutors

TUTORS' TRAINING: On-the-job and non-academic course

TUTORS' EVALUATION: Observation and conferences

TUTORS PAID: Yes

PROGRAM DESIGNED TO SERVE: Students in all disciplines

PROGRAM ACTUALLY SERVES: Students in all disciplines

STUDENTS SEEK HELP WITH: Scientific reports, academic essays, and research papers

PERCENTAGE OF STUDENTS SERVED: Less than 25%

OVER PAST FIVE YEARS THIS PERCENTAGE HAS: Increased

STUDENTS USE CENTER: Throughout the semester on a regular basis

STUDENTS REQUIRED TO USE CENTER: Problem writers

MATERIALS AVAILABLE: Handbooks and exercises

STUDENT ATTITUDE: Somewhat positive

In accordance with state law, the University of Florida demands that students pass two required English courses and two courses with a writing component of six thousand words. These writing component courses are available both inside and outside the English Department. A Developmental English course, which does not award English credit, is also offered to students deficient in basic skills. Most students fulfill the English requirement by taking one composition course and one literature course with a composition component. In many majors (e.g., journalism, engineering, geology, accounting, and recreation), students are required to take an additional upper-level writing course such as technical writing or advanced exposition.

UNIVERSITY OF GEORGIA

Athens, GA 30602

Full-time Students: 8120M/8640W Faculty: 1908

Respondent: Donald E. Barnett, Director of Freshman English

Writing Requirement: 3 required freshman English courses; placement by examination

Writing Center

CENTER HAS EXISTED: 5-10 years HOURS OPEN PER WEEK: 20-40

STAFF: Faculty

PROGRAM DESIGNED TO SERVE: Students in all disciplines

PROGRAM ACTUALLY SERVES: Students in all disciplines, undergraduates and graduates

STUDENTS SEEK HELP WITH: Scientific reports, academic essays, research papers, creative writing, and resumes or business writing

PERCENTAGE OF STUDENTS SERVED: Less than 25%

OVER PAST FIVE YEARS THIS PERCENTAGE HAS: Increased

STUDENTS USE CENTER: Throughout the semester on a walk-in or regular basis

STUDENTS REQUIRED TO USE CENTER: Problem writers

MATERIALS AVAILABLE: Handbooks, exercises, and professional books

STUDENT ATTITUDE: Very positive

The English Department at the University of Georgia has begun to stress a "semi-process" approach to writing by concentrating on the stages of student writing and avoiding formulaic approaches such as the five-paragraph theme. Composition courses continue to stress traditional writing skills, however, and use as a core text the Harbrace College Handbook. Students are required to write themes both in class and out, and must also complete a final composition in these courses. For extra help, students can turn to the faculty-staffed writing center. In the future Georgia will examine computer-aided instruction for writing and teaching grammar.

UNIVERSITY OF HAWAII at HILO

Hilo, HI 96720

Full-time Students: 1336M/1324W Faculty: 206

Respondent: April K. Purcell, Chairperson, English Discipline

Writing Requirement: Required composition course or proficiency examination

Writing Center

CENTER HAS EXISTED: 4 years HOURS OPEN PER WEEK: 40

STAFF: 5-8 faculty and undergraduate tutors

TUTORS' TRAINING: Non-academic course

TUTORS' EVALUATION: Observation and student questionnaires

TUTORS PAID: Yes

PROGRAM DESIGNED TO SERVE: Students in all disciplines

PROGRAM ACTUALLY SERVES: Students in all disciplines

STUDENTS SEEK HELP WITH: Scientific reports, academic essays, and research papers

PERCENTAGE OF STUDENTS SERVED: Less than 25%

OVER PAST FIVE YEARS THIS PERCENTAGE HAS: Increased

STUDENTS USE CENTER: Throughout the semester on an appointment or walk-in basis

STUDENTS REQUIRED TO USE CENTER: Some problem writers

MATERIALS AVAILABLE: Handbooks and exercises

STUDENT ATTITUDE: Somewhat positive

Peer Tutoring Program

PROGRAM HAS EXISTED: 2-5 years

ORGANIZATION: Writing center-based

NUMBER OF TUTORS: Fewer than 10

HOURS THEY WORK PER WEEK: 5-10

TUTORS PAID: Yes

TUTORS' SELECTION: Nominated by English faculty

TUTORS' TRAINING: Non-academic course

TUTORS' EVALUATION: Observation and student questionnaire

PERCENTAGE OF STUDENTS SERVED: Less than 25%

OVER PAST FIVE YEARS THIS PERCENTAGE HAS: Increased

PROGRAM INTENDED TO SERVE: First and second year students in all disciplines

PROGRAM ACTUALLY SERVES: Writing students

STUDENTS SEEK HELP WITH: Academic essays, scientific reports, and research papers

MECHANICS OF TUTORING: Student chooses to discuss papers with tutor

STUDENT ATTITUDE: Somewhat positive

Although new and fairly small, the peer tutoring program at the University of Hawaii at Hilo is reasonably successful, serving mainly writing students. Part of the program's success can be attributed to new management and recently acquired space at the university's Learning Laboratory. The peer tutoring program is expected to grow steadily, along with the number of word processing terminals available, as the Humanities Division at Hawaii at Hilo pays increasing attention to the word processor as a writing tool. Other recent changes include a stricter graduation requirement in composition skills, established in 1977.

UNIVERSITY OF HAWAII/MANOA

Honolulu, HI 96822

Full-time Students: 7334M/7946W Faculty: 1615

Respondent: Roger Whitlock, Director of Composition Program

Writing Requirement: Required freshman English course

Writing Center

CENTER HAS EXISTED: 5-10 years HOURS OPEN PER WEEK: 10-20

STAFF: Fewer than 5 faculty tutors

TUTORS' TRAINING: On-the-job and academic course

TUTORS' EVALUATION: Observation

TUTORS PAID: Yes

PROGRAM DESIGNED TO SERVE: Students in all disciplines

PROGRAM ACTUALLY SERVES: Students in all disciplines

STUDENTS SEEK HELP WITH: Scientific reports, academic essays, research papers, and resumes or business writing

PERCENTAGE OF STUDENTS SERVED: Less than 25%

OVER PAST FIVE YEARS THIS PERCENTAGE HAS: Increased

STUDENTS USE CENTER: Throughout the semester on an appointment or walk-in basis

STUDENTS REQUIRED TO USE CENTER: None

MATERIALS AVAILABLE: Handbooks

STUDENT ATTITUDE: Very positive

Peer Tutoring Program

PROGRAM HAS EXISTED: 5-10 years

ORGANIZATION: Curriculum-based

NUMBER OF TUTORS: 10-20

HOURS THEY WORK PER WEEK: 5-10

TUTORS PAID: Yes

TUTOR SELECTION: Nominated by English faculty

TUTORS' TRAINING: On-the-job

TUTORS' EVALUATION: Observation and questionnaires

PERCENTAGE OF STUDENTS SERVED: Less than 25%

OVER PAST FIVE YEARS THIS PERCENTAGE HAS: Stayed the same

PROGRAM INTENDED TO SERVE: Writing students and freshmen

PROGRAM ACTUALLY SERVES: Writing students and freshmen

STUDENTS SEEK HELP WITH: Essays in freshman English

MECHANICS OF TUTORING: Tutor comments in writing on all papers and discusses them with student

STUDENT ATTITUDE: Very positive

Last year, the freshman English sequence at the University of Hawaii/Manoa adopted a strong process orientation: "Attention is given to all stages of the writing process--generating ideas, drafting, revising, and editing," in the words of Roger Whitlock. Several new composition offerings have also been added to the curriculum, including upper-level courses in career writing and professional editing. A proposal for a composition option within the current M.A. program is now being considered and is likely to be approved. Whitlock anticipates that more cross-curricular writing courses and help for the instructors teaching them will be on the agenda in the near future. In 1974, the university initiated its Writing Workshop and has recently added a peer tutoring program, which serves primarily writing students.

In 1979, the University of Hawaii became a site of the National Writing Project, which trains 20 teachers from all grade levels and from schools throughout the state in a Summer Institute. Devoted to improving teachers' writing and to sharing effective approaches to teaching writing, the Summer Institute also offers in-service training workshops during the school year.

UNIVERSITY OF IDAHO

Moscow, ID 83643

Full-time Students: 3806M/2300W Faculty: 501

Respondent: Richard Hannaford, Director of Writing

Writing Requirement: Required freshman English course; proficiency examination for transfers

Peer Tutoring Program

PROGRAM HAS EXISTED: 10 years

ORGANIZATION: Through Student Advisory Services (SAS)

NUMBER OF TUTORS: 10-20

HOURS THEY WORK PER WEEK: 5-10

TUTORS PAID: Yes

TUTOR SELECTION: By SAS counselor

TUTORS' TRAINING: On-the-job and non-academic training course

TUTORS' EVALUATION: Observation and conferences

PERCENTAGE OF STUDENTS SERVED: Less than 25%

OVER PAST FIVE YEARS THIS PERCENTAGE HAS: Decreased due to budget cut-backs

PROGRAM INTENDED TO SERVE: Students in all disciplines

PROGRAM ACTUALLY SERVES: Students in all disciplines

STUDENTS SEEK HELP WITH: Academic essays, scientific reports, research papers, and resumes or business writing

MECHANICS OF TUTORING: Student may choose to discuss papers with tutor

STUDENT ATTITUDE: Somewhat positive

Writing-Across-the-Curriculum Program

PROGRAM HAS EXISTED: Under 2 years

INSTRUCTORS INVOLVED: English faculty

INSTRUCTORS' SELECTION: By appointment

INSTRUCTORS' TRAINING: Seminars

PERCENTAGE OF FACULTY INVOLVED: 11%

IN PAST FIVE YEARS THIS PERCENTAGE HAS: Increased

STUDENTS INVOLVED IN PROGRAM: Students in all disciplines

PERCENTAGE OF STUDENTS INVOLVED: 25–50%

IN PAST FIVE YEARS THIS PERCENTAGE HAS: Increased

PARTICIPANTS' ATTITUDE: Very positive

In recent years, the University of Idaho's writing program has emphasized thesis-oriented, argumentative prose. Its course offerings in business writing, technical writing, and freshman composition have worked well, and the department has steered away from writing courses "directed at expressing 'the self,' or the 'inner voice,'" according to Richard Hannaford. Although Idaho's ten-year-old peer tutoring program has decreased in size because of recent budget cut-backs, the university still manages to create innovative programs. For example, Idaho plans to initiate a computer-aided instruction program soon, using Bell Laboratories' *Writer's Workbench*, a software package that analyzes texts.

UNIVERSITY OF ILLINOIS at URBANA-CHAMPAIGN

Urbana, IL 61801

Full-time Students: 14,495M/10,914W Faculty: 2796

Respondents: Jim Davis and Susan Pratt, Assistants to the Director of Rhetoric

Writing Requirement: Required freshman English course and humanities electives

Writing Center

CENTER HAS EXISTED: Over 10 years HOURS OPEN PER WEEK: 20-40

STAFF: Fewer than 5 graduate tutors

TUTORS' TRAINING: On-the-job and academic training course

TUTORS' EVALUATION: None

TUTORS PAID: Yes

PROGRAM DESIGNED TO SERVE: Students in all disciplines

PROGRAM ACTUALLY SERVES: Students in all disciplines

STUDENTS SEEK HELP WITH: Academic essays, research papers, and resumes or business writing

PERCENTAGE OF STUDENTS SERVED: Less than 25%

OVER PAST FIVE YEARS THIS PERCENTAGE HAS: Stayed the same

STUDENTS USE CENTER: Throughout the semester on an appointment, walk-in, or regular basis

STUDENTS REQUIRED TO USE CENTER: None

MATERIALS AVAILABLE: Handbooks and exercises

STUDENT ATTITUDE: Unknown

The University of Illinois at Urbana-Champaign has an interesting and varied program. Its writing center, established over ten years ago, serves a small but diverse cross-section of the university community. Illinois has been quite successful with sections of freshmen composition centered on various themes such as "Mass Media and the Rhetoric of Popular Culture" and "Advertising and Film: Images and Ideas For and About Writing." A pilot section that focuses on writing with a word processor is expected to increase the department's emphasis on revision and in–class writing. Illinois has tried and rejected pass/fail writing classes because, as Jim Davis and Susan Pratt believe, "Students seem to need the pressure of grades to motivate them."

UNIVERSITY OF MAINE at MACHIAS

Machias, ME 04654

Full-time Students: 201M/275W   Faculty: 32

Respondent: Geneva Frost, Chairperson, Humanities Division

Writing Requirement: Required freshman English course

Peer Tutoring Program

PROGRAM HAS EXISTED FOR: 5–10 years

ORGANIZATION: Curriculum-based

NUMBER OF TUTORS: Fewer than 5

HOURS THEY WORK PER WEEK: Under 5

TUTORS PAID: Yes

TUTOR SELECTION: Nominated by English faculty

TUTORS' TRAINING: No formal training

TUTORS' EVALUATION: Conferences

PERCENTAGE OF STUDENTS SERVED: Less than 25%

OVER PAST FIVE YEARS THIS PERCENTAGE HAS: Stayed the same

PROGRAM INTENDED TO SERVE: Freshmen and English students

PROGRAM ACTUALLY SERVES: Freshmen and English students

STUDENTS SEEK HELP WITH: Academic essays and research papers

MECHANICS OF TUTORING: Student may choose to discuss any paper with a tutor

STUDENT ATTITUDE: Somewhat positive

The University of Maine at Machias offers its students a small peer tutoring program in addition to English classes. Established over five years ago, the program relies on fewer than five untrained tutors to help freshman English students with their writing. Although less than 25 percent of all students choose to discuss papers with the tutors, those who do generally respond positively.

UNIVERSITY OF MARYLAND

College Park, MD 20742

Full-time Students: 13,263M/11,559W   Faculty: 1837

Respondent: Leigh Ryan, Writing Center Director

Writing Requirement: Required freshman English course, required junior composition course

Writing Center

CENTER HAS EXISTED: 5-10 years   HOURS OPEN PER WEEK: 20-40

STAFF: 16 undergraduate tutors and 16 retired government and business people from the area

TUTORS' TRAINING: On-the-job

TUTORS' EVALUATION: Observation and conferences

TUTORS PAID: Yes

PROGRAM DESIGNED TO SERVE: Freshmen and junior writing students

PROGRAM ACTUALLY SERVES: Writing students (50% freshmen and 50% juniors)

STUDENTS SEEK HELP WITH: Academic essays, research papers, and resumes or business writing

PERCENTAGE OF STUDENTS SERVED: Less than 25%

OVER PAST FIVE YEARS THIS PERCENTAGE HAS: Increased

STUDENTS USE CENTER: Throughout the semester on a walk-in or appointment basis, or by phone

STUDENTS REQUIRED TO USE CENTER: Problem writers

MATERIALS AVAILABLE: Handbooks and exercises

STUDENT ATTITUDE: Very positive

Peer Tutoring Program

PROGRAM HAS EXISTED: 5-10 years

ORGANIZATION: Writing center-based

NUMBER OF TUTORS: 16

HOURS THEY WORK PER WEEK: 5-10

TUTORS PAID: Yes

TUTOR SELECTION: Appointed by director

TUTORS' TRAINING: On-the-job

TUTORS' EVALUATION: Observation and conferences

PERCENTAGE OF STUDENTS SERVED: Less than 25%

OVER PAST FIVE YEARS THIS PERCENTAGE HAS: Increased

PROGRAM INTENDED TO SERVE: Writing students and freshmen

PROGRAM ACTUALLY SERVES: Writing students and freshmen

STUDENTS SEEK HELP WITH: Academic essays, research papers, and resumes or business writing

MECHANICS OF TUTORING: Student may choose to discuss any paper with tutor

STUDENT ATTITUDE: Very positive

Writing-Across-the-Curriculum Program

PROGRAM HAS EXISTED: 2-5 years

INSTRUCTORS INVOLVED: Retired professionals

INSTRUCTORS' SELECTION: Voluntary

INSTRUCTORS' TRAINING: Seminars

STUDENTS INVOLVED IN PROGRAM: All students

PERCENTAGE OF STUDENTS INVOLVED: Less than 25%

IN PAST FIVE YEARS THIS PERCENTAGE HAS: Increased

PARTICIPANTS' ATTITUDE: Very positive

The writing requirement at the University of Maryland ensures that all the students at the school continue to write after their freshman year. First-year students study basic expository writing in freshman composition, while juniors undertake pre-professional writing courses within their major field. The writing center's undergraduate tutors help freshmen with their writing, and the retired professionals, from economists to lawyers to copy editors, are available to provide advice about their fields of study and expertise. These retired professionals occasionally teach as part-time instructors in the junior composition program. Both the peer tutoring and writing-across the curriculum programs have been very popular with Maryland's students.

UNIVERSITY OF MICHIGAN at ANN ARBOR

Ann Arbor, MI 48109

Full-time Students: 11,081M/9439W Faculty: 2660

Respondent: T. Toon, Associate Professor of English, Director of Composition

Writing Requirement: Required freshman English course and required upper level writing course; placement by examination

Writing Center

CENTER HAS EXISTED: 5-10 years HOURS OPEN PER WEEK: 20-40

STAFF: 20-40 faculty

TUTORS' TRAINING: On-the-job and academic course

TUTORS' EVALUATION: Observation, student questionnaire, conferences, and by other tutors

TUTORS PAID: Yes

PROGRAM DESIGNED TO SERVE: Students in all disciplines

PROGRAM ACTUALLY SERVES: Students in all disciplines

STUDENTS SEEK HELP WITH: Scientific reports, academic essays, research papers, and resumes or business writing

STUDENTS USE CENTER: Repeatedly throughout the semester on a walk-in or appointment basis

STUDENTS REQUIRED TO USE CENTER: Problem writers

MATERIALS AVAILABLE: Informal library consisting primarily of handbooks

STUDENT ATTITUDE: Very positive

Writing-Across-the-Curriculum Program

PROGRAM HAS EXISTED: 2-5 years

INSTRUCTORS INVOLVED: Faculty in all disciplines

INSTRUCTORS' SELECTION: Voluntary

INSTRUCTORS' TRAINING: Seminars and team teaching

PERCENTAGE OF FACULTY INVOLVED: 25–50%

IN PAST FIVE YEARS THIS PERCENTAGE HAS: Increased

STUDENTS INVOLVED IN PROGRAM: Students in all disciplines

PERCENTAGE OF STUDENTS INVOLVED: 100%

IN PAST FIVE YEARS THIS PERCENTAGE HAS: Increased

PARTICIPANTS' ATTITUDE: Very positive

In addition to its long-standing and successful writing center, the University of Michigan at Ann Arbor recently began a writing-across-the-curriculum program that serves the entire student body. All students are required to take an upper level writing course during their sophomore or junior years. If possible, students take this course within their areas of concentration. As an outgrowth of this program, Michigan has offered in-service workshops for high schools and community college teachers throughout the state.

UNIVERSITY OF MICHIGAN at DEARBORN

Dearborn, MI 48128

Full-time Students: 1924M/1597W Faculty: 300

Respondent: Sheryl Pearson, Humanities Department, Director of Writing Program

Writing Requirement: Two 3-hour composition courses

Writing Center

CENTER HAS EXISTED: 8 years HOURS OPEN PER WEEK: 30

STAFF: 4-7 undergraduate tutors

TUTORS' TRAINING: On-the job

TUTORS' EVALUATION: Observation, and student and faculty feedback

TUTORS PAID: Yes

PROGRAM DESIGNED TO SERVE: Students in all disciplines, especially writing students

PROGRAM ACTUALLY SERVES: Students in all disciplines, especially writing students

STUDENTS SEEK HELP WITH: Academic essays and research papers

PERCENTAGE OF STUDENTS SERVED: Less than 25%

OVER PAST FIVE YEARS THIS PERCENTAGE HAS: Stayed the same

STUDENTS USE CENTER: Throughout the semester on a walk-in or appointment basis

STUDENTS REQUIRED TO USE CENTER: Those enrolled in remedial course

MATERIALS AVAILABLE: Handbooks, exercises, and professional books

STUDENT ATTITUDE: Positive

Over the past three years the writing program at the University of Michigan at Dearborn has become more diversified, more demanding, and more attentive to "thinking skills along with grammar and mechanics," according to Sheryl Pearson. The required composition sequence, the communications major, and the annual writing awards program have all been successful, partially due to faculty involvement and a strong advising system. Use of the writing center is limited but steady; most students do not seek out the center or use it on a regular basis, but those students who do use it are very positive about the services. Students in the remedial writing course are the most frequent users.

UNIVERSITY OF MICHIGAN at FLINT

Flint, MI 48503

Full-time Students: 1129M/1246W Faculty: 129

Respondents: Wesley D. Rae, Professor of English, Department Chairperson; Frederic Svoboda, member of the Composition Committee

Writing Requirement: Required freshman English course (two semesters for most students); placement into remedial, beginning, or advanced freshman English based on examination

Writing Center

CENTER HAS EXISTED: 5-10 years HOURS OPEN PER WEEK: Over 40

STAFF: 5-20 faculty and undergraduate tutors, and a non-faculty administrator

TUTORS' TRAINING: On-the-job and academic training course

TUTORS' EVALUATION: Observation and conferences

TUTORS PAID: Yes

PROGRAM DESIGNED TO SERVE: Students in all disciplines

PROGRAM ACTUALLY SERVES: Students in all disciplines

STUDENTS SEEK HELP WITH: Academic essays, research papers, and scientific reports

PERCENTAGE OF STUDENTS SERVED: Less than 25%

OVER PAST FIVE YEARS THIS PERCENTAGE HAS: Increased

STUDENTS USE CENTER: Throughout the semester on a walk-in, appointment, or regular basis

STUDENTS REQUIRED TO USE CENTER: Problem writers

MATERIALS AVAILABLE: Handbooks, writing exercises, educational magazines, and professional books

STUDENT ATTITUDE: Somewhat positive

Peer Tutoring Program

PROGRAM HAS EXISTED: 2-5 years

ORGANIZATION: Curriculum-based

NUMBER OF TUTORS: Fewer than 10

HOURS THEY WORK PER WEEK: 10-20

TUTORS PAID: Yes

TUTOR SELECTION: Nominated by English faculty or self-nominated, and appointed by the director

TUTORS' TRAINING: On-the-job and academic training course

TUTORS' EVALUATION: Observation and conferences

PERCENTAGE OF STUDENTS SERVED: Less than 25%

OVER PAST FIVE YEARS THIS PERCENTAGE HAS: Increased

PROGRAM INTENDED TO SERVE: Students in all disciplines

PROGRAM ACTUALLY SERVES: Students in all disciplines

STUDENTS SEEK HELP WITH: Academic essays, research papers, scientific reports, and resumes or business writing

MECHANICS OF TUTORING: Tutor and student discuss papers

STUDENT ATTITUDE: Somewhat positive

In addition to requiring freshmen to take a composition course, the University of Michigan at Flint requires that problem writers seek assistance at the writing center. Open over forty hours each week, the center is well supplied with professional books, educational magazines, and writing exercises, and is staffed by faculty and peer tutors who help students from all disciplines. Though the center and the peer tutors serve less than 25 percent of the university's students, this percentage has been rising steadily over the past five years.

UNIVERSITY OF MINNESOTA at DULUTH

Duluth, MN 55812

Full-time Students: 3411M/2943W Faculty: 413

Respondents: Thomas Bacig, Director of Composition; Kenneth Risdon, Director of Computer-Assisted Instruction in English

Writing Requirement: Word Processing for Writing course, College Writing course, and Advanced Writing course; placement by examination

Writing Center

(Revision planned for Fall 1984)

CENTER HAS EXISTED: 5-10 years in another form

HOURS OPEN PER WEEK: Over 40

STAFF: Fewer than 5 adjunct faculty and graduate tutors

TUTORS' TRAINING: On-the-job and academic course

TUTORS' EVALUATION: Observation and student questionnaires

TUTORS PAID: Yes

PROGRAM DESIGNED TO SERVE: Students in all disciplines

PROGRAM ACTUALLY SERVES: Students in all disciplines

STUDENTS SEEK HELP WITH: Scientific reports, academic essays, research papers, and resumes or business writing

MATERIALS AVAILABLE: Exercises, computers and computer-assisted instruction, slides and tapes, and videotapes

STUDENT ATTITUDE: Unknown

Writing-Across-the-Curriculum Program

(Planned for Fall 1984)

PROGRAM HAS EXISTED: Not yet in operation

INSTRUCTORS INVOLVED: Faculty in all disciplines

INSTRUCTORS' SELECTION: By appointment

INSTRUCTORS' TRAINING: Seminars and team teaching

PERCENTAGE OF FACULTY INVOLVED: Less than 25%

PERCENTAGE OF STUDENTS INVOLVED: Less than 25%

STUDENTS INVOLVED IN PROGRAM: Students in all disciplines

PARTICIPANTS' ATTITUDE: Very positive (in pilot courses)

The writing program at the University of Minnesota at Duluth is undergoing major changes. A cross-curricular program of seminars and team teaching is planned to begin in the fall of 1984, while the university's writing center, which has existed for over five years, will be updated dramatically. This center will soon provide both traditional remedial tutoring and computer-aided instruction in writing. The university's writing curriculum will also be expanded, with many new courses in diverse areas, including Word Processing for Writing, College Writing, and Advanced Writing in various subject areas. Focusing on writing in various academic disciplines, the advanced-level writing courses will be team-taught by composition faculty and faculty in other disciplines.

UNIVERSITY OF MINNESOTA/TWIN CITIES

Minneapolis, MN 55455

Full-time Students: 15,077M/12,574W Faculty: 4655

Respondents: Robert Brown and Donald Ross, Co-Directors, Composition and Communication

Writing Requirement: Required freshman English course and required discipline-related upper level course

Writing Center

CENTER HAS EXISTED: Over 10 years HOURS OPEN PER WEEK: 20-40

STAFF: 5-10 graduate tutors, depending upon enrollments

TUTORS' TRAINING: On-the-job and non-academic course

TUTORS' EVALUATION: Observation, conferences, and by other tutors

TUTORS PAID: Yes

PROGRAM DESIGNED TO SERVE: Writing students and students in all disciplines

PROGRAM ACTUALLY SERVES: Writing students and students in all disciplines

STUDENTS SEEK HELP WITH: All writing

PERCENTAGE OF STUDENTS SERVED: Less than 10%

OVER PAST FIVE YEARS PERCENTAGE HAS: Stayed the same

STUDENTS USE CENTER: Throughout the quarter on a walk-in or appointment basis

STUDENTS REQUIRED TO USE CENTER: Problem writers

MATERIALS AVAILABLE: Handbooks and writing exercises

STUDENT ATTITUDE: Very positive

Writing-Across-the-Curriculum Program

PROGRAM HAS EXISTED: 4 years

INSTRUCTORS INVOLVED: Graduate students

INSTRUCTORS' SELECTION: By appointment

INSTRUCTORS' TRAINING: Seminars

PERCENTAGE OF FACULTY INVOLVED: 75%

IN PAST FIVE YEARS THIS PERCENTAGE HAS: Increased

STUDENTS INVOLVED IN PROGRAM: Students in all disciplines

PERCENTAGE OF STUDENTS INVOLVED: More than 75%; will be 100% by 1985-86

IN PAST FIVE YEARS THIS PERCENTAGE HAS: Increased

PARTICIPANTS' ATTITUDE: Very positive

The large student population at the University of Minnesota/Twin Cities is served by both a writing center and a cross-curricular program. The Composition Program's graduate students teach most of the freshman-level and junior-level composition courses and are trained in several seminars. Minnesota is phasing in a new "split" composition requirement, under which all students will take one quarter of composition in their first year and one quarter as juniors or seniors. Donald Ross and Robert Brown are still not sure how the full-scale program will operate, but the gradual increase in the number of sections (to allow for transfer students) apparently has not harmed the quality of the courses.

UNIVERSITY OF NEW HAMPSHIRE

Durham, NH 03824

Full-time Students: 4354M/4986W Faculty: 614

Respondent: Gary Lindberg, Director of Freshman English

Writing Requirement: Required freshman English course

Some time ago, the University of New Hampshire began to place greater emphasis on critical reading and student writing rather than on literature in the Freshman English classes. Freshman English students submit five pages of writing, read extensively, and meet with their instructors for individual conferences every week. These numerous conferences between faculty and writing students have reinforced the process approach to writing. New Hampshire's English Department also hires professional writers to teach fiction, poetry, and news writing, and these courses have improved both faculty attitudes toward student writing and student writing itself. The university plans to continue developing its process approach to writing, increasing the emphasis on the "processes of thinking and interpretation as these relate to writing."

UNIVERSITY OF NEW MEXICO

Albuquerque, NM 87131

Full-time Students: 6097M/5853W Faculty: 1038

Respondent: M. Hogan, Director, Freshman English

Writing Requirement: Required freshman English course

Writing Center

CENTER HAS EXISTED: 5 years HOURS OPEN PER WEEK: Over 40

STAFF: 30 graduate and undergraduate tutors

TUTORS' TRAINING: On-the-job

TUTORS' EVALUATION: Conferences and student questionnaire

TUTORS PAID: Yes

PROGRAM DESIGNED TO SERVE: Writing students and freshmen

PROGRAM ACTUALLY SERVES: Writing students and freshmen

STUDENTS SEEK HELP WITH: Academic essays

PERCENTAGE OF STUDENTS SERVED: Less than 25%

OVER PAST FIVE YEARS THIS PERCENTAGE HAS: Increased

STUDENTS USE CENTER: Throughout the semester on an appointment or walk-in basis

STUDENTS REQUIRED TO USE CENTER: Problem writers

MATERIALS AVAILABLE: Exercises

STUDENT ATTITUDE: Somewhat positive

With the exception of its writing center, the writing program at the University of New Mexico is fairly traditional. The center is both new and large, with over twenty undergraduates and graduates tutoring a total of over forty hours a week. New Mexico has standardized its freshman composition sequence in the past ten years, intensifying the focus on expository writing and adding a developmental course. The program is not expected to change significantly in the next few years.

UNIVERSITY OF NORTH CAROLINA

Chapel Hill, NC 27514

Full-time Students: 6096M/7999W Faculty: 1887

Respondent: Erika Lindemann, Director of Composition

Writing Requirement: Required freshman English courses and advanced composition for some majors

Writing Center

CENTER HAS EXISTED: Over 10 years HOURS OPEN PER WEEK: 20–40

STAFF: 5–20 undergraduate and graduate tutors

TUTORS' TRAINING: On-the-job

TUTORS' EVALUATION: Observation, conferences, student questionnaires, and by other tutors

TUTORS PAID: Yes

PROGRAM DESIGNED TO SERVE: Students in all disciplines

PROGRAM ACTUALLY SERVES: English students, freshmen, some graduate students, and some students in other disciplines

STUDENTS SEEK HELP WITH: Academic essays and research papers

PERCENTAGE OF STUDENTS SERVED: Less than 25%

OVER PAST FIVE YEARS THIS PERCENTAGE HAS: Increased

STUDENTS USE CENTER: Throughout the semester on a walk-in, appointment, or regular basis

STUDENTS REQUIRED TO USE CENTER: None

MATERIALS AVAILABLE: Handbooks, writing exercises, and professional books

STUDENT ATTITUDE: Very positive

Peer Tutoring Program

PROGRAM HAS EXISTED: Under 2 years

ORGANIZATION: Writing center-based

NUMBER OF TUTORS: Fewer than 10

HOURS THEY WORK PER WEEK: 5-10

TUTORS PAID: Yes

TUTOR SELECTION: Self-nominated and appointed by the director

TUTORS' TRAINING: On-the-job

TUTORS' EVALUATION: Observation, conferences, student questionnaires, and by other tutors

PERCENTAGE OF STUDENTS SERVED: Less than 25%

OVER PAST FIVE YEARS THIS PERCENTAGE HAS: Increased

PROGRAM INTENDED TO SERVE: Students in all disciplines

PROGRAM ACTUALLY SERVES: Students in all disciplines

STUDENTS SEEK HELP WITH: Academic essays and research papers

MECHANICS OF TUTORING: Students discuss papers with tutors or have the tutors comment on the papers

STUDENT ATTITUDE: Somewhat positive

The University of North Carolina approaches the problem of providing adequate writing instruction for its large student body by skillfully organizing its required freshman courses and introducing nontraditional programs. The freshman program is comprised of a basic composition course for inexperienced writers, a standard freshman level course, and a more advanced course that focuses on the process of argument. All three courses are taught in small sections by faculty and ten graduate teaching assistants. Students seeking individual help use the writing center, which is open to all students but is used most frequently by freshmen and English students. Established over ten years ago with only graduate tutors, the center added peer tutors in 1982. The English Department has also recently introduced instruction on prewriting and revision in "draft workshops." In the near future, North Carolina hopes to place greater emphasis on writing outside the English Department.

UNIVERSITY OF NOTRE DAME

Notre Dame, IN 46556

Full-time Students: 5279M/1885W   Faculty: 695

Respondent: Edward A. Kline, Director of Freshman Writing, Chairperson, English Department

Writing Requirement: Required freshman English course

Writing Center

CENTER HAS EXISTED: Over 10 years   HOURS OPEN PER WEEK: Over 40

STAFF: Professional director and 5–20 undergraduate tutors

TUTORS' TRAINING: On-the-job

TUTORS' EVALUATION: Observation and conferences

TUTORS PAID: Yes

PROGRAM DESIGNED TO SERVE: Freshmen

PROGRAM ACTUALLY SERVES: Freshmen

STUDENTS SEEK HELP WITH: Academic essays and research papers

PERCENTAGE OF STUDENTS SERVED: Over 75%

OVER PAST FIVE YEARS THIS PERCENTAGE HAS: Increased

STUDENTS USE CENTER: Throughout the semester on a walk-in and appointment basis

STUDENTS REQUIRED TO USE CENTER: Problem writers

MATERIALS AVAILABLE: Handbooks, exercises, educational magazines, professional books, writing samples, and computer-assisted reviews of grammar and spelling

STUDENT ATTITUDE: Very positive

Writing-Across-the-Curriculum Program

PROGRAM HAS EXISTED: Over 10 years

INSTRUCTORS INVOLVED: English and humanities faculty and graduate students

INSTRUCTORS' SELECTION: By writing director and various chairpersons

INSTRUCTORS' TRAINING: Seminars

PERCENTAGE OF FACULTY INVOLVED: 25-50%

IN PAST FIVE YEARS THIS PERCENTAGE HAS: Decreased

STUDENTS INVOLVED IN PROGRAM: Freshmen

PERCENTAGE OF STUDENTS INVOLVED: 25%

IN PAST FIVE YEARS THIS PERCENTAGE HAS: Stayed the same

PARTICIPANTS' ATTITUDE: Very positive

Notre Dame is particularly concerned with the writing ability of freshmen; both the writing center and the writing-across-the-curriculum program are designed especially for students in this class. As a result, these two programs enjoy popularity and success among the freshmen. Three quarters of all freshmen seek help from the writing center, and the writing-across-the-curriculum program reaches all first-year students. In addition to these longstanding programs, computer-assisted instruction has been used at Notre Dame for nearly ten years. Recently, the computer programs on grammar and editing skills, among others, were adapted to run on micro-computers.

UNIVERSITY OF OKLAHOMA

Norman, OK 73019

Full-time Students: 8352M/5922W Faculty: 753

Respondent: Michael Feehan, Director of Freshman English

Writing Requirement: Required freshman English course; exemption or placement by ACT, SAT, or AP examination

Writing Center

CENTER HAS EXISTED: 2-5 years HOURS OPEN PER WEEK: 20-40

STAFF: 5-20 graduate and undergraduate tutors

TUTORS' TRAINING: On-the-job

TUTORS' EVALUATION: Observation, conferences, and by other tutors

TUTORS PAID: Yes

PROGRAM DESIGNED TO SERVE: Writing students, freshmen, international students, and students in all disciplines

PROGRAM ACTUALLY SERVES: Students in all disciplines, but mostly freshmen

STUDENTS SEEK HELP WITH: Academic essays, research papers, dissertations, and theses

PERCENTAGE OF STUDENTS SERVED: Less than 25%

OVER PAST FIVE YEARS THIS PERCENTAGE HAS: Decreased

STUDENTS USE CENTER: Throughout the semester, primarily on a regular basis, with some walk-ins

STUDENTS REQUIRED TO USE CENTER: Problem writers

MATERIALS AVAILABLE: Handbooks, exercises, student essays, and dissertations

STUDENT ATTITUDE: Very positive

Only recently established, the writing program at the University of Oklahoma is struggling to overcome difficulties that include a 20 percent decrease in freshman enrollment, an overextension of the writing center staff and resources, and an inconvenient physical location for the writing center. The school is reorganizing its freshman writing program, a process that will continue over the next two years. The faculty of the doctoral concentration in Rhetoric are also redesigning writing programs at all levels. Michael Feehan reports that they hope to develop a program similar to the one started by James Kinneavy at the University of Texas at Austin. Oklahoma plans to begin a writing-across-the-curriculum program and will also expand the writing center.

UNIVERSITY OF OREGON

Eugene, OR 97403

Full-time Students: 5670M/5394W Faculty: 1400

Respondent: John Gage, Director of Composition

Writing Requirement: 2 required freshman composition courses

Writing Center

CENTER HAS EXISTED: 5-10 years HOURS OPEN PER WEEK: Over 40

STAFF: 5-20 faculty, graduate, and undergraduate tutors

TUTORS' TRAINING: On-the-job and non-academic training course

TUTORS' EVALUATION: Observation, conferences, and student questionnaires

TUTORS PAID: Yes

PROGRAM DESIGNED TO SERVE: Students in all disciplines

PROGRAM ACTUALLY SERVES: Students in all disciplines

STUDENTS SEEK HELP WITH: Scientific reports, academic essays, research papers, and resumes or business writing

PERCENTAGE OF STUDENTS SERVED: 25-50%

OVER PAST FIVE YEARS THIS PERCENTAGE HAS: Increased

STUDENTS USE CENTER: Throughout the semester on an appointment, walk-in, or regular basis

STUDENTS REQUIRED TO USE CENTER: None

MATERIALS AVAILABLE: Handbooks and exercises

STUDENT ATTITUDE: Somewhat positive

Writing-Across-the-Curriculum Program

PROGRAM HAS EXISTED: 2-5 years

INSTRUCTORS INVOLVED: Faculty in all disciplines

INSTRUCTORS' SELECTION: Voluntary

INSTRUCTORS' TRAINING: Seminars for some

PERCENTAGE OF FACULTY INVOLVED: Less than 25%

STUDENTS INVOLVED IN PROGRAM: Students in all disciplines

PERCENTAGE OF STUDENTS INVOLVED: 25–50%

PARTICIPANTS' ATTITUDE: Somewhat positive

John Gage characterizes the University of Oregon's successful programs as, "a coherent, consistent core of composition, followed by some writing intensive courses." Oregon's programs have shifted recently toward an emphasis on writing as argumentation and "as a means of inquiry and knowing." Although student attitudes toward the writing center have varied, the center serves nearly half of all students each year. Oregon's fairly young writing-across-the-curriculum program reaches a similar percentage of students.

UNIVERSITY OF PENNSYLVANIA

Philadelphia, PA 19104

Full-time Students: 5300M/3400W Faculty: 1800

Respondent: Timothy Martin, Coordinator, Expository Writing Programs

Writing Requirement: One semester required freshman English course for 400 of 2100 freshmen

Writing Center

CENTER HAS EXISTED: 6 years HOURS OPEN PER WEEK: 20-40

STAFF: 6-8 graduate tutors

TUTORS' TRAINING: Previous teaching experience in freshman English

TUTORS' EVALUATION: Student questionnaire

TUTORS PAID: Yes

PROGRAM DESIGNED TO SERVE: Students in all disciplines

PROGRAM ACTUALLY SERVES: Freshmen, humanities students, and English students

STUDENTS SEEK HELP WITH: Any course-related writing

PERCENTAGE OF STUDENTS SERVED: 10%

OVER PAST FIVE YEARS THIS PERCENTAGE HAS: Increased

STUDENTS USE CENTER: Throughout the semester on an appointment or regular basis

STUDENTS REQUIRED TO USE CENTER: None

MATERIALS AVAILABLE: Handbooks and exercises

STUDENT ATTITUDE: Very positive to somewhat positive

Peer Tutoring Program

PROGRAM HAS EXISTED: Less than 2 years

ORGANIZATION: Residentially based

TUTOR SELECTION: Selected from staff of Residential Advisors and appointed by the director

NUMBER OF TUTORS: 25

HOURS THEY WORK PER WEEK: 5-6

TUTORS PAID: Yes

TUTORS' TRAINING: Non-academic series of lectures and workshops

TUTORS' EVALUATION: Tutors give reports at end of term

PERCENTAGE OF STUDENTS SERVED: 20-25%

PROGRAM INTENDED TO SERVE: Students in all disciplines

PROGRAM ACTUALLY SERVES: Freshmen and English students

STUDENTS SEEK HELP WITH: Any academic writing

MECHANICS OF TUTORING: Student may choose to discuss any paper with tutor

STUDENT ATTITUDE: Unknown

Writing-Across-the-Curriculum Program

PROGRAM HAS EXISTED: Less than 2 years

INSTRUCTORS INVOLVED: Faculty in all disciplines and graduate students

INSTRUCTORS' SELECTION: Voluntary

INSTRUCTORS' TRAINING: Seminars for graduate teaching assistants

PERCENTAGE OF FACULTY INVOLVED: 5%

IN PAST FIVE YEARS THIS PERCENTAGE HAS: Increased

STUDENTS INVOLVED IN PROGRAM: Undergraduates in all disciplines

PERCENTAGE OF STUDENTS INVOLVED: 15% of all undergraduates each term

IN PAST FIVE YEARS THIS PERCENTAGE HAS: Increased

PARTICIPANTS' ATTITUDE: Very positive

In 1982, the University of Pennsylvania began a "Writing Across the University" program. Courses in several departments are designated "Writing Enrichment" courses and are separated into three levels: foundation courses in writing, Writing Reinforcement courses, and Advanced Disciplinary courses. Writing Enrichment courses range from freshman seminars to senior thesis colloquia, and are offered in a variety of disciplines from Electrical Engineering to Religious Studies. According to Timothy Martin, the success of such a new program is difficult to evaluate, but many faculty are eager to participate on a continuing basis. The peer tutoring program, which employs twenty-five undergraduate Writing Consultants, has been less successful. These Consultants, who attend a series of lectures and discussions as part of an their training, are also Residential Advisors and live with the students that they tutor. The open and voluntary nature of the program has been one of its problems, but Martin thinks "it will improve as we figure out how to market our Writing Consultants."

UNIVERSITY OF PITTSBURGH

Pittsburgh, PA 15260

Full-time Students: 6109M/5870W   Faculty: 2104

Respondent: Carolyn Ball, Assistant to the Director of Composition

Writing Requirement: Required introductory composition course and two writing-across-the-curriculum courses

Writing Center

CENTER HAS EXISTED: Over 10 years   HOURS OPEN PER WEEK: Over 40

STAFF: 5–20 faculty and graduate tutors

TUTORS' TRAINING: On-the-job and academic course

TUTORS' EVALUATION: Observation, conferences, student questionnaires, tape recordings, and by other tutors

TUTORS PAID: Yes

PROGRAM DESIGNED TO SERVE: Students in all disciplines

PROGRAM ACTUALLY SERVES: Students in all disciplines

STUDENTS SEEK HELP WITH: Scientific reports, creative writing, academic essays, research papers, resumes or business writing, and dissertations

PERCENTAGE OF STUDENTS SERVED: Less than 25%

OVER PAST FIVE YEARS THIS PERCENTAGE HAS: Increased

STUDENTS USE CENTER: Usually once throughout the semester on a walk-in, appointment, or regular basis

STUDENTS REQUIRED TO USE CENTER: Problem writers

MATERIALS AVAILABLE: Handbooks, exercises, professional books, and educational magazines

STUDENT ATTITUDE: Very positive

Writing-Across-the-Curriculum Program

PROGRAM HAS EXISTED: Under 2 years

INSTRUCTORS INVOLVED: Faculty and graduate students in all disciplines

INSTRUCTORS' SELECTION: Voluntary and by appointment

PERCENTAGE OF FACULTY INVOLVED: Less than 25%

STUDENTS INVOLVED IN PROGRAM: Students in all disciplines

PERCENTAGE OF STUDENTS INVOLVED: More than 75%

PARTICIPANTS' ATTITUDE: Positive

Writing programs at the University of Pittsburgh attract a clientele with varied levels of skill. In existence for over ten years and open for over forty hours a week, the writing center is a case in point. The center reaches a wide spectrum of the university community: thirteen percent of the center's clients, for example, are graduate students seeking help with research papers and dissertations. The University of Pittsburgh offers a variety of undergraduate composition courses for students with different levels of writing experience and different writing interests. All of these courses are writing-intensive, require at least forty pages of writing each term, and place the discussion of student essays and the writing process at the center of the classroom experience. The university's focus on writing is also reflected in its cross-curricular writing board program, which has faculty in several departments teaching required courses with a writing component. Although this program has existed for less than two years, it already involves more than 75 percent of the student body.

UNIVERSITY OF RHODE ISLAND

Kingston, RI 02881

Full-time Students: 4430M/4394W Faculty: 702

Respondent: Robert Schwegler, Director, College Writing Program

Writing Requirement: 2 required communications courses, one designated as a writing course

Writing Center

CENTER HAS EXISTED: 5-10 years HOURS OPEN PER WEEK: 10-20

STAFF: 3 part-time instructors and 1 graduate tutor

TUTORS' TRAINING: On-the-job

TUTORS' EVALUATION: Observation

TUTORS PAID: Yes

PROGRAM DESIGNED TO SERVE: Students in all disciplines, especially English and writing students

PROGRAM ACTUALLY SERVES: Students in all disciplines, especially English and writing students

STUDENTS SEEK HELP WITH: Scientific reports, academic essays, research papers, and some resumes or business writing

PERCENTAGE OF STUDENTS SERVED: Less than 25%

OVER PAST FIVE YEARS THIS PERCENTAGE HAS: Increased

STUDENTS USE CENTER: Primarily at mid-semester on an appointment or walk-in basis

STUDENTS REQUIRED TO USE CENTER: None; some strongly encouraged

MATERIALS AVAILABLE: Handbooks, exercises, rhetorics, and readers

STUDENT ATTITUDE: Unknown

Nearly ten years ago, the University of Rhode Island established a separate program in rhetoric and composition within the English Department. Since then, the composition program has created a writing center that serves primarily writing and English students at all levels. The demand for advanced writing courses has increased sharply in the past three years, and URI hopes to expand its upper-level offerings to accommodate this growth. URI has been most successful with advanced scientific and technical writing courses and with expository writing courses that do not include literature. The university is now offering a concentration in rhetoric and composition in its graduate degree program.

UNIVERSITY OF SANTA CLARA

Santa Clara, CA 95053

Full-time Students: 1805M/1601W Faculty: 253

Respondent: Charles Phipps, S. J., Chairperson of English Department

Writing Requirement: 3 required English courses

Peer Tutoring Program

PROGRAM HAS EXISTED: 2-5 years ORGANIZATION: Curriculum-based

NUMBER OF TUTORS: 10-15

HOURS THEY WORK PER WEEK: 5-10

TUTORS PAID: No

TUTOR SELECTION: Based on admission to practicum course; admission by permission of instructor

TUTORS' TRAINING: Academic course

TUTORS' EVALUATION: Observation, conferences, and written reports

PERCENTAGE OF STUDENTS SERVED: Less than 15%

OVER PAST FIVE YEARS THIS PERCENTAGE HAS: Stayed the same

PROGRAM INTENDED TO SERVE: Composition and Rhetoric students referred by instructors

PROGRAM ACTUALLY SERVES: Composition and Rhetoric students referred by instructors

STUDENTS SEEK HELP WITH: Academic essays

MECHANICS OF TUTORING: Tutor comments in writing on all of the student's papers; tutor and student are required to discuss papers

STUDENT ATTITUDE: Very positive

During the past few years, the University of Santa Clara has employed more composition teachers with professional training and experience in the teaching of writing, rather than teachers trained in literature. Charles Phipps feels this shift will greatly benefit students because "Freshman courses must be writing courses. Teachers of writing must be professionally trained writing or literature teachers who are willing and able to teach writing effectively." Introduction to Literature, or Composition and Literature courses have been replaced by Composition and Rhetoric courses, and Phipps feels that this "current freshman program is the best ever." The "Writing Emphasis" within the English major program may include courses in exposition, journalism, creative writing, technical report writing, and argumentation. Peer tutors are available to help students after receiving permission from the students' instructor and enrolling in a "Practicum in Tutoring Composition," a course that includes lectures, reports, and practical experience. Because Phipps believes that a competent staff is the most important element of the writing program, he will continue to improve the hiring procedures during the next few years.

UNIVERSITY OF SOUTHERN CALIFORNIA

Los Angeles, CA 90086

Full-time Students: 7573M/5549W Faculty: 966

Respondent: Michael Holzman, Chairperson, Freshman Writing Program

Writing Requirement: Required freshman English course

Writing Center

CENTER HAS EXISTED: 2-5 yrs HOURS OPEN PER WEEK: Over 40

STAFF: Over 40 graduate tutors

TUTORS' TRAINING: On-the-job and academic course

TUTORS' EVALUATION: Observation

TUTORS PAID: Yes

PROGRAM DESIGNED TO SERVE: Students in all disciplines

PROGRAM ACTUALLY SERVES: Students in all disciplines

STUDENTS SEEK HELP WITH: Academic essays, research papers, and resumes or business writing

PERCENTAGE OF STUDENTS SERVED: 25-50%

OVER PAST FIVE YEARS THIS PERCENTAGE HAS: Increased

STUDENTS USE CENTER: Repeatedly throughout the semester on a walk-in or appointment basis

STUDENTS REQUIRED TO USE CENTER: Freshmen

MATERIALS AVAILABLE: Handbooks and exercises

STUDENT ATTITUDE: Somewhat positive

Writing-Across-the-Curriculum Program

PROGRAM HAS EXISTED: 2-5 years

INSTRUCTORS INVOLVED: Faculty and graduate students in all disciplines

INSTRUCTORS' SELECTION: Voluntary

PERCENTAGE OF FACULTY INVOLVED: Less than 25%

IN PAST FIVE YEARS THIS PERCENTAGE HAS: Decreased

STUDENTS INVOLVED IN PROGRAM: Students in all disciplines

PERCENTAGE OF STUDENTS INVOLVED: Less than 25%

IN PAST FIVE YEARS THIS PERCENTAGE HAS: Decreased

PARTICIPANTS' ATTITUDE: Very positive

The English Department at the University of Southern California has shifted writing instruction away from the classroom and instead encourages individualized writing instruction through private tutorials, independent writing programs, the writing-across-the-curriculum program, and use of the writing center. Although the writing-across-the-curriculum program and the writing center are relatively young, both have been popular with students. In the next few years USC plans to continue its emphasis on tutorials and other innovative writing programs.

UNIVERSITY OF SOUTH FLORIDA

Tampa, FL 33606

Full-time Students: 6192M/6148W Faculty: 1052

Respondent: R.F. Dietrich, Director, Freshman English

Writing Requirement: Required freshman English course and 4 writing-intensive courses that require 6000 words

Writing Center

CENTER HAS EXISTED: Under 2 years HOURS OPEN PER WEEK: 20-40

STAFF: Fewer than 5 faculty and graduate tutors

TUTORS' TRAINING: On-the-job

TUTORS' EVALUATION: Observation and by other tutors

TUTORS PAID: Some are

PROGRAM DESIGNED TO SERVE: Students in all disciplines, primarily freshmen

PROGRAM ACTUALLY SERVES: Students in all disciplines, primarily freshmen

STUDENTS SEEK HELP WITH: Academic essays and research papers

PERCENTAGE OF STUDENTS SERVED: Less than 25%

STUDENTS USE CENTER: Throughout the semester on an appointment or walk-in basis

STUDENTS REQUIRED TO USE CENTER: None

MATERIALS AVAILABLE: Handbooks and exercises

STUDENT ATTITUDE: Unknown

Like many institutions, the University of South Florida is just beginning to develop nontraditional writing programs. Its writing center, designed primarily for first-year students in all disciplines, opened just two years ago. South Florida hopes to expand the center, and perhaps to create other innovative programs. A writing-across-the-curriculum program is a possibility in the near future.

UNIVERSITY OF TEXAS at ARLINGTON

Arlington, TX 76019

Full-time Students: 6958M/4891W Faculty: 677

Respondent: Victor Vitanza, Coordinator of Rhetoric Division

Writing Requirement: Required freshman English course and other required English course

Writing Center

CENTER HAS EXISTED: 5-10 years HOURS OPEN PER WEEK: 20-40

STAFF: Fewer than 5 faculty, graduate, and undergraduate tutors

TUTORS' TRAINING: On-the job and academic training course

TUTORS' EVALUATION: Observation

TUTORS PAID: Yes

PROGRAM DESIGNED TO SERVE: Students in all disciplines

PROGRAM ACTUALLY SERVES: Students in all disciplines

STUDENTS SEEK HELP WITH: Scientific reports, academic essays, and research papers

PERCENTAGE OF STUDENTS SERVED: Less than 25%

OVER PAST FIVE YEARS THIS PERCENTAGE HAS: Increased

STUDENTS USE CENTER: Primarily at mid-semester on walk-in basis

STUDENTS REQUIRED TO USE CENTER: None

MATERIALS AVAILABLE: Handbooks, exercises, and cassette tapes

STUDENT ATTITUDE: Somewhat positive

The University of Texas at Arlington offers students a wide range of writing courses and a writing minor. Students electing this minor can specialize in business and professional writing, creative writing, rhetoric and composition, or technical writing and editing. Texas at Arlington has recently reformulated the sophomore through senior writing courses, developed an M.A. and Ph.D. program in rhetoric and composition, and changed the freshman introduction to literature course to a writing course on exposition and argumentation.

UNIVERSITY OF TEXAS at AUSTIN

Austin, TX 78712

Full-time Students: 20,301M/17,810W Faculty: 2100

Respondent: J. Ruszkiewicz, Director of Freshman English

Writing Requirement: Required freshman English course, upper-division writing course, and 6 hours of courses with a "substantial writing component"

Writing Center

CENTER HAS EXISTED: 2-5 years HOURS OPEN PER WEEK: Over 40

STAFF: 5-20 graduate tutors

TUTORS' TRAINING: On-the-job and non-academic course

TUTORS' EVALUATION: Observation and student questionnaire

TUTORS PAID: Yes

PROGRAM DESIGNED TO SERVE: Freshman English students

PROGRAM ACTUALLY SERVES: Students in all disciplines

STUDENTS SEEK HELP WITH: Academic essays, research papers, and scientific reports

PERCENTAGE OF STUDENTS SERVED: Less than 25%

OVER PAST FIVE YEARS THIS PERCENTAGE HAS: Increased

STUDENTS USE CENTER: Throughout the semester on a walk-in or appointment basis

STUDENTS REQUIRED TO USE CENTER: None

MATERIALS AVAILABLE: Handbooks, exercises, and computer terminals

STUDENT ATTITUDE: Very positive

Writing-Across-the-Curriculum Program

PROGRAM HAS EXISTED: Less than 2 years

INSTRUCTORS INVOLVED: Faculty in all disciplines

INSTRUCTORS' SELECTION: All faculty will participate eventually

INSTRUCTORS' TRAINING: None

PERCENTAGE OF FACULTY INVOLVED: Less than 25%; more courses being added

IN PAST FIVE YEARS THIS PERCENTAGE HAS: Increased

STUDENTS INVOLVED IN PROGRAM: Students in all disciplines

PERCENTAGE OF STUDENTS INVOLVED: Less than 25%; will be 100% in future

IN PAST FIVE YEARS THIS PERCENTAGE HAS: Increased

PARTICIPANTS' ATTITUDE: Unknown

The writing program at the University of Texas at Austin is currently undergoing major changes, the primary focus being a writing-across-the-curriculum program. The writing requirement was three consecutive semesters of English courses, two of which placed a stronger emphasis on literature than writing. The new program requires nine hours of coursework in the English Department and six additional hours of courses with a "Substantial Writing Component" (SWC) These SWC courses may be taken in any department; all colleges in the university will be required to offer them. The nine required hours in the English Department are Rhetoric and Composition in the first year, Masterpieces of Literature in the second year, and Writing in the Disciplines (Natural Sciences, Social Sciences, Humanities) in the third or fourth year. The upper division course, Writing in the Disciplines, is designed to teach students how to communicate their knowledge of their specific discipline to general audiences. The key to implementing this complex program successfully will be the careful coordination of its separate parts, including testing, placement, evaluation, textbook selection, assignments, teacher training, teacher support, tutorial assistance (notably the Writing Lab), student advising, and administration.

UNIVERSITY OF TEXAS at EL PASO

El Paso, TX 79968

Full-time Students: 4703M/4484W Faculty: 430

Respondent: Maureen Potts, Director of Composition

Writing Requirement: Required freshman English course

Writing Center and Peer Tutoring Program

CENTER HAS EXISTED: 5-10 years HOURS OPEN PER WEEK: Over 40

STAFF: 20-40 undergraduate tutors

TUTOR SELECTION: Appointed by director

TUTORS' TRAINING: On-the-job and non-academic course

TUTORS' EVALUATION: Observation, conferences, and by other tutors

TUTORS PAID: Yes

HOURS THEY WORK PER WEEK: 10-20

PROGRAM DESIGNED TO SERVE: Students in all disciplines

PROGRAM ACTUALLY SERVES: Students in all disciplines

STUDENTS SEEK HELP WITH: Academic essays and research papers

PERCENTAGE OF STUDENTS SERVED: Less than 25%

OVER PAST FIVE YEARS THIS PERCENTAGE HAS: Stayed the same

STUDENTS USE CENTER: Primarily at mid-semester and towards the end of the semester on a walk-in basis

STUDENTS REQUIRED TO USE CENTER: None

MECHANICS OF TUTORING: Student may choose to discuss a paper or have tutor comment in writing on any paper

MATERIALS AVAILABLE: Handbooks, exercises, professional books, and educational magazines

STUDENT ATTITUDE: Somewhat positive

Writing-Across-the-Curriculum Program

PROGRAM HAS EXISTED: 2-5 years

INSTRUCTORS INVOLVED: Faculty in all disciplines

INSTRUCTORS' SELECTION: Voluntary

INSTRUCTORS' TRAINING: None

PERCENTAGE OF FACULTY INVOLVED: Less than 25%

IN PAST FIVE YEARS THIS PERCENTAGE HAS: Stayed the same

STUDENTS INVOLVED IN PROGRAM: Students in all disciplines, especially those in the humanities and social sciences

PERCENTAGE OF STUDENTS INVOLVED: Less than 25%

IN PAST FIVE YEARS THIS PERCENTAGE HAS: Stayed the same

PARTICIPANTS' ATTITUDE: Unknown

According to Maureen Potts, the University of Texas at El Paso has "made intensive efforts at faculty development in areas of composition" as part of its writing-across-the-curriculum program. The program encourages students not majoring in English to develop writing proficiency in different areas. The university has also experimented with "paired courses" in which students can register for a non-English course in conjunction with the required freshman composition. Students seeking individual assistance may discuss papers with trained peer tutors at the writing center, which is open over forty hours each week. In addition, ten to thirty faculty members and graduate students teach writing courses exclusively, including those in communications, and creative and expository writing.

UNIVERSITY OF VERMONT

Burlington, VT 05405

Full-time Students: 3107M/4303W Faculty: 552

Respondents: Toby Fulwiler, Director of Writing; Sue Dinitz, Director of Writing Center

Writing Requirement: Required freshman English course, other required writing courses

Writing Center and Peer Tutoring Program

CENTER HAS EXISTED: 2-5 years HOURS OPEN PER WEEK: 40

STAFF: 15-20 undergraduate tutors

TUTOR SELECTION: Appointed by director

TUTORS' TRAINING: On-the-job and academic course

TUTORS' EVALUATION: Observation and student questionnaire

TUTORS PAID: No

HOURS THEY WORK PER WEEK: 3

PROGRAM DESIGNED TO SERVE: Students in all disciplines

PROGRAM ACTUALLY SERVES: Students in all disciplines

STUDENTS SEEK HELP WITH: Academic essays

PERCENTAGE OF STUDENTS SERVED: Less than 25%

OVER PAST FIVE YEARS THIS PERCENTAGE HAS: Increased

STUDENTS USE CENTER: On an appointment basis

STUDENTS REQUIRED TO USE CENTER: None

MATERIALS AVAILABLE: Handbooks and exercises

MECHANICS OF TUTORING: Tutor and student are required to discuss papers

STUDENT ATTITUDE: Very positive

Writing-Across-the-Curriculum Program

PROGRAM HAS EXISTED: Less than 2 years

INSTRUCTORS INVOLVED: Faculty in all disciplines

INSTRUCTORS' SELECTION: Voluntary

INSTRUCTORS' TRAINING: 2-day inductive workshops

PERCENTAGE OF FACULTY INVOLVED: 100% (eventually)

STUDENTS INVOLVED IN PROGRAM: Students in all disciplines

PARTICIPANTS' ATTITUDE: Very positive

To supplement its writing center and peer-tutoring program, the University of Vermont is currently establishing an ambitious writing-across-the-curriculum program. Toby Fulwiler, who has written extensively on the subject of writing-across-the-curriculum, was hired in the fall of 1983 and since then has conducted faculty development workshops that he considers vital to a good cross-disciplinary program. By September 1984, one hundred faculty will have participated in these seminars and sixty more will participate each succeeding year. As part of this program, the Arts and Sciences College is about to adopt an extensive "vertical" writing requirement. Freshmen will take one writing course and all students will take three writing-intensive courses after their first year. Fulwiler describes his plans as a "long-term effort to put writing back in the center of the University of Vermont curriculum."

UNIVERSITY OF VIRGINIA

Charlottesville, VA 22903

Full-time Students: 5614M/5438W Faculty: 1570

Respondent: Charlene M. Sedgwick, Director of Expository Writing

Writing Requirement: Required freshman English course, second writing requirement in courses in other departments; placement by ACH test and essay examination

Writing Center

CENTER HAS EXISTED: 5-10 years HOURS OPEN PER WEEK: 20-40

STAFF: 5-20 graduate tutors

TUTORS' TRAINING: On-the-job, academic course, and non-academic course; some have previous teaching experience

TUTORS' EVALUATION: Student questionnaire and by the director

TUTORS PAID: Yes

PROGRAM DESIGNED TO SERVE: Students in all disciplines, half of whom are writing students

PROGRAM ACTUALLY SERVES: When fully funded, serves students in all disciplines; otherwise, English and writing students are served first

STUDENTS SEEK HELP WITH: Academic essays, research papers, scientific reports, resumes or business writing, and master's and doctoral theses

PERCENTAGE OF STUDENTS SERVED: Less than 25%

OVER PAST FIVE YEARS THIS PERCENTAGE HAS: Stayed the same

STUDENTS USE CENTER: Primarily at mid-semester on a walk-in, appointment, or regular basis, or by phone

STUDENTS REQUIRED TO USE CENTER: None; students with weak writing skills are "strongly urged"

MATERIALS AVAILABLE: Handbooks, exercises, professional books, and educational magazines

STUDENT ATTITUDE: Very positive

The strongest part of the University of Virginia's writing program is a traditional freshman English course that incorporates several innovative techniques. In his outline of the teaching strategies to be employed in the course, E.D. Hirsch states that its aims have been set "by the faculty of Arts and Sciences, not by the English Department. The Faculty wishes mainly to ensure an acceptable level of student writing in examinations, lab reports, short papers and term papers. Whatever our view of this utilitarian goal, we should understand that it is shared also by most of our students." Charlene Sedgwick believes, however, that an official writing-across-the-curriculum program is unlikely because "there is too much departmental autonomy for so-called 'writing across-the-curriculum' to work."

While the University of Virginia may not turn to writing across the curriculum, its writing center helps students overcome writing problems not treated in their classes The graduate tutors working in the center have taught the freshman English course and taken a non-academic training course, and some have also taken the academic courses, "Reading of Composition" and "Teaching Composition." In addition, several of the tutors have experience teaching English at secondary schools. The center is prepared to serve both writing students and students in other disciplines, but Sedgwick reports that the availability of this service varies, depending on funding. He writes, "If we are sufficiently funded, we serve the whole University, including graduate students who need more sophisticated help with their writing. If we are not sufficiently funded we serve writing courses and the English Department first." Although the University of Virginia makes minor adjustments all the time, there are no major plans for the near future. Its current programs have been quite successful.

UNIVERSITY OF WASHINGTON

Seattle, WA 98105

Full-time Students: 11,612M/10,033W Faculty: 2600

Respondent: Joan Graham, Director of Interdisciplinary Writing Program

Writing Requirement: 2 writing-intensive courses in various disciplines

Writing-Across-the-Curriculum Program

PROGRAM HAS EXISTED: 8 years

INSTRUCTORS INVOLVED: Faculty in all disciplines

INSTRUCTORS' SELECTION: Voluntary

INSTRUCTORS' TRAINING: Team teaching

PERCENTAGE OF FACULTY INVOLVED: Less than 25%

IN PAST FIVE YEARS THIS PERCENTAGE HAS: Increased

STUDENTS INVOLVED IN PROGRAM: Students in all disciplines

PERCENTAGE OF STUDENTS INVOLVED: Less than 25%

IN PAST FIVE YEARS THIS PERCENTAGE HAS: Increased

PARTICIPANTS' ATTITUDE: Very positive

The University of Washington's unusually successful and innovative writing-across-the-curriculum program relies on a form of team teaching to spread writing instruction throughout the university. The program's courses, known as "Writing Labs," are expository writing courses linked to specified lecture courses in disciplines as diverse as psychology, art history, economics, and sociology. Participating students take the appropriate Writing Lab course concurrently with its linked content course, write essays drawn from content course readings, and attend frequent individual conferences with the Writing Lab instructor. The Washington faculty plan to expand the program to include faculty training workshops and two-day seminars for those who run the workshops. The university is also considering both a writing center and a peer tutoring program.

UNIVERSITY OF WISCONSIN at MILWAUKEE

Milwaukee, WI 53201

Full-time Students: 6682M/6566W   Faculty: 806

Respondent: T.J. Bontly, Coordinator of Composition

Writing Requirement: English proficiency essay examination

Writing Center

CENTER HAS EXISTED: 2 years   HOURS OPEN PER WEEK: 20-40

STAFF: 5-20 undergraduate tutors

TUTORS' TRAINING: On-the-job and non-academic course

TUTORS' EVALUATION: Observation, student questionnaires, and by other tutors

TUTORS PAID: Yes

PROGRAM DESIGNED TO SERVE: Students in all disciplines

PROGRAM ACTUALLY SERVES: Students in all disciplines, especially freshmen

STUDENTS SEEK HELP WITH: Academic essays and research papers

PERCENTAGE OF STUDENTS SERVED: Less than 25%

OVER PAST FIVE YEARS THIS PERCENTAGE HAS: Increased

STUDENTS USE CENTER: Throughout the semester on an appointment or walk-in basis

STUDENTS REQUIRED TO USE CENTER: Specially admitted students

MATERIALS AVAILABLE: Exercises

STUDENT ATTITUDE: Very positive

The University of Wisconsin at Milwaukee considers its traditional offerings in expository writing to be more satisfactory than its writing center. T.J. Bontly characterizes the problems of labs and tutors as "insufficient control, sporadic use, and uncertain results." Nonetheless, student response to the growing Writing Referral Center has been very positive, especially among first-year students. Wisconsin's writing program has expanded rapidly since 1974, adding business and technical writing, M.A. and Ph.D. degrees, a non-credit remedial course, and several new advanced composition offerings. Bontly hopes to see the remedial courses eventually eliminated as need for them declines.

UNIVERSITY OF WISCONSIN at STEVENS POINT

Stevens Point, WI 54481

Full-time Students: 4310M/4314W Faculty: 488

Respondent: Donald Pattow, Director of Freshman English, Coordinator of Writing Emphasis Program

Writing Requirement: Required freshman English and six credits of writing-emphasis courses

Writing Center

CENTER HAS EXISTED: 10 years HOURS OPEN PER WEEK: 40

STAFF: 10-15 faculty, graduate, and undergraduate tutors

TUTORS' TRAINING: On-the-job and non-academic course

TUTORS' EVALUATION: Observation and conferences

TUTORS PAID: Yes

PROGRAM DESIGNED TO SERVE: Students in all disciplines

PROGRAM ACTUALLY SERVES: Students in all disciplines

STUDENTS SEEK HELP WITH: Academic essays, research papers, and resumes or business writing

PERCENTAGE OF STUDENTS SERVED: Less than 25%

OVER PAST FIVE YEARS THIS PERCENTAGE HAS: Increased

STUDENTS USE CENTER: Throughout the semester on an appointment or walk-in basis

STUDENTS REQUIRED TO USE CENTER: Problem writers

MATERIALS AVAILABLE: Handbooks, exercises, professional books, and educational magazines

STUDENT ATTITUDE: Positive

Writing-Across-the-Curriculum Program

PROGRAM HAS EXISTED: 5 years

INSTRUCTORS INVOLVED: Faculty in all disciplines

INSTRUCTORS' SELECTION: Voluntary

INSTRUCTORS' TRAINING: Seminars

PERCENTAGE OF FACULTY INVOLVED: 40%

IN PAST FIVE YEARS THIS PERCENTAGE HAS: Increased

STUDENTS INVOLVED IN PROGRAM: Students in all disciplines

PERCENTAGE OF STUDENTS INVOLVED: 100%

IN PAST FIVE YEARS THIS PERCENTAGE HAS: Increased

PARTICIPANTS' ATTITUDE: Very positive

The cross-curricular Writing Emphasis Program at the University of Wisconsin at Stevens Point has been very successful. Although participation in the program is voluntary, nearly one half of all faculty elect to participate. In departments throughout the university, these faculty develop their own standards for the amount and type of writing done in the Writing Emphasis courses they offer. During the semester-long training program, participating faculty attend fourteen workshops on teaching writing, and each instructor outside the English Department is paired with an English instructor who functions as a writing consultant for the course. In order to reinforce this training, the Writing Emphasis faculty attend a series of follow-up seminars. Donald Pattow remarks that "writing is perceived as an all-university responsibility" as a result of this program. For unknown reasons, Wisconsin's remedial program has not been nearly as effective. In the future, Wisconsin's cross-curricular efforts will probably extend to residence hall counselors and university staff as well.

UNIVERSITY OF WYOMING

Laramie, WY 82071

Full-time Students: 4069M/3054W Faculty: 868

Respondent: Keith Hull, Assistant Chairperson, English Department

Writing Requirement: Required freshman English course

Writing Center

CENTER HAS EXISTED: 5-10 years HOURS OPEN PER WEEK: 20-40

STAFF: 5-20 faculty tutors

TUTORS' EVALUATION: Observation, conferences, and by other tutors

TUTORS PAID: Yes

PROGRAM DESIGNED TO SERVE: Students in all disciplines

PROGRAM ACTUALLY SERVES: Students in all disciplines, especially freshmen and writing students

STUDENTS SEEK HELP WITH: Scientific reports, academic essays, research papers, and resumes or business writing

PERCENTAGE OF STUDENTS SERVED: Less than 25%

OVER PAST FIVE YEARS THIS PERCENTAGE HAS: Increased

STUDENTS USE CENTER: Mid-semester and at the end of the semester on an appointment, walk-in, or regular basis

STUDENTS REQUIRED TO USE CENTER: None

MATERIALS AVAILABLE: Handbooks, exercises, and professional books

STUDENT ATTITUDE: Very positive

Nearly ten years ago, the University of Wyoming added a writing center to its writing program. This addition reflects Wyoming's change of emphasis from the written product to rhetoric and writing as process. More recently, Wyoming has added a non-credit, pass/fail Basic Writing Course to accommodate those students who do not demonstrate the competency needed to enter regular freshman English. Approximately 13 percent of the university's students are currently served by the course. The Wyoming Conference on Freshman and Sophomore English has continued to contribute improvements to the University of Wyoming's writing program.

URBANA UNIVERSITY

Urbana, OH 43078

Full-time Students: 362M/195W   Faculty: 27

Respondent: David George, Associate Professor of English, Humanities Division

Writing Requirement: Placement by SAT or other examination

Peer Tutoring Program

PROGRAM HAS EXISTED: 5-10 years

ORGANIZATION: Curriculum-based; operated by Student Services

NUMBER OF TUTORS: 10-20

HOURS THEY WORK PER WEEK: Under 5

TUTORS PAID: Yes

TUTOR SELECTION: Nominated by the faculty who request tutors to work with their courses

TUTORS' TRAINING: On-the-job

TUTORS' EVALUATION: Conferences

PERCENTAGE OF STUDENTS SERVED: 15-25%

OVER PAST FIVE YEARS THIS PERCENTAGE HAS: Increased

PROGRAM INTENDED TO SERVE: Students in all disciplines

PROGRAM ACTUALLY SERVES: Students in all disciplines

STUDENTS SEEK HELP WITH: Academic essays and research papers

MECHANICS OF TUTORING: Tutor and student work with specified problems

STUDENT ATTITUDE: Positive

David George finds that the more successful writing programs include "a grammar course with a copy book and a weekly essay." A model essay course requiring imitative skills and increasing independence from the models has also worked well. Students who pass Urbana's "Intermediate English" with an A or a B average are eligible to work as peer tutors in English. Tutors assist English students with problems previously identified by the student's professor. For the next few years, George foresees two possible directions for Urbana's writing programs: "Grammar, syntax, and careful construction may continue to be the leading way, but another school of thought is big on prewriting, rapid composition, and fluency, calling construction and related matters 'merely edited English.' I can't say which will prevail as of now."

UTAH STATE UNIVERSITY

Logan, UT 84322

Full-time Students: 2819M/2170W Faculty: 447

Respondent: William E. Smith, Director of Writing

Writing Requirement: Required freshman English course, other required English course; placement by examination

Writing Center

CENTER HAS EXISTED: 5-10 years HOURS OPEN PER WEEK: 32

STAFF: 2 faculty, 4 graduate tutors, and 12 undergraduate tutors

TUTORS' TRAINING: Academic course and non-academic course

TUTORS' EVALUATION: Observation, conferences, and student questionnaire

TUTORS PAID: Some earn credit, some are paid by the hour, and some receive Education internships

PROGRAM DESIGNED TO SERVE: Students in all disciplines, especially those in English and writing courses

PROGRAM ACTUALLY SERVES: Students in all disciplines, especially those in English and writing courses

STUDENTS SEEK HELP WITH: Academic essays, research papers, scientific reports, and resumes or business writing

PERCENTAGE OF STUDENTS SERVED: Less than 25%

OVER PAST FIVE YEARS THIS PERCENTAGE HAS: Increased

STUDENTS USE CENTER: Repeatedly throughout the quarter on a walk-in, appointment, or regular basis

STUDENTS REQUIRED TO USE CENTER: Problem writers

MATERIALS AVAILABLE: Handbooks, exercises, professional books, tapes, and computer-assisted instruction

STUDENT ATTITUDE: Very positive

Peer Tutoring Program

PROGRAM HAS EXISTED: 6 years

ORGANIZATION: Curriculum-based

NUMBER OF TUTORS: 15–20

HOURS THEY WORK PER WEEK: 10

TUTORS PAID: Some are

TUTOR SELECTION: Nominated by themselves, the English faculty, or college-wide; then appointed by the director

TUTORS' TRAINING: On-the-job and a non-academic course in tandem with an experienced tutor

TUTORS' EVALUATION: Observation, conferences, and student questionnaire

PERCENTAGE OF STUDENTS SERVED: Less than 25%

OVER PAST FIVE YEARS THIS PERCENTAGE HAS: Increased

PROGRAM INTENDED TO SERVE: Students in all disciplines, especially writing students

PROGRAM ACTUALLY SERVES: Students in all disciplines, especially writing and English students

STUDENTS SEEK HELP WITH: Academic essays, scientific reports, research papers, and resumes or business writing

MECHANICS OF TUTORING: Tutor and student discuss papers; student may choose to have tutor comment in writing on any paper

STUDENT ATTITUDE: Very positive

Writing–Across–the–Curriculum Program

PROGRAM HAS EXISTED: Less than 2 years

INSTRUCTORS INVOLVED: English faculty and faculty in all disciplines

INSTRUCTORS' SELECTION: Voluntary

INSTRUCTORS' TRAINING: Seminars

PERCENTAGE OF FACULTY INVOLVED: Less than 25%

IN PAST FIVE YEARS THIS PERCENTAGE HAS: Increased

STUDENTS INVOLVED IN PROGRAM: Humanities and social sciences students (30%), and students in other disciplines (70%)

PERCENTAGE OF STUDENTS INVOLVED: Less than 25%

IN PAST FIVE YEARS THIS PERCENTAGE HAS: Increased

PARTICIPANTS' ATTITUDE: Somewhat positive

Utah State University's vertical writing requirement consists of one freshman, one sophomore, and one junior course. At the beginning of each year, students take an essay placement examination and continue at the appropriate level. William Smith states that the "move from a competency-based program to a student-centered writing program is based largely on James Moffett's work." Faculty resented a competency-based program, and the lecture method was unsuccessful because Utah State's "students have little experience writing until they take our writing courses." Problem writers are required to use the writing center, and any student can drop in for regularly scheduled workshops on peer editing and revision. Smith reports that the writing program recently received $225,000 for computer-assisted instruction, and is currently experimenting with nontraditional courses composed solely of peer group workshops, computer-assisted instruction, and writing done concurrently with specified academic courses.

VANDERBILT UNIVERSITY

Nashville, TN 37235

Full-time Students: 2686M/2787W Faculty: 1985

Respondent: Ellen M. Caldwell, Director of Freshman English

Writing Requirement: 2-3 required writing courses offered in English and other departments; exemptions by a score of 700 on ACH and a score of 4 on AP examination

Peer Tutoring Program

PROGRAM HAS EXISTED: 2-5 years

ORGANIZATION: Operated by the athletic department

NUMBER OF TUTORS: Fewer than 10

HOURS THEY WORK PER WEEK: 5-10

TUTORS PAID: Yes

TUTOR SELECTION: Self-nominated and appointed by the director

TUTORS' TRAINING: No formal training

TUTORS' EVALUATION: General supervision by the academic counselor in the athletic department

PERCENTAGE OF STUDENTS SERVED: Less than 25%

OVER PAST FIVE YEARS THIS PERCENTAGE HAS: Increased

PROGRAM INTENDED TO SERVE: Athletes

PROGRAM ACTUALLY SERVES: Athletes

STUDENTS SEEK HELP WITH: Academic essays and research papers

MECHANICS OF TUTORING: Student may choose to discuss any paper with tutor; tutor gives additional grammar drills and help with outlines, as needed

STUDENT ATTITUDE: Unknown

Writing-Across-the-Curriculum Program

PROGRAM HAS EXISTED: Under 2 years

INSTRUCTORS INVOLVED: Faculty in all disciplines

INSTRUCTORS' SELECTION: Voluntary

INSTRUCTORS' TRAINING: Seminars

PERCENTAGE OF FACULTY INVOLVED: Less than 25%

IN PAST FIVE YEARS THIS PERCENTAGE HAS: Increased

STUDENTS INVOLVED IN PROGRAM: Students in all disciplines

PERCENTAGE OF STUDENTS INVOLVED: Less than 25%

IN PAST FIVE YEARS THIS PERCENTAGE HAS: Increased

PARTICIPANTS' ATTITUDE: Unknown

During the past three years, Vanderbilt University's new College Program in Liberal Education has required that more departments offer writing-intensive courses. Except for the largest science or lab courses, all courses must require writing assignments and revisions. Students must also satisfy a two-semester or three-semester writing requirement that can be fulfilled through core courses in a number of departments, from Classics to Philosophy. Ellen Caldwell feels that these core courses, along with other optional writing courses, have been particularly successful.

VASSAR COLLEGE

Poughkeepsie, NY 12601

Full-time Students: 929M/1290W Faculty: 194

Respondents: William Gifford, Professor of English and Chairperson of Freshman English; Thomas McGlinchey, Writing Specialist, Special Services Program

Writing Requirement: Required freshman English course

Writing Center

CENTER HAS EXISTED: 7 years HOURS OPEN PER WEEK: 50

STAFF: 1 faculty and 2 undergraduate tutors

TUTORS' TRAINING: On-the-job and non-academic course

TUTORS' EVALUATION: Observation, conferences, student questionnaires, tutor contact reports, and final grades in courses

TUTORS PAID: Yes

PROGRAM DESIGNED TO SERVE: Students in all disciplines

PROGRAM ACTUALLY SERVES: Students in all disciplines

STUDENTS SEEK HELP WITH: Academic essays, research papers, scientific reports, creative writing, and resumes or business writing

PERCENTAGE OF STUDENTS SERVED: 10–12%

OVER PAST FIVE YEARS THIS PERCENTAGE HAS: Stayed the same

STUDENTS USE CENTER: Repeatedly throughout the semester, by scheduling an appointment with a specific tutor or with a Writing Specialist for counseling

STUDENTS REQUIRED TO USE CENTER: None

MATERIALS AVAILABLE: Handbooks, exercises, professional books, educational magazines, and an auto-tutorial tape program on basic writing

STUDENT ATTITUDE: Very positive

Peer Tutoring Program

PROGRAM HAS EXISTED: 7 years

ORGANIZATION: Writing center-based

NUMBER OF TUTORS: 2

HOURS THEY WORK PER WEEK: 5-10

TUTORS PAID: Yes

TUTOR SELECTION: Nominated by English and other departments, appointed by the director

TUTORS' TRAINING: On-the-job and non-academic course

TUTORS' EVALUATION: Observation, conferences, student questionnaire, and tutor contact sheets

PERCENTAGE OF STUDENTS SERVED: 1%

OVER PAST FIVE YEARS THIS PERCENTAGE HAS: Stayed the same

PROGRAM INTENDED TO SERVE: Students in all disciplines

PROGRAM ACTUALLY SERVES: Students in all disciplines

STUDENTS SEEK HELP WITH: Academic essays, research reports, scientific reports, and creative writing

MECHANICS OF TUTORING: Student may choose to discuss or have tutor comment in writing on any paper

STUDENT ATTITUDE: Very positive

Writing-Across-the-Curriculum Program

PROGRAM HAS EXISTED: 2 years

INSTRUCTORS INVOLVED: Faculty in all disciplines

INSTRUCTORS' SELECTION: Appointed by departments

INSTRUCTORS' TRAINING: Occasional voluntary meetings

PERCENTAGE OF FACULTY INVOLVED: 20%

IN PAST FIVE YEARS THIS PERCENTAGE HAS: Stayed the same

STUDENTS INVOLVED IN PROGRAM: Students in all disciplines

PERCENTAGE OF STUDENTS INVOLVED: 25% (over 4 years, 100%)

IN PAST FIVE YEARS THIS PERCENTAGE HAS: Stayed the same

PARTICIPANTS' ATTITUDE: Positive

Vassar College's writing-across-the-curriculum program is designed for and required of all freshmen. Instead of a freshman English course, students may take any of a number of writing-intensive "Freshman Courses" offered by various departments. These designated courses emphasize writing in different disciplines. William Gifford and Thomas McGlinchey have found these credit writing courses to be particularly successful. Non-credit writing courses are less successful because, although some students need the work, few have the extra time. Some students voluntarily seek writing counseling, usually through the writing center and the peer tutoring program.

VIRGINIA COMMONWEALTH UNIVERSITY

Richmond, VA 23284

Full-time Students: 3346M/5460W Faculty: 1607

Respondent: James Kinney, Director of Composition and Rhetoric

Writing Requirement: Required freshman English and two upper-level writing-intensive courses

Writing Center

CENTER HAS EXISTED: 5-10 years HOURS OPEN PER WEEK: 20-40

STAFF: Fewer than 5 faculty and graduate tutors

TUTORS' TRAINING: On-the-job and academic course

TUTORS' EVALUATION: Observation and conferences

TUTORS PAID: Yes

PROGRAM DESIGNED TO SERVE: Students in all disciplines

PROGRAM ACTUALLY SERVES: Students in all disciplines, primarily writing students

STUDENTS SEEK HELP WITH: Academic essays and research papers

PERCENTAGE OF STUDENTS SERVED: Less than 25%

OVER PAST FIVE YEARS THIS PERCENTAGE HAS: Increased

STUDENTS USE CENTER: Throughout the semester on an appointment or walk-in basis

STUDENTS REQUIRED TO USE CENTER: Problem writers

MATERIALS AVAILABLE: Handbooks, exercises, professional books, and educational magazines

STUDENT ATTITUDE: Somewhat positive

Writing-Across-the-Curriculum Program

PROGRAM HAS EXISTED FOR: 2-5 years

INSTRUCTORS INVOLVED: Faculty in all disciplines

INSTRUCTORS' SELECTION: Voluntary

INSTRUCTORS' TRAINING: Seminars and team teaching

PERCENTAGE OF FACULTY INVOLVED: Less than 25%

IN PAST FIVE YEARS THIS PERCENTAGE HAS: Increased

STUDENTS INVOLVED IN PROGRAM: Students in all disciplines

PERCENTAGE OF STUDENTS INVOLVED: Less than 25%

IN PAST FIVE YEARS THIS PERCENTAGE HAS: Increased

PARTICIPANTS' ATTITUDE: Very positive

In the past three years, Virginia Commonwealth University has shifted its writing philosophy toward writing-across-the-curriculum. One of the school's most successful writing programs has been the freshman composition program that serves primarily "writing in disciplines other than English," according to James Kinney. In recent years, the freshman program has relied much more heavily on analyzing reading material from many disciplines. Although writing-intensive courses outside of the English Department are "meeting with resistance in some departments," the cross-curricular program continues to grow in size and popularity. This faculty program, which combines faculty training seminars with team teaching, is regarded very favorably by most participants.

VIRGINIA POLYTECHNIC INSTITUTE AND STATE UNIVERSITY

Full-time Students: 12,559M/7705W Faculty: 1923

Respondent: Constance J. Gefvert, Associate Professor, Director of Freshman English

Writing Requirement: Required freshman English courses; other writing courses required by some colleges and departments

Writing Center

CENTER HAS EXISTED: 10 years HOURS OPEN PER WEEK: 30

STAFF: 6 faculty and 1-3 graduate tutors

TUTORS' TRAINING: On-the-job, academic course, and non-academic training course

TUTORS' EVALUATION: Observation

TUTORS PAID: Yes

PROGRAM DESIGNED TO SERVE: Students in all disciplines

PROGRAM ACTUALLY SERVES: Students in all disciplines

STUDENTS SEEK HELP WITH: Scientific reports, academic essays, research papers, theses, dissertations, and resumes or business writing

PERCENTAGE OF STUDENTS SERVED: Less than 25%

OVER PAST FIVE YEARS THIS PERCENTAGE HAS: Increased

STUDENTS USE CENTER: Throughout the quarter on a walk-in or appointment basis

STUDENTS REQUIRED TO USE CENTER: Those required by instructors; most students come voluntarily

MATERIALS AVAILABLE: Handbooks, exercises, magazines, and professional books

STUDENT ATTITUDE: Very positive

Virginia Tech's innovative writing programs are expanding rapidly. Currently, most programs operate out of individual colleges. Each college is responsible for its own graduation writing requirement, although a year of freshman English is required throughout the university for most students. Many of the colleges also employ English consultants or request the writing center staff to conduct workshops on particular skills. Because so many colleges and departments have become more involved in writing over the past few years, Virginia Tech hopes to start a centralized writing-across-the-curriculum program based on these smaller projects. The Teaching Assistant apprenticeship program at the university equips graduate students with a solid theoretical foundation and several practical approaches to teaching writing. The rigorous apprenticeship includes a two-week orientation, a course on teaching college composition, a number of seminars, and individual advising groups. Instructors are carefully supervised in their work and supported by the Writing Center and the Composition Resource Center, a library of writing resources. Writing courses stress the process of composition, pre-writing, and the aims of writing, including audience, stance, and purpose.

WAKE FOREST UNIVERSITY

Winston-Salem, NC 27109

Full-time Students: 1862M/1214W Faculty: 218

Respondent: Nancy Cotton, Associate Professor of English

Writing Requirement: Required freshman English course

Writing Center

CENTER HAS EXISTED: 5-10 years HOURS OPEN PER WEEK: 20-40

STAFF: Fewer than 5 graduate tutors

TUTORS' TRAINING: On-the-job

TUTORS' EVALUATION: Observation

TUTORS PAID: Yes

PROGRAM DESIGNED TO SERVE: Students in all disciplines

PROGRAM ACTUALLY SERVES: Writing students, English students, and underclassmen

STUDENTS SEEK HELP WITH: Academic essays

PERCENTAGE OF STUDENTS SERVED: Less than 25%

OVER PAST FIVE YEARS THIS PERCENTAGE HAS: Stayed the same

STUDENTS USE CENTER: Throughout the semester on a regular basis

STUDENTS REQUIRED TO USE CENTER: Problem writers

MATERIALS AVAILABLE: Handbooks and writing exercises

STUDENT ATTITUDE: Very positive

Peer Tutoring Program

PROGRAM HAS EXISTED: 5-10 years

ORGANIZATION: Curriculum-based

NUMBER OF TUTORS: Fewer than 10

HOURS THEY WORK PER WEEK: 5-10

TUTORS PAID: Yes

TUTOR SELECTION: Nominated by English faculty and appointed by the director

TUTORS' TRAINING: On-the-job

TUTORS' EVALUATION: Observation

PERCENTAGE OF STUDENTS SERVED: Fewer than 25%

OVER PAST FIVE YEARS THIS PERCENTAGE HAS: Stayed the same

PROGRAM INTENDED TO SERVE: Athletes

PROGRAM ACTUALLY SERVES: Athletes

STUDENTS SEEK HELP WITH: Academic essays

MECHANICS OF TUTORING: Tutor and student are required to discuss papers

STUDENT ATTITUDE: Somewhat positive

Since the introduction of the writing center and the peer tutoring program over five years ago, Wake Forest University has found no reason to change its writing program. The English Department has been successful with its traditional freshman composition courses, which are designed to improve students' logic, clarity, and style. Students who enter Wake Forest with proficiency in writing are placed in composition courses that emphasize readings in literature, while those students who have difficulty with grammar and mechanics are given tutorial assistance at the Writing Lab. After freshman year, students who write below the standard of college-level work may be directed by faculty in any department to work in the Writing Lab until they "achieve competency in their writing." The Writing Lab's graduate tutors help students during regularly scheduled hours, and the Lab has received positive responses from students who use it. Wake Forest's unique peer tutoring program consists of a small number of tutors who help only athletes with writing problems.

WASHBURN UNIVERSITY

Topeka, KS 66621

Full-time Students: 1300M/1300W Faculty: 200

Respondent: Robert D. Stein, Professor and Chairperson, English Department

Writing Requirement: 3 hours freshman composition and 3 hours junior composition

Writing Center

CENTER HAS EXISTED: 5-10 years HOURS OPEN PER WEEK: 18-20

STAFF: Fewer than 5 faculty and undergraduate tutors

TUTORS' TRAINING: On-the-job and non-academic training course

TUTORS' EVALUATION: Observation

TUTORS PAID: Yes

PROGRAM DESIGNED TO SERVE: Writing students, freshmen, underclassmen, and people from the community

PROGRAM ACTUALLY SERVES: Primarily composition students

STUDENTS SEEK HELP WITH: Academic essays and other work from freshman composition, Developmental English, and other other composition courses

PERCENTAGE OF STUDENTS SERVED: Less than 25%

OVER PAST FIVE YEARS THIS PERCENTAGE HAS: Increased

STUDENTS USE CENTER: Throughout the semester on a walk-in, appointment, or regular basis

STUDENTS REQUIRED TO USE CENTER: Problem writers

MATERIALS AVAILABLE: Writing exercises

STUDENT ATTITUDE: Positive

Peer Tutoring Program

PROGRAM HAS EXISTED: 2-5 years

ORGANIZATION: Writing center-based

NUMBER OF TUTORS: 1-3

HOURS THEY WORK PER WEEK: 10-20

TUTORS PAID: Yes

TUTOR SELECTION: Appointed by the director (usually selected from the English education program)

TUTORS' TRAINING: On-the-job and supervision from the English Education program

TUTORS' EVALUATION: Observation by the director

PERCENTAGE OF STUDENTS SERVED: Fewer than 25%

OVER PAST FIVE YEARS THIS PERCENTAGE HAS: Increased

PROGRAM INTENDED TO SERVE: Writing students and the community

PROGRAM ACTUALLY SERVES: Writing students

STUDENTS SEEK HELP WITH: Freshman composition and other composition courses

MECHANICS OF TUTORING: Tutor and student discuss paper

STUDENT ATTITUDE: Very positive

According to Robert D. Stein, Washburn University's two traditional writing courses, "Developmental Writing" and "Freshman Composition," have worked well, and students in these courses use the Writing Lab for individualized instruction in addition to classroom work. The English Department has also had success with advanced composition courses in specific disciplines such as pre-law writing, business writing, writing in the humanities, and writing in the sciences. Several of these courses are taught by Washburn's fifteen part-time faculty, while others are taught by full-time English faculty, who must teach composition as half of their course load. In the near future, Washburn plans to continue the one-on-one emphasis of the Writing Lab and to increase the number of adjunct instructors.

WASHINGTON AND JEFFERSON COLLEGE

Washington, PA 15301

Full-time Students: 654M/404W Faculty: 90

Respondent: Clarence L. Branton, Chairperson, English Department and Wallace Professor of Rhetoric

Writing Requirement: Required freshman English course

Peer Tutoring Program

PROGRAM HAS EXISTED: 5-10 years

ORGANIZATION: Curriculum-based

NUMBER OF TUTORS: Fewer than 10

HOURS THEY WORK PER WEEK: 5-10

TUTORS PAID: No

TUTOR SELECTION: Students volunteer and the English faculty then nominate those whom they consider qualified

TUTORS' TRAINING: Academic course

TUTORS' EVALUATION: Observation

PERCENTAGE OF STUDENTS SERVED: Less than 25%

OVER PAST FIVE YEARS THIS PERCENTAGE HAS: Increased

PROGRAM INTENDED TO SERVE: Students in all disciplines

PROGRAM ACTUALLY SERVES: Students in all disciplines

STUDENTS SEEK HELP WITH: Academic essays, research papers, scientific reports, creative writing, and resumes or business writing

MECHANICS OF TUTORING: Student may choose to discuss any paper with tutor

STUDENT ATTITUDE: Somewhat positive

Washington and Jefferson College relies on traditional writing programs for teaching students writing. Clarence L. Branton states, "The only 'programs' in writing that we offer are a course in advanced composition and a course in creative writing. Both work very well." The college's peer tutoring program provides tutorial help in a variety of disciplines, including English.

WASHINGTON AND LEE UNIVERSITY

Lexington, VA 24450

Full-time Students: 1311M Faculty: 150

Respondent: Sidney Coulling, Professor and Chairperson, English Department

Writing Requirement: Required freshman English course; exemption by placement examination

Writing Center

CENTER HAS EXISTED: 2-5 years HOURS OPEN PER WEEK: Under 10

STAFF: Fewer than 5 undergraduate tutors

TUTORS' TRAINING: On-the-job

TUTORS' EVALUATION: Conferences

TUTORS PAID: Yes

PROGRAM DESIGNED TO SERVE: Students in all disciplines

PROGRAM ACTUALLY SERVES: Students in all disciplines

STUDENTS SEEK HELP WITH: Academic essays

PERCENTAGE OF STUDENTS SERVED: Less than 25%

OVER PAST FIVE YEARS THIS PERCENTAGE HAS: Increased

STUDENTS USE CENTER: Throughout the semester on a walk-in basis or by referral

STUDENTS REQUIRED TO USE CENTER: None

MATERIALS AVAILABLE: Handbooks and exercises

STUDENT ATTITUDE: Unknown

Both the classroom and tutorial instruction that constitute Washington and Lee University's writing program have been fairly successful, according to Sidney Coulling. Staffed by peer tutors, the small writing center is used primarily by students referred by faculty. While the number of students using the center is still relatively low, more students come in as they discover this resource. Washington and Lee's future plans include promoting the center and adjusting the writing requirement that was re-instated in 1984. Coulling reports success with small classes within the writing curriculum that combine composition with literature or allow instructors to discuss written work with students on an individual basis.

WASHINGTON UNIVERSITY

St. Louis, MO 63130

Full-time Students: 2670M/1891W Faculty: 1366

Respondent: Robert Wiltenburg, Director of Freshman Composition

Writing Requirement: One semester composition course

Washington University's writing program is in a state of transition. In the past year or so, the university has been standardizing its freshman composition program by promoting greater uniformity in the the way graduate instructors teach, issuing guidelines for the course, holding workshops and observation sessions before the instructors teach, and increasing the rigor of the training seminar and the staff meetings. The reading list for freshman composition has also been modified to include book-length cross-disciplinary readings. Washington hopes to be able to build on these recent changes.

WAYNE STATE COLLEGE

Wayne, NE 68787

Full-time Students: 756M/1005W Faculty: 86

Respondent: Sayre D. Andersen, Department Coordinator, English Department/Humanities

Writing Requirement: Required freshman English course passed with "C" or higher

Writing Center

CENTER HAS EXISTED: 2-5 years HOURS OPEN PER WEEK: 20-40

STAFF: Fewer than 5 faculty

TUTORS PAID: Receive free room accommodations

PROGRAM DESIGNED TO SERVE: Students in all disciplines

PROGRAM ACTUALLY SERVES: Students in all disciplines

STUDENTS SEEK HELP WITH: Scientific reports, academic essays, research papers, resumes or business writing, speeches for communication classes, and copy for radio/TV

PERCENTAGE OF STUDENTS SERVED: 50-75%

OVER PAST FIVE YEARS THIS PERCENTAGE HAS: Stayed the same

STUDENTS USE CENTER: Repeatedly at mid-semester and at the end of the semester on a walk-in or regular basis

STUDENTS REQUIRED TO USE CENTER: Problem writers

MATERIALS AVAILABLE: Handbooks and exercises

STUDENT ATTITUDE: Somewhat positive

The writing program at Wayne State College has undergone several changes over the past ten years. In the mid-1970's the school had a writing lab, but lack of institutional support forced it to close. The school then moved to a more traditional program with modular instruction in basic skills, then to a program requiring that all students' papers be read by a committee. Currently, all freshmen must complete one semester of English composition; this requirement will probably be changed to two semesters in the future. Sayre D. Andersen believes, "Our students need a fairly structured, traditional situation for writing rather than a more open, self-motivated approach."

WAYNE STATE UNIVERSITY

Detroit, MI 48202

Full-time Students: 6025M/6560W Faculty: 1500

Respondent: John Brereton, Director of Composition, English Department

Writing Requirement: Required freshman English course, other required English course, and third year writing proficiency examination

Writing Center

CENTER HAS EXISTED: 25 years HOURS OPEN PER WEEK: 20-40

STAFF: Faculty, part-time staff, and 5-20 undergraduate and graduate tutors

TUTORS' TRAINING: On-the-job and non-academic course

TUTORS' EVALUATION: Observation, student questionnaire, and conferences

TUTORS PAID: Yes

PROGRAM DESIGNED TO SERVE: Students in all disciplines

PROGRAM ACTUALLY SERVES: Primarily writing students and freshmen, with some English and humanities students

STUDENTS SEEK HELP WITH: Academic essays, research papers, and scientific reports

PERCENTAGE OF STUDENTS SERVED: Less than 25%

OVER PAST FIVE YEARS THIS PERCENTAGE HAS: Increased

STUDENTS USE CENTER: Throughout the semester on a regular basis

STUDENTS REQUIRED TO USE CENTER: None; problem writers strongly urged

MATERIALS AVAILABLE: Handbooks and exercises

STUDENT ATTITUDE: Very positive

In operation for twenty-five years, the writing center at Wayne State University is one of the oldest in the country. Staffed by faculty, graduate, and undergraduate tutors, the center forms a solid foundation for the writing program at Wayne State. The school has recently developed a more coherent upper-level curriculum, increased enrollment in technical writing courses, and experienced a decline in remedial writing. In the future Wayne State plans to institute even more stringent standards for writing.

WESLEYAN UNIVERSITY

Middletown, CT 06457

Full-time Students: 1300M/1210W Faculty: 240

Respondent: Anne Greene, Writing Workshop Coordinator

Writing Requirement: None

Writing Center

CENTER HAS EXISTED: 6 years HOURS OPEN PER WEEK: 30

STAFF: 1 faculty and 16 undergraduate tutors

TUTORS' TRAINING: On-the-job and academic course

TUTORS' EVALUATION: Observation, conferences, and self-evaluation

TUTORS PAID: Yes, and they receive course credit

PROGRAM DESIGNED TO SERVE: Students in all disciplines (including ESL students), university administrators, faculty, and staff

PROGRAM ACTUALLY SERVES: Students in all disciplines (including ESL students), university administrators, faculty, and staff

STUDENTS SEEK HELP WITH: Academic essays, research papers, creative writing, and resumes or business writing

PERCENTAGE OF STUDENTS SERVED: Less than 25%

OVER PAST FIVE YEARS THIS PERCENTAGE HAS: Increased

STUDENTS USE CENTER: Throughout the semester on a walk-in, appointment, or regular basis, and by telephone

STUDENTS REQUIRED TO USE CENTER: Students having trouble with course papers

MATERIALS AVAILABLE: Handbooks, exercises, professional books, educational magazines, and a file of student papers written for Wesleyan courses

STUDENT ATTITUDE: Very positive

Peer Tutoring Program

PROGRAM HAS EXISTED: 5–10 years

ORGANIZATION: Curriculum-based

NUMBER OF TUTORS: 50–100

TUTORS PAID: Yes

TUTOR SELECTION: By course professors

TUTORS' TRAINING: On-the-job

TUTORS' EVALUATION: By course professors who supervise tutors' work

PERCENTAGE OF STUDENTS SERVED: 25–50%

OVER PAST FIVE YEARS THIS PERCENTAGE HAS: Increased

PROGRAM INTENDED TO SERVE: Students in all disciplines, especially freshmen

PROGRAM ACTUALLY SERVES: Students in all disciplines, especially freshmen

STUDENTS SEEK HELP WITH: Academic essays, research papers, and assigned papers in the courses where the tutors are working

MECHANICS OF TUTORING: Student may choose to discuss any paper with tutor

STUDENT ATTITUDE: Positive

Approximately 100 undergraduate Teaching Apprentices (TAs) work in Wesleyan University's Writing Workshop, as well as in in courses across the curriculum, reading and commenting on student papers, leading discussion groups, and generally assisting course professors, according to Anne Green. Students can review drafts of papers with their TAs before handing a final version into their professors, and though TAs may comment on a final version, they do not grade any papers. Both the curriculum-based and the writing center-based tutors receive training for their positions through Writing Workshop courses and on-the-job instruction. Those TAs working in courses have usually taken the course to which they are assigned.

Although Wesleyan does not have a formal writing-across-the-curriculum program, writing is stressed in most departments. Greene asserts that "almost all the faculty assign several papers in their courses. Some assign a paper per week. Most students learn to write by taking a range of courses across the curriculum. Periodically, the Writing Workshop offers faculty seminars in which we discuss writing assignments, ways to comment on papers, etc."

WHEATON COLLEGE

Norton, MA 02766

Full-time Students: 1218W   Faculty: 89

Respondent: Beverly Clark, Director, Peer Tutoring Program and Writing Room

Writing Requirement: Proficiency checked by all faculty

Writing Center

CENTER HAS EXISTED: 5-10 years   HOURS OPEN PER WEEK: 20-40

STAFF: 20-40 undergraduate tutors

TUTORS' TRAINING: On-the-job and academic training course

TUTORS' EVALUATION: Observation and conferences

TUTORS PAID: Yes, after completing training course

PROGRAM DESIGNED TO SERVE: Students in all disciplines

PROGRAM ACTUALLY SERVES: Primarily freshman and sophomore English, writing, and humanities students

STUDENTS SEEK HELP WITH: Mostly academic essays and research papers, with some business writing, creative writing, and scientific reports

PERCENTAGE OF STUDENTS SERVED: Less than 25%

OVER PAST FIVE YEARS THIS PERCENTAGE HAS: Increased

STUDENTS USE CENTER: Throughout the semester on a walk-in basis, sometimes by appointment

STUDENTS REQUIRED TO USE CENTER: Problem writers

MATERIALS AVAILABLE: Handbooks, writing exercises, professional books, campus publications, and educational magazines

STUDENT ATTITUDE: Positive

Peer Tutoring Program

PROGRAM HAS EXISTED: 5–10 years

ORGANIZATION: Writing center-based and residentially based

NUMBER OF TUTORS: 20–40

HOURS THEY WORK PER WEEK: 2–5

TUTORS PAID: Yes, after completing training course

TUTOR SELECTION: Self-nominated, nominated by English faculty, and nominated college-wide

TUTORS' TRAINING: On-the-job and academic training course

TUTORS' EVALUATION: Observation and conferences

PERCENTAGE OF STUDENTS SERVED: Fewer than 25%

OVER PAST FIVE YEARS THIS PERCENTAGE HAS: Increased

PROGRAM INTENDED TO SERVE: Students in all disciplines

PROGRAM ACTUALLY SERVES: Primarily freshman and sophomore English, writing, and humanities students

STUDENTS SEEK HELP WITH: Mostly academic essays and research papers, with some business writing, creative writing, and scientific reports

MECHANICS OF TUTORING: Student may choose to discuss any paper with tutor

STUDENT ATTITUDE: Positive

Writing-Across-the-Curriculum Program

PROGRAM HAS EXISTED: 5–10 years

INSTRUCTORS: Faculty in all disciplines

INSTRUCTORS' SELECTION: Voluntary

INSTRUCTORS' TRAINING: Faculty training seminars

PERCENTAGE OF FACULTY INVOLVED: 50–75%

IN PAST FIVE YEARS THIS PERCENTAGE HAS: Increased

STUDENTS INVOLVED IN PROGRAM: Students in all disciplines

PERCENTAGE OF STUDENTS INVOLVED: 76-100%

IN PAST FIVE YEARS THIS PERCENTAGE HAS: Increased

PARTICIPANTS' ATTITUDE: Very positive

Spurred on by a FIPSE grant in 1977, Wheaton College introduced a writing center-based peer tutoring program, a writing-across-the-curriculum program, new writing courses, and an innovative writing requirement. The extensive and successful peer tutoring program requires all tutors to take a training course specifically designed for them. After completing this course, tutors work between two and five hours in the writing center each week, helping students from all disciplines. Wheaton's well-established writing-across-the-curriculum program trains faculty through seminars on the teaching of writing. The program has been so successful in past years that between 50 and 75 percent of Wheaton's faculty have voluntarily taken the faculty training seminar. The training they receive in this seminar helps all faculty enforce the writing requirement, which currently states that any student deemed deficient in writing skills by any faculty member must demonstrate proficiency to the satisfaction of the English Department. The English Department recently added a basic writing course, ESL instruction, and a course in ESL tutoring. The department also employs part-time and full-time faculty who teach journalism, ESL, and expository and creative writing classes. In the future, the English Department staff will consider revising the writing requirement and using its teacher training experience to develop an internship program in the teaching of writing.

WHITMAN COLLEGE

Walla Walla, WA 99362

Full-time Students: 582M/623W Faculty: 80

Respondent: Irvin Hashimoto, Director of Writing Center

Writing Requirement: None

Writing Center

CENTER HAS EXISTED: 2-5 years HOURS OPEN PER WEEK: 20-40

STAFF: Fewer than 5 faculty and undergraduate tutors

TUTORS' TRAINING: On-the-job

TUTORS' EVALUATION: Observation and conferences

TUTORS PAID: Yes

PROGRAM DESIGNED TO SERVE: Students in all disciplines

PROGRAM ACTUALLY SERVES: Students in all disciplines

STUDENTS SEEK HELP WITH: Scientific reports, academic essays, research papers, and resumes or business writing

PERCENTAGE OF STUDENTS SERVED: Less than 25%

OVER PAST FIVE YEARS THIS PERCENTAGE HAS: Increased

STUDENTS USE CENTER: Throughout the semester on a walk-in or appointment basis

STUDENTS REQUIRED TO USE CENTER: None

MATERIALS AVAILABLE: Handbooks and exercises

STUDENT ATTITUDE: Very positive

Writing-Across-the-Curriculum Program

PROGRAM HAS EXISTED: 2-5 years

INSTRUCTORS INVOLVED: Faculty in all disciplines

INSTRUCTORS' SELECTION: Voluntary

INSTRUCTORS' TRAINING: Seminars

PERCENTAGE OF FACULTY INVOLVED: 25-50%

IN PAST FIVE YEARS THIS PERCENTAGE HAS: Stayed the same

STUDENTS INVOLVED IN PROGRAM: Humanities students

PERCENTAGE OF STUDENTS INVOLVED: More than 75%

IN PAST FIVE YEARS THIS PERCENTAGE HAS: Stayed the same

PARTICIPANTS' ATTITUDE: Unknown

Whitman College's writing-across-the-curriculum program has been highly successful. In existence for nearly five years, the program includes both a freshman-level and a senior-level humanities course team-taught by instructors from all academic disciplines. In these courses, teachers require four to eight papers and spend considerable time helping their students learn to write academic discourse. Whitman is unusual in that it has chosen not to establish or re-establish a writing requirement. The school's writing program is expected to change very little in the next few years, except for an increase in intermediate and advanced composition offerings.

WILLIAMS COLLEGE

Williamstown, MA 01267

Full-time Students: 1081M/841W Faculty: 154

Respondent: Suzanne Graver, Assistant Professor of English, Coordinator of Student Writing Tutorials

Writing Requirement: None

Writing Center

CENTER HAS EXISTED: 2-5 years HOURS OPEN PER WEEK: 20-40

STAFF: 5-20 undergraduate tutors

TUTORS' TRAINING: On-the-job and non-academic course

TUTORS' EVALUATION: Student questionnaire, conferences, and tapes of tutorial sessions

TUTORS PAID: Yes

PROGRAM DESIGNED TO SERVE: Students in all disciplines

PROGRAM ACTUALLY SERVES: Students in all disciplines

STUDENTS SEEK HELP WITH: Academic essays, research papers, scientific reports, honors theses, resumes, and fellowship and graduate school applications

PERCENTAGE OF STUDENTS SERVED: 20%

OVER PAST FIVE YEARS THIS PERCENTAGE HAS: Increased

STUDENTS USE CENTER: Throughout the semester on a walk-in, appointment, or regular basis

STUDENTS REQUIRED TO USE CENTER: None

MATERIALS AVAILABLE: Handbooks, exercises, and handouts

STUDENT ATTITUDE: Very positive

Housed in the library and staffed by trained undergraduate tutors, the Writing Workshop at Williams College successfully combines the services of a writing center, peer tutoring program, and writing-across-the-curriculum program. The tutors, who are recruited from among the best students at the college, attend weekly training seminars and serve during their junior and senior years. Several tutors also work as writing assistants in selected courses across the curriculum. Williams encourages faculty participation in the teaching of writing in all courses, and during the past few years has regularly offered workshops for the faculty on improving student writing.

WILMINGTON COLLEGE

New Castle, DE 19720

Full-time Students: 328M/355W Faculty: 79

Respondent: Raymond Miller, Associate Professor of English

Writing Requirement: Required freshman English course

Peer Tutoring Program

PROGRAM HAS EXISTED: 2-5 years

ORGANIZATION: Residentially based

NUMBER OF TUTORS: 10-20

HOURS THEY WORK PER WEEK: 5-10

TUTORS PAID: Yes

TUTOR SELECTION: Nominated college-wide

TUTORS' TRAINING: On-the-job

TUTORS' EVALUATION: Observation

PERCENTAGE OF STUDENTS SERVED: Fewer than 25%

OVER PAST FIVE YEARS THIS PERCENTAGE HAS: Increased

PROGRAM INTENDED TO SERVE: Students in all disciplines

PROGRAM ACTUALLY SERVES: Students in all disciplines

STUDENTS SEEK HELP WITH: Academic essays, scientific reports, research papers, and resumes or business writing

MECHANICS OF TUTORING: Tutor and student are required to discuss papers

STUDENT ATTITUDE: Somewhat positive

The basis of Wilmington College's writing program is its composition courses, but an increasing percentage of the student body has been seeking individualized help from the peer tutoring program. The peer tutors and the successful composition courses will be supported by a new writing center, scheduled to open in the spring of 1984. The peer tutors who will staff the center will be trained on-the-job and evaluated by observation and in conferences. Like the peer tutoring program, the center will help students in all disciplines with essays, research papers, and scientific reports. Wilmington hopes to expand the scope of all of its writing programs over the next few years.

WITTENBERG UNIVERSITY

Springfield, OH 45501

Full-time Students: 1066M/1199W Faculty: 141

Respondent: Terry Otten, Chairperson, English Department

Writing Requirement: Required freshman English course; exemption by AP test, SAT, or local test; entry and exit level proficiency requirements

Writing Center

CENTER HAS EXISTED: 2-5 years HOURS OPEN PER WEEK: Over 40

STAFF: 3 part-time faculty and 30 undergraduate tutors

TUTORS' TRAINING: On-the-job and non-academic training course

TUTORS' EVALUATION: Observation and weekly sessions with the director

TUTORS PAID: Yes

PROGRAM DESIGNED TO SERVE: Students in all disciplines

PROGRAM ACTUALLY SERVES: Students in all disciplines

STUDENTS SEEK HELP WITH: All types of writing

PERCENTAGE OF STUDENTS SERVED: 18-20%

OVER PAST FIVE YEARS THIS PERCENTAGE HAS: Increased dramatically

STUDENTS USE CENTER: Throughout the semester on a walk-in or regular basis

STUDENTS REQUIRED TO USE CENTER: Students referred by professors, students failing junior proficiency test, and problem writers in freshman writing courses

MATERIALS AVAILABLE: Handbooks, writing exercises, professional books, educational magazines, and some computer material

STUDENT ATTITUDE: Very positive

Peer Tutoring Program

PROGRAM HAS EXISTED: 2–5 years

ORGANIZATION: Writing center-based

NUMBER OF TUTORS: 30–35

HOURS THEY WORK PER WEEK: 5–10

TUTORS PAID: Yes

TUTOR SELECTION: Nominated college-wide and appointed by the director

TUTORS' TRAINING: On-the-job and non-academic training course

TUTORS' EVALUATION: Observation and weekly sessions with director

PERCENTAGE OF STUDENTS SERVED: Fewer than 25%

OVER PAST FIVE YEARS THIS PERCENTAGE HAS: Increased

PROGRAM INTENDED TO SERVE: Students in all disciplines

PROGRAM ACTUALLY SERVES: Students in all disciplines

STUDENTS SEEK HELP WITH: All types of writing

MECHANICS OF TUTORING: Tutor comments on writing and discusses papers with student

STUDENT ATTITUDE: Very positive

With its five-year-old writing proficiency requirement, Wittenberg University ensures that all students receive writing instruction. Students are tested for proficiency when they enter and again before they are allowed to graduate. Any students not designated proficient by the entrance examination are required to take and pass English 101: Expository Writing. Continued writing proficiency is checked in all courses, since faculty must grade each student's writing as satisfactory or unsatisfactory. Students whose writing is judged unsatisfactory are referred to the Writing Workshop for the help needed to improve their writing skills. Any student who receives two or more "unsatisfactories" is required to use the Workshop until his writing is satisfactory. In addition, students who score below the acceptable level on the junior year proficiency test must raise their writing proficiency through the Writing Workshop program. The entry and exit proficiency program requires all poor writers to seek help, and has raised writing consciousness at Wittenberg significantly, while the successful Workshop and its peer tutors have replaced less successful course requirements as the basis of Wittenberg's writing program. Since its opening three years ago, the Workshop has offered instruction on different types of writing, on special writing assignments in courses in all disciplines, and on many other facets of writing. Faculty throughout the university also participate in workshops on assigning writing in the classroom; many have subsequently revised courses, in consultation with the Workshop director, to include significantly more writing. The English Department expects the Writing Workshop to expand and create more new programs in the next few years.

WORCESTER POLYTECHNIC INSTITUTE

Worcester, MA, 01609

Full-time Students: 1950M/450W Faculty: 201

Respondent: Lance Schachterle, Professor of English, Humanities

Writing Requirement: Three major projects must be acceptably written

Writing Center

CENTER HAS EXISTED: 8 years HOURS OPEN PER WEEK: 15-20

STAFF: 2 part-time professionals

PROGRAM DESIGNED TO SERVE: Students in all disciplines, especially those working on projects

PROGRAM ACTUALLY SERVES: Students in all disciplines, especially those working on projects

STUDENTS SEEK HELP WITH: Scientific reports, academic essays, research papers, and business correspondence

PERCENTAGE OF STUDENTS SERVED: 25%

OVER PAST FIVE YEARS THIS PERCENTAGE HAS: Increased slowly

STUDENTS USE CENTER: 75% throughout the semester, 25% at the end of the semester on a walk-in or appointment basis

STUDENTS REQUIRED TO USE CENTER: Certain speech and writing courses require students to use center; otherwise students are referred by faculty or come in voluntarily

MATERIALS AVAILABLE: Handbooks and exercises

STUDENT ATTITUDE: Positive

Worcester Polytechnic Institute requires that all students complete three major projects in order to graduate. Since these projects must be well written, students are encouraged to seek help writing through the Writing Resources Center. The center features a staff of professional writing tutors who counsel students on an appointment basis, and it also provides videotapes, handouts, and writing texts. Periodically the center offers non-credit mini-courses on specific writing problems. Worcester Polytechnic has recently added a new course to its writing curriculum entitled "Elements of Writing." In this course, students study various prose styles, rhetorical devices, and techniques of logical persuasion.

XAVIER UNIVERSITY OF LOUISIANA

New Orleans, LA 70125

Full-time Students: 685M/1122W Faculty: 119

Respondent: Judith Haydel, Director, Writing Center

Writing Requirement: 2 semesters required freshman English; placement by SAT or ACT

Writing Center and Peer Tutoring Program

CENTER HAS EXISTED: Over 6 years HOURS OPEN PER WEEK: 25

STAFF: 1 faculty member, 1 staff member, and 3 undergraduate tutors

TUTOR SELECTION: Nominated by themselves, by English faculty and faculty college-wide; appointed by director

TUTORS' TRAINING: On-the-job

TUTORS' EVALUATION: Observation and student questionnaires

TUTORS PAID: Yes

HOURS THEY WORK: 10-20

PROGRAM DESIGNED TO SERVE: Students in all disciplines

PROGRAM ACTUALLY SERVES: Students in all disciplines

STUDENTS SEEK HELP WITH: Scientific reports, creative writing, academic essays, research papers, and resumes or business writing

PERCENTAGE OF STUDENTS SERVED: 25-50%

OVER PAST FIVE YEARS THIS PERCENTAGE HAS: Increased

STUDENTS USE CENTER: Throughout the semester on a walk-in or regular basis

STUDENTS REQUIRED TO USE CENTER: Problem writers

MATERIALS AVAILABLE: Handbooks and writing exercises

STUDENT ATTITUDE: Very positive

Writing-Across-the-Curriculum Program

PROGRAM HAS EXISTED: Under 2 years

INSTRUCTORS: Faculty in all disciplines

INSTRUCTORS' SELECTION: Voluntary

INSTRUCTORS' TRAINING: None

PERCENTAGE OF FACULTY INVOLVED: 2-3%

STUDENTS INVOLVED IN PROGRAM: Students in all disciplines

PERCENTAGE OF STUDENTS INVOLVED: 5%

PARTICIPANTS' ATTITUDE: Unknown

The writing requirement at Xavier University of Louisiana insures that all of its students receive classroom writing instruction, while three nontraditional programs provide writing instruction outside the classroom. The writing center staff and the peer tutors help students in all disciplines, including students referred by faculty. In all, over 25 percent of the university's students use the tutoring programs. The English Department has no major plans for the near future other than the continuation and development of the existing programs.

YALE UNIVERSITY

New Haven, CT 06520

Full-time Students: 2958M/2170W Faculty: 1486

Respondent: Joseph Gordon, Director, Bass Writing Program

Writing Requirement: None

Writing Center

CENTER HAS EXISTED: 5 years HOURS OPEN PER WEEK: 10–20

STAFF: 12 professional writers and editors

TUTORS' TRAINING: On-the-job

TUTORS' EVALUATION: Conferences, student questionnaires, and by other tutors

TUTORS PAID: Yes

PROGRAM DESIGNED TO SERVE: Students in all disciplines

PROGRAM ACTUALLY SERVES: Students in all disciplines

STUDENTS SEEK HELP WITH: Creative writing, essays, research papers, resumes and business writing, and applications to graduate and professional schools

PERCENTAGE OF STUDENTS SERVED: 10–15%

OVER PAST FIVE YEARS THIS PERCENTAGE HAS: Increased

STUDENTS USE CENTER: On an appointment, walk-in, or regular basis

STUDENTS REQUIRED TO USE CENTER: None

MATERIALS AVAILABLE: Handbooks and exercises

STUDENT ATTITUDE: Very positive

Writing-Across-the-Curriculum Program

PROGRAM HAS EXISTED: 5 years

INSTRUCTORS SELECTED: Faculty and graduate students in all disciplines

INSTRUCTORS' SELECTION: Voluntary

INSTRUCTORS' TRAINING: Seminars and team teaching

PERCENTAGE OF FACULTY INVOLVED: 10–15%

IN PAST FIVE YEARS THIS PERCENTAGE HAS: Increased

STUDENTS INVOLVED IN PROGRAM: Students in all disciplines

PERCENTAGE OF STUDENTS INVOLVED: Less than 25%

IN PAST FIVE YEARS THIS PERCENTAGE HAS: Increased

PARTICIPANTS' ATTITUDE: Somewhat positive

Yale University's Bass Writing Program has grown in the past ten years "from a nothingness to a full, elaborate program," according to its director, Joseph Gordon. The writing center consists of residentially based centers in each of Yale's twelve colleges, each center staffed with a professional writer or editor. Yale also offers tutorials in Daily Themes, an upper-level intermediate composition course that requires daily assignments of approximately 300 words. The writing-across-the-curriculum program, which trains faculty and graduate students who teach writing intensive courses, has also worked effectively. The writing intensive courses in thirteen departments tend to attract students who might not take one of the six standard freshman composition offerings; thus the cross-curricular program fulfills precisely the role it was intended to fulfill.

YORK COLLEGE

York, PA 17405

Full-time Students: 930M/1309W Faculty: 103

Respondent: R. Batteiger, Chairperson, English and Speech Department

Writing Requirement: 2 semesters required freshman English

Writing Center

CENTER HAS EXISTED: 2-5 years HOURS OPEN PER WEEK: Over 40

STAFF: 8 faculty, non-student, and undergraduate tutors

TUTORS' TRAINING: On-the-job

TUTORS' EVALUATION: Observation

TUTORS PAID: Yes

PROGRAM DESIGNED TO SERVE: Students in all disciplines

PROGRAM ACTUALLY SERVES: Students in all disciplines

STUDENTS SEEK HELP WITH: All types of writing

PERCENTAGE OF STUDENTS SERVED: Less than 25%

OVER PAST FIVE YEARS THIS PERCENTAGE HAS: Increased

STUDENTS USE CENTER: Throughout the semester on a walk-in, appointment, or regular basis

STUDENTS REQUIRED TO USE CENTER: Those referred by faculty

MATERIALS AVAILABLE: Handbooks and exercises

STUDENT ATTITUDE: Positive

Like many other schools, York College has recently introduced computer-assisted instruction to the teaching of writing. The college plans to increase the use of computers and word processing in teaching composition and is investigating the role of computers in heuristics and critical thinking. In the future York plans to begin a writing-across-the-curriculum program.

YOUNGSTOWN STATE UNIVERSITY

Youngstown, OH 44555

Full-time Students: 5286M/4613W Faculty: 406

Respondents: Gratia Murphy, Coordinator of Basic Composition; Sherri Zander, Coordinator of the Writing Center

Writing Requirement: Required freshman English course

Writing Center

CENTER HAS EXISTED: 10 years HOURS OPEN PER WEEK: 35

STAFF: 15–18 faculty, graduate, and undergraduate tutors

TUTORS' TRAINING: On-the-job and weekly workshops

TUTORS' EVALUATION: Observation, conferences, student questionnaires, by other tutors, and by faculty of Basic Writing course

TUTORS PAID: Yes

PROGRAM DESIGNED TO SERVE: Students in all disciplines

PROGRAM ACTUALLY SERVES: Students in all disciplines

STUDENTS SEEK HELP WITH: Scientific reports, creative writing, academic essays, research papers, and resumes or business writing

PERCENTAGE OF STUDENTS SERVED: 20–25%

OVER PAST FIVE YEARS PERCENTAGE HAS: Increased

STUDENTS USE CENTER: Throughout the quarter on an appointment or workshop basis

STUDENTS REQUIRED TO USE CENTER: Students enrolled in Basic Writing Workshop

MATERIALS AVAILABLE: Handbooks, filmstrips, videos, exercises, professional books, and cassettes

STUDENT ATTITUDE: Very positive

In the past ten years, Youngstown State University's writing program has developed a strong emphasis revision and on the process of writing. Youngstown State has structured its freshman composition courses according to this philosophy, encouraging students to consider audience and rhetorical situation as they write. As Gratia Murphy explains, most of these composition classes include "guided practice in revision and drafting." Aside from writing courses, the major focus of Youngstown State's program is its Writing Center. Staffed by faculty, graduate, and undergraduate tutors, the Writing Center serves students at all levels, particularly students enrolled in the Basic Writing Workshop. The center emphasizes communication between tutors by holding weekly staff meetings and by encouraging tutors to record their observations in a staff journal kept in the center. Youngstown State has been equally successful with a team-teaching program that links freshman composition with social science courses.

VI. COMPREHENSIVE INDEX TO TYPES OF SERVICES

In order to help readers use this guide efficiently, we include an index listing schools with writing centers, peer tutoring, writing-across-the-curriculum programs, ESL programs, and all those using or anticipating using computer-assisted instruction and word processing.

Writing Centers

Adelphi University (future)
Albany State College
Alfred University
Allegheny College
Amherst College
Arizona State University
Auburn University
Baylor University
Beaver College
Beloit College
Bentley College
Bethel College
Bloomsburg University
Boise State University
Bowling Green State University
Brenau College
Bridgewater State College
Brigham Young University
Brigham Young University/Hawaii Campus
Brown University
Bucknell University
California Polytechnic Institute
California State University at Fullerton
California State University at Long Beach
Capital University
Carleton College
Carnegie-Mellon University (Fall 1985)
Case Western Reserve University
Central Missouri State University
Central Wesleyan College
Chaminade University of Honolulu
Chicago State University
The Citadel
City University of New York/Brooklyn College
City University of New York/The City College
City University of New York/Hunter College
City University of New York/College of Staten Island
City University of New York/LaGuardia Community College
City University of New York/Queens College
Clarion University
Clark College
Clark University
College of the Holy Cross
College of William and Mary
Colorado State University
Columbia University
Dartmouth College
Defiance College
De Paul University
Drake University
Drew University
Drexel University
Duke University
Eastern Illinois University
Eastern Montana College
Emmanuel College
Emory University
Emporia State University
Eureka College
Evergreen State College
Fitchburg State College
Florida Institute of Technology
Frostburg State College
Geneva College
George Mason University
Georgetown University
Georgia Southern College
Georgia State University
Goldey Beacom College
Grinnell College
Guilford College
Hamilton College (future)
Harding University
Harvard University
Hope College
Husson College
Illinois Institute of Technology

Illinois State University
Indiana State University at Terre Haute
Ithaca College
Jamestown College
Johnson State College
Kansas State University
Knox College
La Roche College
Lawrence University
Le Moyne College
Lewis and Clark College
Lincoln University (Missouri)
Lincoln University (Pennsylvania)
Louisiana College
Lynchburg College
Macalester College
Mankato State University
Marquette University
Massachusetts Institute of Technology
Mercer University
Miami University
Mills College
Mississippi College (Fall 1984)
Muhlenburg College
National College of Education
New College of California
New Hampshire College
New York University
North Carolina State University
Northeastern University
North Texas State University
Oklahoma City University
Oakland University
Oregon State University
Ottawa University
Pennsylvania State University
Pine Manor College
Providence College
Purdue University
Ramapo College
Randolph-Macon College
Reed College
Rensselaer Polytechnic Institute
Rochester Institute of Technology
Roosevelt University
Rutgers University/Cook College
Rutgers University/Rutgers College
St. John's University
St. Mary's College
St. Olaf College
Salem State College
San Francisco State College
Scripps College
Seton Hall University
Simon's Rock of Bard College
Skidmore College
Slippery Rock University
Smith College
Southwestern at Memphis
Springfield College
Stanford University
State University of New York at Albany
State University of New York at Binghamton
State University of New York at Buffalo
State University of New York at Stony Brook
State University of New York/College at Fredonia
Stonehill College
Sweet Briar College
Temple University
Texas A & M University
Tougaloo College
Trinity College (Connecticut)
Trinity College (Vermont)
University of Albuquerque
University of California at Berkeley
University of California at Davis
University of California at Los Angeles
University of California at San Diego
University of Colorado at Colorado Springs
University of Delaware
University of Florida
University of Georgia
University of Hawaii at Hilo
University of Hawaii/Manoa
University of Illinois at Urbana-Champaign
University of Maryland
University of Michigan at Ann Arbor
University of Michigan at Dearborn
University of Michigan at Flint
University of Minnesota at Duluth (Fall 1984)
University of Minnesota/Twin Cities
University of New Mexico
University of North Carolina
University of Notre Dame
University of Oklahoma
University of Oregon
University of Pennsylvania
University of Pittsburgh
University of Rhode Island
University of Southern California
University of South Florida
University of Texas at Arlington
University of Texas at Austin
University of Texas at El Paso

University of Vermont
University of Virginia
University of Washington (future)
University of Wisconsin at Milwaukee
University of Wisconsin at Stevens Point
University of Wyoming
Utah State University
Vassar College
Virginia Commonwealth University
Virginia Polytechnic Institute and State University
Wake Forest University
Washburn University
Washington and Lee University
Wayne State College
Wayne State University
Wesleyan University
Wheaton College
Whitman College
Williams College
Wittenberg University
Worcester Polytechnic Institute
Xavier University of Louisiana
Yale University
York College
Youngstown State College

Peer Tutoring Programs

Adelphi University
Alfred University
Baylor University
Bentley College
Bloomsburg University
Boise State University
Boston College
Brigham Young University
Brown University
Bucknell University
California State University at Fullerton
Carleton College
Carnegie-Mellon University
Central Wesleyan College
Centre College
Chaminade University of Honolulu
The Citadel
City University of New York/Brooklyn
College
City University of New York/College of Staten Island
City University of New York/LaGuardia Community College
Clarion University
Clark College
Clark University
College of Insurance
Dakota Wesleyan University
Dartmouth College
Defiance College
De Paul University
Drew University
Emporia State University
Eureka College
Evergreen State College
Fitchburg State College
Georgetown University
Georgia Southern College
Goldey Beacom College
Grand Canyon College
Guilford College
Harvard University
Hope College
Husson College
Illinois State University
Johnson State College
Lawrence University
La Roche College
Lincoln University (Missouri)
Louisiana College
Lynchburg College
Macalester College
Miami University
Mississippi College
New College of California
New York University
Northeastern University
Oakland University
Ottawa University
Pennsylvania State University
Pitzer College
Pomona College
Purdue University
Ramapo College
Randolph-Macon College
Reed College
Rochester Institute of Technology
Rutgers University/Cook College
St. John's University
St. Joseph's University

St. Mary's College
St. Olaf College
Salve Regina
Scripps College
Seton Hall University
Simon's Rock of Bard College
Skidmore College
Smith College
Springfield College
State University of New York at Buffalo
Stonehill College
Sweet Briar College
Tougaloo College
Trinity College (Vermont)
University of Albuquerque
University of California at Berkeley
University of California at Los Angeles
University of California at San Diego
University of Colorado at Colorado Springs
University of Hawaii at Hilo
University of Hawaii/Manoa
University of Idaho
University of Maine at Machias
University of Maryland
University of Michigan at Flint
University of North Carolina
University of Pennsylvania
University of Santa Clara
University of Texas at El Paso
University of Vermont
University of Washington (future)
Urbana University
Utah State University
Vanderbilt University
Vassar College
Wake Forest University
Washburn University
Washington and Jefferson College
Wesleyan University
Wheaton College
Wilmington College
Wittenberg University
Xavier University of Louisiana

Writing-Across-the-Curriculum Programs

Allegheny College
Beaver College
Beloit College
Bentley College
Boise State University
Brigham Young University
Brown University
Bucknell University
California Maritime Academy
California State University at Fullerton
Carleton College
Carnegie-Mellon University (future)
Centre College (future)
Chaminade University of Honolulu (future)
City University of New York/Brooklyn College
City University of New York/College of Staten Island
City University of New York/LaGuardia Community College
Clark College
Clark University
College of the Holy Cross
College of William and Mary
De Paul University
Eastern Illinois University
Emmanuel College (future)
Evergreen State College
George Mason University
Georgetown University
Grinnell College
Hamilton College
Harvard University
Illinois State University
Ithaca College
Knox College
La Roche College
Lewis and Clark College
Lincoln University (Missouri)
Lincoln University (Pennsylvania) (future)
Lynchburg College
Macalester College
Mankato State University
Massachusetts Institute of Technology
National College of Education
Northeastern University (future)
Oklahoma City University
Oakland University
Oregon State University (future)
Ottawa University
Pine Manor College
Pitzer College (future)

Polytechnic Institute of New York
Providence College (future)
Ramapo College
Randolph-Macon College
Roosevelt University
Rutgers University/Cook College
St. John's University
St. Mary's College
St. Olaf College
San Francisco State College
Scripps College
Seton Hall University
Shimer College
Simon's Rock of Bard College
Skidmore College
Slippery Rock University (Fall 1984)
Stanford University
State University of New York at Albany
State University of New York at Binghamton
State University of New York/College at Fredonia
State University of New York/Empire State College
Stonehill College
Tougaloo College
University of California at Davis
University of Colorado at Colorado Springs
University of Idaho
University of Maryland
University of Michigan at Ann Arbor
University of Minnesota at Duluth (Fall 1984)
University of Minnesota/Twin Cities
University of Notre Dame
University of Oklahoma (future)
University of Oregon
University of Pennsylvania
University of Pittsburgh
University of Southern California
University of South Florida (future)
University of Texas at Austin
University of Texas at El Paso
University of Vermont
University of Washington
University of Wisconsin at Stevens Point
Utah State University
Vanderbilt University
Vassar College
Virginia Commonwealth University
Wheaton College
Whitman College
Xavier University of Louisiana
Yale University
York College (future)

Instruction in English as a Second Language

Brigham Young University/Hawaii Campus
California Polytechnic Institute
Case Western Reserve University
City University of New York/College of Staten Island
Evergreen State College
Hawaii Pacific College
Indiana State University at Terre Haute
Lincoln University (Pennsylvania) (future)
Mercer University
Mills College
New Hampshire College (future)
Oregon State University (future)
Rensselaer Polytechnic Institute
Southwestern at Memphis
University of Albuquerque
Wesleyan University
Wheaton College

Computer-Assisted Instruction and Word Processing

Alfred University
Bloomsburg University
Brenau College (future)
Brigham Young University (Fall 1984)
Bryn Mawr College
California State University at Fullerton
Carnegie-Mellon University
Case Western Reserve University (future)

City University of New York/Brooklyn College
City University of New York/LaGuardia Community College
College of the Holy Cross
Colorado State University
Columbia University (future)
Drexel University (future)
Eastern Illinois University
Eureka College
Evergreen State College
Guilford College
Husson College (future)
Illinois Institute of Technology
Kansas State University (future)
Louisiana College
Macalester College (future)
New College of California
Oklahoma City University (future)
Oakland University
Oregon State University (future)
Pennsylvania State University
Providence College
Randolph-Macon College
Rensselaer Polytechnic Institute
Rochester Institute of Technology (future)
Springfield College (future)
State University of New York/Empire State College
Stonehill College
Sweet Briar College
Temple University
University of California at Berkeley
University of California at Davis
University of California at Los Angeles
University of Georgia (future)
University of Hawaii at Hilo
University of Idaho
University of Illinois at Urbana-Champaign
University of Minnesota at Duluth
University of Notre Dame
University of Texas at Austin
Utah State University (future)
Wittenberg University
York College